EMPIRE DE/CENTERED

Empires and the Making of the Modern World, 1650–2000

Series Editors:
Philippa Levine, University of Southern California, USA
John Marriott, University of East London, UK

This monograph series seeks to explore the complexities of the relationships among empires, modernity and global history. In so doing, it wishes to challenge the orthodoxy that the experience of modernity was located exclusively in the west, and that the non-western world was brought into the modern age through conquest, mimicry and association. To the contrary, modernity had its origins in the interaction between the two worlds. In this sense the imperial experience was not an adjunct to western modernization, but was constitutive of it. Thus the origins of the defining features of modernity – the bureaucratic state, market economy, governance, and so on – have to be sought in the imperial encounter, as do the categories such as race, sexuality and citizenship which constitute the modern individual.

This necessarily complicates perspectives on the nature of the relationships between the western and non-western worlds, nation and empire, and 'centre' and 'periphery'. To examine these issues the series presents work that is interdisciplinary and comparative in its approach; in this respect disciplines including economics, geography, literature, politics, intellectual history, anthropology, science, legal studies, psychoanalysis and cultural studies have much potential, and will all feature. Equally, we consider race, gender and class vital categories to the study of imperial experiences.

We aim, therefore, to provide a forum for dialogues among different modes of writing the histories of empires and the modern. Much valuable work on empires is currently undertaken outside the western academy and has yet to receive due attention. This is an imbalance the series intends to address and so we are particularly interested in contributions from such scholars. Also important to us are transnational and comparative perspectives on the imperial experiences of western and non-western worlds.

Empire De/Centered
New Spatial Histories of Russia and the Soviet Union

Edited by

SANNA TUROMA
University of Helsinki, Finland

AND

MAXIM WALDSTEIN
Amsterdam University College, The Netherlands

ASHGATE

© Sanna Turoma, Maxim Waldstein and contributors 2013

All rights reserved. No part of this publication may be reproduced, stored in a retrieval system or transmitted in any form or by any means, electronic, mechanical, photocopying, recording or otherwise without the prior permission of the publisher.

Sanna Turoma and Maxim Waldstein have asserted their moral right under the Copyright, Designs and Patents Act, 1988, to be identified as the editors of this work.

Published by
Ashgate Publishing Limited
Wey Court East
Union Road
Farnham
Surrey GU9 7PT
England

Ashgate Publishing Company
110 Cherry Street
Suite 3-1
Burlington, VT 05401-3818
USA

www.ashgate.com

British Library Cataloguing in Publication Data
Empire de/centered : new spatial histories of Russia and the Soviet Union. – (Empires and the making of the modern world, 1650–2000)
1. Soviet Union – History. 2. Imperialism – Social aspects – Soviet Union.
I. Series II. Turoma, Sanna. III. Waldstein, Maxim.
947'.084–dc23

The Library of Congress has cataloged the printed edition as follows:
Empire de/centrered : new spatial histories of Russia and the Soviet Union / edited by Sanna Turoma and Maxim Waldstein.
   pages ; cm. – (Empires and the making of the modern world, 1650–2000)
Includes index.
ISBN 978-1-4094-4786-3 (hbk) – ISBN 978-1-4094-4787-0 (ebk PDF) – ISBN 978-1-4094-7329-9 (ePUB) 1. Space – Political aspects – Russia. 2. Space – Political aspects – Soviet Union. 3. Space – Political aspects – Russia (Federation)
4. Space – Political aspects – Eurasia. 5. Geopolitics – Russia. 6. Geopolitics – Soviet Union. 7. Geopolitics – Russia (Federation) 8. Geopolitics – Eurasia. 9. Eurasian school.
10. Imperialism. I. Turoma, Sanna, editor. II. Waldstein, Maxim, editor. III. Series: Empires and the making of the modern world, 1650–2000.
DK18.E46 2013
947–dc23   2013000830

ISBN 9781409447863 (hbk)
ISBN 9781409447870 (ebk – PDF)
ISBN 9781409473299 (ebk – ePUB)

Printed in the United Kingdom by Henry Ling Limited, at the Dorset Press, Dorchester, DT1 1HD

Contents

Series Editors' Preface vii
List of Figures ix
List of Contributors xi

Introduction: Empire and Space: Russian and the Soviet Union in Focus 1
Sanna Turoma and Maxim Waldstein

PART I: EURASIANISM AND INTELLECTUAL CONSTRUCTION OF SPACE

1 The Empire of Language: Space and Structuralism in Russian Eurasianism 31
   Sergey Glebov

2 Between Russia, Ukraine, and Eurasia: Georgii Vernadskii's Search for Identity 61
   Igor Torbakov

3 Space as a Destiny: Legitimizing the Russian Empire through Geography and Cosmos 85
   Marlène Laruelle

PART II: SPATIAL SCIENCE AND GEOGRAPHICAL KNOWLEDGE

4 The Mapping of Illiberal Modernity: Spatial Science, Ideology and the State in Early Twentieth-century Russia 105
   Nick Baron

5 Regionalization, Imperial Legacy, and the Soviet Geographical Tradition 135
   Marina Loskutova

PART III: POLITICAL AND CULTURAL ECONOMY OF THE (POST-)SOVIET SPACE

6   The Controlled Space of Socialist Internationalism and its
    Transgression: COMECON Energy Projects between 1970
    and 1990   159
    Ulrich Best

7   The Rearrangement of the Post-Soviet Space and the
    Representation of Russia as a Eurasian Bridge   173
    Katri Pynnöniemi

8   Debating Soviet Imperialism in Contemporary Poland:
    On the Polish Uses of Postcolonial Theory and Their
    Contexts   191
    Tomasz Zarycki

PART IV: REPRESENTING EMPIRE: MEDIA, ART, LITERATURE

9   Playing Games with Empire: Finnish Political Imaginaries on
    the Early Soviet State   219
    Anni Kangas

10 *Imperiia* Re/Constructed: Narratives of Space and Nation in
    1960s Soviet Russian Culture   239
    Sanna Turoma

11 Picturing Infinity: Space Race and the Cosmic Landscape   257
    Iina Kohonen

12 Eccentric Orbit: Mapping Russian Culture in the Near
    Abroad   271
    Kevin M.F. Platt

Bibliography   *297*
Index   *335*

Series Editors' Preface

The landmass of modern Russia has posed many challenges for thinkers and politicians in Europe and the United States. Empire or nation? East or west? Communist or totalitarian? Czardom or modern state? These are among the questions that have taxed influential minds, and yet a satisfactory resolution has proved elusive. Indeed, if anything, the collapse of the Soviet Union has complicated the task, for many of the old certainties in Western perceptions suddenly and dramatically evaporated. Even if it could be argued, for example, that the matter of empire has now been rendered obsolete, precisely how "post-imperial" Russia can be thought remains highly problematic.

The historical experiences of Russia and the Soviet Union thus pose productive questions for students of empire, questions that are richly exploited in this intriguing collection of essays edited by Sanna Turoma and Maxim Waldstein. Recent debates over whether Russian expansion even constituted an example of modern imperialism have largely been resolved, as historians have come to accept that empires can be defined beyond those narrow maritime conceptions that once dominated the field. But, as Turoma and Waldstein note in their introduction, Russia continues to be marginalized in the histories of modern empires, when compared with the empires of Western Europe. One of the goals of the contributors to this volume is to demonstrate how a continued Eurocentrism, even in the wake of postcolonial studies, has not only encouraged this marginalization but also perpetuated the view that the imperial experiences of Russia and the Soviet Union were wholly exceptional and peculiar. In keeping with that optic, much of their concern is to decenter conceptions of European dominance by thinking of empire not as an abstract, universal category or as a tightly defined political unit, but rather as a set of historically specific practices that can provide evidence of imperial formations. Thus, instead of asking whether Russia or the Soviet Union was an empire, they explore how their discourses, institutions, and practices worked, and how they might be seen as "imperial situations."

Turoma and Waldstein's primary vehicle for achieving this is an attention to the importance of spatiality in imperial history, a focus that makes this volume a highly original and productive contribution to the scholarship on empire. With their awareness of centre–periphery relations, and their tendency to separate nation from empire in precisely the ways that the contributors set out to challenge, considerations of space go to the very core of imperial histories. In calling into question the tenacious underpinnings of imperial history, this collection offers a refreshing counterview that emphasizes the inequalities enshrined in the role of empire while letting go of a fixed hierarchy between metropole and colony. This allows us to read both Russia and the Soviet Union as empires with overlapping but distinctive communities and societies, contact zones rather than merely subservient outposts, in which imperial power could be exercised severally through violence or through negotiation. The significance of geographies to this refreshingly original analysis of the historical questions of empire cannot be underestimated.

The deft combination of the so-called imperial and spatial "turns" evident in the volume speaks not only to the experience of modern Russia and the Soviet Union but to historians of empire more generally, allowing us to reflect on empires through the analytical category of space, and to utilize that category as a way to reimagine the hierarchies we so closely associate with modern imperial formations.

Philippa Levine
John Marriott

List of Figures

4.1	General map of factory industry of the Russian Empire, 1896.	112
4.2	Map of Russia. Compiled by V.P. Gushchnyi and A.G. Mikh'evyi on the instructions of D.I. Mendeleev, 1906.	114
4.3	Economic centres of the USSR and their movements.	123
4.4	Movements of centres of Russia and Soviet Union, 1858–1932.	124
4.5	Diagram of the movements of several industries, 1900–1927.	125
4.6	Centres of gross output, 1927/28, and of capital investment in the First Five-Year Plan.	127
6.1	Plan of the Sojuz project (1974–1978), with national subdivisions (I–V: Poland, CSSR, Hungary, GDR, Bulgaria).	165
7.1	Advertisement for the DVTG Group.	176
7.2	Moscow—a port of five oceans.	177
9.1	Eetu Isto, *The Attack* [*Hyökkäys*], 1899, Finnish National Museum, Helsinki.	222
9.2	'The failed "attack" of Kullervo Akilles Manner and Oskar Tokoi' [*Kullervo Akilles Mannerin ja Oskari Tokoin epäonnistunut hyökkäys*] (extract).	224
9.3	'Russian friends of the fatherland in cooperation' [*Venäläiset isänmaanystävät yhteistyössä*].	225
9.4	'Knight and deserters, or The last bastion of humanity crumbling' [*Riddare och desertörer eller mänsklighetens sista front bröts*].	227
9.5	'Overview of the year 1925' [*Katsaus vuoteen 1925*].	228
9.6	'Union of independence and Alexander II' [*Itsenäisyysliitto ja Aleksanteri II*].	230
9.7	'The fifth anniversary jubilee of communism in Russia' [*Kommunismin viisivuotisriemujuhla Venäjällä*].	231
9.8	*Nya Fyren*, New Year's Issue (January 1918), untitled cover art (extract).	232

9.9	'A Finnish communist in Moscow' [*Suomalainen kommunisti Moskovassa*].	234
9.10	'The fate of small nations' [*Pienten kansain kohtalo*].	236
9.11	'The Bolsheviks and us' [*Bolschevikerna och vi*].	237
10.1	Advertisement for Sputnik, the Soviet travel agency for youth. The map shows Moscow as the center from which other Soviet cities and capitals of republics radiate. The thinner lines represent the network of roads interconnecting the other cities.	242
11.1	*Sputnik 1*.	258
11.2	An artists interpretation of how *Luna 2* impacts the surface of the Moon.	263
11.3	The far side of the Moon.	265

List of Contributors

Nick Baron is an Associate Professor in History at the University of Nottingham, UK. He works on 20th century Russian and East European history and historical geography, and has particular interests in questions of space and place and in migration. Recent books include 'Soviet Karelia. Politics, Planning and Terror in Stalin's Russia' (2007; Russian transl. 2011), 'Warlands. Population Resettlement and State Reconstruction in the Soviet–East European Borderlands, 1945–50' (2010) and 'Nurturing the Nation: Displaced Children, State Ideology and Social Identity in Eastern Europe and the USSR, 1918-1953' (2013). He is currently working on a cultural history of Soviet cartography.

Ulric Best is a DAAD Visiting Professor in Geography at York University's Canadian Centre for German and European Studies. In addition to research on the Soviet-era pipeline projects that are the subject of his chapter in this book, he also works on American-Soviet youth exchange and current border issues in the EU.Recent publication: Transgression as a Rule. German-Polish Cross-border Cooperation, Border Discourse and EU-enlargement (Münster: Lit, 2007).

Sergey Glebov is Assistant Professor of History at Smith and Amherst Colleges in Massachusetts and a founding editor of *Ab Imperio: Studies of Nationalism and Empire in the Post-Soviet Space*. He specializes in the history of the Russian Empire and is currently working on the history of the Eurasianist movement.

Anni Kangas is an Academy of Finland Post-Doctoral Researcher in International Relations at the University of Tampere, School of Management. She has published articles on Finnish-Russian relations, semiotics and pragmatism in International Relations in journals such as Cooperation and Conflict, International Political Anthropology, and Millennium: Journal of International Studies. Dr. Kangas is also a partner in the Finnish Centre of Excellence in Russian Studies - Choices of Russian Modernisation.

Iina Kohonen has a doctorate in photography (2012) from the Aalto University, School of Art, Design and Architecture Helsinki, (Finland). Her recent publications address the visual history of the Soviet Space program. Research interests: Soviet visual history and Cold War culture; Soviet space program; photographic theory and history of cosmic art.

Marlène Laruelle is a Research Professor of International Affairs, The Institute for European, Russian and Eurasian Studies (IERES), The Elliott School of International Affairs, George Washington University, Washington DC. She has published *Russian Eurasianism: An Ideology of Empire* (Woodrow Wilson Press/Johns Hopkins University Press, 2008), and *In the Name of the Nation: Nationalism and Politics in Contemporary Russia* (Palgrave, 2009).

Marina Loskutova is a senior researcher at the St. Petersburg branch of the Institute for the history of science and technology, the Russian Academy of Sciences. She works on the history of the exploration of natural resources in the 19th century Russia, Russian learned societies and local studies movement at the turn of the 19th - 20th centuries. She is also a researcher at the Centre for historical research, History department of the National Research University Higher School of Economics, St. Petersburg.

Kevin M.F. Platt is Edmund J. and Louise W. Kahn Term Professor in the Humanities, and Graduate Chair of the Comparative Literature Program at the University of Pennsylvania. He is the author of Terror and Greatness: Ivan and Peter as Russian Myths (Cornell UP, 2011) and History in a Grotesque Key: Russian Literature and the Idea of Revolution (Stanford, 1997; Russian edition 2006), and the co-editor (with David Brandenberger) of Epic Revisionism: Russian History and Literature as Stalinist Propaganda (Wisconsin UP, 2006). His current projects include a critical historiography of Russia and a study of contemporary Russian culture in Latvia.

Katri Pynnöniemi is a researcher at the Finnish Institute of International Affairs. In her latest book she discusses Russian policies on development of international transport corridors. She is currently working on Russian critical infrastructures and critical infrastructure protection.

Igor Torbakov is Senior Fellow at the Center for Russian and Eurasian Studies at Uppsala University, Sweden. A trained historian, he specializes in Russian and Eurasian history and politics. His most recent publications explored the politics of history and memory wars in Eastern Europe.

Sanna Turoma is Academy of Finland Research Fellow at Aleksanteri Institute (University of Helsinki). She is the author of *Brodsky Abroad: Empire, Tourism,*

Nostalgia (University of Wisconsin Press, 2010) and the co-editor and co-author of the Finnish-language *History of Russian Literature* (Gaudeamus University of Helsinki Press, 2011). She is also a researcher at the Finnish Center of Excellence in Russian Studies – Choices of Russian Modernization.

Tomasz Zarycki is associate professor and director of the Robert B.Zajonc Institute for Social Studies at the University of Warsaw, Poland. His latest book is 'Ideologies of Eastness in Central and Eastern Europe' (forthcoming at Routledge).

Maxim Waldstein teaches sociological theory at Amsterdam University College. He received his PhD in Sociology from the University of Illinois at Urbana-Champaign in 2005. He taught at the University of Pennsylvania, the University of Helsinki, and the University of Leiden, and conducted post-doctoral research at the Helsinki Collegium for Advanced Studies. His teaching and research interests include classical and contemporary sociological theory; history and theory of nationalism and empire; sociology of media, art and cinema; and the social and political history of Russian/Soviet human sciences and intellectuals.

Introduction
Empire and Space: Russian and the Soviet Union in Focus

Sanna Turoma and Maxim Waldstein

Twenty years ago the Soviet Union—"the last empire"—collapsed and thus, arguably, the phenomenon of empire was at last shelved as a purely historical matter. Yet, ironically, as a topic of public debate and academic research, empire is still alive and well. As the rise and expansion of such fields as postcolonial and imperial studies indicate, empire and its legacies are increasingly topical intellectual concerns far beyond the domain of purely historical research. This is in part due to the fact that the collapse of colonial and communist empires overlapped with such processes as globalization, European integration, and the rise of new nationalisms that are often very violent and directed against not only old empires but also established nation-states. These processes have cast considerable doubt on the assumption that national identity and nation-state are natural, universal, and/or normative forms of social relations. Consequently, the idea that empire and imperialism may not be as much behind us as many of us have hoped has gained ground.

This endurance of empire is particularly apparent with respect to Russia, the history of which has been marked by the close and ambiguous relationship between nation- and empire-building, national and imperial identities. In this context, it is hardly surprising that the global surge of interest in empire has resonated especially strongly among scholars of Russian and Soviet history, society, and culture. And yet Russia, and much of Eurasia, continues to be marginal in contemporary discourse on empire, including postcolonial studies and new imperial histories.

This volume pursues the same intellectual goal as other recent efforts to bring Russia and the Soviet Union to the focus of academic discussions about empire.[1]

---

[1] For recent discussions of Russia and empire, see Jane Burbank and Frederick Cooper, *Empires in World History: Power and Politics of Difference* (Princeton, NJ, 2010); Jane Burbank, Mark von Hagen, and Anatolyi Remnev (eds.) *Russian Empire: Space, People, Power* (Bloomington, IN, 2007); Francine Hirsch, *Empire of Nations: Ethnographic Knowledge and the Making of the Soviet Union* (Ithaca, NY, 2005); Ronald Grigor Suny and Terry Martin

It participates in the recent concerted effort to "de-provincialize" Russia as an object of study, to bring its history, present day, and intellectual traditions into the center of contemporary theory and research in social sciences and the humanities.[2] This effort is part of a larger project of "provincializing Europe" understood as a work of deconstructing, or decentering, the Eurocentric optics that still dominate much of contemporary theory and research.[3] The work of provincializing and decentering involves two distinctive but interrelated sub-projects: unsettling the claims of classical Western grand narratives on their universal and normative status and "writing ambivalence" into the history of Western modernity.[4] As far as the history and theory of imperial formations is concerned, this general agenda boils down to questioning the unconditional legitimacy and normativity of dominant Western practices and narratives of nation-building and imperial expansion, the nation-state, and colonial empire. This has been done, in particular, by demonstrating the extent to which European national identities were constituted *by*, and not isolated from, imperialism and colonial encounters.[5] Methodologically, this agenda implies moving "toward

---

(eds.), *A State of Nations: Empire and Nation-making in the Age of Lenin and Stalin* (Oxford, 2001); Terry Martin, *The Affirmative Action Empire: Nations and Nationalism in the Soviet Union, 1923–1939* (Ithaca, NY, and London, 2001). See also the contributions to *Ab Imperio. Studies of New Imperial History and Nationalism in Post-Soviet Space*, a journal that established itself rapidly as the leading forum for discussions about empire in Russian and Soviet studies after its foundation in 2000.

[2] Most of the editorials and publications in *Ab Imperio* aim at this goal. See also Maxim Waldstein, "Theorizing the Second World: Challenges and Prospects," *Ab Imperio* 1 (2010): 98–118.

[3] For this, see Dipesh Chakrabarty, *Provincializing Europe: Postcolonial Thought and Historical Difference* (Princeton, NJ, new edn 2007). According to Jacques Derrida, the process of *de-centering* has played an essential role in intellectual change. He says, for example, that "ethnology could have been born as a science only at the moment when a de-centering had come about: at the moment when European culture … had been dislocated, driven from its locus, and forced to stop considering itself as the culture of reference." Derrida, "Structure, Sign, and Play in the Discourse of the Human Sciences. Discussion," in Richard Macksey and Eugenio Donato (eds.), *The Structuralist Controversy: The Languages of Criticism and the Science of Man* (Baltimore, MD, 2007), p. 251. See also Peter Burke, *History and Social Theory* (Cambridge, 2005), p. 180.

[4] Dipesh Chakrabarty defines "provincializing Europe" as a project of writing "into the history of modernity the ambivalence, contradictions, the use of force, and tragedies and ironies that attend it." See Chakrabarty, *Provincializing Europe*, p. 43.

[5] As Julian Go has observed, "[R]ather than taking binaries between East/West and colonizer/colonized for granted, it [postcolonial historiography] explored how two sides were mutually constituted," in Julian Go, "The 'New' Sociology of Empire and Colonialism," *Sociology Compass* 3 (2009): 2.

a shared analytical space for forms of rule not predicated on a West/northern Europe vs. the Rest dichotomy."[6] Substantively, this means a "decentered" focus on non-national forms of modern political identity and on non-Western imperial experiences. Considered in this context, Russian and Soviet imperial experiences appear to be not exceptional, unique or abnormal—as they are usually treated in both popular and academic literature—but, on the contrary, quite paradigmatic of the practices and identifications that are often silenced and suppressed in dominant modern Western narratives. By extending the decentering agenda on Russia and the Soviet Union, this volume brings their histories and the present day to the fore as a source of theoretical insights into the nature of political and cultural identity, belonging, and modernity.

The collection sets out to explore imperial and/or anti-imperial discourses and institutions not *in abstracto*, but in the thick of historically specific social and cultural settings and practices. In doing so, we proceed from the distinction between empire as a "category of analysis" and as a "category of practice," or a category of everyday social experience, developed and deployed by ordinary social actors.[7] By distinguishing between these two usages of "empire," we attempt to avoid the uncritical translation of politically charged, negative or positive, deployments of "empire" into the language of research. Skeptical about the possibility of a universal and objective definition of empire, we subscribe to the approaches, which view empire as a "research context rather than a structure, a problem rather than a diagnosis."[8] The contributions to this volume focus not so much on the question of whether a certain political unit is "really" an empire but rather on various instances of an "imperial situation," that is, a set of patterns that can be observed in various degrees of evidence in various political and cultural formations.[9] In short, this volume performs the work of conceptual decentering of the established ways in which the category of empire has been used.

---

[6] Ann Laura Stoler, "Considerations on Imperial Comparisons," in Ilya Gerasimov, Jan Kusber, and Aleksandr Semyonov (eds.), *Empire Speaks Out: Languages of Rationalization and Self-description in the Russian Empire* (Boston and Leiden, 2009), pp. 39–40.

[7] Rogers Brubaker and Frederick Cooper, "Beyond Identity," *Theory and Society* 29 (2000): 1–47.

[8] Ilya Gerasimov, Sergey Glebov, Aleksandr Kaplunovski, Marina Mogil'ner, and Aleksandr Semyonov, "In Search of a New Imperial History," *Ab Imperio* 1 (2005): 53.

[9] *Ab Imperio* authors define an imperial situation as "a situation of undetermined boundaries and mutually open channels of influence that emanate not only from the culturally and technologically dominant center, but also from imperial periphery." Ibid., p. 44. Ann Laura Stoler has proposed a related category of "imperial formations," defined as "not fixed macropolitical entities but ongoing processes that produce gradations of

Empire De/Centered brings together spatial and imperial "turns," two major paradigmatic shifts in contemporary social sciences and humanities, and focuses both lenses on twentieth-century Russia and the Soviet Union. It combines new imperial histories with new spatial histories, two fields of interest that are topical to social sciences and humanities in general, and Russian and Soviet studies in particular. The understanding of space as social construction vital to historical narratives and cultural production has generated a bulk of interdisciplinary scholarship with a spatial orientation, informed by the work of such theoreticians as Michel Foucault, Jacques Derrida, Henri Lefebvre, Edward Soja, and David Harvey.[10] The editors of the recent edited volume entitled *The Spatial Turn* describe this "turn" as a shift from center to periphery, from capitals to boundaries, from structures to contexts, and from sovereign nation-states to transnational networks and flows.[11] This is a "post-Fordist" shift from "an absolute, Cartesian notion—static, fixed, and lying outside of society, or space as container—to relative and relational space, space as socially constructed by people, and thus fluid, folded … the view of space as networks."[12] The dialogue between the studies of empire and space with the focus on Russia and the Soviet Union offers a venue for truly comparative and relational analyses, as opposed to thinking in terms of various implicit or explicit binary schemes such as West–East and norm–deviation.

In particular, the contributors to *Empire De/Centered* question the dominant imagery of the space of empire as structured along the binary distinction between two hierarchically subordinated but clearly distinct and internally homogeneous polities and populations. This dualistic imagery is not a universal norm, as this volume manifests. Instead, this volume proposes to shift the focus to spaces and situations of nested centrality and subalternity. The contributions

---

sovereignty, not as exceptions to their architecture but as constitutive of them." See Stoler, "Considerations," p. 35.

[10] For a brief overview of how discourse on spatiality developed in critical social and cultural theory in the post-World War II period Europe and US, see Edward D. Soja's account in "Taking Space Personally," in Barney Warf and Santa Arias (eds.), *The Spatial Turn: Interdisciplinary Perspectives* (London, 2009), pp. 11–35.

[11] The editors of *The Spatial Turn* capture this "turn" in the following way: "Recent works in the fields of literary and cultural studies, sociology, political science, anthropology, history, and art history have become increasingly spatial in their orientation. From various perspectives, they assert that space is a social construction relevant to the understanding of the different histories of human subjects and to the production of cultural phenomena. In some ways, this transformation is expressed in simple semantic terms, i.e. the literal and metaphorical use and assumptions of 'space,' 'place,' and 'mapping' to denote a geographic dimension as an essential aspect of the production of culture". Barney Warf and Santa Arias, "Introduction: The Reinsertion of Space in the Humanities and Social Sciences," in Warf and Arias, *The Spatial Turn*, p. 1.

[12] Barney Warf, "From Surfaces to Networks," in Warf and Arias, *The Spatial Turn*, p. 74.

focus on hybrid, networked, decentered discourses, identities, strategies, and social formations. This approach does not seek to undermine the fact that the distinction between center and periphery continues to constitute the poles of social, cultural, and spatial inequality between individuals, institutions, and groups. The distinction between center and periphery is not only an ideological construct but also a social reality. And yet, it is the ambiguity and the dynamics of the imperial situation that we seek to draw attention to.

In short, *Empire De/Centered* aims at illuminating the articulations between empire and space by performing a series of displacements and decenterings with respect to the dominant conceptual frameworks and empirical foci. Not wishing to limit ourselves to this critical, or negative, project, the editors and contributors to this volume also offer specific suggestions on how such traditionally marginal conceptual concerns and empirical domains as social and cultural hybridity, borderlands, continental empires, and Russia can be de-provincialized, or "centered," that is, transferred into the focus of contemporary academic debates on nation, empire, and modernity.

New Imperial Histories

The 1990s and early 2000s saw a burst of innovative research on, primarily, British imperial history that became tagged as a "new imperial history."[13] These studies often applied interdisciplinary approaches, which drew from cultural, postcolonial, feminist, and subaltern studies. In the introduction to *The New Imperial Histories Reader* Stephen Howe sums up these new approaches as "centered on ideas of culture, and often, of discourse; ones with strong attention to gender relations and/or to racial imaginings; ones which emphasize the impacts of colonialism's cultures on metropole as well as on the colonized, and tend also to urge its continuing effects after the end of formal colonial rule."[14]

The core agenda of the new approaches to the study of imperial histories can be best understood by contrasting them to more traditional theories

---

[13] See, for instance, Antoinette Burton (ed.), *After the Imperial Turn: Thinking with and through the Nation* (Durham, NC, 2003); Kathleen Wilson (ed.), *A New Imperial History: Culture, Modernity, and Identity* (Cambridge, 2004); Stephen Howe (ed.), *The New Imperial Histories Reader* (London, 2010).

[14] Howe, *New Imperial*, p. 2. See also Barbara Bush's reading of new imperial histories as a "major historiographical shift in conceptualizations of empires and imperialism" catalyzed by postcolonial studies, in her review of *The New Imperial Histories Reader*: http://www.history.ac.uk/reviews/review/989 (accessed April 13, 2012).

of empire, colonialism, and imperialism.[15] These theories usually defined empires as composite polities based on hierarchical interrelations between two types of pre-existing, well-formed, internally homogeneous entities—metropolis and colonies, or core and periphery nations. For instance, in his now classic *Empires*, Michael Doyle discusses empire as a system of "control of a subordinated society by an imperial society."[16] Ronald Suny, an expert on Armenian history and a leading authority on empire and nation in post-Soviet studies, defines empire similarly as "a particular form of domination or control between two units set apart in a hierarchical, inequitable relationship, more precisely as a composite state in which a metropole dominates a periphery to the disadvantage of the periphery."[17]

The epistemological presumptions behind traditional definitions of empire have recently been under attack for their "methodological nationalism," or "the assumption that nation/state/society is the natural and transhistorical form of social relations."[18] In fact, these assumptions and perspectives are deeply rooted in the peculiar modern-age experiences of European/Western nation-building, Western colonization and colonial empires. In this framework, Western colonial empires, with their explicit codification of the difference between the colonizer and the colonized nations, serve as heuristic and even normative models for understanding composite polities in other times and places, including traditional aristocratic empires of the premodern age or modern continental empires that managed to survive till the twentieth century—Russian, Austro-Hungarian, Ottoman empires, as well as the Soviet Union and even China and the US.[19]

Of course, there has been a competing tradition that tended to limit "methodological nationalism" to West-dominated modernity. Here, "empire" is essentially a premodern sociopolitical form defined not through the conflict between nations and states but through the social conflict between various elites, such as the conflict of kinship-based aristocracy vs. bureaucracy and

---

[15] The target of the critique launched by the champions of "new imperial histories" in the study of British Empire was, above all, *The Oxford History of the British Empire*; see, for instance, Antoinette Burton, "Thinking beyond the Boundaries: Empire, Feminism and the Domains of History," *Social History* 26/1 (2001): 60–71.

[16] Michael Doyle, *Empires* (Ithaca, NY, 1986), p. 30.

[17] Ronald Grigor Suny, "Empire Strikes Out," in Suny and Martin, *A State of Nations*, p. 25.

[18] Go, "The 'New' Sociology of Empire and Colonialism," p. 9. See also Burton, "Thinking beyond the Boundaries."

[19] See the criticism of this thinking in Craig Calhaun, Frederick Cooper, and Kevin W. Moore (eds.), *Lessons of Empire: Imperial Histories and American Power* (New York and London, 2006).

mercantile elites.²⁰ Similarly, Benedict Anderson's historiographical scheme can be reduced to the opposition between modern nations, imagined as "limited" (bounded), "sovereign," and "horizontal" communities, and premodern dynastic empires, which Michael Doyle defined as "a sovereignty that lacks community."²¹ Western colonial empire, in this context, is more of a transitional stage toward the complete domination of nation as the only quintessentially modern way of imagining a political community. Even more "abnormal" in the modern order of things are continental empires, which have been treated as mere survivals of the related premodern polities.

Despite their differences, all of these traditional frameworks share nation-centric and Eurocentric biases, reify the (European) "nation form," and privilege the view from (Western) imperial centers. The empirically observable geographical, institutional, and cultural distance between the metropole and the colonies is interpreted in such a way that, for instance, the British nation and a colonized nation pre-exist the empire and enter a number of external relationships such as "subjugation," "civilization," and eventually "liberation." Nation- and empire-building are treated as essentially two separate processes, while the processes of colonization are seen as external to the societies of the metropolis.

Since the 1970s this framework has been criticized from many quarters, especially by the proponents of postcolonial theory and "new imperial history." Following Edward Said's pioneering work on the discourse of Orientalism, they proposed a number of alternative ways of understanding nationhood, empire, and colonialism, ways not premised on essentialized binaries between West and East, and the colonizer and the colonized. This is especially the achievement of the post-Saidian generation of students of postcoloniality and empire, the generation of the "revisionists" critical of Said's residual tendency to reinforce the discursive boundaries he seeks to deconstruct.²²

In a striking departure from received wisdom, the representatives of this trend have demonstrated the relativity of the boundaries between the metropole and the colony, and explored the processes of "mutual constitution" in which their social and cultural identities and institutions historically emerged. Furthermore, the contemporary students of empire and postcoloniality have relativized the very distinction between nation and empire in a number of interesting ways. By treating nation-building in both Europe and in colonies as an "imperial process,"

---

[20] See Shmuel Eisenstadt, *Political Systems of Empires* (New York, 1963).
[21] Benedict Anderson, *Imagined Communities: Reflections on the Origin and Spread of Nationalism* (London, rev. edn. 2006), pp. 6–7; Doyle, *Empires*, p. 36.
[22] See the critique of Said and mainstream postcolonial theory in Cooper, *Colonialism in Question*, pp. 14–17; Gerasimov et al., "In Search of a New Imperial History," pp. 43–4. See also Waldstein, "Theorizing the Second World," pp. 105–7.

they have explored how, for instance, Britishness was emerging in the course of confronting, dominating, and producing knowledge about the colonized Other. They have also demonstrated that a nation-state can be seen as effectively a former empire that has more or less successfully "nationalized" itself (through such processes as "peasants into Frenchmen" and "internal colonization"). In the words of Eugen Weber, "[t]he famous hexagon [continental France] can itself be seen as a colonial empire shaped over the centuries: a complex of territories conquered, annexed, and integrated into a political and administrative whole, many of them with strongly developed national or regional personalities, some of them with traditions that were specifically un- or anti-French."[23]

These advances imply "provincializing Europe" and decentering of the concept of modernity: "Europe" is considered in relation to its non-European sources, while modernity appears to be constituted not only by liberal democracy and the unprecedented rate of social and economic development but also by racialized exclusion, violence, and the invention of such traditions as the "Hindu caste system."[24] This decentering of modernity helps to make the concept of modernity more analytical and less ideological by making lighter the positive value load usually associate with it.

Some of the best passages in the texts of contemporary theorists of empire and postcoloniality are dedicated to "hybridity" that is both repressed and often generated by nationalistic and colonial discourses and policies.[25] The "discovery" of this pervasive hybridity behind the screen of colonial and nationalistic dichotomies problematizes what seems to be the basic assumption of the colonial domination—the impenetrable difference between the colonizer and the colonized, whether understood as the difference between the civilizer and the savage, the master and the subject, or the oppressor and the resistance fighter. The identities of all actors involved in the colonial/imperial encounter appear to be, in postcolonial analysis, notoriously fragile, unstable, contested, and negotiated, marred by doubts, repressions, sublimations, and fears of

---

[23] Eugen Weber, *Peasants into Frenchmen: The Modernization of Rural France, 1870–1914* (Stanford, CA, 1976), p. 485. Etienne Balibar has contextualized nation-building as an aspect of empire-building in the following way: "In a sense, every modern nation is a product of colonization: it has always been to some degree colonized or colonizing, and sometimes both at the same time." See Etienne Balibar, "The Nation-Form: History and Ideology," in Etienne Balibar and Immanuel Wallerstein (eds.), *Race, Nation, Class: Ambiguous Identities* (London, 1991), p. 89.

[24] Nicholas B. Dirks, *Castes of Mind: Colonialism and the Making of Modern India* (Princeton, NJ, 2001).

[25] A key study of postcolonial hybridity is Homi K. Bhabha's *The Location of Culture* (London, 1994).

contamination.²⁶ Simultaneously—contemporary theorists and historians of empire argue—despite the regime of racial exclusion and the status of imperial subjects, local colonial elites and Europeanized middle classes exercised many of the civilizer and even colonizer functions with respect to "their own" populations. Thus, the answer to the question "whose empire?" appears to be rather more complicated than previously perceived.

On the empirical plane, these perspectives imply the shift of scholarly attention from privileging clearly bounded political bodies, national myths of origin, and the othering "gaze" from the imperial center to the preoccupation with peripheries, margins, and borderlands of all sorts, whether they are indeed located at the geographical outskirts of empires or occupy the fringes and "cracks" in the body of the imperial and national identities and institutions. In other words, postcolonial analysis and new imperial history de-provincializes all sorts of "meeting points" or "contact zones," that is, the sites where the hybridity of the social world are thrown into open relief, and thus we have direct access to ways in which supposedly monolithic and primordial identities and dichotomies come into being.

Russia and the Soviet Union as Empire

The collapse of the Soviet Union engendered a vivid debate about the nature of Russian Empire and the Soviet Union. Was pre-revolutionary empire "the prison of the people" or a regime that successfully accommodated ethnic and religious diversity? Was it a modern colonial empire like its Western competitors or a survival of a traditional and Oriental despotic polity? Was the Soviet Union an empire at all, or was it rather a nation-state in making? One of the most enlightening conclusions that were reached as a result of the two decades of these debates was the realization that traditional Eurocentric categories are simply not sufficient for understanding the historical experiences in question. This is due to the pronounced ambiguity of the borderlines and distinctions between nation and empire, metropolis and "colonies," East and West, and modern and premodern in Russian and Soviet history.²⁷ With their amorphous inner

---

²⁶ Despite the visible racial difference between the British and the African or Indian, the burden of empire was only seemingly light and easy for Britons: many of them—proletarians, women, the Irish, in particular—used to find themselves in the situation of being effectively "subalterns" not less often than in the situation of masters and citizens of the metropole nation-state. As for the elites, they never fully achieved monolithic agreement on the "how," "what for," and "is this worth it" of the imperial expansion.

²⁷ Mark Beissinger has argued that the Soviet Union blurred the line between nation-state and empire and was "one of the first of a new form of empire whose crucial contributions

borderlines and expansive borderlands, polyethnicity and cultural diffusion, repeated modernization attempts and the interpenetration between imperial centers and peripheries, Russian and Soviet empires were hybrid "contact zones," or zones of "transculturation," *par excellence*.[28]

These hybrid experiences appear as "abnormalities" and "deviations" only if considered against the background of privileged categories of Western theory.[29] When methodological nationalism and West/East binaries are no longer accepted uncritically, continental empires like Russia appear to be sources of inspiration and even heuristic models for an alternative, post-traditional understanding of the broader dimensions of the imperial situation, beyond its embodiment in Western colonial empires. As the works of Frederick Cooper, Jane Burbank, Ann L. Stoler, Alexei Miller, and *Ab Imperio* editors and authors demonstrate, new critical perspectives on empire lead to the transformation of colonial studies/histories, narrowly focused on Western empires, into more comprehensive imperial studies, which include a larger comparative sample of premodern, traditional, and non-classical modern empires.[30]

The perspective represented by new imperial histories of Russian empire and the Soviet Union can be best illustrated by contrasting it to two traditional strategies of dealing with the hybrid nature of corresponding historical experiences. First, there is the tradition of dismissing the ambiguities as insignificant and reducing Russia to one of Western "pure types"—for example the Soviet Union as a nation in formation (modernization theory) or as empire in denial, or Russia as "normal" European superpower and Western-style colonial empire, or Russia as a continental empire understood as a survival of premodern (Oriental and despotic) imperial formations. The other traditional

---

were its denial of its imperial quality and its use of the very cornerstones of the modern nations-state system [...] as instruments of nonconsensual control over culturally distinct populations." See Mark Beissinger, "Rethinking Empire in the Wake of Soviet Collapse," in Zoltan Barany and Robert G. Moser (eds.), *Ethnic Politics after Communism* (Ithaca, NY, 2005), p. 17.

[28] E.g. Burbank and Cooper, *Empires*; Aleksei Miller, *The Romanov Empire and Nationalism: Essays in the Methodology of Imperial Research* (Budapest and New York, 2008). Cf. Stephen Howe's description of the Russian empire as a "hybrid, with the balance of its mixture of types shifting constantly over time. There were 'traditional' patterns of conquest, more 'modern' efforts of commercial and indeed post-industrial expansion, regions where imperial rule was handled by the military or by small numbers of exported administrators, ones where something like an indirect rule system operated, and ones involving large-scale settlement." Stiven Khou [Stephen Howe], "Iz Manchestera v Moskvu" [From Manchester to Moscow], *Ab Imperio* 1 (2011): pp. 89–90.

[29] Stoler, "Considerations," p. 43.

[30] See, for instance, *Ab Imperio* manifestos in *Ab Imperio* 1 (2005) and *Ab Imperio* 1 (2011).

interpretation of Russia's hybridity is to see it as a sign of being a peculiar, Eurasian civilization. Here hybridity is interpreted as Russia's uniqueness, its *Sonderweg*, sometimes as Russian messianism. Whether celebrated or blamed for all Russia's historical misfortunes, this uniqueness is usually interpreted as secondary, or derivative, with respect to the "purity" of the social and cultural types presumably embodied in the "West" and the "East."[31]

The fact of the enduring coexistence and competition between these strikingly contrasting perspectives within Russian intellectual history and in the field of Russian studies has repeatedly foregrounded the gap between the essentialist conceptual frameworks and the messy empirical reality of Russian and Soviet society and culture. In other words, this empirical reality has always contained potential for powerful critique of dominant paradigms. Yet, this potential was rarely consistently realized and, when realized, it rarely achieved theoretical sophistication or was expressed in language that would make it accessible to the broader international intellectual and academic public.[32] Most importantly, as the case of Russian Eurasianism demonstrates, this potential was often thwarted under the weight of taken-for-granted or even openly proclaimed assumptions of (methodological) nationalism and essentialism. As long as scholars and thinkers continue to expect to find "pure" Europe and Asia beyond the boundaries of Russia's hybrid social and cultural space, the radical "decentering" potential of the region's history and present day can easily be neutralized.

This has begun to change over last two decades, with the extension of postcolonial theory and new imperial history to Russian studies. What used to be dismissed as a theoretically inconsequential empirical complexity, or essentialized as a revelation of Russia's *Sonderweg*, turns out of be an exemplary case for understanding what used to be marginalized in traditional histories of the nation-state and colonial empire. Russian history and, in a distinctive manner, Soviet history exemplify the characteristics of other empires highlighted in the course of the recent imperial turn. In Ann L. Stoler's words: "Those features that provide the template of European colonial empires and the scholarship about them—sharp distinction between metropole and colony, and abiding preoccupation with race over other exclusions, the incessant proliferation of distinction in the pursuit of profit—look less like imperial universals when considered across the thicker swath of imperial ground."[33]

[31] Waldstein, "Theorizing the Second World," pp. 102–3.
[32] There are exceptions, of course, such as Mikhail Bakhtin's considerable impact on the contemporary theories of hybridity. Yet, these occasional breakthroughs have had limited impact on conceptualizing Russian (imperial) history, until recently at least. See Bhabha, *The Location of Culture*; Robert Young, *Colonial Desire: Hybridity in Theory, Culture, and Race* (London, 1995).
[33] Stoler, "Considerations," p. 45.

When looked at through the lens of the Russian experience, empire is not a mere one-nation-dominated polity—despite Russia's elites' occasional Russifying policies.[34] Russian history demonstrates the key principle of empire, that is, differentiation of non-equivalent and non-equal territories and populations, which does not necessarily accord with fixed binary oppositions. In fact, the importance of the experience of Russia and other continental empires is explicitly acknowledged in Burbank and Cooper's definition of empires as "large political units, expansionist or with a memory of power extended over space, polities that maintain distinction and hierarchy, as they incorporate new people... The concept of empire presumes that different people within the polity will be governed differently."[35] Like no other, Russian history exemplifies the idea that empire is about managing, accommodating, not eradicating, difference. Modern colonial empires were more explicit about codifying difference in a binary way but otherwise they were far more like Russian empire than it was previously acknowledged.[36]

Neither the Russian empire nor the Soviet Union was merely a survival of traditional aristocratic empire or "purely" modern political formations. Nor were they merely transitional forms between the two. Rather, conceptualizing Russian and Soviet history and present involves the substantial revision of "ideal-typical" binary distinctions like the one between (premodern or colonial) empire and (modern, post-imperial) nation. In particular, this history calls for problematizing Benedict Anderson's "assumption that the category 'nation' is the sole available slot for an imagined community after the advent of print capitalism."[37] Unburdened by essentialist and binary assumptions, the studies of Russia and the Soviet Union foreground the diversity of other imagined collectivities in the modern world, an imperial community included. These studies demonstrate that nation is not the only possible way of imagining a modern political community; that the imperial principle can be experienced as legitimate and can compete for legitimacy with the national principle (metropolitan or subaltern).

Russian history offers, thus, an empirical critique of the influential, anticolonial nationalist assumptions about empire defined as "a sovereignty that lacks

---

[34] As Jane Burbank and Frederick Cooper remind us, the Ottoman, Romanov, and Habsburg empires "were not Turkish, Russian, and Germanic peoples ruling 'others,' even if there were people within these empires who advocated Turkifying, Russifying, or Germanizing policies." *Empires*, p. 368.

[35] Ibid., p. 8. The "rule of exception" is another formulation of the concept of differential rule: "imperial states by definition operate as states of exception that vigilantly produce exceptions to their principles and exceptions to their laws." Stoler, "Considerations," p. 43.

[36] See Waldstein, "Theorizing Second World," pp. 107–8.

[37] Nancy Condee, *The Imperial Trace: Recent Russian Cinema* (Oxford, 2009), p. 10.

community" (Doyle) and "domination without hegemony" (Ranajit Guha).[38] Rather than by default illegitimate and imposed, empire could function as a cosmopolitan "moral space, the unit in regard to which righteous political behavior was debated."[39] The legitimacy of empires as modern imagined communities, along with nations, has an important theoretical implication: The concept of community does not necessarily entail homogeneity. "Imperial communities—in the French, Ottoman, or Habsburg empires [or Russian empire and the Soviet Union]—were not coterminous with a single society but could still entail a strong sense of belonging among part of their populations."[40]

Everything that has been said above about the Russian Empire could be said about the Soviet Union with an addition that it was, like a nation-state, an attempt to forge a modern anticolonial and non-imperial political identity. It was modern in a sense that it aimed at "rationalizing" Russian space, the space of overlapping and inconsistent differences and loyalties. This rationalization/modernization included a considerable effort of forging politically and ideologically—but not ethnically or "culturally"—homogeneous "peoplehood" (Soviet people). This rationalization, however, led to a rather rare form of "institutionalized multinationality": If colonial empires codified the binary difference, the Soviets pursued "the thoroughgoing codification and institutionalization of nationhood and nationality exclusively on a sub-state rather than a state-wide level."[41] As such, this system is quite exceptional but its inner tensions and its fate attest to a more universal characteristics of modernity and modern political identities: Any attempt to modernize and rationalize the exercise of power comes not so much *instead* of the previous exercises of power but *on top* of them; it is superimposed on the residues of the previous attempts

---

[38] Doyle, *Empires*, p. 30; Ranajit Guha, *Dominance without Hegemony: History and Power in Colonial India* (Cambridge, MA, 1997).

[39] Cooper, *Colonialism in Question*, p. 163. The "morality" of this space is not a matter of objective "righteousness" but of its legitimacy in the eyes of a sizable number of an empire's subjects. Even such totalitarian societies as the Soviet Union were, at various points of their histories and within various populations, the objects of debates and struggles for their definition, development, and improvement, rather than simply for their abolition and liberation from them.

[40] Ibid., p. 289.

[41] Rogers Brubaker, *Nationalism Reframed: Nationhood and the National Question in the New Europe* (Cambridge, 1996), pp. 26–7. See also Suny and Martin (eds.), *A State of Nations* and Martin, *The Affirmative Action Empire*.

to rationalize social relations. This is, in essence, Foucault's idea of archaeology of knowledge, in this case "archaeology of knowledge about empire."[42]

Overall, Russian history, and some of the existing thinking about it, offers plenty of material for rethinking the traditional Eurocentric assumptions about empires, nations, belonging, and modernity. Yet, until recently, this potential was hardly realized (or, it was realized inconsistently, not radically enough). The emergence of postcolonial theorizing and its more contemporary extensions and applications makes possible an alternative use of these resources. Within these novel fireworks, Russia's hybridity is not only a sign of its national exceptionality and "abnormality" within the context of the nation-centric imagination. It is also representative, even exemplary of the broadly understood imperial situation. Russian and Soviet history appears to be an exemplary case of the dimensions of the imperial situation, which are often obscured or even suppressed within dominant Western narratives. This is especially true to "imperial spatiality," the distinctive topic of this volume, which comes to light in the course of the dialogue between the imperial turn and the spatial turn in social sciences and the humanities.

Imperial Space

There is what one may call a distinctive Russian obsession with space in social practice and in academic research. The vastness of space has been an inspiration and a product of the practices and images of empire and nation-building throughout Russian and Soviet history. Space has meant mobility and expansion, while it has also meant "slowness" of communication, insufficient infrastructure, and deceleration of historical change. Russia's vast geographical expanses have been regarded as an obstacle to modernization, while they have also been understood, by historical actors and scholars alike, as an asset, a boundless and ceaseless resource of industrial, economic, and technological progress. Once released of its traditional association with the narratives of the Russian *Sonderweg*, this "obsession" with space may serve as a particularly enlightening lens on the nature of Russian imperial experience and empire in general.

The recent upsurge of interest in Russian and Soviet space—what Nick Baron has labeled "new spatial histories" of Russia—is heavily indebted to "the

---

[42] The idea of the "archaeological" nature of new imperial history has been developed in more detail by *Ab Imperio* editors, e.g. "The archaeology of knowledge permits the restoration of the palimpsest of social identities (regional, confessional, estate, etc.) that are usually narrated into the teleological and mono-logical paradigm of the building of a nation, class, or confession." Gerasimov et al. "In Search of a New Imperial History," p. 54.

spatial turn" in social sciences and humanities. This historiography, according to Baron, "engage[s] critically with the interaction of human agency and space, and with the mediating role of culturally-defined spatial practices and spatially-configured cultural practices."[43] Baron links the emergence of the new field to accelerated globalization in trade, travel, and communication, and to the collapse of the cold war world order, with its realities and metaphors of "Iron Curtain" and "containment." These processes have triggered scholars to probe into the "precarious nature of the configurations of territory, populations, and power."[44] The editors of *Space, Place, and Power in Modern Russia: Essays in the New Spatial History* have pointed to the interaction of the spatial turn and the interest in space in Russian studies by observing that "these new analytical perspectives encountered their 'perfect storm' in the aftermath of the collapse of the Soviet Union".[45] The destabilization, fragmentation, fluidity, and instability of boundaries turned post-Soviet Russia into "a veritable laboratory for the study of ... the changing patterns of spatial interaction."[46]

This volume aims at generating a dialogue between two currently vibrant fields, new imperial history and new spatial history. The essays in the volume bring empire and space together on two levels: Firstly, they combine in their perspective and methodology the insights from recent imperial and spatial "turns" in social sciences and humanities, and, secondly, they analyze the entanglements between the images and conceptions of empire and space in Russian and Soviet intellectual traditions, public debates, and discourses in the past and in the present. In other words, empire and space are entangled in the volume in both methodology/theory and subject matter. The remaining part of this section focuses on the distinctive features of the conceptual dialogue between imperial and spatial studies, as orchestrated in this volume.

---

[43] Nick Baron, "New Spatial Histories of Twentieth-century Russia and the Soviet Union: Surveying the Landscape," *Jahrbücher für Geschichte Osteuropas* 55 (2007): 374. See also Nick Baron, "New Spatial Histories of 20th-century Russian and the Soviet Union: Exploring the Terrain," *Kritika: Explorations in Russian and Eurasian History* 9/2 (2008): 433–47. Among these studies, Baron mentions Evgeny Dobrenko and Eric Naiman (eds.), *The Landscape of Stalinism: The Art and Ideology of Soviet Space* (Seattle, WA, 2003); Emma Widdis, *Visions of a New Land: Soviet Film from the Revolution to the Second World War* (New Haven, CT, 2003); Karl Schlögel, *Im Raume lesen wir die Zeit: Über Zivilisationsgeschichte und Geopolitik* (Munich, 2003). See also Jeremy Smith (ed.), *Beyond the Limits: The Concept of Space in Russian History and Culture* (Helsinki, 1999).
[44] Baron, "New Spatial Histories," p. 376.
[45] Mark Bassin, Christopher Ely, and Melissa Stockdale (eds.), *Space, Place, and Power in Modern Russia: Essays in New Spatial Histories* (DeKalb, IL, 2010), p. 4.
[46] Ibid.

There is a formidable literature on the spatial character of imperial formations and imaginings, "the space of empire," and the spatial dimensions of specific empires, imaginative geographies of imperial and/or colonial expansion, and the social patterns of economic exchange and political domination (metropolis vs. provinces/colonies; core vs. periphery; imperialism; globalization).[47] The contribution of this volume to the bulk of this literature is an elaboration of *imperial space* as a distinctive object of study and, simultaneously, a distinctive perspective of analyses. Although heavily informed by the analyses of various historical empires, the concept of imperial space is not limited to empire as a distinctive political entity or a distinct historical entity. No claim is made to argue that all dimensions of mental or social space in historical empires have actually been "imperial." What is at stake is the question of what makes particular spatial arrangements "imperial" as opposed to making them "national."

In the nation-centric ontology, as Michel Foucault characterized it, space is "dead, fixed, immobile," as opposed to time with its "richness, fecundity, life and dialectics."[48] Space is presumed to be a neutral Cartesian system of coordinates, which lies outside of history and social relations. Conceived of as homogeneous and "empty," it is analogous to its representation on contemporary political maps. The space of the nation-centric universe is a flat surface covered by multiple "squares," or "boxes" and "containers" of different size. These boxes are "filled" with distinctive "stuff" of their own, which differs in amounts (the size of populations) and "character" (national cultures, ways of life). Within each box, each "place" is fundamentally equivalent to the other, just as all citizens are equal before the sovereign.

While the national sovereignty is, as Benedict Anderson put it, "fully, flatly, and evenly operative over each square centimeter of legally demarcated territory," an imperial realm is "defined by centers" that are surrounded by imperial borderlands, "relatively porous and indistinct, [where] sovereignties imperceptibly faded into one another."[49] Frederick Cooper, Ann Stoler, Jane Burbank, and other authors credit "empire" with such features as the ability to accommodate, rather than eradicate, difference; the differential rule

---

[47] See, for instance, David Harvey, *Spaces of Global Capitalism: A Theory of Uneven Geographical Development* (London, 2006); Edward Said, *Orientalism* (New York, 1978) and *Culture and Imperialism* (New York, 1994), esp. pp. 3–14; Edward Soja, *Postmodern Geographies: The Reassertion of Space in Critical Social Theory* (London, 2011); Maria Todorova, *Imagining the Balkans* (New York, 1997); and Larry Wolff, *Inventing Eastern Europe: The Map of Civilization on the Mind of the Enlightenment* (Stanford, CA, 1994).

[48] Michel Foucault, *Power/Knowledge: Selected Interviews and other Writings, 1972–1977* (New York, 1980), p. 70.

[49] Anderson, *Imagined Communities*, p. 19.

over nonequivalent populations, and the incorporation of overlapping and gradated sovereignties and identities, differentiated along multiple incongruous criteria.[50] Considered in these terms, empires are not simply *in* (abstract and homogeneous) space but *are* (dynamic and heterogeneous) spaces. Empire is about ranks and gradations inscribed in space. Empire *is* space, a space of hierarchically interconnected places.

Imperial space is not only an attribute of a political unit called "empire" but also of the broader "imperial situation." Here, "imperial situation" refers to political, social, and cultural patterns and relations that cross over the boundaries between specific nations (including the dominant and the dominated) and between "nation" and "empire." "Any society," as the editors of *Ab Imperio* write, "can be 'thought of' as an empire, just as features characteristic of nation-states can be discerned in any empire."[51] That is, the differential and hierarchical organization of space—for example when it is organized around the distinction between the capital and the province—can be associated not only with a formal "empire" but also with a paradigmatic nation-state like France.

If one wishes to point out the single attribute that distinguishes imperial space from any other spatiality, the distinction between center and periphery comes immediately to mind. In fact, the dynamics between center and periphery can be seen as a minimal condition of imperial spatiality. Capital vs. province or metropole vs. colony are just historically specific realizations of this invariant pattern, which does not necessarily presuppose the distinction between two homogeneous units (nations, states, people). The distinction between center and periphery is not a substantial but a functional or relational distinction.[52] This distinction may itself be indispensable but its realization in the world is ambiguous and precarious. A particular center–periphery relationship can change and reverse in time.[53] A central or peripheral position of any given social actor or unit

---

[50] Cooper, *Colonialism in Question*, p. 55; Cooper and Burbank, *Empires*, p. 8; Stoler, "Considerations," pp. 35–43.

[51] Gerasimov et al., "In Search," p. 53.

[52] Elaborating on his idea about an intellectual or ideological center in response to a query from Serge Doubrovsky, Jacques Derrida wrote: "I didn't say that there was no center, that we could get along without a center. I believe that the center is a function, not a being – a reality, but a function. And this function is absolutely indispensable." See Jacques Derrida, "Structure, Sign, and Play," p. 271.

[53] For Yuri Lotman, a predecessor of the perspective on center–periphery relations advocated here, center and periphery are semiotic/cultural constructions and relational entities. They exist as extreme poles in the turn-taking process of text- and culture-production, the process of "a changeover between center and periphery" (145). This is "the process whereby the periphery of culture moves into the center, and the center is pushed out to the periphery"

is never absolute; it depends on the web of relations in which it is embedded. For instance, a political center can be a cultural backwaters/dependency with respect to its own political periphery; it can also be a political dependency of another center or cultural center of another cultural periphery. That is, instead of clearly defined units and binary oppositions, we have a relational continuum, a field of border drawing and "classification struggles" (in Pierre Bourdieu's terms).[54] In sum, to decenter the essentialist and binary understanding of empire means to reinterpret it as a surface, or space, of relationships, the basic structure of which is a *nested* opposition between center and periphery.[55]

Hence, the space of empire is built of overlapping and superimposed fields, practices, and symbols, where each field has a center–periphery structure. The axes of corresponding relationships usually do not fit together neatly; they overlap, clash, and are nested in one another; they have different temporalities so that the movement in space is often (quite legitimately) experienced as the movement in time. For instance, far from being a monolithic whole, Soviet society "consisted of multiple sub-societies, located as if in different temporal spaces, in different historical epochs and, furthermore, localized territories."[56]

These statements should not be misunderstood. This multidimensionality and heterogeneity of empires does not contradict their often violent and oppressive character. The center–periphery relationship is, after all, a hierarchical, asymmetrical relationship, a relationship of inequality and nonequivalence. Yet, it cannot be reduced—not even in colonial empires—to the binary relationship between two political units and populations. This, again, does not mean that attempts to homogenize an imperial space and codify differences, for instance, by

---

(141). Even when embodied in physical territory and separated by a spatial boundary, they are distinguishable not in any absolute terms but only with respect to specific cultural contexts or "coding systems." Center in one "system" may be a periphery in another. The geographical frontier may coincide with the ideological and political center of the state" (141). Yuri Lotman, *Universe of the Mind: A Semiotic Theory of Culture* (Bloomington, IN and Indianapolis, IN, 1990). See also Maxim Waldstein, *The Soviet Empire of Signs* (Saarbrucken, 2008), pp. 155–61

[54] Pierre Bourdieu, *The Logic of Practice* (Cambridge, 1990).

[55] Philosophers and logicians define the concept of a nested opposition as "a conceptual opposition each of whose terms contains the other, or each of whose terms shares something with the other." See Jack M. Balkin, "Nested Oppositions," in *Yale Law School Legal Scholarship Repository. Faculty Scholarship Series.* Paper 281, http://digitalcommons.law.yale.edu/fss_papers/281 (1990), p. 8.

[56] Anatolii Vishnevskii, *Serp i rubl': Konservativnaia modernizatsiia v SSSR* (Moscow, 1998), p. 288.

Cf. the following formula: "The concept of empire presumes that different peoples within the polity will be governed differently," in Burbank and Cooper, *Empires in World History*, p. 8.

reducing multiple and still-overlapping and fluctuating differences to a common denominator such as race, always fail. Yet, their success is not predetermined and cannot be assumed either, as is assumed in many classical approaches. This success (or failure) requires case-by-case interpretation and explanation.[57]

The contributions to this volume aim at providing not only examples but also *exemplars* of what these interpretations and explanations based on decentering traditional perspectives and the "de-provincialization" of continental empires and Russia might look like. The chapters are sorted not chronologically or by region but thematically and methodologically. The first two sections are composed of the pieces that explore the entanglements between empire and space in the Russian intellectual tradition, in the works of the nineteenth- and twentieth-century Russian philosophers, economists, linguists, historians, and geographers. The contributors to the third section apply social-scientific perspectives to explore "imperial" and "spatial" aspects of various types of social interactions, public discourses, and academic debates. The final section explores a variety of ways of representing empire and imperial spatiality in literature, art, and popular media.

An Outline of the Contributions

The volume starts by introducing a chapter in Russian intellectual history that produced the political movement of Eurasianism and its unique doctrine of empire and space. Founded in the post-revolutionary years by émigré scholars, Eurasianism surfaced again in the late Soviet period and gained currency in Russia in the 1990s after the disintegration of the Soviet Union. In its classic version Eurasianist ideology opposed European modernity and cultural colonialism, whose influence the founders saw as having led to the October Revolution. In an effort to rethink Russian Empire and its role in the new post-revolutionary world, they hailed the future of Russia–Eurasia as a distinctive empire-civilization and, simultaneously, super-ethnic nation, the leader of colonized people.[58]

Eurasianist thinkers pioneered a number of "decentering" strategies in their work—for example, they focused on the Eurasian imperial experience that

---

[57] Frederick Cooper gives an example of such explanation with respect to Western colonial empires: "Modern empires were in some ways more explicit about codifying difference – and particularly codifying race – than aristocratic empires, for the giving way of status hierarchies to participation in a rights-bearing polity raised the stakes of inclusion and exclusion." Cooper, *Colonialism in Question*, p. 23.

[58] See Sergei Glebov's discussion of the anticolonial rhetoric of the Eurasianist movement in "Granitsy imperii kak granitsy moderna. Antikolonial'naia ritorika i teoriaa kul'turnykh typov v evraziistve," *Ab Imperio* 3/2 (2003): 267–91.

seemed aberrant and marginal within the framework of the then dominant Eurocentric perspectives, and, in analyzing this experience, they moved off-center, from imperial centers to peripheries and borderlands, from the capitals to the steppe. By focusing on the heterogeneity, or "federalism," of Eurasian space and the hybridity of the cultural identities that this space engenders, Eurasianists legitimized Russian empire and its characteristic spatiality as a theoretically consequential object of study. Yet, they also celebrated Eurasian spatiality as a basis for their brand of Russian "imperial nationalism" and the *Sonderweg* theory. In effect, the decentering potential of their studies remained underexplored and even undercut by the effective reversal to more traditional patterns of thought.[59]

Part I, entitled "Eurasianism and Intellectual Construction of Space," brings together three scholars of the Eurasianist movement. Sergey Glebov ties the Eurasianists' spatial and imperial visions to the development of Western structuralism through the figure of Roman Jakobson. Glebov discusses the work of the geographer Petr Savitskii and the linguist Nikolai Trubetskoy, two founding fathers of Eurasianism, and the influence they had on Roman Jakobson's understanding of structuralist linguistics, which, in turn, had a great impact on Claude Lévi-Strauss. The Eurasianist spatializing approach is felt particularly in Jakobson's ideas about linguistic boundaries and language unions. Glebov's essay uncovers the previously unexplored intellectual roots of structuralism and highlights the impact of Russian spatial and imperial imagination on the production of a major Western scholarly paradigm. The language of structuralism combined the "Russian tradition of counter-Enlightenment and anti-evolutionism with a vision of a grand, universal project of a systemic supra-science—an ideal language for empire in the 20th century," as Glebov concludes.

Igor Torbakov approaches Eurasianist imagination through Georgii Vernadskii's life and work. Son of the famous scientist Vladimir Vernadskii, he was born in St. Petersburg but had Ukrainian roots. After the October Revolution and civil war he lived for some time in Europe and then immigrated to the US, where he made an academic career as the professor of Russian history in Yale University. Vernadskii played a vital role in an effort to produce an Eurasianist historiography. Torbakov takes Vernadskii's ambiguous position between Russian and Ukrainian heritages as his starting point and projects Vernadskii's

---

[59] Cf. Mark von Hagen, "Writing the History of Russia as Empire: The Perspective of Federalism," in Catherine Evtuhov et al. (eds.), *Kazan, Moscow, St. Petersburg: Multiple Faces of the Russian Empire* (Moscow, 1997), pp. 393–410; Mark von Hagen, "Empires, Borderlands, and Diasporas: Eurasia as Anti-paradigm for the Post-Soviet Era," *The American Historical Review* 109/2 (2004): 445–68; Stephen Kotkin, "Mongol Commonwealth? Exchange and Governance across the Post-Mongol Space," *Kritika* 8/3 (2007): 487–532.

personal quest for identity on his visions of empire, nation, and Ukrainian and Russian history. Torbakov's discussion of the making of Vernadskii's hybrid identity illuminates poignantly the multidimensionality of imperial space, the fluidity of center–periphery boundaries, and the contested character of the definitions of national identity in the context of an imperial situation.

Marlène Laruelle discusses the configurations of empire and space in three ideological narratives she discerns in Russian twentieth-century intellectual debates. These narratives are structured around geographical determinism and Cosmism and have been mainly elaborated by classic Eurasianists and their followers. She highlights the cosmic visions in Lev Gumilev's thought and analyzes the ideas of such post-Soviet neo-Eurasianist intellectuals as Evgenii Troitskii, Aleksandr Panarin, and Aleksandr Dugin. They have been influential in promoting the idea of Russia's imperial destiny, which, as Laruelle argues, is a version of Russian messianism legitimized by the conviction of the country's specific relation to space.

Part II, entitled "Spatial Science and Geographical Knowledge," focuses on the interrelationships between political ideologies, economic and administrative policies, and geographical knowledge in late imperial Russia and the prewar Soviet Union. Nick Baron explores the conflicting views among Russian and Soviet intellectuals on how the territorial space of empire was to be analyzed, apprehended, accounted for, and acted upon. He focuses on the ideas of Dmitrii Mendeleev and his Soviet followers on the large-scale spatial planning. Mendeleev, better known as a chemist, took keen interest in czarist territorial planning and published a series of writings in which he proposed a number of initiatives for spatial policymaking. His political and economic ideas came into vogue again in post-Soviet years, and he has been lauded as an economic visionary, a geopolitical thinker, and a "national prophet." While Baron's main concern is with ideologies and policies of "illiberal modernization," he contrasts Mendeleev's conservative and statist but also scientifically rigorous and empirically based vision of imperial space with Stalinist "teleological planning," which was based on the primacy of ideologically informed cartographic imagination over material reality. Overall, Baron's essay highlights the struggle between materialist and idealist conceptions in Russian spatial discourse and practice.

Marina Loskutova analyzes the underexplored aspects of the development of the Russian geographical tradition, especially the spatial dimensions of the production of geographical knowledge. She explores the debates among Russian geographers, statisticians, ecologists, and economists in the context of their cooperative involvement in the regional cadastral surveys and in other government-sponsored projects. What brings Loskutova's study particularly close to Baron's contribution is their shared focus on "regionalization," a distinctive preoccupation of Russian and Soviet scholars and politicians. "Regionalization" refers to the task of identifying, mapping, and describing regional variations within the country, understood as a unified and integrated political and economic space. A key concern of Mendeleev and Russian geographers, regionalization was also recognized by (especially Soviet) authorities as a tool for strengthening central state control over the periphery. Yet, as Loskutova argues, the distinctive Russian focus on regionalization has been a product of the more or less explicit admission by the elites of a continental empire that their mastery over space cannot be achieved by means of eradicating difference or by subsuming it under the binary distinction between the metropole and the periphery. Instead, Russian authorities and intellectuals had continually to negotiate and renegotiate the strategies of rationalizing and controlling the social and natural inner boundaries within the empire's space, and this resulted in conflicting projects of regionalization. Despite the statist and loyalist motivations of most authors of these projects—as we learn from Baron and Loskutova—most of these regionalization projects reflect the basic structure of imperial space, a space of multiple "nested" centralities and peripheries.

Part III, "Political and Cultural Economy of the (Post-)Soviet Space," brings together social scientists who contribute their disciplinary perspective and methodologies to understanding spatial practices and discourses in the Soviet Union, post-Soviet Russia, and Eastern Europe. The section opens with Ulrich Best's contribution, in which he looks at the oil pipeline building sites within the socialist block in the context of the wider cultural and geopolitical transformations of the 1970s. Variously described as the transition to postmodernity, post-Fordism, and/or post-Westphalian order, these transformations are usually analyzed strictly in the Western context. In his ethnography of international building sites under Soviet socialism, Best adds an exciting comparative case to the existing body of literature on the topic. He argues that the tendencies of breaching the "container model"—the model according to which social relations and cultural patterns can be "contained" within the borders of nation-states and political "camps"—have been equally in evidence in the socialist East as they were in the capitalist West. Moreover, these tendencies could rely on such distinctive resources as the ideology and practice of socialist internationalism. Yet, as Best shows by analyzing everyday life in the international building sites, the trend toward the different regimes of territoriality and control only amplified the inherent contradictions in the discourses and practices of the regulation of socialist space. On the one hand, these sites and the discourse of internationalism offered opportunities for a limited transgression of national and cultural boundaries (adventure, male bonding, opportunities for smuggling, etc.). On the other hand, these sites and discourses were also associated with heightened control and surveillance: Free movement and free encounter of people was not encouraged. In effect, the international building sites were both transgressions and extensions of national spaces; they were national spaces beyond national territories. In the short term, the workers' experiences in these sites helped to legitimate socialist regimes in a specific nation-state—often, paradoxically, by promoting the reversal of the ideologically mandated hierarchies between the Soviets and East Europeans. Eventually, however, these ambivalent experiences revealed the failure of the socialist states to maintain official hierarchies and control boundaries effectively. Ulrich Best concludes by suggesting that the fall of state socialism can be illuminated in the context of the socialist states' inability to shift to a more contemporary regime of territoriality and control.

"Post-Soviet space," a common phrase in public and academic debates, is often used to differentiate the space occupied by the post-Soviet successor states from the territory of contemporary Russia proper. Yet, Katri Pynnöniemi's empirical focus zooms in on post-Soviet Russia and highlights the concept's materially embedded aspects. She defines post-Soviet space in terms of the infrastructure network of post-Soviet Russia. The infrastructure network— road and rail linkages, oil and gas pipelines, and electricity network—forms the backbone of the Russian economy, and embeds a particular political order in space. Analyzing public and institutional debates, among them Vladimir Putin's and other high-ranking Kremlin politicians' speeches about the transportation network, Pynnöniemi argues that what is at stake in these debates is the question of the Soviet regime's economic legacy. This legacy is seen either as means and/ or an obstacle for the integration of Russia into global economy. The post-Soviet space of infrastructure carries within it the incompleteness of the Soviet modernization project but also the potential for its renewal. What was once a monument to Soviet power is now a means for Russia to engage in the global economy. Meanwhile, the idea of Russia as a Eurasian continent has fed into the vision of Russia's global importance as a transport corridor between Europe and Asia. Eventually, the modernization of the transportation network in post-Soviet Russia raises three issues: the integration of Russia into the global markets and the EU, the reorganization of Russian polity as a whole, and the fragmentation of the post-Soviet space. Overall, Pynnöniemi's analysis of the transportation policies and discourses "decenters" the studies of Russian economy by focusing our attention on inherently unstable and ambiguous aspects of the spatial order in which this economy is embedded.

In his contribution, Tomasz Zarycki explores the role of the political and geopolitical context in shaping the reception of the ideas and the very language of postcolonial theory in post-socialist Poland. He shows that, despite the developed discourse of Poland's victimhood under Russian and Soviet rule, the conceptualization of the corresponding power relations in terms of colonization and Orientalism played a minor role in Polish academic and public debates until the second half of the first decade of the twenty-first century. Zarycki explains this, in part, by references to the project of European integration, which preoccupied Polish elites for most of the post-socialist period. In the context of this project, the association of Poland under Soviet hegemony with the status of a "colony"—the status associated with historical passivity, cultural inferiority, and non-Europeanness—had to be rejected or downplayed. The emphasis was made on the opposition to, and liberation from, communism, not on colonial dependence from the Russian "metropole." Zarycki further argues that the more recent recognition of Poland's dependence on the West, the inequalities in their relations, had an effect of raising interest in postcolonial readings of the relations with Moscow. Interestingly, the reception of Western postcolonial theories is dominated by right-wing, nationalistic intellectuals, who, paradoxically, use the ideas of Edward Said and other early postcolonial theorists to bring together their traditional Russophobia with more recent and "hip" Euro-skepticism.

While providing a number of incisive criticisms of this appropriation of postcolonial thinking, Zarycki suggests that the contradictory reception of postcolonial thinking in contemporary Poland is itself an exciting case in point for developing a post-nationalistic "new imperial history" of Poland's complex geopolitical and cultural position in the world. He emphasizes how this reception reveals the historical ambivalence of Poland's intertwined dependencies and identifications, the ambivalence that still shapes the relationships between Poland (and Eastern Europe) and its western and eastern neighbors. Instead of continuing to essentialize the opposition between the Russian "colonizers" and the Polish "colonized," as some recent Polish and Western postcolonial scholars tend to do, Zarycki makes a case for analyzing the dynamic and "nested" properties of the categories employed in contemporary academic and public debates in Eastern Europe, categories like "West" and "East," as well as center and periphery.

Part IV, "Representing Empire: Media, Art, Literature," includes four contributions that explore the discursive and visual constructs of empire. In addition to Tomasz Zarycki's contribution in the previous section, there are two other chapters that offer a perspective from a Western frontier to the Russian imperial formation: Anni Kangas's analysis of Finnish political cartoons with Russian topics and Kevin M.F. Platt's discussion of the Russian-speaking community in Latvia.

Anni Kangas analyzes Finnish political imaginary of Russia and the Soviet Union during the interwar period 1918–39. The chapter focuses on distinctive ways in which the idea of Russia and the Soviet Union as an empire featured in and shaped Finnish political debates and discussions. Arguing for the continued importance of empire as a category of practice, Kangas adopts Wittgenstein's concept of "language game" to examine how historical actors adapted an imperial frame of interpretation to articulate a relationship with Soviet Russia at a time when a re-articulation of the relationship with Russia was central to the political identity of the newly independent Finland.

Before analyzing Finnish representations of Soviet power, Kangas discusses the 1899 painting titled *Attack*, which has since then been incorporated into Finnish national iconography and depicts a young maiden (the personification of Finland) protecting the book of law (the Finnish constitution) from the attack of a double-headed eagle (Russian administration). This painting articulated in visual terms the Finnish opposition to Russification measures. In a careful rereading of the painting, Kangas argues that the image, with its gendered significations of submission and domination, actually exhibits an understanding of a symbiotic relationship between nationhood and empire, which, in turn, was a common interpretation of the Finnish nineteenth-century imperial situation. The Russification measures posed a threat not only to Finnish autonomy as a grand duchy but also to the political symbiosis in which nation and empire were not perceived as mutually exclusive but rather as constitutive of each other. After the revolution Finnish cartoonists often represented the new Soviet state as a veiled Russian Empire. The Russian eagle continued to signify expansion and omnipresence. At the same time, the cartoonists also evoked the idea of *Pax Russica*, an interpretive frame for Finnish history in which the hundred years of Russian rule were seen as bourgeoning economic and cultural development contrasted with Finland's previously marginalized position as a periphery of the Swedish Empire. These conflicting interpretations coexisted in Finnish political imagery: The imperial character of Russia and the Soviet state was increasingly seen as a violation of the "natural" condition of national self-determination, as Kangas concludes, but the "pre-national" conceptualization of a symbiotic relation between an empire and a nation also continued to feed Finnish political imagination in the interwar period.

Sanna Turoma's contribution analyzes the role of spatial imagery in the formation of Soviet identity in the post-Stalin period of the late 1950s and early 1960s. Taking her clue from the popular Soviet phrase of the country encompassing "one-sixth" of the earth's landmass, she shows how popular books and magazine articles about Soviet geography and natural zones, travel accounts of expeditions in Siberia, and glorifying reportage of the country's massive modernization projects participated in the building of a unified Soviet identity, articulated often in terms of spatial and geographical imagery. The vastness of Soviet territory was understood as a point of identification, as something all Soviet citizens shared. Working outside the official cultural production, writers and dissenting intellectuals, too, communicated their authorial identity within the spatial paradigm and the metropolitan hierarchy it implied. But despite the decentering impetus of travel and mobility, the metropolitan hierarchies of Soviet spatial ideology were seldom questioned, as Turoma argues. This said, the exploration and relative freedom of itineraries and routes suggested an interconnectedness of peripheral regions, independent of their link to the imperial center. The 1960s dash to periphery, which recalled the early Soviet period, invokes a conceptualization of a multidimensional and heterogeneous imperial spatiality that deconstructed the strict hierarchy of Stalinist spatial ideology.

Ultimately, Turoma's chapter attempts to shed light on the origins of post-Soviet attitudes to Soviet and Russian territory. The cultural politics of the 1960s shaped the worldviews of those Russians who in mid-life, at the height of their careers and personal lives, were faced with the fall of the socialist system and the disintegration of the Soviet Union. Turoma's analysis of the narratives of empire, nation, and identity seeks to uncover the roots of the cultural authority that spatial imaginings exercised on Russian-language intellectual formations and the endurance of a uniform spatial identity that these imaginings produced. The chapter takes issue with the boundary between "national" and "imperial," demonstrating how the Soviet spatial identity as a discursive construct blurred the boundaries between these seemingly binary conceptualizations.

Iina Kohonen extends the discussion of the 1960s Soviet spatial imagery to concern space exploration and visual representations of outer space. She sheds light on the uses of the philosophy of Cosmism in the Soviet Union by demonstrating how photographic practices and visual aesthetics played a crucial role in expressing the ideologies of cosmic utopianism that pervaded Soviet culture in the 1950–60s. Analyzing the photographs of the Luna program—the first three robotic spacecraft missions sent to the Moon in 1959—she shows how the Soviet Union produced and projected its new cosmic scale through visual descriptions of the first cosmic triumphs. Through the launch of a massive media program and controlled selection of cosmic imagery, outer space became a vital part of the Soviet landscape in the Khrushchev period. Mapping and naming the Moon, and propagating the cosmic imagery, was a way of incorporating outer space into Soviet imperial space.

Kevin M.F. Platt reconstructs the diverging strategies of representing "Russian culture" in contemporary Latvia by analyzing the Russian-language media and the works of Russian-language poets and other artists. One strategy combines the pretensions to global significance—as opposed to the supposed "smallness" of Latvian culture—with nostalgia for the bygone empire-size ethnic unity, faithfulness to the canonical forms of Soviet Russian high culture (ballet, opera, Pushkin, etc.), and, simultaneously, the assertion of the rootedness of the Russians in Latvia. Defensively contrasted with Latvian nationalistic discourse, which pictures "Russians" as non-European and foreign "invaders," and patronized by the Russian government, this self-victimizing and self-provincializing strategy dominates the Russian-language media and reflects the nearly hermetic isolation of Russian-language communication circuits from Latvian ones. Another strategy, exemplified by the multimedia artistic output of the "Orbit group," implies practicing cosmopolitan hybridity, rather than the nostalgic loyalty to ethnocentrically imagined bygone empire, and departure from artistic traditions, rather than loyalty to the officialized canons. In its politics and practice, the Orbit group produces Russian identity not by means of a return to the imagined "origins" but by gesturing toward margins, peripheries, borders, and limits of established linguistic and cultural forms as well as geographical territories. Marginal to the "mainstream" culture of the Russian community in Latvia, the group is broadly recognized within the bohemian cultural scene of Riga (Latvia's capital), often represents Latvia on the international cultural stage and, simultaneously, thrives on elite publishing contracts and contacts in Moscow and St. Petersburg. Hence, Platt concludes, precisely by distancing itself from ethnic and political definitions and centers of Russianness, the Orbit group succeeds in recuperating the transnational, or "universal," significance of Russian cultural output and preserving the cultural geography of the late Soviet period where "Russian culture" was not reducible to the culture of ethnic Russians and where Riga was a privileged site of cultural production, a "center on the ('Western') periphery."

Kevin Platt's study is exemplary in its manner of deconstructing and decentering the nationalistic assumption in understanding the spatiality and temporality of "culture." He demonstrates that the tendency to think of "cultures" in a unitary and bounded way is just one strategy of practicing and representing group identities. He also provides a case study, which illustrates the particular epistemic potential of post-Soviet space as an object of study. (Any) culture's perpetual non-coincidence with itself, its internal spatial and temporal fragmentation is particularly visible in the cultural significance of space and the spatial mapping of culture—the characteristics of Platt's case and the (post-)Soviet imperial space as whole. Even the ethnocentric discourse of post-imperial nostalgia, which dominates the cultural media of the Russian community in Latvia, is based on the premise of non-coincidence of political and cultural centrality of "Moscow"/"Russia" and on the (bygone) prestige of the Western Soviet peripheries as centers of Russian cultural innovation and European-style "civilization." Part of the explanation of the success of the works of the Orbit group members may be in their considerable reflexivity with respect to the nestedness of center–periphery relationships, the heterogeneity of different geographies and different temporal modalities, of which the space of culture is composed.

PART I
Eurasianism and Intellectual Construction of Space

CHAPTER 1

The Empire of Language: Space and Structuralism in Russian Eurasianism

Sergey Glebov

> Augen gab uns Gott ein Paar,
> Daß wir schauen rein und klar;
> Um zu glauben was wir lesen,
> Wär ein Auge gnug gewesen.
> Gott gab uns die Augen beide,
> Daß wir schauen und begaffen
> Wie er hübsch die Welt erschaffen
>
> Heinrich Heine, "ZurTeleologie"

For most Western scholars, the East European roots of structuralism remain, at best, a vague notion. Many authors have noted the influence of Roman Jakobson and of structuralist linguistics of the Prague Circle on Claude Lévi-Strauss and Jacques Lacan, and the two scholars repeatedly acknowledged the fundamentally important role of Jakobson's structural phonology in providing theoretical foundations for their own work. The role of linguistics as a "model" for the emerging structuralist paradigm of the post-World War II period has thus been sufficiently documented.[1] Still, it would probably come as a great surprise to most Western scholars that some of the ideas that Roman Jakobson communicated to his French counterparts in the 1940s and 1950s took shape in the context of his collaboration with participants in the Russian émigré Eurasianist movement, a complex and multifaceted attempt to reinvent—and recuperate—the former Russian Empire as Eurasia, a distinct civilization that developed out of the interaction between the Slavs and "Turanians."

This collaboration is the subject of this chapter. I am going to analyze the paradoxical intellectual alliance between two Eurasianist thinkers, the linguist Nikolai Trubetskoi and the geographer and economist Petr Savitskii, on the one hand, and Roman Jakobson on the other in the course of the 1920s and 1930s. The alliance emerged across many lines of division and was predicated on shared

---

[1] François Dosse, *History of Structuralism. Vol. I.The Rising Sign, 1945–1966*, trans. Deborah Glassman (Minneapolis, MN, 1997), esp. ChaptersII–IV, VIII.

commitments of the participants to what Patrick Sériot in his path-breaking study so aptly termed "national epistemology."[2] Jakobson, Savitskii, and Trubetskoi subscribed to a vision of a unique Russian scholarly tradition based on holistic approach, teleology, and resistance to positivism and evolutionism. Developing alongside the anti-colonialist rhetoric of the Eurasianist thinkers, the national epistemology also allowed the trio to question and subvert the perceived hierarchy in the production of knowledge in Europe. Although Jakobson and the Eurasianist thinkers arrived at that consensus from vastly different political and intellectual backgrounds, they all were critical of European modernity: for Jakobson, "Europe" stood for bourgeois conformism resistant to intellectual innovation, while for the Eurasianist thinkers it remained the source of much feared and detested revolution.[3]

The relationship between the emerging structuralist approaches in linguistics and Eurasianism was not a straightforward one. As Roman Jakobson and Nikolai Trubetskoi developed the structuralist approach in phonology, they increasingly relied on the rhetoric of "systemic" study of Eurasia produced by the Eurasianist thinkers. One can discern how certain concepts were shared between Eurasianism and emerging phonology in what we can call, following Pierre Bourdieu, "political ontology" of the scholarly and ideological language of the Eurasianist scholars.[4] For instance, the idea of the language union introduced by Trubetskoi and developed by Jakobson fitted well with phonology's concern for priority of acquired characteristics over the genetic ones and satisfied the Eurasianist insistence on the unity and historical convergence of Eurasia's groups. Similarly, the Eurasianist scholars rose against what they saw as the standardizing and leveling work of modernity and mourned the destruction of God-given differences. The understanding of phonemes as "bundles of distinctive features" fulfilling the basic meaning producing function in the language became one of the building blocks of rising phonology. Finally, the Eurasianist commitment to the notion of teleological and law-governed (*gesetzmäßig* (Ger.), *zakonomernyi* (Russ.) evolution—the idea upon which the concept of Eurasia as a historically constituted entity rested—was paralleled by the centrality of teleology to phonology's shift of focus to the function of distinctive elements of the system of sounds in the language.

---

[2] Patrick Sériot, *Structure et totalité: Les Origines intellectuelles du structuralisme en Europe centrale et orientale* (Paris, 1999). Further references are to the Russian edition:*Stru kturaitselostonost'. Ob intellektual'nykhistokakhstrukturalizma v Tsentral'noiiVostochnoiEvrope, 1920–1930* (Moscow, 2001).

[3] Natalia Avtonomova and Mikhail Gasparov, "Jakobson, Slavistics and the Eurasian Movement: Two Moments of Opportunity, 1929–1953," in Henryk Baran et al. (eds.), *Roman Jakobson. Teksty, dokumenty, issledovania* (Moscow, 1999), pp. 334–40.

[4] Pierre Bourdieu, *L'Ontologie politique de Martin Heidegger* (Paris, 1988).

My point in tracing these mutual ties is not just to prove yet another remarkable legacy of Eurasianism, albeit a useful task. As historians of Russia insist on exploring their subject within the "comparative framework of European modernity," I also want to draw attention to how an ideology that developed as a reaction to the dissolution of the Russian imperial space and stressed Russia's *Sonderweg* turned out to be an important influence in shaping an international scholarly movement.[5] Eurasianism's peculiar role in the birth of structuralism also raises questions about how intellectual concerns connected to challenges of conceptualizing imperial spaces (concerns that are largely hidden behind the powerful image of the nation-state as a "natural" form of the organization of political space) were in fact central to European intellectual history of the twentieth century. As scholars increasingly uncover imperial contexts of anthropology, sociology, geography, or historical writing, tracing imperial roots of such highly technical and abstract a discipline as linguistics proved to be a more challenging task and I hope to contribute to the growing literature on how empires and their legacies shaped the production of disciplinary knowledge.[6]

Specialists in linguistics, no doubt, will find my treatment of their field superficial. Historians, on the other hand, will question the inroads into a highly technical discipline such as linguistics. Yet, the exercise seems useful to me, as it helps uncover one of the most fascinating aspects of the history of the Eurasianist movement and its attempt to develop a language to describe the Russian imperial space through history, geography, linguistics, andethnography. Reflecting the imperial situation of Russia (that is, of a continental, relatively backward multiethnic state), Eurasianism stands out within the comparative framework of European modernity above all because it centered on the defense of the empire's unity and on subverting perceived hierarchies of development and civilization within Europe rather than on constructions of hierarchies within the imperial spaces.

* * *

---

[5] Yanni Kotsonis, "Introduction," in David L. Hoffman and Yanni Kotsonis (eds.), *Russian Modernity: Politics, Knowledge, Practices* (New York, 2000), p. 3; on the *Sonderweg* interpretations of Russian history see *Ab Imperio* 2/1(2002): 15–101 (contributions by Carl E. Schorske, Hans van der Loo, Gunilla-Friederike Budde, Jurgen Kocka, and Manfred Hildermeier).

[6] Literature on these imperial contexts is rapidly growing. See a review in "Introduction," in IlyaGerasimov, Jan Kusber, and AleksandrSemyonov(eds.), *Empire Speaks Out: Languages of Rationalization and Self-description in the Russian Empire* (Leiden, 2009); for sociology, see George Steinmetz (ed.),*Sociology and Empire* (Durham, NC, 2010); for an excellent review of anthropology in imperial contexts, see Marina Mogil'ner, *Homo Imperii. Istoriia fizicheskoi antropologii v Rossii (konets XIX–nachalo XX vv.)*(Moscow, 2008).

Lévi-Strauss met Roman Jakobson in New York, at the École Libre des Hautes Études established under the Charter from de Gaulle's government in exile (the École Libre was formally inaugurated on February 12, 1942).[7] Among many refugee scholars who came to the United States to join the École Libre there were several Russian émigrés: the political theorist Boris Mirkine-Guetzevitch (whom Lévi-Strauss credited with the idea of the École in exile), Alexandre Koyre (a historian of philosophy and the École Libre's secretary), and the linguist Roman Jakobson.

Alexandre Koyré introduced Claude Lévi-Strauss to Jakobson.[8] Their discussions continued in the summer of 1942 on the campus of Mount Holyoke College in South Hadley, Massachusetts, where Jean Wahl revived the interwar tradition of the Pontigny seminars.[9] As Claude Lévi-Strauss himself admitted, the encounter with Jakobson was crucial for his intellectual biography. He explained that he "was at the time a kind of a naïve structuralist." Lévi-Strauss confessed that he "did structuralism without knowing it. Jakobson opened for me the doctrine already constituted in a discipline: it was linguistics, which I never practiced. For me, it was a revelation."[10] Elsewhere, Lévi-Strauss engaged the work of Jakobson and Trubetskoi (calling the latter "the illustrious founder of structural linguistics") to demonstrate his own method of synchronic analysis of kinship systems as opposed to "individualist" and "atomistic" interpretations based on history.[11] He also told the story of Jakobson's contacts with Jacques Lacan, who was already influenced by another former Eurasianist, Alexandre Kojeve, whose lectures on Hegel Lacan had attended.[12] Jakobson inspired Lévi-Strauss to write *The Elementary Structures of Kinship*, the work that revolutionized anthropology by moving it from genetic analyses of ethnic cultures to the study

---

[7] Aristide R. Zolberg, "The Ecole Libre at the New School, 1941-1946,"*Social Research* 65/4 (1998): 921.

[8] Claude Lévi-Strauss, *De près et de loin* (Paris, 1988), pp. 62-5.

[9] Andrew Lass, "Poetry and Reality: Roman O. Jakobson and Claude Lévi-Strauss," in ChristoferBenfey and Karen Remmler (eds.), *Artists, Intellectuals and World War II: The Pontigny Encounters at Mount Holyoke College, 1942-1944* (Amherst, MA, 2006), pp. 173-84.

[10] Lévi-Strauss, *De près et de loin*.

[11] Claude Lévi-Strauss, "L'Analyse structurale en linguistique et en anthropologie," in *Word* 1 (1945): pp. 1-22; Claude Lévi-Strauss,"Structure et dialectique," in *For Roman Jakobson: Essays on the Occasion of His Sixtieth Birthday* (The Hague, 1956), pp. 289-94; Claude Lévi-Strauss, *Structural Anthropology*, vol. 2, trans. Claire Jacobson and Brooke Grundfest Schoepf (New York, 1963), pp. 33-4. The term "atomistic" is one of the key markers used by Eurasianist scholars to describe positivism in opposition to their own "systemic" methods.

[12] Lévi-Strauss, *De près et de loin*, pp. 62-5.

of structures of culture and of acquired characteristics. The encounter between Lévi-Strauss and Jakobson did not end with the former's departure for France after the war. Until Jakobson's death in 1982, the two corresponded actively and met regularly both in the US and in Europe.[13]

While there can be little doubt that Jakobson (and, via Jakobson, Trubetskoi) had a profound influence on the key structuralist, the element that is missing conspicuously in this story is a study of the intellectual and political context in which the structuralist rhetoric of Jakobson and Trubetskoi emerged in interwar Europe. When Jakobson met Lévi-Strauss, he had just arrived from Europe as a refugee. He also came with a history of almost two decades long collaboration with two Eurasianist scholars, N.S. Trubetskoi and P.N. Savitskii.

This collaboration complicated the structure of the Eurasianist movement to the extent that the latter was led by a larger group of four: N.S. Trubetskoi, P.N. Savitskii, P.P. Suvchinskii (Pierre Souvtchinsky), and P.S. Arapov. The scholarly troika of Trubetskoi, Savitskii, and Jakobson thus did not coincide neatly with the Eurasianist leadership. The cooperation between Jakobson, Trubetskoi, and Savitskii began in earnest with the foundation of the Prague Linguistic Circle in 1926,[14] and continued throughout the 1930s, while the Eurasianist movement as an organized political group disintegrated in 1929. Nevertheless, the scholarly project of substantiating the existence of Eurasia continued and even intensified in the 1930s.

---

[13] See correspondence between Jakobson and Lévi-Strauss in MIT Archives.MC 72 (Roman Jakobson Papers), Box 43, Folders 33 and 34. For correspondence between Jakobson and Jacques Lacan, see MIT Archives.MC 72 (Roman Jakobson Papers), Box 43, Folder 28.

[14] The literature on the Prague Linguistic Circle is very voluminous. Some of the most important works include Jean Pierre Faye et Léon Robel, *Le Cercle de Prague* (Paris, 1969); František W. Galan, *Historic Structures: The Prague School Project, 1928–1946* (Austin, 1984); Philip A. Luelsdorff(ed.), *The Prague School of Structural and Functional Linguistics: A Short Introduction* (Philadelphia, 1994). Especially important is Jindrich Toman, *The Magic of a Common Language: Jakobson, Mathesius, Trubetzkoy, and the Prague Linguistic Circle* (Cambridge, MA, 1995), because it pays attention to the ideological foundations of the linguistic thought of the Prague thinkers. Perhaps the best work that outlines these ideological foundations is Boris Gasparov, "The Ideological Principles of Prague School Phonology," in KrystynaPomorska et al. (eds.), *Language, Poetry and Poetics. The Generation of the 1890s: Jakobson, Trubetzkoy, Majakovskij. Proceedings of the First Roman Jakobson Colloquium, at the Massachusetts Institute of Technology, October 5–6, 1984* (New York and Berlin, 1987), pp. 49–78. Savitskii's contribution was P.N.Savickij, "Les problèmes de la géographie linguistique du point de vue du géographe," in *Travaux du Cercle linguistique de Prague* I (1929): 145–56.

"Not entirely ours": Roman Jakobson and the Eurasianists

Roman Osipovich Jakobson was born in Moscow in 1896 to a Russian Jewish family.[15] His father, an immigrant from the Habsburg Empire, was a prominent chemist, engineer, and industrialist. Roman Jakobson studied at the gymnasium of the Lazarev Institute of Oriental Languages, a prestigious school in Moscow (initially founded as an Armenian school but later emerging as a leading school of Oriental scholarship). The institute was directed by the Academician Vsevolod Fedorovich Miller, one of Russia's leading folklorists and specialists in Iranian languages. Jakobson entered Moscow University in 1914. At the university he became involved with an extraordinary group of philologists and linguists and founded the Moscow Linguistic Circle in 1915, of which he served as chair until 1919.[16] He also became fascinated with the poetry of the Futurists Velimir Khlebnikov and Vladimir Mayakovskii, and published, together with famous Aleksei Kruchenykh, trans-rational poetry of his own under the pseudonym Aliagrov.

It was in Moscow that he met and befriended a fellow student of philology, Prince Nikolai Sergeevich Trubetskoi. Jakobson recalled in the 1970s how he and Trubetskoi regularly returned from meetings of the MLC or the Dialectological Commission together and spent hours discussing linguistics, history, and literature.

This friendship developed into a lifelong intellectual collaboration. Jakobson remained deeply committed to the memory of Trubetskoi and to the promotion of his work after the latter's death in June 1938. It is difficult to imagine how this strange intellectual alliance emerged and developed transcending differences of origin, social position, and political views, not to mention psychological traits of both scholars. Trubetskoi was personally conservative, extremely religious, and deeply nationalist. He also was a fervent anti-Semite who associated Jews with the destructive force of the all-leveling modernity (Jakobson tended to dismiss Trubetskoi's anti-Semitism as a cultural atavism of the Russian aristocracy).[17] His literary tastes were, to say the least, unexciting: Trubetskoi thought little of Ilya Ehrenburg's experimental novels and famously dismissed Boris Pasternak as

---

[15] Among many works on Roman Jakobson's life and work, one can note Elmar Holenstein, *Roman Jakobson's Approach to Language. Phenomenological Structuralism* (Bloomington, 1976); Richard Bradford, *Roman Jakobson. Life, Language, Art* (New York, 1994); *A Tribute to Roman Jakobson, 1896–1982* (Berlin and New York, 1983); Stephen Rudy, *Roman Jakobson, 1896–1982: A Complete Bibliography of His Writings* (New York, 1990); and the excellent volume *Roman Jakobson. Teksty, dokumenty...*

[16] Grigorii Vinokur, "Moskovskii Lingvisticheskii Kruzhok," *Nauchnyelzvestia Akademicheskogo Tsentra Narkomprosa*, vol. 2 (Moscow, 1922).

[17] Viacheslav V. Ivanov, "BurianadN'iufaundlendom. Izvospominanii o Romane Jakobsone," in *Roman Jakobson. Teksty.dokumenty...*, p. 252.

a "star of tenth degree." Jakobson, on the contrary, was revolutionary, innovative, experimental, cosmopolitan, and left-wing. Trubetskoi's life appears to have been compartmentalized to a great extent as he functioned in two different planes of existence, the one in which he sought to recover the lost foundations of life, culture, and religion through the holistic teaching of Eurasianism, and the other in which he pursued a radically innovative scholarly agenda. Jakobson's biographical trajectory was less schizophrenic: He made innovation and change into his most important intellectual and even biographical pursuit. His involvement with Russian modernist poetry, formalism, Eurasianism, Slavic studies in the US, and structuralism colored those intellectual ventures with a reddish shade of revolutionary turmoil.[18] While Trubetskoi often reflected pan-European *Kulturpessimismus* and saw modernity as a leveling and standardizing force that eliminated differences, Jakobson's texts radiated with cultural optimism and futuristic pathos.

In the spirit of this cultural optimism, Jakobson attempted to work in Russia in the early years of Soviet power in the hopes that the Revolution would open up new paths for creativity. He continued to serve as the chair of the Moscow Linguistic Circle until 1919 and took an active part in the work of OPOJAZ, the informal group of literary scholars who laid the foundations for the formalist school. The Revolution did not disrupt Jakobson's focus on the Futurists and in 1919 he wrote his first book on Velimir Khlebnikov, the famous author of startling "trans-rational" poetry.

However, as the Bolshevik grip on the country tightened, Jakobson went abroad and became the head of the press bureau of the Soviet Red Cross mission in Prague. His position in the Russian émigré circles was precarious: he was working for the Soviets, he remained a Soviet citizen, he was Jewish, and he was left-wing. Although he departed from Russia, he was not a full-fledged participant in the émigré life. After the publication of his famous article "On the Generation that Spent Its Poets" in 1930, Jakobson chose not to return to the Soviet Union. By that time he had already embarked on a scholarly career abroad. In the early 1920s Jakobson developed close ties with the Czech literary milieu and published scholarly studies of Czech poetry.

---

[18] Sometimes this aura of a left-wing intellectual got Jakobson into trouble: In Czechoslovakia, the press ran a campaign in which he was depicted as a Soviet agent, and in the US he barely escaped an encounter with the McCarthy Commission. In the latter case, Michael Karpovich's intervention and witnessing of Jakobson's "anti-Communist credentials" saved him. In another instance, Eisenhower's brief tenure of the presidency of Columbia University while Jakobson worked there seems to have helped him when he was questioned by FBI. See Stephen Rudy, "Jakobson pri makkartizme," in *Roman Jakobson. Teksty, dokumenty...*, pp. 192–200.

In 1930, following Trubetskoi's advice, Jakobson defended his doctoral dissertation at the German University in Prague (where P.N. Savitskii taught geography and economics) and soon received a position at the University of Brno, which he occupied until 1939. Jakobson's dissertation was a study of the historical evolution of phonological changes in Russian, which, together with Trubetskoi's *Grundzüge der Phonologie* laid foundations for phonology as a distinct field preoccupied with differentiating functions of sounds in the language.

The Nazi occupation of Central Europe interrupted Jakobson's scholarly career. A mind-boggling flight from Czechoslovakia to Denmark in April 1939, then Norway (where Jakobson arrived as Europe officially descended into World War II on September 1, 1939) and Sweden (where he fled literally before the advancing Nazi occupation forces from Norway and where he completed his famous work on aphasia) followed. In May 1941 Jakobson and his wife departed from Sweden to the United States on a cargo ship (Ernst Cassirer was another refugee passenger).[19]

Jakobson and Trubetskoi began their correspondence in 1920, as soon as they arrived in Czechoslovakia and Bulgaria respectively, and continued it until Trubetskoi's death in 1938. They also met regularly, even if not often, in person. Jakobson visited Trubetskoi in Vienna, while Trubetskoi came to Prague on various occasions. Their very last meeting occurred on February 12, 1938, when the Austrian Chancellor Schuschnigg met Hitler at Berchtesgaden in the vain attempt to prevent the Anschluss.[20] This final meeting was focused on discussions regarding interpretations of distinctive features in phonology, with Jakobson sharing with the skeptical Trubetskoi his idea of the binary nature of all distinctive features in phonemes.

Judging from their correspondence, one cannot say that Trubetskoi regularly informed Jakobson on Eurasianist developments. He nevertheless felt obliged to explain his first book, *Europe and Mankind*, as soon as it came out in 1920 and discuss it with Jakobson. Soon, Trubetskoi sent Jakobson the first Eurasianist collection of articles (*Exodus to the East*) and introduced him to the tenets of Eurasianism:

> it would be very interesting to know your opinion about it [the collection]. Its essence is in finding and probing new paths for some new direction that we call Eurasianism [*evrazistvo*], a term that might not be entirely apt but it strikes the

---

[19] Bengt Jangfeldt, "Roman Jakobson v Shvetsii, 1940–1941," in *Roman Jakobson. Teksty, dokumenty...*, pp. 167–74.

[20] Moris Halle, "On the Origins of Distinctive Features," in M. Halle (ed.), *Roman Jakobson: What He Taught Us* (Columbus, OH, 1983), p. 83.

eye, it is provocative and therefore suitable for agitation purposes. This direction is in the air, I sense it in the poetry of M. Voloshin, A. Blok, Esenin, in "Russia's Paths" by Bunakov-Fundaminskii, and, at the same time, in conversations with some extreme right-wingers and even with an inveterate Kadet.[21]

Trubetskoi presented Eurasianism to Jakobson not as a local Russian ideology redefining the country's identity vis-à-vis Europe but as a part of some universal and critical revolution in the *Zeitgeist*, which undoubtedly was appealing to Jakobson:

> it looks like a shift in the consciousness of the intelligentsia is about to arrive, it may well sweep off all the old directions and will create new ones, on entirely new foundations. All this is too indefinite at this point but undoubtedly "something is coming, something is being prepared," and in these conditions it is necessary to arouse thought, to shake it out of slumber, to awaken it, to move it from the dead point, to tease it with unacceptable paradoxes, to stubbornly reveal what people attempt to hide from themselves...[22]

During their meetings throughout the 1920s Trubetskoi attempted to convert Jakobson to Eurasianist ideas and the Eurasianist spirit. In the winter of 1926 P.P. Suvchinskii sought Trubetskoi's advice on potential authors for the literary journal *Versty*, which Suvchinskii co-founded with D.S. Mirsky in Paris. Jakobson's candidacy immediately came up and Trubetskoi cautioned Suvchinskii: "I would wait with inviting Jakobson. After all, he has a certain reputation and the appearance of his name in the first issues of the journal would create a presumption. With time, though, you need to invite him: he is very talented." This advice was followed by a typically anti-Semitic diatribe by Trubetskoi: "In general, fewer kikes. You shouldn't pursue Pasternak: I think his reputation is overrated."[23] Trubetskoi wrote to Suvchinskii again after a Prague meeting with prominent Soviet philologists organized by Jakobson: 'I am especially close to and united with Jakobson. In the realm of scholarship he is, probably, the person closest to me. Even about everyday life [*byt*] he is now saying those "right" words. He is going to write about it for the *Versty*, although he asks not to reveal his name.[24] Trubetskoi's proselytizing efforts seemed to have been in vain and he confessed to Suvchinskii in the fall of

---

[21] Roman Jakobson (ed.), *N.S. Trubetzkoy's Letters and Notes* (The Hague, 1975), pp. 21–2.
[22] Ibid., p. 22.
[23] Nikolai Trubetskoi to Petr Suvchinskii, February 15, 1926. Bibliotheque Nationale de France (BNF), Department de Musique (DdM). Not catalogued at the time of access.
[24] Nikolai Trubetskoi to Petr Suvchinskii, n.d. (fall 1927). BNF,DdM. Not catalogued.

1927 that "unfortunately, [Jakobson] is hopeless not only with respect to religion but also with respect to his political convictions. He accepts neither ideocracy nor etatism, however much I try."[25]

The Eurasianists were clearly ambivalent about Jakobson's full participation in the movement. His Jewish origin was an important consideration for them in the context of their attempts to secure broad support among the generally conservative and anti-Semitic émigrés. Similarly, Jakobson's association with the Futurists such as Vladimir Mayakovskii, his left-leaning sympathies, and, above all, his work for the Soviet mission in Prague were barely acceptable for the Eurasianists and their conservative émigré audience. Still, Trubetskoi saw Jakobson as his immediate ally in the scholarly battles that accompanied the emergence of structural phonology. As Trubetskoi grew increasingly disenchanted with Eurasianism's political entanglements, which he blamed for taking up his scholarly time, he also grew closer to Jakobson, with whom he shared his linguistic ideas.

Trubetskoi introduced Jakobson to P.N. Savitskii, another Eurasianist scholar. Since Jakobson and Savitskii both lived in Prague (where Jakobson resided until he assumed a position at the Masaryk University in Brno), they became close and actively exchanged ideas. When the Eurasianist movement as a political organization and a publishing venture disintegrated in 1928–29, and the same fate befell the Eurasianist leading troika of Savitskii, Suvchinskii, and Trubetskoi, a new alliance emerged. This time, it was informal and scholarly, and consisted of Jakobson, Savitskii, and Trubetskoi. The new alliance had little taste for the Eurasianist ambitions of converting the Soviet leadership or participating in underground networks of spies and terrorists. Yet, intellectually it focused on the same issues that preoccupied the Eurasianists in the 1920s: the unity of the Eurasian space as reflected in geography, linguistics, or history, and the new, "systemic" and "structural" methods of describing that unity. As Savitskii wrote to Jakobson in 1930, their work had to be based on the understanding of "Russian studies as a "system" and "autarkic regularity" [*samozakonnost'*]."[26]

Trubetskoi left in his correspondence certain clues that allow us to reconstruct the attitude of the Eurasianist leaders to Jakobson. The latter himself, though, left very few specific clues as to what attracted him in the circle of the Eurasianists. He posthumously called Savitskii "a genius inventor

---

[25] Nikolai Trubetskoi to Petr Suvchinskii, n.d. (fall 1927). BNF,DdM. Not catalogued. According to archival evidence, Jakobson became interested in religion in the early 1930s and was baptized in 1936.

[26] Petr Savitskii to Roman Jakobson, August 7, 1930. MIT Archives, MC 72, Box 119, Folder 95.

of structuralist geography" and made the propagation of Trubetskoi's legacy his personal task. Beyond that, we know very little about Jakobson's ideas with respect to Eurasianism as a whole. We can speculate that he found himself in relative isolation in the Russian-speaking world (as a former Soviet employee, he was suspicious for the émigrés, and as an émigré he was a *persona non grata* for the Soviets). Although Jakobson established close and lasting ties to Czech intellectuals, especially in the period of the Prague Linguistic Circle, the Eurasianists were the only Russians in the immediate proximity with whom he socialized. Certain biographical details—such as Jakobson's baptism in 1936 into Orthodox Christianity (Savitskii was his godfather) and the warmth and intensity of personal correspondence—seem to confirm this notion. Jakobson's lifelong rift with Viktor Shklovskii centered on the question of where a Russian philologist should reside, and Jakobson's connection to the fiercely nationalist Eurasianists might have been a recompense for the inability to practice Russian philology "normally," that is, in Russia proper.

On the other hand, Jakobson undoubtedly sensed and appreciated the Eurasianist rhetoric of drastic innovation and reconsideration of established ideas and assumptions. Eurasianism was a radically innovative movemen t that promoted a conservative vision of Eurasia as an antimodernist utopia. Jakobson was attracted to the radically innovative method if not to the vision itself. His lasting commitment to some Eurasianist ideas may substantiate this point. In 1972 Jakobson suggested to an Italian publisher in Turin a translation of Trubetskoi's early ideological work, *Europe and Mankind*, and wrote a preface to this publication. In this text, Jakobson fondly interpreted Trubetskoi's vicious attack on the European civilization and his critique of European cultural imperialism as informed by his search for innovation in humanities: 'The negative position of this platform (which was further developed by the author's ideology) essentially corresponds to the pathos of fundamental revision of the foundations of traditional linguistics, a revision that Trubetskoi had feverishly elaborated since 1917 despite all external troubles.'[27]

Jakobson thus occupied an unusual place among Eurasianism's many and diverse adherents. On the one hand, he did not—and could not—fully participate in all aspects of the movement. At the same time, he shared some of Eurasianism's key interests. In particular, Jakobson found its rhetoric of innovation and its scholarly edge appealing. Undoubtedly, Jakobson creatively reinterpreted Eurasianism's ideology to suit his own overarching interest: with its critique of the hierarchies of cultural and scholarly production, Eurasianism,

---

[27] MIT Archives, MC 72, Box 28, Folder 103. "Po povodu knigi N.S. Trubetskogo 'Evropa i Chelovechestvo'" (manuscript).

not unlike phonology, was above all a field capable of revolutionizing epistemological foundations of scholarly research. Last but not least, Jakobson found the Eurasianist vision of a specifically Russian scientific tradition appealing and took part in its elaboration.

In Search of Russian Science

For all Eurasianist thinkers the new scientific era of which they were the harbingers was connected with ideas and methods rooted in the Russian intellectual tradition. They viewed their scholarly debates in respective disciplines—such as linguistics—in light of the epistemological differences between "cultures." As Trubetskoi reminded Jakobson in 1934, the French dislike of Jakobson's scholarly work was related to a "certain repulsion of the French from those forms of Eurasian-Danubian culture in which contemporary phonology expresses itself."[28] Reflecting the new intellectual mood of the 1920s that stressed national scholarly traditions, they spoke of the specific "Russian science" that differed from its West European counterpart by preferences in the object of study and a specific method.[29] That method—"systemic" or "structuralist"—was opposed to the "atomistic" science of the nineteenth century. "Russian science" was teleological, and it embraced the entirety of facts and attempted to find regularities that governed the ocean of data. The Eurasianists offered an unprecedented attempt to translate their ideological doctrine of Russia's "special path" into a conception (a range of conceptions, to be precise) of a "Russian science" as the source of a new scholarly paradigm.

Petr Savitskii, a geographer, was probably the first Eurasianist thinker to offer a vision of national science. His own geographical method was derived from the Russian tradition of *Naturphilosophie* and Russian geographical scholarship, in particular, from Vasilii Dokuchaev's systemic study of soils.[30] Savitskii spatialized scholarly thought by suggesting that Dokuchaev's approach was determined by its very location (which, in this case, was also the object of study) in Russia. This

---

[28] *N. S. Trubetzkoy's Letters and Notes...*, p. 300.

[29] For an argument about "nationalization" of science in the context of World War I, which focuses on the activities on Vladimir Vernadskii, see Alexei Kojevnikov, "The Great War, the Russian Civil War, and the Invention of Big Science," in *Science in Context* 15/2 (2002): 239–75; D.A. Aleksandrov, "Pochemu sovetskie uchenye perestali pechatat'sia zarubezhom: stanovlenie samodostatochnosti I izolirovannosti otechestvennoi nauki, 1914–1940," in *Voprosy istorii estestvoznania I tekhniki* 3 (1996): 3–24.

[30] Petr Savitskii, *Geograficheskie osobennosti Rossii* (Prague, 1927), pp. 9–20.

idea fitted neatly with Savitskii's key geographical concept of "place-development" [*mestorazvitie*] designed to instrumentalize Eurasia as a close and autarkic system.

For the Eurasianist scholar, the connections between Russian geography's allegedly unique methods and its unique object of study were obvious and natural. He suggested that in European geography there existed a geomorphologic focus defined by Europe's intense geomorphologic structure, whereas in the Russian geography the emphasis is upon geo-biology and the study of soils. Morphology, due to the lack of mountains, is relatively unimportant. The lack of significant mountain ranges that could have changed the climatic conditions across the country as well as Russia's vast expanses made it possible to observe the zonal structure of soils and flora (the structure dependent on the south–north direction of climatic change) at is clearest. In a way, Russia was a polygon for the study of climate and vegetation zones running uninterruptedly from the Atlantic seabed to the Pacific. That is why, Savitskii believed, the study of forests became so prominent here, and that is why the science of soil conditions was born.

While specifically Russian geographic methods and objects stressed the uniqueness and wholeness of Eurasia as a natural complex, they also illustrated the opposition between Europe and Eurasia. Savitskii even asserted that it was possible to speak of two different worlds of geography, the Russian and the European, each with its specific poetics and language. Was it not true that Russians borrowed from the Germans most of the terms used in geomorphology, whereas Russian words that designate soils and natural zones, such as "chernozem" or "steppes," gained currency abroad?

But Russian geographical science was not just a "place-development." For Savitskii, it was methodologically unique because it also promoted a synthetic method of studying natural and social phenomena.[31] In the Russian geographic tradition Savitskii saw the tendency of Russian geography not to limit itself to descriptions of "atomized objects" (we can note the appearance of this term in Savitskii's work here and follow it through Trubetskoy to Lévi-Strauss) but to engage in a systemic exploration of interrelationships between different forms of organic and nonorganic nature on the given territory, including humans and their societies. In his 1927 work on Russia's geographic specifics Savitskii quoted Dokuchaev's work *On the Teaching of Natural Zones*, in which the latter comes very close to formulating what appears as a structuralist approach focusing on the relationship between elements in the system:

---

[31] Savitskii, *Geograficheskieosobennosti...*, pp. 21–8.

> It cannot be doubted that the knowledge of nature—of its forces, its elements, its phenomena and its physical bodies—has made such gigantic steps in the course of the nineteenthcentury that the century itself is often called the age of natural sciences and natural scientists. However, it was mostly separate bodies that were studied, such as minerals, rocks, plants, and animals, and separate phenomena, separate elements, such as fire (volcanism), water, earth, air. We shall repeat that in that science may have reached astounding results. But it did not study their interrelationships, this genetic, eternal and always regular [*zakonomernyi, gesetzsmäßig*] connection that exists between forces, bodies, and phenomena, between organic and nonorganic nature, between the realms of plants, animals, and minerals on the one hand, and the man, his life, and even his spiritual world, on the other. Yet, it is these interrelationships, these regular mutual interactions that form the essence of our cognition of nature, the kernel of true *Naturphilosophie*, the best and highest charm of natural sciences!³²

One of the key elements of Savitskii's work was his attempt to substantiate the specificity and geographical unity of Russia/Eurasia. To do so, he constructed a series of regularities that allegedly governed that unity and sharply separated Eurasia from Europe. One such regularity consisted in the principle of climatic change (temperature and humidity) along the axis north–south, which in turn established the regular transition from the zone of the tundra to that of the forest and finally the steppe. This regularity was interpreted by Savitskii as an increase in "continental characteristics" in the heart of Eurasian steppes.

Savitskii's work that outlined his geographical views was published in 1927 as part of the Eurasianist ambitious publishing venture. As soon as it appeared, Trubetskoi rushed to report about it to Roman Jakobson: "Savitskii's *Geographical Specifics* [*of Russia*] has been published. Do read it. It's interesting. It's the first attempt to bring *structure* [cursive mine, SG] to a field that has traditionally been marred by chaos…"³³ As we shall see later, Jakobson did read it and assimilated Savitskii's methodological "system," which assumed the existence of a deep structure underlying the visible surface of "atomistic" facts and governing the configuration of territoriality.

While Savitskii primarily elaborated on the legacy of the German *Naturphilosophie* and especially the work of Friedrich Ratzel with its conception of the "territorial complex" in Russian geography, for Roman Jakobson Russian Slavic studies represented the field that promised innovation in scholarly research. In the first, programmatic article that he published in the *Slavische*

---

³² Quoted in Savitskii, *Geograficheskie osobennosti…*, p. 28.
³³ *N. S. Trubetzkoy's Letters and Notes…*, p. 227.

Rundschau in 1929 (the article was originally solicited from Trubetskoi, who did not live up to the promise to deliver the text), Jakobson outlined his vision of the Russian Slavic studies as a locomotive of structuralism.[34] According to Jakobson, "Studies of Russia [*Russlandkunde*] witness the fact that in an entire range of disciplines, for example, in literary studies, art history, linguistics, very heated discussions are taking place on crucial theoretical issues…," and, correspondingly, "one senses an uplifting and a teleological movement of Russian studies to their future significance."[35] Jakobson noted—in a clear reference to Eurasianist geo-cultural preferences—that in Russian scholarship exploration of Romano-Germanic languages and cultures was in disarray compared to the very developed Oriental studies.

Eurasianist influences were visible in other arguments by Jakobson as well. The most important, indeed crucial, feature of modern Russian studies for Jakobson consisted in that "Russia was explored as a structured whole." Any province tends to become autarkic within its territory, Jakobson admitted, "but in the Russian scientific thought the desire to embrace the entire Russian world and to view its temporary and spatial representations from the point of view of the whole was prevalent."[36] Thus, Jakobson made clear that in his view the new epistemological approach—structuralism—was intrinsically linked to the holistic conception of Russia and its territory and culture. To make his preferences and sources clear, he immediately listed examples of these new structuralist studies: Savitskii's conception of Russia as a "special geographic world" and Trubetskoi's works that revealed "the unity of the Eurasian cultural circle" [*Eurasische Kulturzyklus*].[37] Jakobson also noted, in a reference to his own work, that an exploration of the "structural unity of Eurasian languages originally not tied by genetic bonds was being prepared."[38]

The fact that in his 1929 article Jakobson inserted those very lines of Dokuchaev that had been quoted by Savitskii in his 1927 book on the geographic characteristics of Russia in order to illustrate the holistic and all-embracing

---

[34] Roman Jakobson, "Über die heutigen Voraussetzungen der russischen Slavistik," in *Slavische Rundschau* 1 (1929): 629–46. Hereafter quoted from the Russian translation by Natalia Avtonomova: Roman Jakobson, "O sovremennykh perspektivakh russkoi slavistiki," in *Roman Jakobson.Teksty, dokumenty…*, pp. 21–33.

[35] Ibid., p. 22.

[36] Ibid., p. 23.

[37] Here Jakobson's choice of words is unusual. This is probably a reference to the anthropology of *Kulturzyklen* developed by the Austrian scholar Wilhelm Schmidt.

[38] Apart from Savitskii, Jakobson listed the geographer Tanfil'ev, the ethnographer Zelenin, and the linguists Bubrikh, Selishchev, and Georgievskii. All these scholars he will quote in his work on the Eurasian union of languages. Ibid., p. 23.

nature of the Russian scholarly tradition, point to the fact that Jakobson's thought was under the direct influence of the "systemic" science promoted by Savitskii.³⁹ If the latter believed that Russian science was focused on the unity of the universe, Jakobson argued that "for the fundamental and deeply original line of development of contemporary Russian science the following is characteristic: The correlation [*Korrelativität*] of separate rows of facts is not viewed in terms of causal dependence...the main concept with which [Russian] science operates is a system of correlating rows of facts, a structure immanent for the observer, and subjected to its own internal laws."⁴⁰

Jakobson's publication came out at an interesting juncture in the history of Eurasianism. The long-running conflict between Savitskii and Suvchinskii, shattering revelations of the extent of the Soviet secret services' penetration of the emigration through the fake monarchist organization Trest and the Eurasianist involvement with the underground operations of the GPU, and the increasingly pro-Soviet orientation of the newspaper *Eurasia* that Suvchinskii operated from Paris finally caused the movement to implode. Outraged by its "dangerous flirtation with Marxism," Trubetskoi publicly withdrew from organized Eurasianism in January 1929 (confirming, however, his commitment to all his Eurasianist writings). Informed by Savitskii about the pro-Soviet publications in *Eurasia*, Henry Norman Spalding cut funding to the Parisian Eurasianist group. Petr Arapov, the central figure in the organized political movement of the Eurasianists and a Soviet agent, secretly left for the USSR in 1930. All this left the movement in tatters, yet gave Savitskii a unique opportunity to reshape what was left according to his own taste.

The resurrection of Eurasianism à *la* Savitskii began with the publication of the volume of collected essays. Savitskii wrote to Jakobson that he sensed "a general cultural uplifting in the Eurasianist milieu" a year after the collapse of the movement and suggested that the new volume "would in its content equal 'Exodus to the East' [the first Eurasianist publication that appeared in 1921]."⁴¹ When the volume saw light of day, it carried the title *Tridtsatye*

---

³⁹ Ibid.

⁴⁰ Ibid., pp. 24–5. It should be noted that in the article Jakobson also wrote about the formalists as representatives of the new structuralist paradigm that privileged acquired characteristics over the genetic ones. He also demanded that Slavic cultures be studied in the light of the new paradigm focusing on their convergence and divergence and not on their genetic affinities. On Jakobson's article in the context of different scholarly and ideological contexts, see Avtonomova and Gasparov, "Jakobson, Slavistics and the Eurasian Movement."

⁴¹ PetrSavitskii to Roman Jakobson, August 7, 1930. MIT Archives, MC 72, Box 119, Folder 95.

Gody. Utverzhdeniia evraziitsev [The 1930s. Affirmations of the Eurasianists], echoing the title of the first collective Eurasianist manifesto.[42] It contained 17 contributions, of which six Savitskii wrote himself (under three different names). The rest belonged to the Kalmyk scholar Erzhen Khara-Davan ("On Nomadic Customs"), the well-known philologist Petr Nikolaevich Bogatyrev (under the pseudonym Ivan Savel'ev; "The Specifics of Russian Folkloric Studies"), Georgii [George] Vernadskii ("Notes on Lenin"), Vladimir Nikolaevich Il'in on science and dialectics, N.N. Alekseev on Eurasianist interpretations of law, Ia. Bromberg ("On Jewish Eurasianism"), and Konstantin Chkheidze on geopolitics. Markedly absent were typical Eurasianist texts of the 1920s on Orthodoxy and modernity, usually penned by Suvchinskii, and the general character of the collection was in line with "scholarly" Eurasianism.

The overall goal of the collection was "planning the decade" of Eurasianist studies in the 1930s. Scholarship and "systemic" study of Eurasia was central to the revival of Eurasianism. In this spirit, Savitskii began to approach Jakobson about his contribution in the spring of 1930, but, as of August, Jakobson failed to deliver and the volume appeared without his work. Sometime in October Jakobson shared with Savitskii the draft of his planned chapter and it was decided that it was to appear as a separate publication under the title *K Khrakteristike evraziiskogo iazykovogo soiuza* [On the Eurasian Language Union], which it did in late 1931.

The Empire of Language: Space and the Study of Structures

The overlapping interests and concerns of rising structuralist phonology and Eurasianism became highly visible with the publication of Roman Jakobson's work on the Eurasian language union. Written while Jakobson's cooperation with the Eurasianists reached its peak, the work set out to demonstrate that languages spoken on the territory of Eurasia developed similarities that crossed the boundaries of genetic linguistic families. In analyzing those characteristics, Jakobson utilized the methods of phonology and the structuralist principles elaborated by the geographer Savitskii.

To be sure, the very notion of the "language union" [*Sprachbund, iazykovoi soiuz*] was developed by Trubetskoi in 1923. The context in which Trubetskoi developed this concept is in itself quite interesting. It did not appear in a specialized linguistic journal, where Trubetskoi regularly published his linguistic studies. Rather, it was introduced in the article "The Tower of Babel and the

---

[42] The first Eurasianist collection was titled *Exodus to the East. Forebodings and Achievements. Affirmations of the Eurasianists*.

Mixing of Languages," which appeared in the third annual almanac of the Eurasianist movement.[43] In the article, Trubetskoi not only attacked the possible monolingual international culture as a sin against the God-given diversity of tongues and cultures, a guarantee of the spiritual richness of humanity. He also suggested a new linguistic concept that spelled out a break with the linguistic tradition of the nineteenth century that insisted on analyzing languages according to the "genetic tree":

> Apart from the genetic grouping, the geographically close languages often can be grouped independently of their origins. It happens that several languages of one geographic and cultural-historical region reveal features of particular similarity despite the fact that these similarities are not conditioned by common descent but only by prolonged spatial proximity and parallel development. For such groups based not on the genetic principle we propose the term of "language unions."[44] Such language unions exist not only between single languages but also between language families, that is, it happens that several linguistic families, which are not genetically related to each other but which occupy one geographic and cultural-historical zone, are united into a union of linguistic families by a range of common features...[45]

The Eurasianist context of Trubetskoi's argument is evident: The replacement of the genetic model with that of historical convergence offered a possibility to remap Eurasia's linguistic makeup. Instead of the conglomeration of languages belonging to the Indo-European, Uralic, and Altaic families, one could attempt to find language unions that would endow Eurasia with a degree of linguistic homogeneity. Language unions also have the potential to construct boundaries that would coincide with other lines of division, such as confessional, between, for example, the Czechs and the Russians, both of whom belong to the Slavic group of the Indo-European family of languages but are divided by the boundary between Latin Christendom and Greek Orthodoxy.

This is exactly what Jakobson undertook in his work on the Eurasian language union. He provided linguistic material for Trubetskoi's concept and outlined

---

[43] Nikolai Trubetskoi, "Vavilonskaia Bashnia I smeshenie iazykov," *Evraziiskii Vremennik* 3 (1923): 116–17.

[44] Trubetskoi's footnote: "A clear example of a language union in Europe is presented by the Balkan languages, such as Bulgarian, Romanian, Albanian, and the modern Greek: Although they belong to completely different branches of the Indo-European family, they nevertheless are united with each other by an entire range of common features and detailed coincidences in the sphere of grammatical construction."

[45] Trubetskoi, "Vavilonskaia Bashnia...," pp. 116–17.

the existence of a distinct region characterized by the presence of phonologically determined characteristics. For Jakobson, this work was part of a greater scholarly task, which was "to capture correlations of phenomena of different planes and to discover in these correlations a regular [*zakonomernyi*] order."[46] Jakobson termed his approach as "method of correlations" [*metod uviazki*].[47] This method consisted in comparing data from various disciplines and was based on Savitskii's attempt to put side by side the position of Russian dialects on the map with the lines marking major climactic and orographic changes. Trubetskoi and Jakobson were impressed by Savitskii's work that was presented to the Prague Linguistic Circle in 1928, motivating Jakobson to pursue his study of the Eurasian language union.[48] As Jakobson suggested, "the unexpected fact that the Russian dialectological map reproduces characteristic features of the zonal composition of the Eurasian geographical map stimulates us to expand the framework of our studies and to subject, along with the Russian language, the entire diversity of the languages of Eurasia to a confrontation with data of geography."[49]

For Jakobson, the discussion of the language union was predicated on the notion of convergence. Linguists had long discovered similarities between territorially adjacent but genetically unrelated languages and explained them through borrowing. Jakobson argued that this outdated approach was due to "the preeminence of the genetic interests above functional problematic."[50] Yet, with the help of the new synthetic approach and a structuralist understanding of the development of language.scholars can determine that "borrowing and convergence do not exclude one another and cannot be categorically opposed to each other."[51] It is crucial to understand whether a specific borrowing is "sanctioned by the system" and whether it "corresponds to the system's needs and evolution."[52] Convergence of languages, then, can only be determined if scholars are capable of discovering the intrinsic laws governing each language's development.

While any language, according to Jakobson, is a system of systems, "the most fruitful research of similarities between neighboring languages can be achieved in the science of the linguistic sound order" because of the advances in phonology. Jakobson defined the latter as a study of phonological systems, each of which is

---

[46] Roman Jakobson, *K kharakteristike evraziiskogo iazykovogo soiuza* (Paris, 1931), p. 5.
[47] Ibid.
[48] Savitskii's work was published as P.N. Savickij, "Les problèmes de la géographie linguistique du point de vue du géographe," in *Travaux du Cercle linguistique de Prague* 1 (1929): pp. 145–56.
[49] Jakobson, *K kharakteristike*..., p. 6.
[50] Ibid., p. 6.
[51] Ibid., p. 7.
[52] Ibid., p. 8.

"the inventory of such acoustic differences that make differentiation of meaning possible."[53] Such an inventory was based on the phoneme, the smallest acoustic element capable of distinguishing meaning in the language. The phonemes are "combined in certain relations in the language and form a system."[54] These relations are repeatable and may become systemic or structural correlations. For instance, Czech, Magyar, Latin, and Serbian are characterized by the quantitative correlations of vowels: Oppositions between long and short vowels are capable of distinguishing meaning. In Russian, such correlations include stressed vs. unstressed vowels, timbre correlation of consonants (hard vs. soft), and so on.

One such phonological correlation, according to Jakobson, is the changes in the musical tone of the voice. As long as such changes form part of oppositions and are capable of producing differences in meaning, one can speak of "polytonic" languages. Jakobson discovered the existence of the Baltic polytonic union, which included "Swedish, Norwegian, most Danish dialects, some German Baltic dialects, Northern Kashubian, Lithuanian, Latvian, and Estonian."[55] Albeit these languages did not use polytony to the same extent as the great Pacific polytonic language union, Jakobson claimed that "Eurasia appears to be symmetrically delimited from two sides by the polytonic language unions, by the Baltic from the North-West and by the Pacific from the South-East."[56] To the languages of Eurasia itself, then, "polytony is entirely alien."[57]

This vision of Eurasia, though, was vague. After all, most languages of Europe and Asia were monotonic. Jakobson suggested that another phonological distinction—the timbre distinction between the presence and the absence of soft vs. hard consonants—should be utilized to define the linguistic map of Eurasia. The key example of the language characterized by the phonological juxtaposition of soft vs. hard consonants was, of course, Russian. The western boundary of the language union based on the timbre correlation ran according to Jakobson between Ukrainian and Slovak dialects, with Polish dialects representing a transition from those where the correlation of soft vs. hard consonants had a phonological function to those (in the West) where it did not. In the south, Jakobson found that "only eastern Bulgarian speech knows the phonological juxtaposition of soft and hard consonants but even there it is the area where its use is very limited."[58] The timbre

---

[53] Ibid., p. 8.
[54] Ibid., p. 9.
[55] Ibid., p. 15.
[56] Ibid., p. 17.
[57] Ibid., pp. 16–17.
[58] Ibid., p. 24.

correlation thus created a boundary separating genetically close Czech, Polish, Slovak, Serbian, Croatian, and Bulgarian from Russian, Ukrainian and Belarusian.

Similarly, the only Romance language in Eastern Europe, Romanian, was divided by this line: "Correlation of softness characteristic of Moldavian dialects and literary language is unknown in Romanian literary language."[59] As in other cases in Eastern Europe, Jakobson determined that "in the direction from the east to the west this correlation first diminishes and then disappears altogether."[60] Finno-Ugric languages demonstrated a similar picture according to Jakobson. Languages within Eurasia—such as Komi, Udmurt, Mordovian, Karelian—all know phonological oppositions between soft and hard consonants, "unlike the language of Saami and most dialects of Suomi (that is, the language of Finns in Finlandia)... and Magyar."[61]

Turkic languages presented a more difficult challenge for Jakobson. These languages are characterized by the harmony of vowels, where all vowels in a word belong to the same category. Jakobson claimed that a recent discovery confirmed the presence of the timbre correlation in some Turkic languages, and argued that these languages are characterized by what he called "syllabic harmony."[62] In the Turkic languages of Eurasia, according to Jakobson, it is more appropriate to talk about the timbre correlation of syllables, where the oppositions between types of vowels is inseparable from the oppositions between hard and soft consonants. Jakobson believed that the presence of timbre correlation of syllables is established beyond doubt in the Tatar, Kazakh, Bashkir, Turkmen, and Azerbaijani languages and in the speech of Bessarabian Gagauz, as well as in most Uzbek dialects.[63]

In Jakobson's work visions of Eurasia as a geographical unity, an ethno-psychological whole, a leader of anti-colonialist uprising against European cultural dominance or a site of scientific modernity were supplanted with another hypostasis. It became the first language union discovered with the help of structuralist linguistics as a world populated by speakers of languages characterized by monotony and the correlation of soft and hard sounds. These languages

> fully cover three great plains—the White Sea—Caucasian, the Western Siberian, and the Turkestan plains, that is the very main core where we observe the most characteristic geographic particularities of the Eurasian world. The southwestern

---

[59] Ibid., p. 27.
[60] Ibid., p. 27.
[61] Ibid., p. 29.
[62] Ibid., p. 30.
[63] Ibid., p. 31.

periphery of this phonological union occupies the western edge of Eurasian steppes, hanging along the coast of the Black Sea from Odessa to the Balkans. Finally, in the east, the monotonic languages with timbre correlation apparently cover "the Mongolian core of the continent" which belongs to Eurasia on the basis of several features.[64]

To be sure, certain areas that belonged to the former Russian Empire and formed part of the USSR could not be included into the Eurasian linguistic design. For instance, "the languages of Transcaucasia (the Armenian language and the Kartvelian group) do not possess the timbre correlation of consonants."[65] Similarly, Iranian languages such as Ossetian or Tadjik did not display phonological oppositions between hard and soft sounds, and so did not many languages of the Far East, such as the Chukchee or the Yukagir. The Eurasianists, however, were not concerned with minor exceptions and dismissed them as a confirmation of the correctness of the map of Eurasia: "already now we have the right to speak of a Eurasian language union, without predicting, however, the exact correlation of its isophones with other geographical lines."[66]

Jakobson attempted to draw a rough picture of the diachronic development of the Eurasian language union. Characteristically, he chose as one of his examples the loss of the correlation of soft and hard consonants in medieval Czech to illustrate the impact of Europeanization:

> Jan Hus was the witness to the elimination of the last remainders of the differentiation of soft and hard consonants. He defended the original antiquity, with pathos he declared that "those Pragians and other Czechs who speak half-Czech half-German" and remove the difference between li and ly... deserve flogging. Gus's indignation was in vain and those Czechs who spoke *more Teutonicorum* emerged victorious."[67]

This example was fully in line with the Eurasianist rebellion against Europeanization and loss of authenticity under the assault of difference eliminating European cultural expansion. Jakobson's work appeared at the time when Soviet linguists largely completed the implementation of Latin scripts for Soviet Turkic and Finno-Ugric languages and discussions were underway about the introduction of Latin script for Ukrainian, Russian, and Belarusian.

---

[64] Ibid., p. 36.
[65] Ibid., p. 37.
[66] Ibid., p. 38.
[67] Ibid., p. 42.

Jakobson found Latinization to be a "pointless waste to please Westernizers."[68] Transcribing a Belarusian text with Latin script would increase the number of symbols by 7.5 percent in comparison to Cyrillic, because Latin is not designed to reflect the timbre correlation between soft and hard consonants and other phonological specificities of Eurasian languages.[69]

Jakobson also paralleled the Eurasianists in how he described the role of the Russians in the Eurasian space. As Eurasianist thinkers described non-Christian peoples of Eurasia as "potentially Orthodox" and Eurasianist historians saw the history of Eurasia as the history of Russian expansion, Jakobson envisioned Russian language as paradigmatic and dominant in the Eurasian language union:

> The Great Russian timbre correlation of consonants sets the standard. It is regularly used in the interest of differentiating meanings, both in words and grammatically. It is realized on the greatest scale before almost all consonants and at the end of the word...tendencies that characterize the Eurasian language union found their most complete expression in Russian. It is not a coincidence that the Great Russian phonology formed the basis of the Russian literary language, that is, the language with the all-Eurasian cultural mission.[70]

Jakobson's work on the language union was not without a consequence in linguistics. While linguists did not find much in the idea of the Eurasian language union as such, elsewhere the concept proved to be a useful tool to conceptualize similarities between genetically unrelated languages, in particular in the Balkans or in India. Jakobson himself continued to promote the concept and associated apparatus for most of his career. In his *Dialogues* with Krystyna Pomorska, Jakobson explained that in the 1930s he "published a number of studies proving the existence of a vast 'Eurasian linguistic alliance,' which encompassed Russian, the other languages of Eastern Europe, and the majority of the Uralic and Altaic languages, all of which make use of the phonemic opposition of palatalized and non-palatalized consonants."[71] Jakobson stressed that these ideas were parallel to the work of Franz Boas, "who revealed the existence of phonic and grammatical phenomena common to the Amerindian languages and encompassing large zones of these languages without regard to origin..."[72] In a sweeping move characteristic of Jakobson's thought, he related the

---

[68] Ibid., p. 48.
[69] Ibid., p. 49.
[70] Ibid., p. 46.
[71] Jakobson and Pomorska, *Dialogues*..., p. 85.
[72] Ibid., p. 84.

problem of the language union and the resulting issue of acquired characteristics to a range of topics, such as bilingualism or aphasia. Jakobson argued that "with every step, one finds in the ever growing number of these secondary linguistic affinities [*Wahlverwandschaften*] an entire series of problems which have yet to be resolved. In much that at one time appeared to be a mosaic of chance events we now perceive geo-linguistic regularities awaiting explanation."[73] He added, in a reference to Savitskii's method, that "only the creation of atlases will oblige linguists to reflect in a consistent manner upon such isoglosses as the boundary line between the West European mass of languages with articles and the East European languages without articles…"[74]

Jakobson insisted that linguistic boundaries determined by acquired characteristics do often coincide with, although not necessarily depend upon, the sphere of particular language domination, or with a sociocultural zone as such: "We should also point out that these widespread isoglosses generally coincide with other puzzling lines encountered in the geographical distribution of anthropological traits. These often unexpected connections require a many-sided analysis in accordance with the methodological theses advanced by the ingenious scholar Petr Nikolaevich Savitskii, the precursor of structural geography."[75]

In 1936 Jakobson presented his conception of the language union to the IV International Congress of Linguists in Copenhagen and included the text of his presentation in the French translation of Trubetskoi's *magnum opus*.[76] He also included this text in his selected writings and in the key Soviet publication of Jakobson's work.[77] These inclusions confirm that Jakobson clearly did not see his Eurasianist encounter as a passing or deviant moment in his intellectual evolution and remained committed to the centrality of the Eurasianist spatializing approach to the development of structuralism.

Political Ontology of Eurasian Structures: Goal, Convergence, Evolution, Religion

The Eurasianist scholars saw their own approach to substantiating the existence of Eurasia as part of an epistemological revolution that replaced genetic ties with

---

[73] Ibid., p. 88.
[74] Ibid., p. 88.
[75] Ibid., p. 89.
[76] Roman Jakobson, "Sur la théorie des affinités phonologiques entre les langues," in N.S. Troubetzkoy, *Principes de phonologie* (Paris, 1949), pp. 351–66.
[77] Roman Jakobson, "O teorii fonologicheskikh iazykovykh souiuzov mezhdu iazykami," in Roman Iakobson, *Izbrannye raboty* (Moscow, 1985), pp. 92–115.

acquired characteristics and the nineteenth-century observation of "atomistic" facts with discovering structural regularities. When P. Savitskii complained to Trubetskoi about critical reception of his work on depression in pre-capitalist societies, Trubetskoi responded that "the problem is that until now history has been a very atomistic discipline and it taught all historians its atomistic approach. Your attempt to apply structuralist [*struktural'nyi*] approach to historical facts therefore remains unappreciated by 'professional' historians."[78] In a letter to Vera Guchkova-Suvchinskaia, who had begun studying linguistics under Antoine Meillet and sought Trubetskoi's opinion on the teacher, Trubetskoi wrote: "Meillet indeed quite deserves this respect that you pay him. He is the best linguist of our time. Of course, he represents a certain epoch in the history of linguistics, an era that maybe will have to end soon and to be replaced by another one..."[79]

The new era that opened up with the retreat of the "atomistic" scholarship was characterized by the change in perspective. If the nineteenth-century scholars explored causality, the structuralist approach focused on teleology: "In the current hierarchy of values the question 'where to?' is ranked higher than the question 'where from?'"[80] "The goal," wrote Jakobson, "this Cinderella of the ideology of the recent past, is being rehabilitated everywhere."[81] Human collectivities were to be viewed differently in accordance with the new parameters: "Instead of the genetic indicators self-determination becomes a feature of nationality, the idea of caste is replaced with the idea of class, and both in societal life and scholarly constructions commonality of origin retreats into the background in comparison with the unity of common goal."[82]

For Jakobson the predisposition of the national epistemology toward structuralism relied on the Russian philosophical tradition that was characterized by animosity to positivism. Jakobson listed as his lineage the works by thinkers as different as Nikolai Danilevskii, Fedor Dostoevskii, Nikolai Fyodorov,

---

[78] Nikolai Trubetskoi to Petr Savitskii, n.d. [1935]. BAR, George Vernadsky Papers, Box 8, Folder "Petr Nikolaevich Savitskii 1935." The article in question is P.N. Savitskii, "'Pod'em' i 'depressia' v drevnerusskoi istorii," *Evraziiskaia Khronika* 9 (1935): 65–100.

[79] Nikolai Trubetskoi to Vera Guchkova-Suvchinskaia (later Traill), n.d. [before 1926]. BNF, DdM. Not catalogued. Antoine Meillet (1866–1936), a student of Ferdinand de Saussure and an outstanding linguist, was often seen by the Eurasianists as their opponent. It is remarkable that both Trubetskoi and Jakobson paid respects to Meillet publicly, while in private correspondence they often pointed out the backwardness and outdated views of de Saussure's student who was the main representative of the neo-grammarians, whom they considered incapable of grasping new ideas in scholarship.

[80] Jakobson, *K kharakteristike*..., p. 3.

[81] Ibid., p. 3.

[82] Ibid., p. 3.

Konstantin Leont'ev, and Vladimir Solov'ev, all of whom pursued religious philosophy. In another remarkable reference, Jakobson suggested that Russian teleology manifested itself in the works of the geographer Karl von Baer, the Orthodox critic Nikolai Strakhov, the biologist Nikolai Vavilov, and, finally, the bio-geographer Lev Semenovich Berg. The striking list of names is united only by the adherence to the critical reception of Darwin's thought in Russia.[83]

Of this list, the name of Lev Semenovich Berg is especially telling. A student of the leading ethnographer and anthropologist in late imperial Russia, D. Anuchin, Berg was a universalist scholar with contributions ranging from biology to geography and history, who continued Dokuchaev's work by establishing the "natural zones of the Soviet Union," which became the foundation of Soviet geographic textbooks in the twentieth century.[84] His best-known and controversial legacy was the work on "nomogenesis," a law-governed, regular evolution. For Berg, differences between his theory and Darwinism consisted in that he believed in multiple origins of evolutionary development; species developed both by divergence and convergence, with the prevalence of the latter; species are strictly delimited; and evolutionary convergent development is in essence based on preexisting conditions.

Albeit the Eurasianists were not aware of Berg's work until 1926 (and Jakobson until 1929),[85] they immediately recognized an intellectual affinity. In a letter to Suvchinskii dated by March 5, 1926, Trubetskoi wrote:

> Savitskii told me of two interesting books that were published in Russia. The first is "Nomogenesis" by Berg... It is especially interesting because Berg proclaims himself as a follower of Danilevskii and in his theses he develops propositions that are close to ours (in particular to my ideas developed in *Europe and Mankind* and *The Tower of Babel*)...[86]

Trubetskoi's admission is important because he clearly identifies the areas where the Eurasianists found their ideas resonating with those of Berg. Trubetskoi's *Europe and Mankind* focused on the role of evolutionism in European history

---

[83] For an overview of this reception, see Alexander Vucinich, *Darwin in Russian Thought* (Berkeley, CA, 1988); also Daniel P. Todes, *Darwin without Malthus: The Struggle for Existence in Russian Evolutionary Thought* (New York, 1989); for the role of evolutionary ethnography in the making of the Soviet nationalities policies, see Francine Hirsch, *Empire of Nations: Ethnographic Knowledge and the Making of the Soviet Union* (Ithaca, NY, 2005).

[84] Lev S. Berg, *Ocherki po istorii russkikh geograficheskikh otkrytii* (Moscow, 1946); Lev S. Berg, *Natural Regions of the U. S. S. R.* (New York, 1950).

[85] Sériot, *Struktura i Tselostonost'...*, p. 202.

[86] Nikolai Trubetskoi to Petr Suvchinskii. March 5, 1926. BNF,DdM. Not catalogued.

and ethnology as a masque for Europe's colonial domination of the world. It also suggested, following the nineteenth-century pan-Slavist Nikolai Danilevskii, that there exist large cultural units, "cultures," and that cultural borrowings from one to another are harmful and destructive. Trubetskoi's *Tower of Babel*, apart from proposing the concept of the language union, also offered a theological take on differences: According to Trubetskoi, "attempts to create a universal culture *eo ipso* are godless." Berg's "alternative evolutionism" reverberated with the Eurasianist insistence on plurality of cultural worlds and multiple origins of human culture. We can note here Trubetskoi's famous presentation on the Indo-European problem, which questioned the original unity of Indo-European languages and proposed that the Indo-European family might have been an outcome of convergent development.[87] Berg's ideas fitted well with the grand Eurasianist task of turning what Arthur Lovejoy called "diversitarianism" into a central ideological premise of Eurasianism.[88] At the same time, Berg's anti-Darwinist model connected Eurasianism with a range of native theories and constructions, from Karl von Baer's to Danilevskii's, in which a critique of Darwinism and evolutionism was closely interwoven with attempts to construct an extra-European, autochthonouscivilization in Russia.

Berg's "nomogenetic" evolutionism saw biological changes as following a goal-oriented pattern. As Berg pointed out in the introduction to his key work on evolution, "teleology is the main characteristic of all living beings."[89] For the Eurasianists, teleology was a key principle upon which the unity of Eurasia rested: Its cultural, ethnic, and geographical homogeneity was regular and corresponded to a series of laws, of which some were yet to be discovered. The goal of Eurasianism—and of all scholarship—was to uncover those yet-to-be-revealed teleological "regularities." When Savitskii received the manuscript of Jakobson's work on phonological union in Eurasia, he responded with excitement: "I just sent you a letter, received your manuscript, read it, and became drunk from happiness. I congratulate you: Russia's phonology as a

---

[87] Nikolai Trubetskoi, "Mysli ob indo-evropeiskoi problem,"*Voprosy iazykoznaniia* 1 (1958): 65–77.

[88] Arthur O. Lovejoy, *The Great Chain of Being: A Study of the History of an Idea* (Cambridge, MA, 1936), pp. 293–4.

[89] The Russian term *tselesoobraznost'* has no equivalent in English. It was a calque from the German *Zweckmässigkeit* and *Zielstrebigkeit*, the latter one of the favorite terms of Jakobson. Lev S. Berg, "Nomogenez, iliEvoliutsianaosnovezakonomernostei," in Lev S. Berg, *Trudy po teorii evoliutsii, 1922–1930* (Leningrad, 1977), p. 99. Berg's work was first published as *Nomogenez, ili Evoliutsia na osnove zakonomernostei*, Trudy Geograficheskogo Instituta, vol. 1 (Petrograd, 1922). Remarkably, in 1926 an English edition was published: Leo S. Berg, *Nomogenesis; or, Evolution Determined by Law* (London, 1926).

system has been created by you. I was taken over by a storm of thoughts and ideas during two hours..."[90] Savitskii found Jakobson's work to be "uncovering an entirely new sphere of life." Nothing in the lines drawn by Eurasianist scholars on the maps was accidental: "If you could only imagine, Savitskii wrote to Jakobson, with what precision every single line you describe correlates with geographical and historical background!" Savitskii immediately drew a picture of a synthesis: "Apparently, there is a close parallelism between the tasks of Eurasian phonology and the tasks of general Eurasian history (political, social, cultural). As Russia's history needs to expand to become history of Eurasia, to acquire Eurasian horizons and Eurasian perspectives, so Russian linguistics—a branch of Slavic linguistics—has to become a chapter in Eurasian studies of language."[91]

As Patrick Sériot has recently demonstrated, Eurasianist scholars viewed Eurasia as an ontological reality, whose diverse manifestations revealed themselves to an attuned eye in limitless numbers.[92] Lines of climate change, geological elevations, types of soil and vegetation coincided with nomadic and settled civilizations. The discovery of phonological lines of division that so neatly matched with other data just proved, yet again, the validity of the ontological reality of Eurasia.These coincidences, or, as Jakobson called them, "correlations of rows of data" were interpreted by Savitskii within his "periodic system of being," a structured and strictly organized methodology of uncovering repetitions and coincidences in history, geography, or linguistics. After his release from the Soviet camp in Mordovia in 1956,Savitskii sent to George Vernadskii his poems, written in the camp, and added the following clarification: "These poems cover my conception of the periodical system of being, which you know. This system includes the periodic conception of [geographical] zones and the periodical rhymes of history."[93] The "system" combined a scientific search for regularity with a deep commitment to the religious foundations of knowledge. As Savitskii himself noted,

> The entire ideological system of Eurasianism is deduced from the idea of personality: the idea of personal God, the idea of Russia–Eurasia as a "symphonic personality,"

---

[90] Petr Savitskii to Roman Jakobson, August 9, 1930. MIT Archives, MC 72, Box 119, Folder 119.

[91] Ibid.

[92] Sériot, *Structure et totalité*...; for a discussion of this problem from a historical perspective, see S. Glebov, "Whither Eurasia: History of Ideas in Imperial Situation," in *AbImperio* 8/2 (2008): 345–76.

[93] Petr Savitskii to Georgii Vernadskii. 9 December 1956. BAR, George Vernadsky Papers, Box 8, Folder "Mordovskaia ASSR 1945–46 gg."

the idea of personality as the creator of life. Without the idea of personality the religious transformation of life for which Eurasianism strives is impossible.[94]

It was Orthodox religiosity that provided Eurasianist scholars with philosophical—or, rather, theological—foundations for their "systemic" study of Eurasia. As Eurasianism envisioned as its ideal a society permeated by the spirit of totalizing religiosity, so its scientific pursuits relied on Neoplatonic visions of "discovery" of ontological reality of "structure" through the iconic representation by rows of data. Eurasia's existence was not in question: The task was to uncover the almost miraculous "correlations" revealed in ever-increasing quantities.

Curiously, Trubetskoi actually described this method when he subjected medieval Russian texts produced by pilgrims to formal analysis:

> The greatest happiness that may befall a Christian is the heavenly beatitude thatconsists in supra-sensory perception of God. This highest happiness a Christian can achieve only after death under the condition of a sinless life. Here, on Earth, one can only incompletely approach this happiness in the form of visions… A necessary spiritual condition could be achieved by a pilgrim as the pilgrim stood before the external world as before an icon, as he "iconized" the world inside himself. In everything that a pilgrim encountered on his path he only noted what he could connect, though his supra-sensory vision, with his religious thoughts and ideas of the Heavenly Kingdom. He passed the rest without noting it and without reacting to it. The land of his pilgrimage was for him a great temple with many bright icons.[95]

In this context, Jakobson's conversion in 1936 to Orthodoxy (Savitskii was his godfather) appears in a new light. It underscored his encounter with Eurasianist thought and its Neoplatonic currents well and above his personal relations with Eurasianist scholars. His work on Eurasianist language union, if taken in the context of Jakobson's encounter with the movement, appears to have been based on assumptions that drew on religious interpretations of Eurasia. Jakobson might not have accepted some political implications of Eurasianism but he shared in the Eurasianist "systemic discovery" of Eurasia's multiple characteristics while taking the object's primordial existence as a matter of faith.

---

[94] PetrSavitskii, "Introduction," in *TridtsatyeGody. Utverzhdeniia evraziitsev* (Prague, 1931).

[95] Nikolai Trubetskoi, *Istoriia. Kul'tura. Iazyk* (Moscow, 1995), pp. 580–81.

It was this peculiar structuralism—with its stress on the relations between different elements in a structure underlying the visible phenomena—that Jakobson conveyed to his French interlocutors in the 1940s. Boris Gasparov described this structuralism as "systemic principle," which "emphasized the interconnectedness of all the elements within a system and the impossibility of defining the features of any element without considering its relation to other elements and its position in the system as a whole."[96] Its political ontology revealed itself in persistent attempts to recuperate the space of the former Russian empire by reinventing it as "Eurasia."

To be sure, in the following decades Jakobson himself moved structuralism in a number of different directions. He followed "the constructive principle, which noted diverse phenomena of human communication in their elusive multiplicity through a surface, empirical examination, and it then proceeds to pick out the key features of internal structure, the study of which is the specific matter and prerogative of linguistics and semiotics…"[97] It was exactly this constructive element in structuralism that secured the "widespread dissemination of structuralist poetics and semiotics" after World War II, whereas the "systemic branch of structuralism receded in the past and could be perceived as its prehistory, a preliminary and insufficiently focused stepping-stone to what later became the dominant theme of linguistic and semiotic structuralism."[98]

However deviant or passing, though, it was the holistic, teleological, and "systemic" structuralism of the Eurasianists that provided the material and the apparatus for the emerging international intellectual movement. The new language of structuralism served Eurasianist scholars well: with its seeming ability to resolve the impasse between unity and diversity, with its stress on the wholeness and all-embracing nature of the structure, it combined Russian tradition of counter-Enlightenment and anti-evolutionism with a vision of a grand, universal project of a systemic supra-science—an ideal language for empire in the twentieth century.

---

[96] Boris Gasparov, "The Ideological Principles of Prague School Phonology," in K. Pomorska et al. (eds.), *Language, Poetry and Poetics. The Generation of the 1890s: Jakobson, Trubetzkoy, Majakovskij. Proceedings of the First Roman Jakobson Colloquium, at the Massachusetts Institute of Technology, October 5–6, 1984* (New York, 1987), p. 72.

[97] Ibid.

[98] Ibid, p. 75.

CHAPTER 2

Between Russia, Ukraine, and Eurasia: Georgii Vernadskii's Search for Identity

Igor Torbakov

Over the last decade, the body of scholarly literature on "classical" Eurasianism has been steadily growing.[1] The broadest reason for this interest is obvious. Following the collapse of the Soviet Union and the emergence of the new geopolitical landscape in what has come to be designated—tellingly—as Eurasia, scholars and the general public alike have experienced crises of identity not unlike those that tormented the Eurasianists themselves in the wake of the unraveling of the Russian Empire, and are still grappling with how best to analyze the new reality. The recent essay by the American historian Mark von Hagen is both a manifestation of those crises and a helpful attempt to show the way out of them.[2] Remarkably, not only did von Hagen invoke the iconoclastic spirit of classical Eurasianists but he also advanced Eurasia as the "anti-paradigm for the post-Soviet era."[3]

---

[1] The literature on Eurasianism is voluminous. For the works written before 2000, see Aleksandr Antoshchenko (ed.), *O Evrazii i evraziitsakh (bibliograficheskii ukazatel')* (Petrozavodsk, 2000). Among the recent publications, the following are particularly useful: Dmitry Shlapentokh (ed.), *Russia between East and West: Scholarly Debates on Eurasianism* (Leiden, 2007); Marlène Laruelle, *Russian Eurasianism: An Ideology of Empire* (Washington, DC, 2008); Marlène Laruelle, *Ideologiia russkogo evraziistva ili mylsi o velichii imperii* (Moscow, 2004) (this work first appeared in French in 1999 as *L'Idéologie eurasiste russe ou comment penser l'empire*); Aleksandr Antoshchenko, *Evraziia ili "Sviataia Rus"? Rossiiskie emigranty v poiskakh samosoznaniia na putiakh istorii* (Petrozavodsk, 2003); Mark Bassin, "'Classical' Eurasianism and the Geopolitics of Russian Identity," *Ab Imperio* 2 (2003): 257–66; Vladimir G. Makarov, "'Pax Rossica'. Istoriia evraziiskogo dvizheniia i sud'by evraziitsev," *Voprosy filosofii* 9 (2006): 102–17; Valeriia Khachaturian, "Istoki i rozhdenie evraziiskoi idei," *Tsivilizatsii* 6 (2004): 187–201; Igor Ionov, "Puti razvitiia tsivilizatsionnogo soznaniia v Evrazii i problema evraziistva," *Tsivilizatsii* 6 (2004): 158–87.

[2] Mark von Hagen, "Empires, Borderlands, and Diasporas: Eurasia as Anti-paradigm for the Post-Soviet Era," *American Historical Review* 109 (April 2004): 445–68.

[3] Glennys Young, "Fetishizing the Soviet Collapse: Historical Rupture and the Historiography of (Early) Soviet Socialism," *Russian Review* 66/1 (2007): 95–122.

The study of Eurasianism, however, has produced mixed results so far. As one contemporary student of this fascinating school of thought observes, "As a body of doctrine, Eurasianism has been much more frequently summarized than critically examined."[4] The Eurasianism-related archival materials, in particular the voluminous correspondence between the participants of the movement, still need to be studied. Moreover, the interest in Eurasianism has been traditionally skewed toward the geopolitical (the "Exodus to the East"), the sociopolitical (Eurasianism's authoritarian leaning toward "ideocracy"), and, to a lesser extent, the historiosophic. Recently, a number of useful studies of Eurasianist theory of culture have appeared.[5] But the Eurasianists' attempts at rethinking empire and nation and at crafting a new historical narrative in which Russia's multiethnic character would find a more thorough treatment have not been sufficiently explored.[6]

This brings me to the figure of Georgii [George] Vernadskii, who is rightly regarded as Eurasianism's principal historian. There is, it would appear, a virtual flourishing of Vernadskii studies in today's Russia. Most of the works of the émigré historian have been reprinted in his historical homeland and there is a

---

[4] Gerald Smith, *D.S. Mirsky: A Russian-English Life, 1890–1939* (Oxford, 2000), p. 138.

[5] Sergei Glebov, "Granitsy imperii kak granitsy moderna: Antikolonial'naia ritorika i teoriia kul'turnykh tipov v evraziistve," *Ab Imperio* 2 (2003): 267–92; Leonid Liuks, "Zametki o 'revoliutsionno-traditsionalistskoi' kul'turnoi modeli 'evraziitsev,'" *Forum noveishei vostochnoevropeiskoi istorii i kul'tury* 2 (2004): 1–17; David Chioni Moore, "Colonialism, Eurasianism, Orientalism: N.S. Trubetzkoy's Russian Vision," *Slavic and East European Journal* 41/2 (1997): 321–40.

[6] A useful discussion of Eurasianist views on national question is to be found in the exchange between Viktor Shnirel'man and Viktor Karlov; see Shnirel'man, "Evraziiskaia ideia i teoriia kul'tury," *Etnograficheskoe obozrenie* 4 (1996): 3–16; Karlov, "Evraziiskaia ideia i russkii natsionalizm: Po povodu stat'i V.A. Shnirel'mana 'Evraziiskaia ideia i teoriia kul'tury,'" *Etnograficheskoe obozrenie* 1 (1997): 1–13; Shnirel'man, "Evraziistvo i natsional'nyi vopros. Vmesto otveta V.V. Karlovu," *Etnograficheskoe obozrenie* 2 (1997): 112–25; Karlov, "O evraziistve, natsionalizme i priemakh nauchnoi polemiki," *Etnograficheskoe obozrenie* 2 (1997): 125–32. See also Viktor Shnirel'man, "The Fate of Empires and Eurasian Federalism: A Discussion between the Eurasianists and Their Opponents in the 1920s," *Inner Asia* 3 (2001): 153–73. Shnirel'man's main conclusion, however, is that Eurasianism did not have too much that was original to offer and was basically an intellectual continuation of Russian imperial nationalism and "Great Power chauvinism." On Eurasianism as an ideological response to the concepts of pan-Turkism and pan-Turanism, see Stefan Wiederkehr, "Eurasianism as a Reaction to Pan-Turkism," in Dmitry Shlapentokh (ed.), *Russia between East and West: Scholarly Debates on Eurasianism* (Leiden, 2007), pp. 39–60. Margarita Vandalkovskaia's *Istoricheskaia nauka rossiiskoi emigratsii: 'Evraziiskii soblazn'* (Moscow, 1997) focuses mainly on the Russian émigré thinkers' critique of the Eurasianists' historical concept.

seemingly endless stream of monographs and articles on his life and scholarship.[7] "Surprisingly," the eminent Harvard historian Richard Pipes recently remarked, "since its emancipation from communism a kind of cult of Vernadskii has emerged in Russia."[8] This atmosphere of adulation has also prompted the senior Russian historian Nikolai Bolkhovitinov, Vernadskii's most recent biographer, to comment that, while in Soviet times Vernadskii was a popular "whipping boy," mercilessly criticized for his non-Marxist understanding of the historical process, in post-communist Russia, he has become an object of almost "limitless lauding."[9]

But despite the impressive range of scholarly research on Vernadskii, the question persists: How well do we understand his intellectual legacy—in particular, the links among his own national identity (identities?), his choice of Eurasianist paradigm, and his historical scholarship?

George Vernadskii is generally regarded as a historian of Russia.[10] At first blush, this seems quite understandable: His multivolume magnum opus is titled *A History of Russia*, and his last big study, published posthumously, was *Russian Historiography*. Yet this traditional perception of the scholar obscures the fact that Vernadskii's ambition was to write not the history of Russia as a nation-state but the history of Russia-Eurasia—the vast territory, virtually a world unto itself, inhabited, to borrow his Eurasianist friend Petr Savitskii's words, by an "assembly of peoples" [*sobor narodov*]. Thus, Vernadskii tried to create a master narrative that would incorporate the histories of all major peoples living on the Eurasian plains—both the eastern nomads ("the peoples of the steppe") and the western neighbors of the Great Russians, first of all the Ukrainians. In doing this, he would naturally draw heavily upon the Russian imperial historiography in whose tradition he was steeped at the Moscow and St. Petersburg universities. But Vernadskii would also introduce the new vision of "Russian history" obviously inspired by his

---

[7] A list of works on Vernadskii published in the 1990s can be found in *O Evrazii i evraziitsakh*. The two recent biographical studies are by Nikolai Bolkhovitinov: "Zhizn' i deiatel'nost' G.V. Vernadskogo (1887–1973) i ego arkhiv," *Slavic Research Center Occasional Papers* 82 (2002): 1–63, and *Russkie uchenye-emigranty (G.V. Vernadskii, M.M.Karpovich, M.T.Florinskii) i stanovlenie rusistiki v SShA* (Moscow, 2005). The short biographical essay by Sergei Rybakov is too descriptive and mainly restates the well-known facts; see Sergei Rybakov, "Istorik-evraziets Georgii Vernadskii," *Voprosy istorii* 11 (2006): 157–64.

[8] See *Kritika: Explorations in Russian and Eurasian History* 7/2 (Spring 2006): 386.

[9] Bolkhovitinov, "Zhizn' i deiatel'nost' G.V. Vernadskogo," p. 47.

[10] The Harvard historian Serhii Plokhii, for example, bluntly calls Vernadskii "the scion of the Russian imperial historiographic school." Plokhii notes, though, that "In his Russian history courses Vernadsky paid unprecedented attention to the history of Ukraine." See Serhii Plokhii, *Unmaking Imperial Russia: Mykhailo Hrushevsky and the Writing of Ukrainian History* (Toronto, 2005), p. 151.

Eurasianism. In 1933, in a letter to his father, Vladimir Ivanovich Vernadskii, he described his work on *An Essay on the History of Eurasia*: "In the general concept of Russian history, I try to devote much more attention than has ever been given before to Western Rus' and Ukraine."[11] In the same vein, in his study of Russian historiography one finds the scholarly portraits of the leading Ukrainian historians of the nineteenth and twentieth centuries such as Mykola Kostomarov, Mykhailo Drahomanov, Volodymyr Antonovych, and Dmytro Bahalii.

Also, Vernadskii appeared to view the history of Ukraine as a legitimate subject per se. He authored an English-language biography of Hetman Bohdan Hmelnytsky and wrote an introduction and did editorial work for a translation of Mykhailo Hrushevsky's one-volume history of Ukraine. The historian seemed to be especially fascinated by the personality of Mykhailo Drahomanov. In the mid-1930s he urged a fellow émigré, Aleksandra Golshtein, a family friend and longtime acquaintance of Drahomanov, to write a memoir about him.[12] Later, Golshtein sent him the manuscript of her reminiscences and her copious correspondence with Drahomanov.[13]

Among Vernadskii's works that are preserved in his archive[14] there are two typescripts underscoring his professional interest in the history of Ukraine—"The Kievan and Cossack Periods in Ukrainian History" and "Prince Trubetskoi and the Ukrainian Question."[15] Also, in his archival collection are two folders of materials titled "The Ukrainian Question before and during the Second World War." It would be only proper to add here that as early as 1941 Vernadskii, in an interview with an English-language Ukrainian publication, spoke in favor of the plans to set up a Ukrainian research institute in the United States, which would publish a Ukrainian-language journal.

So I guess a pretty strong case can be made for the need to revisit George Vernadskii's understanding of what he himself called a "Russian history." Particularly intriguing seems to be the exploration of how Vernadskii's

---

[11] George Vernadskii, *Russkaia istoriografia* (Moscow, 1998), p. 439.

[12] On the relationship between Aleksandra Golshtein and the Vernadskiis, see A. Sergeev and A. Tiurin, "Istoriia poluvekovoi druzhby," *Minuvshee: Istoricheskii almanakh* 18 (1995): 353–425.

[13] George Vernadskii's interest in Drahomanov was likely generated by both his family ties—his father befriended Drahomanov in the late 1880s in Paris—and the Eurasianists' interest in federalist theories.

[14] Bakhmeteff Archive of Russian and East European History and Culture, Columbia University [hereafter BAR]. George Vernadsky Collection.

[15] BAR, George Vernadsky Collection, Box 96. These two documents were recently published in *Ab Imperio* 4 (2006).

Eurasianism relates both to his own struggles with identity and to his thinking on empire, nation, and Russian and Ukrainian history.

Thus, in this article I propose to place Vernadskii's historical research on Russian and Ukrainian history within the context of his biography and Eurasianist worldview. My central argument is that George Vernadskii's post-1917 historical scholarship was influenced by one powerful motive—namely, his personal search for national identity, the search that was obviously made more complicated by his exile. Internal contradictions and resultant tensions between Ukrainian origin and imperial *Weltanschauung*, between the ardent love of "historic Russia" and his wretched status of an émigré deprived of his beloved homeland by the victorious Bolshevik regime made the grappling with the issue of identity emotionally agonizing but also fruitful in terms of producing new and unorthodox solutions.[16]

Like other Eurasianists, Vernadskii understood that after the 1917 Revolution it was simply impossible to turn the former Russian Empire into a classic nation-state. The early Soviet practices aimed at managing multiethnicity only confirmed him in this view. At the same time, Vernadskii, in keeping with the Eurasianist intellectual tradition, put an immense value into the preservation of that unique geopolitical and geocultural space that this school of thought called Russia-Eurasia. The need to re-conceptualize the notion of nation and the way national history should be written was thus inevitable. I argue that Eurasianism was precisely the intellectual framework to achieve this goal.

Two key Eurasianist ideas were instrumental in shaping Vernadskii's historical vision. The first was the concept of Eurasian nationalism advanced by Prince Nikolai Trubetskoi, who contended that the nationalism of each people of Eurasia should be combined with pan-Eurasian nationalism. Being a precursor of the theory of multiple identities, this concept not only helped resolve the problem of Vernadskii's personal soul-searching but also appeared to show the way how to preserve the precious unity of "historic Russia." The other fundamental idea, set forth by Petr Savitskii, was the image of Eurasia as a natural "developmental space" [*mestorazvitie*] for the host of various ethnic groups that reside in those vast expanses. Eurasia, being a highly cohesive geographical world, molds those groups into a unique "assembly of nationalities and religions" and, in its turn, is being reshaped in the process of those peoples' economic and cultural activity.

---

[16] Literary historians have demonstrated the fruitfulness of research that explores the links between discordant national identity and an author's creativity. In her recent study of Nikolai Gogol's internally contradictory (Ukrainian-Russian) identity, Edyta Bojanowska observes how the two different halves of Gogol's self evolved in his writing and traces the relationship between them. See Edyta Bojanowska, *Nikolai Gogol: Between Ukrainian and Russian Nationalism* (Cambridge, MA, 2006).

Eurasianists asserted that the political unity of the former Russian Empire was the result not only of the efforts of the Great Russians alone but that of many peoples of Eurasia. That vision had prompted Vernadskii to steer away from the traditions of Russian imperial historiography that tended to write the history of Russia as that of a nation-state. In contrast, Vernadskii was among the first to try to craft a historical narrative of Russia as a *Nationalitätenstaat*. The Eurasianist conceptual limitations, however, prevented him from writing a truly comprehensive history of Russia as a multiethnic *empire*.

Biographical Context

Given all the current interest in classical Eurasianism, what appears to be really surprising is the dearth of explanation of what exactly prompted George Vernadskii (and, for that matter, all other leading members of the movement) to adopt such an unorthodox outlook on the Russian historical process. Some researchers (such as, for instance, Nikolai Bolkhovitinov) simply state the fact of Vernadskii's association with the Eurasianist movement without bothering to investigate the reasons underlying Vernadskii's affiliation with Eurasianism. Other scholars (such as Natalia Alevras) try to prove that Vernadskii was somehow predestined to become a Eurasianist, given his pre-revolutionary scholarly interests in Russia's eastward expansion and colonization of Siberia.[17] Alevras refers to the early, pre-1917 works by George Vernadskii and Petr Savitskii,[18] calling them the "proto-Eurasianist" essays that prefigured the authors' post-revolutionary embracing of Eurasianist historiosophy.[19] There are also scholars who, while acknowledging the tremendous importance of Vernadskii's choice of the Eurasianist paradigm for his subsequent historiographic development,

---

[17] Natalia Alevras, "G.V. Vernadskii and P.N. Savitskii: Istoki evraziiskoi kontseptsii," in *Rossiia i Vostok: problemy vzaimodeistviia / Tezisy dokl. i soobshch. k mezhdunar. nauch. konf.* (Cheliabinsk, 1995), pp. 121–4; Natalia Alevras, "Nachala evraziiskoi kontseptsii v rannem tvorchestve G.V. Vernadskogo i P.N. Savitskogo," *Vestnik Evrazii* 1 (1996): 5–17.

[18] See Georgii Vernadskii, "O dvizhenii russkikh na vostok," *Nauchno-istoricheskii zhurnal* 2 (1914); Vernadskii, "Protiv solntsa: Rasprostranenie russkogo gosudarstva k vostoku," *Russkaia mysl* 1 (1914): 56–79; Vernadskii, "Gosudarevy sluzhilye i promyshlennye liudi v Vostochnoi Sibiri XVII veka," *Zhurnal Ministerstva narodnogo prosveshcheniia* 4 (1915): 352–4.

[19] True, before the Revolution, Vernadskii displayed a keen interest in certain particular features of Russian colonialism. But "even if some of the Eurasian ideas had their genesis before 1917, it was the experience of the Revolution and Civil War that caused these ideas to be taken up by the Russian émigrés." See Catherine Andreyev and Ivan Savický, *Russia Abroad: Prague and the Russian Diaspora, 1918–1938* (New Haven, CT, 2004), p. 141.

claim that we will probably never know the true reasons that were behind his Eurasianist affiliation. "Only detailed biographical information about individual Eurasianists can illuminate the distinct characteristics of those original minds which led them to non-normative beliefs," wrote Charles Halperin, Vernadskii's American biographer. "For Vernadsky," he added, "and perhaps for all the Eurasian epigones, such information is lacking."[20] Indeed, Halperin is right when he noted that Vernadskii "was not a self-revealing man and did not dwell in his memoirs upon this momentous intellectual event"—that is, his joining the Eurasianist movement in mid-1920s. But I think the lack of direct evidence should still not prevent a researcher from an attempt at reconstructing George Vernadskii's intellectual evolution in the aftermath of the 1914–1921 "Russian catastrophe." My starting point here will be the analysis of all available information that might shed light on Vernadskii's struggles with the problem of his own national identity following the collapse of the Russian Empire, the defeat of the Whites in the civil war, and his flight into European exile.

In his seminal 1967 article "The Emergence of Eurasianism," Nicholas Riasanovsky noted that it is probably not accidental that the main Eurasianist theorists had Ukrainian roots.[21] He didn't elaborate on this valuable intuition and it was largely neglected in the subsequent scholarly literature.[22] Indeed, it doesn't seem a mere coincidence that three of the four founding members of the movement—Petr Savitskii,[23] Petr Suvchinskii[24] and Georgii Florovskii[25]— originated in Ukraine and/or spent some time there in their childhood and

---

[20] Charles Halperin, "George Vernadsky, Eurasianism, the Mongols, and Russia," *Slavic Review* 41/3 (1982): 483. See also Halperin, "Russia and the Steppe: George Vernadsky and Eurasianism," *Forschungen zur Osteuropäischen Geschichte* 36 (1985): 55–194.

[21] Nicholas Riasanovsky, "The Emergence of Eurasianism," *California Slavic Studies* 4 (1967): 39–72.

[22] Sergei Glebov briefly discusses the Ukrainian origin of the leading Eurasianists in Glebov, "Granitsy imperii."

[23] For information on Savitskii's life and work, see Sergei Glebov, "A Life with Imperial Dreams: Petr Nikolaevich Savitsky, Eurasiansim and the Invention of 'Structuralist' Geography," *Ab Imperio* 3 (2005): 299–329; Vladimir Makarov and Aleksandra M. Matveeva, "Geosofiia P.N. Savitskogo: mezhdu ideologiei i naukoi," *Voprosy filosofii* 2 (2007): 123–35.

[24] See Alla Bretanitskaia (ed.), *Petr Suvchinskii i ego vremia* (Moscow, 1999) and John Malmstad, "K istorii 'evraziistva': M. Gorky and P.P. Suvchinskii," *Diaspora: Novye materialy* 1 (2001): 327–47.

[25] Georgii Florovskii distanced himself from Eurasianism as early as the mid-1920s. See his critique of the movement's cultural-philosophical tenets in Georgii Florovskii, "Evraziiskii soblazn," *Sovremennye zapiski* 34 (1928): 312–46.

youth. Prince Nikolai Trubetskoi,[26] Eurasianism's fourth founding father, was the descendant of Gedymin, the Grand Prince of Lithuania, and his keen interest in all things Ukrainian was, in Vernadskii's words, a manifestation of an ancestral instinct.[27] And George Vernadskii himself (who joined the movement somewhat later), although he grew up in Moscow, could boast of a long and illustrious Ukrainian pedigree. This "Ukrainian connection" appears to be crucially important indeed. On the one hand, the attachment to Ukraine and its culture would distinguish Vernadskii and other key Eurasianists (particularly Savitskii) from the bulk of their fellow Russian émigrés who continued dreaming of Russia's resurrection as a "unified state"—"one and indivisible"—and who were bent on denying the Ukrainians even a modicum of a distinct identity that might make them look somewhat different from the Russians and result in some sort of Ukrainian autonomy.[28] On the other hand, Vernadskii and his fellow Eurasianists

---

[26] See Vladimir Toporov, "Nikolai Sergeevich Trubetskoi—ucheny, myslitel', chelovek," in *Pis'ma i zametki N.S. Trubetskogo* (Moscow, 2004) (Russian edn: *N.S. Trubetzkoy's Letters and Notes*, prepared for publication by Roman Jakobson with the assistance of Henryk Baran, Omni Ronen, and Martha Taylor (The Hague and Paris, 1975)); Nikita Tolstoy, "N.S. Trubetskoi i evraziistvo," in N.S. Trubetskoi, *Istoriia. Kul'tura. Iazyk* (Moscow, 1995), pp. 5–30; Anatoly Liberman, "N.S. Trubetzkoy and His Works on History and Culture," in Nikolai Trubetzkoy, *The Legacy of Genghis Khan* (Ann Arbor, MI, 1991), pp. 293–375.

[27] George Vernadskii, "Kn. Trubetskoi i ukrainskii vopros," BAR, George Vernadsky Collection, Box 96.

[28] On the Russian White movement and the Ukrainian question during the Civil War, see Anna Procyk, *Russian Nationalism and Ukraine: The Nationality Policy of the Volunteer Army during the Civil War* (Edmonton and Toronto, 1995). For a more general discussion of the nationality question within Russian émigré communities in interwar Europe, see Askold Doronchenkov, *Emigratsiia 'pervoi volny' o natsional'nykh problemakh i sud'be Rossii* (St. Petersburg, 2001). It is quite symptomatic that Pavel Milyukov, the Russian liberal politician who, arguably, was most sympathetic toward "national minorities," accepted a possibility of a "federal solution" only by the end of 1920, when it was obviously too late. At the same time, the views of the legal scholar and liberal imperial administrator Baron Boris Nolde (who like Milyukov was a member of the Kadet party) appear to be quite representative of the prevailing perspective of Russian émigrés on the nationality question. "In Russia," Nolde asserted, "the nationality question will be decided either by the non-Russians [*inorodtsy*] cutting our throats, or us cutting theirs... Once the revolutionary wave recedes, Russia will again become a unified state, so long as it does not break apart into its component parts and cease being Russia." Nolde specifically noted that there could be no compromise with the Ukrainians: "Either Ukraine will devour Great Russia, or we will uproot Ukrainian separatism." Nolde, however, greatly admired the way the Russian Empire was ruled for centuries before the "unfortunate" advent of the age of nationalism; specifically, he referred to the peculiar imperial system of informal "federalism" that would preserve local autonomies in the borderlands. For a detailed and thoughtful discussion of Nolde's views,

held that the Russian–Ukrainian unity forged throughout several centuries of intensive interaction within one state produced the tremendously beneficial results for both East Slavic peoples. Most important among them was the high culture of the late imperial epoch that was, in Vernadskii's view, both Russian and Ukrainian—a magnificent product of the two peoples' fruitful collaboration. This dual loyalty—Ukrainian *Landespatriotismus* and appreciation of the imperial high culture that flourished under the conditions of political unity of "historic Russia"—created the internal tension that had to be reconciled. This reconciliation appeared to have involved the re-conceptualization of empire and nation within the Eurasianist philosophical framework.

The Vernadskiis' Ukrainian roots are very well documented, including by George Vernadskii himself. Shortly before his death in 1973 Vernadskii started publishing his memoirs: several chapters were serialized in *Novyi Zhurnal*.[29] A fascinating manuscript in the Vernadskii archival collection titled "The Story of the Vernadskii Family as Related by My Father" is particularly interesting in that both Vernadskiis, father and son, had made an attempt to reconstruct their Ukrainian lineage and trace the ties that connected Vernadskiis with other illustrious old Ukrainian families such as the Korolenkos and Konstantinoviches.[30] The extremely valuable information on the Vernadskiis' Ukrainian roots and interests can also be gleaned from Vladimir Vernadskii's diaries.[31]

But, of course, place of origin or ethnic roots do not necessarily define one's national identity and loyalty. More importantly, most scholars within the humanities today hold that national identity is

> not a fixed category, but a fluctuating process, in the course of which one or more identities can evolve side by side in the same person, in greater or lesser tension with each other… [N]ational identity can be multiple or compound… an individual can be both Scottish and British, or Ukrainian and Russian. The two (or more)

---

see Peter Holquist, "Dilemmas of Progressive Administrator: Baron Boris Nolde," *Kritika: Explorations in Russian and Eurasian History* 7/2 (Spring 2006): 241–73.

[29] Some important parts of his reminiscences, however—an account of his life in Athens in 1921–22 and his description of the crucial Prague period, 1922–27—still remain unpublished.

[30] George Vernadskii, "O rode Vernadskikh," BAR, George Vernadsky Collection, Box 98.

[31] Vladimir Vernadskii, *Dnevniki. 1917–1921. Oktiabr' 1917 – ianvar' 1920* (Kiev, 1994); Vladimir Vernadskii, *Dnevniki. 1917–1921. Ianvar' 1920 – mart 1921* (Kiev, 1997); Vladimir Vernadskii, *Dnevniki. Mart 1921 – avgust 1925* (Moscow, 1998); Vladimir Vernadskii, *Dnevniki. 1926–1934* (Moscow, 2001); Vladimir Vernadskii, *Dnevniki. 1935–1941*, 2 vols. (Moscow, 2006).

national identities are not just superimposed on one another, but may complement each other, since the defining features of each nation differ from case to case.³²

In this sense, the Vernadskiis' case is particularly instructive in that it shows how complex, contradictory, and vague the issue of national identity and political loyalty was in imperial Russia's twilight years.

Most contemporary historians seem to agree that, since the 1860s, when the slow but steady rise of Ukrainian ethnic nationalism prompted the imperial regime in St. Petersburg to come up with its own "nationalizing project," and till the Russian Empire's collapse in 1917, Ukraine represented an administrative territory where a whole gamut of loyalties and identities existed simultaneously.³³ To be sure, the bulk of Ukraine's population, the local peasants, had not been affected yet by this new nationalist discourse; for the most part, they remained in the premodern stage till approximately the late 1910s, defining themselves just as "locals," good followers of the Orthodox Church, and loyal subjects of the czar. Ukraine's "nationalist front" was represented by a tiny group of activists, mostly members of local intelligentsia, who consciously called themselves *Ukrainians*—in contrast to *malorosy* [Little Russians], an official appellation of the region's population that did recognize certain insignificant regional differences but generally presupposed the unity of *malorosy* and *velikorosy* [Great Russians]—and advanced the idea that Ukrainian people were a full-blown nation, linguistically and culturally distinct from the *velikorosy*. For its part, the imperial establishment, which was until the mid-nineteenth century very wary of pursuing a nationalizing policy (as any authority presiding over a multinational empire would be), decided that the time had come to confront the challenge posed by what it labeled "Ukrainian separatism." Thus it launched a set of measures that some scholars characterize as a "greater Russian nation project"—a policy that ideally was supposed to lead to the formation of the Russian Empire's core nation comprising all three East Slavic peoples—the Great Russians, Little Russians, and Belarusians.³⁴

Now, this nationalizing activism on the part of St. Petersburg authorities, with its incoherent and poorly executed policies of Russification and persecution

---

³² Geoffrey Hosking, "First through Kiev," *Times Literary Supplement*, June 1, 2007.

³³ See a stimulating discussion on loyalties and identities in the Russian Empire at the forum held by the journal *Ab Imperio*: "Alfavit, iazyk i natsional'naia identichnost'" v Rossiiskoi imperii," *Ab Imperio* 2 (2005): 123–319 as well as its continuation in *Ab Imperio* 1 (2006).

³⁴ Aleksei Miller, *Imperiia Romanovykh i natsionalizm* (Moscow, 2006); Aleksei Miller, "Ukrainskii vopros" v politike vlastei i russkom obshchestvennom mnenii (vtoraia polovina XIX v.) (St. Petersburg, 2000).

of the nationalist-minded members of the Ukrainian intelligentsia, made the picture of local identities and loyalties even more complex.[35] Depending on how they perceived the imperial government's policies, we can discern—apart from the mostly passive and premodern peasantry and those members of local society who retained a pre-nationalist, dynastic type of loyalty—at least four other social types that existed in the pre-revolutionary Ukraine. First, there were the Ukrainian nationalists, who, quite naturally, opposed Russification and rejected the idea of a single Russian nation. (This attitude, however, didn't prejudge the vision of further political relationship with the Russians: Some Ukrainian nationalists advocated complete separation, while others were ready to settle for a federation.) Second, those people in Ukraine (of whatever ethnic origin) who believed they were Russians wholeheartedly supported the authorities' attempt to forge a "greater Russian nation." Third, there were ethnic Ukrainians who persisted in proudly calling themselves *malorosy* and who perceived themselves as constituting an inseparable Russian triad together with the Great Russians and Belarusians. They were supportive of the government's efforts to form the empire's "core nation" and castigated the Ukrainian nationalists for their perceived desire to break the "historic" East Slavic unity. Finally, there were people, mostly ethnic Ukrainians, who had a hybrid or dual identity, who described themselves as "both Ukrainian and Russian" or as "Ukrainians belonging to the world of Russian [high] culture." This group, arguably the smallest in comparison with the other three, found itself in the most difficult situation since its relations with the Ukrainian nationalists on the one hand and the Russian nationalists on the other were equally strained. Its members were appalled by the crude Russification measures and the stubborn reluctance of the imperial government to recognize Ukrainians as a nation in its own right, possessing its own language and culture. But they also found the Ukrainian nationalists' drive toward political separation as counterproductive and believed that Ukraine would be much better served if it stayed united in one powerful state with Russia, sharing in the magnificent riches that the late imperial culture had produced.

As the Russian Empire's days drew to a close and the struggle over the "Ukrainian question" became more acute, this group found itself between a rock and a hard place, being forced by circumstances to make a political choice and define what their ultimate loyalties and identities were. It was a choice that they would rather avoid making.

All the evidence we have suggests that the Vernadskiis likely belonged to this small group of ethnic Ukrainians who had a dual "Russian–Ukrainian

---

35   See the discussion of the issue of identities in the pre-revolutionary Ukraine in Aleksei Miller, "Dualizm identichnostei na Ukraine," *Otechestvennye zapiski* 1 (2007): 84–96.

identity."³⁶ There were some interesting nuances, though. The paths that led Vladimir and George Vernadskii to the dual "Ukrainian–Russian" identity differed markedly. There is a general consensus among scholars that, from very early on, Vladimir Vernadskii (who, although born in St. Petersburg, did live as a young boy with his parents in Ukraine—in the city of Kharkiv) was conscious of his Ukrainian origin.³⁷ He kept a keen interest in Ukrainian affairs after he moved to St. Petersburg and Moscow,³⁸ and during the decade preceding the Russian Revolution participated in all the important debates on the "Ukrainian question" in his dual role as prominent academic and influential politician.³⁹ But

---

36   Ernest Gyidel, "Ob 'ukrainofil'stve' Georgiia Vernadskogo, ili variatsiia na temu natsional'nykh i gosudarstvennykh loial'nostei," *Ab Imperio* 4 (2006): 329–46.

37   In several diary entries dated from September 1924, Vladimir Vernadskii describes the "Ukrainophile" atmosphere that was characteristic of his Kharkiv milieu. "Ukrainian tendencies," Vernadskii was reminiscing, "were undoubtedly strong in many families—not just in the families belonging to the ancient [Ukrainian] clans that took part in the historical life during the recent centuries, but also in such families belonging to the local intelligentsia as our family... Deep in his heart, [my father] always remained a Ukrainian and sharply distinguished between Ukrainians and Russians. Both he and my mother had a very strong sense of Ukrainian nationality, and my father was conscious of the deep differences between the Ukrainian people [and the Russians]... In my childhood years, I got from him a different perspective on [Hetman] Mazepa than the one that had been predominant within Russian society. He held that Mazepa was right, not Peter [the Great]. From him I learned about Shevchenko; he told me that St. Petersburg had been built on the bones of the [Ukrainian] Cossacks... In our household there were Ukrainian books but they were kept in a disorganized way. In Kharkov, due to the hard times [in the 1870s, thanks to the anti-Ukrainian imperial legislation] there were no Ukrainian books. My father received everything that could be subscribed, through the Main Post-office, from Galicia [in Austria-Hungary]... During my trip to foreign lands in 1873–76, my father was telling me not only about the Slavs (Prague) but also about Lvov and Galicia and about the freedom that Ukrainian literature enjoyed there... He tremendously loved Ukrainian songs and my mother sang them beautifully. At night parties in Kharkov, in our big house—my father was the manager of the [State] bank's [Kharkov] branch—she would organize choirs: The windows would be opened and the Ukrainian songs would flow... As though in a dream, I also remember Ukrainian plays and Ukrainian poems being discussed in Kharkov." See V. Vernadskii, *Dnevniki. Mart 1921 – avgust 1925*, pp. 176–7.

38   Before Vladimir Vernadskii decided to take up a professorship at Moscow University he was thinking of settling down in Ukraine. On July 15, 1941 he reminisced in his diary that, upon completion of his two-year-long research trip to Europe in 1890, he "returned from Paris ... and was going to move to one of the Ukrainian universities—in Kiev or in Kharkov." See V. Vernadskii, *Dnevniki. 1935–1941*, vol. 2, p. 268.

39   See Kendall E. Bailes, *Science and Russian Culture in the Age of Revolutions: V.I. Vernadsky and His Scientific School, 1863–1945* (Bloomington, IN, 1990). Bailes's is the only comprehensive biography of Vladimir Vernadskii in English.

with George Vernadskii the situation appears to be much trickier. It is only now that the evidence found in his personal papers allows us to reconstruct the long and winding odyssey in the course of which he developed what appears to be a dual "Russian–Ukrainian" identity.

It would seem that throughout his life in Russia—the period between 1887, the year he was born, and November 1920, when he fled together with the remnants of the Baron Petr Wrangel's army to Constantinople—George Vernadskii thought of himself as Russian. There is fascinating evidence to this effect provided by none other than his father, when, in 1920, Vladimir Vernadskii wrote in a letter to his Parisian friend Aleksandra Golshtein: "I am tremendously happy with my kids… [But] the children, though they're good friends, turned out to be quite different. My son is Orthodox and Russian, lacking any Ukrainian sympathies whatsoever, while my daughter is Ukrainian and in this sense she is spiritually closer to me."[40] George Vernadskii himself was quite explicit when, in an unpublished passage of his memoirs, he described his trip in the summer of 1908 to the Slavic congress in Prague and encounters with the Ukrainian students there. Being one of the three delegates elected to the congress from the Moscow student body, George met, at the gathering presided over by Professor Masaryk, the student representatives of other Slavic peoples, including the Ukrainians. The latter, Vernadskii pointedly notes, "treated *us Russians* in a particularly unfriendly way."[41]

The collapse of the Russian *ancien régime* followed by the string of political upheavals that irretrievably buried the "historic Russia" couldn't fail to deeply shake George Vernadskii and affect his perceptions of personal identity. Between November 1920 and February 1922 George Vernadskii and his wife Nina were literally struggling for survival, leading the difficult life of refugees at the eastern periphery of postwar Europe. The painful sense of being "stateless persons" undoubtedly exacerbated their angst and deepened their identity crisis. "We will likely never return to Russia—we're already a cutoff piece [*my otrezannyi lomot'*]," Nina Vernadskii wrote in her diary. "We had left Russia because we could not accept [the rule of the Communist] International but now we have lost any nationality ourselves."[42] From Constantinople, the Vernadskiis moved in 1921 to Athens and then, in 1922, to Prague where the Masaryk government had just launched the so-called "Russian Initiative" [*Ruska akce*], having provided funds to support a number of Russian scholarly and educational

---

[40] BAR, Aleksandra Golshtein Collection, Box 3.
[41] BAR, George Vernadsky Collection, Box 97.
[42] Ibid., Box 141.

institutions in Czechoslovakia.⁴³ It was also in Prague that George was reunited with his parents almost two years after they had parted from one another, in a most dramatic way, in the Crimea on the eve of the Bolshevik seizure of the peninsula. (In May 1922, the Soviet government allowed Vladimir Vernadskii to go abroad to take up a teaching position at the Sorbonne. As soon as they were issued foreign passports, he, accompanied with his wife and daughter, traveled to Paris via Prague.)

I would argue that this family reunion—particularly, the reestablishment of ties with his father, which would be never broken again until the latter's death in 1945—played a crucial role in the transformation of George Vernadskii's personal identity. Reflections on Russia's—and his own—trials and tribulations following the 1917 Revolution, coupled with Vladimir Vernadskii's powerful influence, appear to have reshaped George's perception of self, steering him away from an exclusively Russian identity and toward a compound "Russian-Ukrainian" one.

Archival documents provide evidence illustrating this fascinating process. While Vladimir Vernadskii was staying in Paris, from 1922 to 1925, father and son appeared to have used the opportunity of personal meetings to discuss, among other things, matters pertaining to family history and the Ukrainian connection.⁴⁴ George Vernadskii's interest in the issue seemed to grow constantly as he would frequently return to it in his diaries and notes in the 1930s. For

---

⁴³ See George Katkov, "Masaryk's Guests," in Michael Glenny and Norman Stone (eds.), *The Other Russia* (London, 1990); Elena Chinyaeva, "Ruska emigrace v Ceskoslovensku: vyvoj ruske pomocne akce," *Slovansky prehled* 1 (1993); Zdenek Sladek, "Prag: Das 'russische Oxford,'" in Karl Schlogel (ed.), *Der Grosse Exodus. Die russische Emigration und ihre Zentren 1917 bis 1941* (Munich, 1994), pp. 218-33.

⁴⁴ Vladimir Vernadskii's personal experiences in Ukraine during the turbulent times of the civil war—in particular, in his capacity as founder and first president of the Ukrainian Academy of Sciences in 1918-19—appeared to confirm both his sense of Ukrainian identity and his understanding of how crucially important the "Ukrainian question" was. Upon his return from the Crimea to Moscow in March 1921, he, according to his diary, was "consciously raising everywhere the Ukrainian issue." He was dismayed at how "here [in Russia] its significance was so poorly understood: Deep in their hearts many people believe that this is a kind of transitory phenomenon that is destined to disappear quite soon!" See Vernadskii, *Dnevniki. Mart 1921 – avgust 1925*, 15. On April 20, 1921 Vladimir Vernadskii wrote, in a letter to his friend the Ukrainian Academician N.P. Vasilenko: "You know how precious Ukraine is for me and how deeply the Ukrainian rebirth is penetrating my entire national and personal *Weltanschauung*... Russian culture should become a Russian-Ukrainian culture..." See S.N. Kirzhaev and V.A. Tolstov (eds.), *Iz epistoliarnogo naslediia V.I. Vernadskogo: Pis'ma ukrainskim akademikam N.P. Vasilenko i A.A. Bogomol'tsu* (Kiev, 1991), pp. 13-14. On Vladimir Vernadskii's ties with Ukraine and Ukrainian scholars, see

instance, in 1932 George had a chance to see his father again—incidentally, in Prague, which they chose as a meeting place because one (George) was coming from the United States and the other (Vladimir) from Leningrad (St. Petersburg). An entry in George's diary for that year begins: "These last days, both Dad and Mom were telling a lot about the lives of their parents and families. All this is precious and very interesting. It's a pity that previously I knew so little and paid little attention, but now I want to learn every single detail." Then he adds: "In general, everyone has to know the history of his family and kin, and I—a historian—even more so… And I knew so little."[45]

A document that George finished compiling in 1936—but which was based, as he himself specifies, on the conversations he had with his father in Paris in August 1923—gives us a good idea of what George Vernadskii learned about his Ukrainian ancestors and their political attitudes. Here is a noteworthy description of George's grandfather, Ivan Vasilyevich Vernadskii, who at one time was an economics professor at Kiev University. Ivan Vernadskii, writes George in this genealogical memo, "knew Ukrainian very well and loved this language. He was on friendly terms with Shevchenko, Kulish, Kostomarov [the leading members of the Ukrainian movement in the mid-nineteenth century] and his pro-Ukrainian sympathies had likely increased partially under their influence." George also notes that Ivan, even when he was a young boy, criticized his father for the failure to learn Ukrainian. Later, George adds, Ivan Vasilyevich passed on his Ukrainophile sentiments to his son Vladimir, George's father. George ends the description of his grandfather with a short but telling outline of his historical–political views: "Ivan Vasilyevich believed that [Hetman] Mazepa was one of the last fighters for Ukraine's independence. And he had a negative view of Peter the Great because of his [ruthless] Ukrainian policy."[46] Among many additions and corrections that Vladimir Vernadskii personally introduced into this genealogical text, one is particularly remarkable. Its heading, in Vladimir's own handwriting, reads: "About our family as Ukrainians, *not* Russians." Vladimir stressed in these notes that both his father and his mother "felt very acutely their distinctiveness from the Russians. [They] knew from legends and books the history of Ukraine. [I] heard a lot [about it] in my childhood."[47]

Konstantin Sytnik, Stepan Stoiko, and Elena Apanovich, *V.I. Vernadskii: Zhizn' i deiatel'nost' na Ukraine* (Kiev, 1984).

[45] BAR, George Vernadsky Collection, Box 103.
[46] Ibid., Box 98.
[47] Ibid. Vladimir Vernadskii was acutely interested in the genealogical roots of the Vernadskii family. "In connection with the 'biological' studies of my own genealogy and that of my children," Vernadskii wrote in one of his diary entries, "I did research on the families" with which the Vernadskiis were connected. This research gave Vernadskii a "strange

Boosted by the renewed close association with his father, whom he revered, George Vernadskii's reevaluation of his identity appeared to be moving apace in 1924, as a diary entry by Vladimir Vernadskii from September 5 of that year indicates, in which Vladimir refers to the "Ukrainian tendencies of [my] son."[48] That those tendencies persisted and probably grew even stronger over time we know from George Vernadskii himself. In January 1940, in a letter to an editor of the Ukrainian émigré publication in America, he wrote (in Ukrainian!), "[I] regard myself as both Ukrainian and Russian and also believe that the strength of the Russian and Ukrainian peoples lies in cooperation and not in separation of one from the other."[49] These were precisely the words that his father could have used to describe his own identities and loyalties.

It would be pretty safe to conclude, then, that throughout the 1920s the positions of George and Vladimir Vernadskii on the "Ukrainian question" grew closer together until they became basically identical. The stance they shared can be summed up in five points:

1. Both the Great Russians [*velikorosy*] and the Ukrainians are closely related but still distinct peoples in their own right, each with its own language and culture.
2. At the same time, their close association throughout the ages, their common endeavors and their shared sacrifices have given rise to a great imperial state—a global power with a world-class culture that can be truly called pan-Russian [*obshcherusskii*] in that it is the result of the close collaboration of the Great Russian and Ukrainian peoples.
3. Russian–Ukrainian unity can rest only on mutual understanding and respect, including the appreciation of national (cultural and linguistic) peculiarities.
4. Both the attempts to suppress national distinctiveness and the desire to separate one people from the other politically are equally lethal for the unity of the pan-Russian state and the wholeness of pan-Russian culture.
5. Thus, the worst enemies of Russian–Ukrainian unity are (a) the radical Russian nationalists, who deny the very existence of the Ukrainian people and hold that the "Ukrainian question" is a mere instrument in the perfidious geopolitical designs of Russia's European neighbors, and (b) the Ukrainian separatists, who, by seeking to tear Ukraine away

---

impression: all were Ukrainians... [There were] no Great Russians at all." See V. Vernadsky, *Dnevniki. 1935–1941*, vol. 2, p. 132.

[48] V. Vernadskii, *Dnevniki. Mart 1921 – avgust 1925*, p. 176.
[49] BAR, George Vernadsky Collection, Box 50.

from Russia, doom Ukrainian culture to wretched provincialism and Ukrainians to a parochial existence.⁵⁰

It seems plausible that, having shaped the perspective outlined in these five points, George Vernadskii would find the previous approaches to Russian history—as well as the previous interpretations of what "Russia" and "Russian" mean—inadequate. What type of loyalty do these terms describe—imperial, political, or cultural? Do historians of Russia and historians of the Russian Empire study the same subject? If not, how then do these different subjects correlate?

To answer those questions, a thorough reconceptualization of the Russian historical process was needed. But what would be the proper analytic framework for such a rethink? Incidentally, in February 1922 George Vernadskii was living in Prague—the Central European city that, in the first postwar decade, was turning into the principal center of the Eurasianist movement.⁵¹ It wouldn't take too long for Vernadskii, who was looking for a new paradigm to better understand Russia's past and present, to realize that Eurasianism was exactly the framework he sought.

---

⁵⁰ In a characteristic passage from the article titled "Ukrainian Question and Russian Society" (1916), Vladimir Vernadskii basically put Russian and Ukrainian ethnic nationalisms on an equal footing in terms of how negatively both nationalisms affected the cause of Russian–Ukrainian unity. "The government policy at that time [1870s–80s]," noted Vernadskii, "was striving to achieve a certain goal—namely, to bring about the full merger of Ukrainians with the ruling [Russian] nationality and eliminate the awareness of national distinctiveness within the Ukrainian population perceived as being dangerous for the Great Russians. In its essence, this policy of Great Russian national centralism was, consequently, no less separatist than the Ukrainian movement that had always been suspected of separatism. Only the official separatism was Great Russian in its nature and sought to transform the enormous multilingual and multicultural state into a country fashioned according to the Great Russian model. [Such transformation would amount to turning] Great Russia into *Velikorossiya* [the ethnic Russian state]." See Vladimir Vernadskii, *Publitsisticheskie stat'i* (Moscow, 1996), p. 214.

⁵¹ There is a growing literature on the Russian émigrés in Prague in general and on the Prague Eurasianist circle in particular. See Andreyev and Savický, *Russia Abroad*; Ivan Savický, *Praga i zarubezhnaia Rossiia* (Prague, 2002); Elena Chinyaeva, *Russians outside Russia: The Emigré Community in Czechoslovakia, 1918–1938* (Munich, 2001); Elena Serapionova, *Rossiiskaia emigratsiia v Chekhoslovatskoi respublike (20–30 gody)* (Moscow, 1995). Also useful are the symposium proceedings *Russkaia, ukrainskaia i belorusskaia emigratsiia v Chekhoslovakii mezhdu dvumia mirovymi voinami. Rezul'taty i perspektivy issledovanii. Fondy Slavianskoi biblioteki i prazhskikh arkhivov* (Prague, 1995).

The Eurasianist Framework

Two Eurasianist concepts are particularly relevant here. The first one, advanced by the geographer Petr Savitskii, was the vision of Eurasia—whose borders, incidentally, roughly coincide with those of the pre-1917 Russian Empire—as a highly cohesive landmass. The integrity of this vast geo-massif, Savitskii argued, is an objective fact of physical geography since it is based on the region's specific natural "structure": the correlation between the horizontally shaped ecological zones and vertically shaped river systems.[52] "Eurasia is indivisible," Savitskii asserted. Being a "special geographical world," it serves as a natural *mestorazvitie* [developmental space] for the numerous peoples residing in Eurasia.[53] The Eurasianists held that there exists an organic connection between geographical territory, the peoples (ethnic groups) that reside in this territory, and the character of cultural development. Environment and culture constantly interact, experiencing mutual influences and tensions. So *mestorazvitie*, a key Eurasianist category, was coined specifically to embody this complex process of interaction between various types of natural and socio-historical milieu. "For us," Savitskii asserted, "socio-historical milieu and its territory should merge into a single unified whole—into a geographical individual or a landscape."[54] The Eurasianists argued that this "geographical individual," as it was supposedly born of the intimate interaction between culture/history and territory, was in fact a live organism—a "symphonic personality."

---

[52] For an excellent discussion of Savitskii's "structuralist" geography, see Glebov, "A Life with Imperial Dreams." It was none other than Roman Jakobson who, not long before his death, called Petr Savitskii "a highly gifted intellectual precursor of structuralist geography." See Roman Jakobson and Krystyna Pomorska, *Besedy* (Jerusalem, 1982), p. 68.

[53] Petr Savitskii, *Rossiia – osobyi geograficheskii mir* (Prague, 1927).

[54] It's noteworthy that Savitskii advanced the idea of Eurasia's cultural uniqueness very early on—even before the first formal Eurasianist collection of articles was published in 1922. Already in 1921, in his review of Trubetskoi's *Europe and Mankind*, Savitskii contended that the type of relations that existed between the Russian nation and other nations of Eurasia differed radically from that which "existed in the parts of the world involved in the sphere of European colonial policies." For him, Eurasia "is a region where there is certain equality and certain brotherhood between nations—phenomena that don't have any analogies in the international relations [within] the colonial empires." Furthermore, according to Savitskii, over millennia of close and usually friendly interaction, the Eurasian peoples shaped what can be called a common culture: "One can posit the existence of a Eurasian culture that, to a certain extent, is a common product and common asset of the peoples of Eurasia." See Petr Savitskii, "Evropa i Evraziia. (Po povodu broshiury kn. N.S. Trubetskogo 'Evropa i Chelovechestvo')," *Russkaia mysl* 2 (1921): 135.

The other crucial concept—the idea of Eurasian nationalism—was advanced by Nikolai Trubetskoi. Trubetskoi, a brilliant linguist and ethnographer, took the Eurasianist reconceptualization of nation one step further and suggested—in an almost Gellnerian manner—that a "peculiar" Eurasian nation might, in fact, be created. He developed his arguments most fully in the short essay titled "Pan-Eurasian Nationalism."[55] The Revolution and the collapse of the Russian Empire, asserted Trubetskoi, had radically changed the position of the Russians within the former imperial space. The borderland peoples had attained broad new rights that they would never give up voluntarily, while the Russians appeared to have forever lost their role of the "master race" within the realm. At the same time, the political upheaval that followed the Revolution and imperial implosion had caused only the temporary fragmentation of the Eurasian space, and its unity had been quickly restored—a fact that, according to Trubetskoi, should serve as yet another proof that "Eurasia constitutes a geographical, economic and historical whole." But here was a dilemma: "[T]here is no return to the situation in which Russians were the sole owner of the state territory, and, clearly, no other people can play such a role." Trubetskoi boldly resolves this conundrum in a famous passage. "Consequently," he asserted, "the national substratum of the state formerly known as the Russian Empire and now known as the USSR can only be the totality of peoples inhabiting that state, taken as a peculiar multiethnic nation and as such possessed of its own nationalism. We call that nation Eurasian, its territory Eurasia, and its nationalism Eurasianism."[56]

To prevent the rise within the borderland peoples of political nationalism (separatism), Trubetskoi suggested that all ethnic groups residing in Eurasia should develop a hierarchy of loyalties that would be interconnected and complementary. Every individual people in Eurasia should combine its own local nationalism with the overarching Eurasian nationalism. By the same token, "all citizens of the Eurasian state"[57] should be conscious of and take pride in the fact that they simultaneously belong both to a given people and the Eurasian nation. (Trubetskoi conceded, though, that this "Eurasian nation" was still a work in progress since the understanding of the common destiny of the Eurasian peoples had yet to become a "significant part of their consciousness."[58])

---

[55] Nikolai Trubetskoi, "Obshcheevraziiskii natsionalizm," *Evraziiskaia khronika* 9 (1927): 24–31. The English translation is in Nikolai Trubetzkoy, *The Legacy*, pp. 233–44.
[56] Trubetzkoy, *The Legacy*, p. 239.
[57] Ibid., p. 241.
[58] Ibid.

George Vernadskii and the History of Russia–Eurasia

The Eurasianist vision of the former imperial space as the geographical, economic, and historical whole as well as the idea of the overarching Eurasian nationalism obviously appealed to George Vernadskii. These concepts appeared to have neatly resolved—at least on a theoretical level—the Russian–Ukrainian dilemma that was troubling him. Within the Eurasianist paradigm, there couldn't be any such Russian–Ukrainian problem at all. Because Eurasia is indivisible from the geographic-historical point of view, Ukraine, being a component part of it (along with, for that matter, any other parts of this "special world"), *objectively* belongs to the Eurasian space, while the cultivation of the overarching Eurasian nationalism (along with the nationalisms of the individual peoples residing in Eurasia) provides the Ukrainians, Tatars, or Georgians with the *subjective* feeling of belongingness in a "multiethnic nation." Thus, for a Ukrainian, it is possible to retain the local Ukrainian loyalty, see himself as part of the broader Russian (East-Slavic) unity, and have affinity with a still-larger Eurasian entity at one and the same time. This arrangement suited Vernadskii perfectly.

But for history writing, the concept of "Russia–Eurasia" clearly presented both advantages and problems. To be sure, the Eurasianist approach significantly broadened the geographical horizon of research and boldly shifted the perspective, challenging the well-established Eurocentric interpretation of Russian history that presented Russia as a "Europeanizing" country, undergoing the same evolutionary process as other European nations but held back by Russian peculiarities. At the same time, however, the very term "Russia–Eurasia" has also obscured the object of research because in this category Russia and Eurasia found themselves inseparably merged, thus completely blurring the distinction between them. A brief analysis of the methodological foundations of Vernadskii's historical writing demonstrates how he grappled with this problem, trying to both delineate Russian and Eurasian history and at the same time preserve the opaque situation where they would remain virtually indistinguishable.

In his first major Eurasianist work, the *Outline of Russian History*, Vernadskii presents the Russian historical process as the expansion of the Russian state across the Eurasian landmass. "The history of the expansion of the Russian state is to a significant extent the history of the adapting of the Russian people to its *mestorazvitie*—Eurasia; it is also the history of the adapting of the entire territory of Eurasia to the historical-economic needs of the Russian people."[59] Thus, the history of Russian people was basically identified with the history of the state and included in the general history of Eurasia. In its turn, the history of Eurasia

---

[59] George Vernadskii, *Nachertanie russkoi istorii* (Prague, 1927).

was understood as a series of persistent attempts by various peoples to form a Eurasia-wide state—starting from the Scythians, Huns, and Mongols. The book seemed to imply, though, that as soon as the Russians completed their expansion across Eurasia and formed *their* pan-Eurasian state, the history of Russia and the history of Eurasia became identical.

Vernadskii tried to refine his thesis in a number of subsequent works[60] and finally arrived at a formula that was included in a short memorandum entitled "A Concise Exposition of the Eurasianist View on Russian History" (1938).[61] Of course, he again reasserted the Eurasianists' main credo that Eurasia as a whole constitutes the historical *mestorazvitie* of the Russian people. But there was also one important nuance. "The history of the Russian people, however, doesn't incorporate in its narrative the histories of other Eurasian peoples who for a long period of time both cooperated with the Russian people and competed with it," noted Vernadskii. "Thus," he continued, "if Russian history is increasingly merging with the history of the entire Eurasia geographically as we are approaching the contemporary epoch, this doesn't exclude the other approach to the history of Eurasia [seen] as the history of all the peoples of Eurasia, including the Russian people." Remarkably, though, in this programmatic text he subsumed the histories of the East Slavs (the Great Russians, Ukrainians, and Belarusians) under the general rubric of "Russian history." Vernadskii's concluding passage reads as follows: "Russian history is, consequently, the history of the peoples of the entire East Slavic (Russian) family... seen against the backdrop of the history of their relations with other peoples of Eurasia and [developing] on the geographical basis of the entirety of Eurasia as the Russian historical *mestorazvitie*."

This formula was, no doubt, a big step forward since Vernadskii, for the first time in Russian historiographic tradition, fully appreciated the multiethnic character of "Eurasia" and its complex interaction with "Russia,"[62] a process that was steadily leading to a new conceptualization, that of "Russia–Eurasia." But his approach remained ambiguous, given that he began largely to disregard the multiethnic factor when the merger between "Russia" and "Eurasia" became fully realized. As the Russians reach in their eastward thrust the "end of the earth" on the Pacific, multiethnic Eurasia somehow dissolves into the pan-Eurasian Russian state. This state, Vernadskii asserts, is a "gigantic historical-

---

[60] See, for example, Vernadskii, *Opyt istorii Evrazii* (Berlin, 1934).

[61] Vernadskii, "Kratkoe izlozhenie evraziiskoi tochki zreniia na russkuiu istoriiu."

[62] "Even now," Vernadskii noted, "the notion 'history of Eurasia' doesn't fully coincide with the notion 'Russian history' as today in Eurasia there live, besides the Russian people, also many other peoples whose [historic] development has been closely connected with the development of the Russian people but who are not identical with the Russians." See Vernadskii, *Opyt istorii Evrazii*, p. 5.

cultural organism" and "the world power." The inclusion into this Russian state of the "individual regions and peoples gave them the invaluable economic and cultural benefits" and made them the "co-participants in world history."[63]

Vernadskii's ultimate reluctance—all his theoretical maneuverings notwithstanding—to decouple "Russia" and "Eurasia" and clearly distinguish Russian history from that of the Eurasian peoples is highly symptomatic since it reveals the Eurasianist agenda: to preserve the unity of the former imperial space at all costs.[64] This task presupposed the strategy of avoiding any descriptions of pre-revolutionary Russia that might invite unwelcome comparisons with the European colonial empires. To write a truly comprehensive "Russian history" in its interrelation with the history of the peoples of Eurasia, one would have to pose the questions that Vernadskii paid little attention to or ignored altogether: What methods were used to facilitate Russian expansion in Eurasia? What policies were employed to incorporate the territories with ethnically, religiously, and culturally diverse populations? How did the subjugated peoples and their elites react to the Russian advance? How did Russian rule affect the local government, social structure, economic life, and culture of the peoples who were drawn into the orbit of the Russian state? While discussing these issues, one would have to treat the borderland peoples not as mere objects of Russian government policies but as actors who to a large extent define the course of history.

But to write such an analysis would mean to write the history of Russia as a multiethnic *empire*—the objective Vernadskii definitely didn't pursue. He and his Eurasianist friends had witnessed the power of ethnic nationalism and sincerely hoped that the new Eurasian identity that they had fashioned in their bitter exile would help them preserve the integrity of "historic Russia" (be it the pre-1917 Romanov empire or the Soviet Union) in an age when empires appeared to be out of place. Their reasoning was indeed original if somewhat utopian: "if the Russian empire were a symphonic unity of people—more than that, if there were no Russian empire at all but only organic Eurasia—the issue of separatism would lose its meaning."[65]

However, George Vernadskii was not a mere ideologue but a serious scholar. Unlike all his great nineteenth-century predecessors beginning with Nikolai

---

[63] Vernadskii, *Nachertanie russkoi istorii* (Prague, 1927), p. 231.

[64] At one point, Vernadskii would concede that a "separate," "national" history of the Russian people does have the right to exist. "Russian history," he wrote, "is [just] a subdivision of the [general] history of the Eurasian peoples." But, he immediately added, "Russian history had, *nolens volens*, to include into its field of vision geopolitically ever broader expanses as the Russian people, in its historical development, would increasingly spread over [its] Eurasian *mestorazvitie*." See Vernadskii, *Opyt istorii Evrazii*, p. 8.

[65] Nicholas Riasanovsky, *Russian Identities: A Historical Survey* (Oxford, 2005), pp. 234–5.

Karamzin and ending with his teachers Vasili Kliuchevskii and Sergei Platonov, who were treating Russian history as a *national* history, Vernadskii clearly saw the Russian Empire's *multiethnicity* and tried to analyze the complex interplay between the "history of the Russian people" and the "history of the peoples of Eurasia." Vernadskii's Eurasianist approach toward Russian history appears to have been one of the possible ways out of the tangled historiographical dilemma formulated by von Hagen—

> the dilemma, which, on the one hand ignores the multinational character of the Russian Empire and the Soviet Union and chooses thereby to treat the Russian past as the history of a nation-state, or, on the other hand, highlights the multinational character of those two state formations only to condemn them, in the name of national liberation and nationalism, as anachronistic and thereby inevitably fated to collapse as such.[66]

It is precisely this search for an alternative vision "between, or beyond, empire and nation-state"[67] that Vernadskii and his fellow Eurasianists referred to as their attempts at building a "true" theory of nationalism.[68]

---

[66] See Mark von Hagen, "Writing the History of Russia as Empire: The Perspective of Federalism," in Catherine Evtuhov et al. (eds.), *Kazan, Moscow, St. Petersburg: Multiple Faces of the Russian Empire* (Moscow: 1997), p. 397.

[67] Ibid., pp. 397–8.

[68] The left-wing Eurasianist Prince Dmitrii Sviatopolk-Mirskii praised Eurasianism because, "despite the inherent propensity to nationalism, from the very outset it showed the way toward overcoming Russian nationalism [and] underscored the supranational character of its task by its very name." See Dmitrii Sviatopolk-Mirskii, "Natsional'nosti SSSR," *Evraziia* 22 (1929).

CHAPTER 3

Space as a Destiny: Legitimizing the Russian Empire through Geography and Cosmos

Marlène Laruelle

In European historiography, Russia has been often analyzed through the paradigm of empire. Throughout the nineteenth century, the image of the Czarist empire as a "prison of peoples" constituted a key element of European political life and a fetish topic of liberal currents, which denounced St. Petersburg both for its autocracy as well as for its refusal to grant more national autonomy to the peoples under its grip. In the twentieth century, the ambiguous nature of the Soviet regime, which refused to institutionalize Russian dominance but was concerned by national communisms, contributed to ongoing questioning on the imperial nature of the Soviet construction. Since the disappearance of the USSR, debates have raged in the newly independent states, swift to blame the former colonial power for all their evils.[1] In Western historiography innovative comparisons have been made between "The last Empire" and the Habsburg and Ottoman Empires, as well as between European and Soviet decolonizations.[2] In Russia, the subject of empire occupies a paradoxical discursive field. The pride of state historical continuity, conceived as natural, goes hand in hand with the feeling that Russia has been an involuntary and unexpected victim of the declarations of independence of 1991. The stakes are not only affective: Legally, present-day Russia is the heir of the Soviet Union, but territorially it is heir only to the Russian Federation (RSFSR), which is not without ambiguity, for example in Moscow's treatment of the Russian minorities of the "near abroad".

Valid or not, this imperial paradigm has been investigated in many ways: Is Russia a European-style empire divided between a metropole and its peripheries;

---

[1] Tadayuki Hayashi (ed.), *The Construction and Deconstruction of National Histories in Slavic Eurasia* (Sapporo, 2003); Viktor Shnirel'man, *Who Gets the Past? Competition for Ancestors among Non-Russian Intellectuals in Russia* (Washington, DC, 1996).

[2] See, in particular, the school created around the journal *Ab Imperio*, and Ilya Gerasimov et al. (eds.), *Novaia imperskaia istoriia postsovetskogo prostranstva* (Kazan, 2004).

a homeland or prison of peoples for Soviet nationalities; an egalitarian plurinational state in which all peoples share a same Eurasian destiny? Empire is also a key element of the national narrative, in which it completes and rivals the notion of the "Russian Idea" [*russkaia ideia*]. This latter term conventionally refers to the late nineteenth and early twentieth-century intellectual debates that were centered on the idea that the essence of the Russian nation could be characterized by certain timeless features, including messianism, Orthodox spirituality, and a sense of symphony or community [*sobornost'*]. However, the concept of the Russian Idea has been gradually expanded to encompass all debates on national identity, extending from those among the first Slavophiles of the early 1830s to contemporary doctrines on how the nation can reassume its sense of mission. Debated by some currents among the Russian emigration of the 1920s and 1930s, and then among the nationalist dissidence of the 1960s–80s, the topic of empire has been subject to many contemporary reinterpretations: currents that express nostalgia for Czarism, as well as neo-communist movements, theoreticians of the Eurasian nature of Russia, defenders of Russian diasporas in the near abroad, not to mention supporters of the "liberal empire," such as Anatoli Chubais, the father of liberal reforms of the Yeltsin era.

The theme of empire has traversed the entire Russian twentieth century, crossing over at several points with the other key component of the national narrative, the weight of geography in Russia's destiny, and the relation to the cosmos. Ever since the first texts inquiring into the nature of the Russian state, written in the second half of the eighteenth century under the impetus of early Romanticism—those of Mikhail V. Lomonosov (1711–65), for example— numerous references have been made to Russia's geographical characteristics. Present since ancient times, geographical determinism constituted a legitimate mode of reflection on nations at the time. It was notably Montesquieu who developed the theory of it in his famous *Esprit des lois* (1748), in which he claimed that climates do not only strongly influence human activities, but also the nature of political regimes.[3] This notion remained very present in twentieth-century reflections on Russia's specificity, and partly intersected with the other key theme, namely, the relation to the cosmos, a theme inspired by Orthodox theology.

This chapter analyzes the articulations between empire as a nationalist discursive construction and the idea of a unique link of Russia to space, both in the sense of geography and of cosmos. It considers that the nationalist focus on the concept of "space" allows a decentering strategy for imagining the imperial

---

[3] Patrick Sériot, *Discours sur la langue et souffrance identitaire en Europe centrale et orientale* (Paris, 2010).

tradition of Russia. It therefore examines the theme of empire from the angle of an ideological narrative inspired both by forms of geographical determinism, such as Eurasianism, and by so-called Cosmist theories. To demonstrate this articulation between space and empire, it studies three categories of narrative: first, classic Eurasianism, which, elaborated in the émigré world of the 1920s–30s, can be analyzed as a geographist ideology; then, the work of Lev Gumilev (1912–92), a theoretician who combined Cosmist[4] and Eurasianist statements; and, third, some post-Soviet intellectual figures who are linked either to neo-Eurasianism or to Communist nostalgia and espouse the notion that Russia's imperial nature is legitimized by its specific relation to space. These three groups make it possible to grasp how a "decentering" strategy based on the presuppositions of Russia's specific link between humanity and cosmos, have been integrated into geographical theories about Russia and gave birth to a new legitimacy for the imperial destiny of the country.

Defining the Russian Empire by Spatial Features

Eurasianist ideology was developed in the early 1920s inside the Russian intellectual circles that emigrated to Western Europe after the October Revolution and the civil war.[5] Its founders were relatively young at the time of their emigration and came from intellectual circles that had been privileged under the former regime. Settled in various European capitals, they tried to apply political ideas that were fashionable in Europe ("the third way", "the

---

[4] Cosmism's boundaries and founding fathers are quite variable, depending upon whether one takes into account the strict interest in spatial conquest, or a more global belief in an intrinsic link between man and cosmos, between the micro- and macrocosm. If one sticks to an intellectual genealogy that heeds various historical times and theoretical presuppositions, the paternity of Cosmism, properly speaking, can be ascribed to Konstantin Tsiolkovskii (1857–1935). However, it is also possible to understand Cosmism as a more general current that emphasizes the interdependence—conceived either in philosophical or biological terms—of man with the universe, and which is based, among others, in the Orthodox theological tradition and on the works of Nikolai Fyodorov (1828–1903) about the resurrection of the dead and the birth of an all-knowing Cosmic humanity that is no longer limited in time or space, as well as on those of Vladimir Vernadskii (1863–1945) concerning the biosphere and the noosphere.

[5] On classic Eurasianism, see Marlène Laruelle, *Russian Eurasianism: An Ideology of Empire* (Washington, DC, 2008); Sergei Glebov, "The Challenge of the Modern: The Eurasianist Ideology and Movement, 1920–29," unpublished Ph.D. (Rutgers, The State University of New Jersey, 2004); Otto Böss, *Die Lehre des Eurasier. Ein Beitrag zur russischen Ideengeschichte des 20. Jahrhunderts* (Wiesbaden, 1961).

conservative revolution") to a Soviet Russia to which they no longer had access.[6] The Eurasianist movement appeared in Sofia in 1921, but quickly found its center in Prague with the settlement of some of its main theoreticians: geographer and economist Petr Savitskii (1895–1968), historian Georgii (George) Vernadskii (1887–1973), and linguist Nikolai Trubetskoi (1890–1938), a professor at the University of Vienna and an eminent member of the Prague Linguistic Circle.[7] Some of the organization's important figures could also be found in Paris, such as the philosopher and historian of culture Lev Karsavin (1882–1952), and the musician and music critic Petr Suvchinskii (1892–1985). One of the main publishing houses for Eurasianist literature was in Berlin, although the most famous members of the movement did not live in Germany.

The influence of Fydorovian thinking on classical Eurasianism is complex: While Nikolai Fyodorovian's texts on the resurrection of dead were known and debated among the emigration, they did not directly inspire the Eurasianist theories.[8] However, one "leftist" Eurasianist current, symbolized by the weekly *Evraziia*, which was published in the Parisian suburb of Clamart in 1928–29, wanted to link Eurasianism's historical conception of Russia with the emerging Marxist political conscience and did not hide its affiliations to Fyodorov's arguments on the unity between micro- and macrocosmos.

Eurasianism is part of a tradition of thought about the "median world" [*srednii mir*], a notion that was elaborated by pan-Slavist linguist Vladimir Lamanskii (1833–1914), who was the first to give the empire's geographic location and ethnic diversity a major role in the definition of Russian identity: Russia is neither Europe nor Asia, but a specific median world.[9] Lamanskii's contemporary Konstantin Leont'ev (1831–91) went even further and opened up the definition of Russia to the Asian world.[10] He anticipated, albeit in a still-equivocal fashion, the Eurasianists' future eastward turn. These so-called Orientalizers [*vostochniki*] were also among the first to take the country's imperial

---

[6] Martin Beisswenger, "Konservativnaia revoliutsiia v Germanii i dvizhenie evraziitsev—tochki soprikosnoveniia," *Konservatism v Rossii i v mire* 3 (2004): 49–73; Leonid Luks, "Evraziistvo i konservativnaia revoliutsiia. Soblazn antizapadnichestva v Rossii i Germanii," *Voprosy filosofii* 6 (1996): 57–69.

[7] On the role of Eurasianism in the birth of structuralism, see Patrick Sériot, *Structure et totalité: Les Origines intellectuelles du structuralisme en Europe centrale et orientale* (Paris, 1999).

[8] Cf. n. 4.

[9] Lamanskii's works have been republished: Vladimir Lamanskii, *Geopolitika panslavizma* (Moscow, 2010).

[10] Stephen Lukashevich, *Konstantin Leontev: A Study in Russian 'Heroic Vitalism'* (New York, 1967); Viktor Koshik, *Konstantin Leont'ev, razmyšlenija na slavjanskuju temu* (Moscow, 1997).

character into account in the definition of its identity.¹¹ However, it would not be until the catharsis of the Revolution that radical arguments emerged about the non-Europeanness of Russian identity.

Eurasianism claimed to provide a global explanation of the world based on a condemnation of the "epistemological imperialism" of the West: By applying its own concepts to the rest of the world, Europe was said to obfuscate the diversity of civilizations and establish a benchmark for measuring political and economic backwardness. However, Europe did not represent a *state* of development that all nations had to reach, but a specific *mode* of development that could not be reproduced. Seen through the historicist Western prism, Russia was a backward country; but the Eurasianists suggested that Russia should unlearn the West and perceive itself *geographically*: History, they argued, is the mode in which Europe expresses its identity; Russia's is geography. Eurasianism endeavored therefore to theorize its ideology geographically to an extent that made this "territorialized" aspect one of the main targets of its critics. Prince Yuri Shirinskii-Shikhmatov, for instance, accused the Eurasianists of naturalism and criticized the fact that, to them, "it seems that [...] Russia's path is determined not by a spiritual, but by a material factor (geography)."¹²

To interpret Eurasia in terms of its spatial relations was thus the core intellectual activity of the movement's geographer and economist, Petr Savitskii. Strongly influenced by Petr Struve (1870–1944), whose courses he attended, Savitskii lined up with the White Army during the civil war. In 1920 he was the personal secretary of Struve, who at the time was the Foreign Affairs Minister of the government of General Petr Wrangel. After the Crimea, he joined General Anton Denikin, with whom he emigrated via Turkey and Gallipoli. Once in Sofia, he coedited *Russkaia mysl'* and then in 1921 abandoned Struve's newspaper and settled in Prague, where he occupied the chair of Economy at the Russian Agrarian Institute. Arrested after the Liberation by the Soviet secret services, he was deported to Moscow and sentenced to ten years in camps. In 1956 he was discretely rehabilitated and he left again for Czechoslovakia.¹³

---

11 See Marlène Laruelle, "A-t-il existé des précurseurs au mouvement eurasiste? L'obsession russe pour l'Asie au tournant du siècle," *Revue des études slaves* 3-4 (2004): 437–54.

12 Yuri Shirinskii-Shikhmatov, "Rossiiskii natsional-maksimalizm i evraziistvo," *Evraziiskii sbornik* 6 (1929): 28.

13 See Martin Beisswenger, *Petr Nikolaevich Savitskii (1895–1968): A Bibliography of His Published Works* (Prague, 2008) and Sergei Glebov, "A Life with Imperial Dreams: Petr Nikolaevich Savitsky, Eurasianism, and the Invention of 'Structuralist' Geography," *Ab Imperio* 3 (2005): 299–329.

According to Savitskii's precepts, territory has a "transparent" [*prozrachnyi*][14] structure that reveals Russia's nature and destiny: There is an organic link between a territory, the specific development of a culture, and the peoples living on this soil. Savitskii's concept of topogenesis—or "place-development" [*mestorazvitie*]— aimed to prove scientifically the mystical link that the Eurasianists projected between territory and culture, and illustrated their teleological conception of the relationship between man and nature. From this encounter between history and territory, a geographical being was born, Eurasia, which was presented as a living organism. For the Eurasianists, geosophy—philosophy of geography, a Russian word coined on the model of historiosophy—confirmed the idea of a distinct historical destiny that was explainable by geography. They claimed that the soil exposed the hidden meaning of events and destinies, and that the unity of Eurasian territory was visible in its geometric and systemic nature (*zakonomernost'*, from the German *Gesetzmäßigkeit*), that is, to the extent that it lends itself to rationalization and explanation, as well as in its subjection to demonstrable scientific principles.[15]

According to Savitskii, Eurasia obeys a specific nonlinear temporal dynamic, one that is cyclical. This cyclicality can be explained by the importance of the geographical factor and nomad culture. As he put it, "The history of the nomad world provides rich material for building a theory of the repetitiveness of events."[16] Accordingly, the history of Eurasia, he claimed, is summed up by its constant attempts at internal unification: whether this is from east to west, as occurred during the great Turkic–Mongol migrations, or from west to east, as took place under a Russian Empire in expansion. "The line of continuity is so clear-cut that it is possible to claim a geopolitical repetitiveness of events."[17] Through this discourse on the cyclical history of the steppe the preeminence given to space is affirmed. In this way, the heart of Eurasia was said to beat in geographical form, insofar as history can materialize in the soil and be determined territorially. At the center of these geographical rhythms one finds stages or dialectic rhythms unifying the forest and the steppe. Russian–Eurasian history is thus a double pendulum of forest/steppe, unification/division movements. "Thanks to the predominance, either of centrifugal forces,

---

[14] Petr Savitskii, "Geograficheskie i geopoliticheskie osnovy evraziistva," in *Kontinent Evraziia* (Moscow: 1997), p. 300.

[15] More in Marlène Laruelle, *L'Idéologie eurasiste russe ou comment penser l'empire* (Paris, 1999). Trans. in Russian: *Ideologiia russkogo evraziistva. Mysli o velichii imperii* (Moscow, 2004).

[16] Petr Savitskii, *O zadachakh kochevnikovedeniia. Pochemu skify i gunny dolzhny byt' interesny dlia russkogo?* (Prague, 1928), p. 18.

[17] Ibid.

or of centripetal ones, the process of creation and life of state entities on the Eurasian territory has taken on the nature of a periodical rhythm."[18]

The idea that there is an historical time that depends upon spatial characteristics specific to Russia was also expressed by the Yale-based future historian of medieval Russia, George Vernadskii. His first publication, "Against the Sun: The Russian State's Expansion into the Orient," published in 1914 in *Russkaia mysl'*, seeks to demonstrate the simultaneous existence of different historical times. In it, Vernadskii claims that

> what is already in the past for Muscovite Russia can still be present in Siberia depending on the remoteness from Moscow. This fact expresses the law of correspondence of time and space as a factor of the historical process. A social phenomenon obeys analogous changes, which surmount space and time. For one and the same time a social phenomenon differs depending upon its occurrence in space. [...] The further we see, the more we see the repercussions of that which was once in the center and is long since dead.[19]

Vernadskii went so far as to specify this relation to space-time: the distance of 1,000 *verstes* is equal to a return to the past of a hundred years. As a result, there is not only an asynchrony between center and periphery, which live in different eras, but a countable and material materialization of Russia's various times. In this way, Eurasia can become an object of astronomical science, in that it also has the same properties that are specific to the universe: The further one sees, the more one goes back in time.

Depending on which founding father—Savitskii, Vernadskii, or Trubetskoi—is adhered to, Eurasianists combine various spatial arguments in order to legitimate the empire. They state that Russia is unable to enter into the European schema of linear history, since it combines several temporalities within it; that it has a cyclical temporality, stamped by population flows from east to west and from west to east; and that it is subject not to temporality but solely to spatiality. Thus, does Russia's geographical expanse and horizontality directly stands in for Europe's historicity, or does it only enable the expression of a temporality that is neither linear nor progressive, but cyclical and repetitive? Does Eurasia announce a different possible formulation of history, or does it have to refuse all temporal approaches and remain limited to the domain of the spatial?

---

[18] Georgii Vernadskii, *Opyt istorii Evrazii* (Berlin, 1934), p. 14.
[19] Georgii Vernadskii, "Protiv solntsa. Rasprostranenie russkogo gosudarstva k Vostoku," *Russkaja mysl'* 1 (1914): 4.

Whichever response was advanced to such questions, this horizontal feature was supposed to be imbued with political meaning. The European countries were said to have found a "vertical" embodiment of their political identity (in the development of democratic systems), whereas Russia, the Eurasianists claimed, found its fulfillment in "horizontality," whose political expression they identified with the country's autocratic and imperial structure: Being *geographic*, Russia's territorial expansion is thus the *natural* expression of its identity. Trubetskoi maintained, for instance, that Turkic thought was driven by "a striving for expansion,"[20] which was a subtle way of legitimating the expansion of Russian territory and its organic "horizontality" through a drawing of parallels between ethnography and politics. If Eurasia is a natural space, then it cannot accept the severance of any of its parts. As he put it: "The nature of the Eurasian world offers as little scope as possible for different kinds of 'separatisms,' be they political, cultural, or economic."[21]

The crucial goal of Eurasianist thought was therefore to demonstrate that the territory Russia covers is naturally its own, and that the need for an imperial structure is self-evident. Russia's history would be the history of its expansion to the east, to the north, and to the south. Control over a huge territory is synonymous with self-awareness—the Eurasianists' calls for self-awareness were nothing but calls to recognize empire as the only viable structure for Russia.

Geography and Biosphere at the Service of the Empire

In the second half of the twentieth century, some theories inspired by Eurasianism developed in the underground spaces of Soviet society, in particular around Lev Gumilev, who maintained a semi-dissident, semiofficial status that earned him many admirers, especially in Leningrad.[22] Gumilev was partly inspired by one of the Eurasianist founding fathers, Savitskii, with whom he entertained a lengthy correspondence, and to a lesser extent by Vernadskii. He contributed to popularizing not only Eurasianist ideas of the cultural and political unity of Eurasian peoples, but a specific conception of the interaction between peoples and nature.

Defining Eurasia as "the Great Steppe that stretches from the Yellow River almost to the banks of the Arctic Ocean,"[23] Gumilev stated that two so-called

---

[20] Nikolai Trubetskoi, "O turanskom elemente v russkoi kul'ture," *Istoriia, kul'tura, yazyk* (Moscow, 1995), p. 150.

[21] Petr Savitskii, "Geograficheskie i geopoliticheskie osnovy evraziistva," p. 301.

[22] On Gumilev's biography, see Alexander Titov, "Lev Gumilev, Ethnogenesis and Eurasianism," Ph.D. diss. (University College London, School of Slavonic and Eastern European Studies, 2005), and Mark Bassin's forthcoming book on Gumilev.

[23] Lev Gumilev, *Ritmy Evrazii. Epokhi i tsivilizatsii* (Moscow, 1993), p. 77.

super-ethnos, the Russian and the Steppic, dominated the Eurasian territory. On this view, then, the history of the Russian Empire is tantamount to the history of these two super-ethnoses' slow convergence in the steppe, whose geographic centrality is unique in the world. Gumilev constantly upheld the unity, and irreducible distinctiveness, of the Eurasian world, and claimed that its permanence guaranteed it a glorious future. The entirety of Eurasianist historiography served to demonstrate that Russia's eastward expansion was not a conquest, but a natural phenomenon. Indeed, Gumilev claimed that "any territorial question can only be resolved on the basis of Eurasian unity."[24] Any kind of secessionism was condemned in advance as a violation of nature. Like all the other Eurasianist theorists, Gumilev did not believe in the universality of man. He thought that, once Russia became aware of its Eurasianist (i.e. imperial) destiny, its mission would consist in rebutting that universalism. However, he differed from the founding fathers of Eurasianism insofar as he transformed theoretically the influence of geography on human destiny into an extreme biological determinism, one based on Cosmist assumptions.[25]

Indeed, Gumilev found inspiration in Cosmic theories, and in particular in the notions of biosphere and noosphere, which he borrowed from Vladimir Vernadskii, George Vernadsii's father, who was a geochemist by training and director of the biochemistry laboratory of the Soviet Academy of Sciences from the late 1920s until his death.[26] Confined to the camps in the 1940s, Gumilev met future astronomer Nikolai Kozyrev (1908–83), who convinced him of the superiority of the hard sciences over the humanities and stirred his interest in the cosmos and in Vernadskii's theories. Renowned throughout Europe, Vernadskii was especially interested in the energy of living matter. In the 1920s he developed the notions of noosphere—or sphere of thought, which he presented as the third level of the earth's development after the geosphere (inanimate matter)—and the biosphere (biological life).[27] The terrestrial envelop, he claimed, would soon be the object of regulation by human reason, which was itself beginning to appear as a form of energy, as it had the ability to change hitherto material processes.[28]

---

[24] Ibid., p. 65.

[25] More in Laruelle, *Russian Eurasianism*, pp. 50–82.

[26] Kendall E. Bailes, *Science and Russian Culture in an Age of Revolutions: V.I. Vernadsky and His Scientific School, 1863–1945* (Bloomington, IN, 1990).

[27] The term "noosphere" was employed for the first time by a disciple of Bergson, Edouard Le Roy, during his courses at the Collège de France in 1927, as well as by Pierre Teilhard de Chardin. Cf. Svetlana Semenova and Anastasiia Gacheva (eds.), *Russkii kosmizm. Antologiia filosofskoi mysli* (Moscow, 1993).

[28] Vladimir Vernadskii, *Biosfera i noosfera* (Moscow, 2002).

The original Eurasianists were subtle determinists: Rather than seeing man as unilaterally dependent on nature, they believed that the two interact. Gumilev deviated from this tradition, for, despite his talk of the ethnos's intrinsic dependence on its landscape, he carried out little geographical analysis. For him, territory is but the first element of a more complex determinism, and one of the least important ones at that. He believed that the characteristic features of the ethnos are grounded not in soil, but in physics, chemistry, biology, and genetics. In several of his books he criticized the geographical determinism of classic authors such as Montesquieu, Bodin, or Herder, who thought that national psychology depends on the natural milieu. His only elaborate theory on this question, described in *One Thousand Years around the Caspian,* concerned the interaction between the movements of nomads, on the one hand, and variations of humidity and climate in the steppe, on the other. Gumilev tried to establish whether the presence of nomads in that region depended on climate change. He thought that in this way he could draw up a comparative table to show the coincidence between climatological data and historical facts.[29]

For Gumilev, territory is not a sufficient condition for the emergence of an ethnos. Man depends on the entire cosmic and terrestrial environment, of which territory is only a minor part.[30] Unlike the founding fathers of Eurasianism, Gumilev did not seek to establish the Eurasian totality with the help of geographic arguments. His determinism was a physical rather than a geographical one: For him, man had to be studied not as part of his immediate spatial environment, but from a planetary and cosmic perspective. He claimed that ethnoses originate from natural phenomena: They are born of a burst of energy coming from the creatures that inhabit the surface of the earth, as well as from geological and mineral activity, from the circulation of energy between plants and animals, not to mention from solar activity.

Gumilev's writings are interspersed with physical and chemical metaphors that are intended to explain the nature of men and nations.[31] He believed that he had founded a new discipline, which he called "socio-natural history." He claimed that whereas the humanities could only graze the surface of human nature, socio-natural history went to its very core, insofar as the ethnos "is not only biological, but also physical and chemical, i.e. part and parcel of planetary

---

[29] See Lev Gumilev, "Izmenenie klimata i migratsii kochevnikov," *Priroda* 4 (1972): 44–52.

[30] "Therefore I will put the question differently. I will ask, not only how the geographical milieu affects people, but also in what way people themselves are constitutive parts of that outer layer of the earth that is now called the biosphere?" Lev Gumilev, *Etnogenez i biosfera zemli* (Leningrad, 1990), p. 37.

[31] Lev Gumilev, *Drevniaia Rus' i Velikaia step'* (Moscow, 1989), p. 77.

patterns."³² According to him, the biosphere, defined as the interaction between animate and inanimate matter, is currently entering a new geological era, that of the noosphere, which is based on the power of the human intellect.³³ Gumilev offered no detailed discussion of the idea that mankind's original force is of cosmic origin, but it may be wondered whether this idea was not a cautious way of asserting the existence of God or a vague belief in the existence of extraterrestrial forces, a conviction that was later held by many of his disciples. Some of his ideas do indeed seem to be inspired by a pantheist sentiment, such as his stating that "We are not alone in the world! The Cosmos participates in the protection of nature, and it is our duty not to destroy it. It is not only our home; it is us."³⁴

Also part of this current are the works of Aleksandr Chizhevskii (1897–1964), who was Konstantin Tsiolkovskii's (1857–1935) friend and disciple. Chizhevskii spent eight years in the Gulag between 1942 and 1950, and was then imprisoned in Karaganda until 1958. Not until 1995 was the most complete version of his manuscript *Zemlia v ob"iatiiakh solntsa* [The Earth in the Embrace of the Sun] finally published.³⁵ Chizhevskii sought to prove that cosmic phenomena, and in particular solar eruptions, have demonstrable socio-historical effects. He therefore contributed to developing two scientific domains that he called heliobiology—the study of the impact of solar flare cycles on human history—and heliotaraxy—the study of the effect of solar activity on the biosphere.³⁶ According to him, the earth's physical fields, the variations of solar activity, solar magnetism, and the corresponding geomagnetic oscillations, all impact on human life. Analyzing sunspot records and proxies as well as battles, revolutions, riots and wars for the period 500 BCE to 1922 CE, he found that 80 percent of the most significant events occurred around the sunspot maximum. The history of humankind, he therefore claimed, responded to cosmic regularities [*zakonomernost'*]. In his "historiometric" works, Chizhevskii claimed that human history is shaped by the 11-year cycles in the sun's activity, and is manifest in political events (revolts, wars, revolution), as well as other events such as power shortages or plane crashes. This new discipline, called "historiometry," claimed to have ascertained the existence of solar cycles, which accordingly divided human

---

32   Lev Gumilev, "Pis'mo v redaktsiiu 'Voprosov filosofii,'" *Voprosy filosofii* 5 (1989): 161.
33   Lev Gumilev, "Menia nazyvaiut evraziitsem," *Nash sovremennik* 1 (1991): 24.
34   Lev Gumilev, "Etnogenez i biosfera zemli," *Priroda i chelovek* 4 (1992): 59.
35   Available at http://www.chizhevski.ru/zemla
36   Boris Vladimirskii and N.A. Temuryants, *Solar Activity and the Biosphere: Heliobiology. From A.L. Chizhevsky to the Present* (Moscow, 1999).

history into political periods that ranged from stability to war or revolution, a statement shared by Gumilev.

Neo-Cosmist Assumptions and the Post-Soviet Quest for an Empire

During post-Soviet times, reflections on the topic of empire based on arguments borrowed from historical geography became fashionable, and some works like those of Vadim Tsymburskii (1957–2009) contributed to the revival of critical geopolitics.[37] In addition to the fashion that surrounded the rediscovery of Fyodorov, the rereading of the great texts of the Silver Age gave more scope to Cosmist allusions that were based on references to Orthodoxy. Indeed, among many Russian philosophers, such as Vladimir Solov'ev (1853–1900), Sergei Bulgakov (1871–1944), or Pavel Florenskii (1882–1937), Orthodoxy was interpreted as a religion that both grants particular attention to the territory (through the notion of canonical territory and the philosophical interpretations that were provided of it) and that seeks to ground its harmony with the universe (through the idea of kingdom of the spirit or of the heavens). These two elements, territorial and cosmic, emerged to complete the palette of the spatial arguments that were advanced in order to legitimate the Russian Empire among Russian nationalist circles.[38]

Aleksandr Panarin (1940–2003), for example, one of the great theoreticians of neo-Eurasianism, employed an argument about the existence of a link between the empire's territorial expansion and a specific relation to the cosmos. Head of the chair of Political Science in the Faculty of Philosophy at Moscow State University, he was a prolific essayist, well known for his erudition, and respected among political scientists with nationalist leanings. In 1998 he published a highly successful book called *Revansh istorii* [The Revenge of History], which, as its name indicates, was intended to provide a response to Francis Fukuyama's famous thesis about the "end of history."[39] In 2002, only a few months before his death, he was awarded the prestigious Solzhenitsyn Prize for his book *Orthodox Civilization in a Globalized World*, in which he announced the revenge of an economically backward but spiritually advanced Russia over a West that he claimed is losing itself in a technological frenzy.

---

[37] His works have been republished: Vadim Tsymburskii, *Ostrov Rossii. Geopoliticheskie i khronologicheskie raboty* (Moscow, 2007).

[38] More in Ivan Mitin and Dmitry Zamiatin (eds.), *Voobrazhenie prostranstva, prostranstvo voobrazheniia* (Moscow, 2009).

[39] See the review by Valentin Bazhanov, "A Note on A.S. Panarin's *Revansh Istorii*," *Europe-Asia Studies* 51/4 (1999): 705–8.

On Panarin's view, Russia acts as a global safeguard of polycentrism: By its very existence it demonstrates that the West is not the sole driving force of development. For him, Europe gives primacy to individual rights to the detriment of collective rights, be they regional, ethnic, or religious. It upholds pluralism for individuals, but has a unitarian and hegemonic approach to relations between nations. Eurasia is the exact opposite of the European model: The absence of Western-type political democracy is tantamount to the recognition of the empire "as a political form of organization of the coexistence of a heterogeneous ethnic and confessional conglomerate, of peoples who do not have any other basis for a set of universal norms and a legal order."[40] This imperial essence of Russia is thus allegedly a political embodiment of the horizontal nature and spatial extension of Eurasia. From a Western point of view, Panarin argued, only temporality (with "lags" and "advances") can account for differences between civilizations, which can be classified on a scale going from the archaic to the modern. By contrast, he proposed to restore the category of space to analytic favor and use it in support of non-European nations' right to differ: For him, cultural specificity is not temporal or vertical, but spatial and horizontal.

Panarin believed that the predominance of territory over time makes Russia evolve cyclically: He called this the "idiom of space."[41] He claimed that the difference between Western and Russian culture lies precisely in the connection between man and cosmos. Whereas Western culture has broken the links between microcosm and macrocosm, the Russian world continues to see God in nature. Whereas the West views the cosmos as a dead and mechanical phenomenon, Russia views it as a living being. According to Panarin, Russia's preeminence here can be explained by its territorial reality: It is only possible to feel harmony with God in the big Russian plain, whereas the other Orthodox states in the Balkans are too insular to be aware of that.

In his *Orthodox Civilization*, Panarin presents the Russians not as a "horizontal" people, as did the founding fathers of Eurasianism, who insisted on the spatial expanse of their conquests, but as a "vertical" one, in reference to the character of Orthodox civilization, which, he held, tends toward the divine, in contrast to Western man, who is horizontal by virtue of being inscribed in the materiality of life. Marked by anti-Semitic statements, Panarin devoted many pages to comparing Russians and Jews, and describing the former as nomads in

---

[40] Boris Erasov, "O geopoliticheskom i tsivilizatsionnom ustroenii Evrazii," *Evraziia* 5 (1996): 30.
[41] Viktor Il'in and Aleksandr Panarin (eds.), *Rossiia: opyt natsional'no-gosudarstvennoi ideologii* (Moscow, 1994), p. 128.

time and the latter as nomads in space.⁴² He believed that the two peoples are different from the rest of humanity, but also in competition with each other, since both are bearers of a messianic idea and claim to be a chosen people. According to Panarin, however, the messianism of the Jews became "normalized" when they accepted the West's lifestyle and way of thinking and established their own country.⁴³ Thus the Russian people are now the only bearers of hope for a different type of humanity: Russia cannot become a normal and pragmatic state guided by national egoism, since the Russians are inherently messianic.⁴⁴

The cosmist allusions are less clear-cut in the work of that most media-prominent proponent of Eurasianism, Aleksandr Dugin. After having attempted to enter into the ruling circles, Dugin tried to create his own Eurasianist political party, and today teaches in the Department of Sociology at Moscow State University. A prolix and eclectic author, he combines multiple intellectual traditions: the traditionalist thought of René Guénon and Julius Evola; some elements of the Orthodox religious philosophy; Aryanist and occultist theories; parts of National Bolshevism and German fascism; and Eurasianist geopolitical conceptions. Dugin only rarely mentions the role of geography in Russian destiny, insofar as it is to be a continental empire, but he has nonetheless made allusions to the spatial factor in building national identities, especially in his Aryan and anti-Semitic statements. He refers for instance to Hermann Wirth (1885–1981) and to his occultist theories about the Arctic homeland of the original Aryan peoples. According to Dugin, the Hyperborean civilization was not in Scandinavia but further to the east. In his *The Mysteries of Eurasia* (1991), he presents Siberia and its enormous Nordic continental mass as the original cradle of the Aryans, as well as the magical center of the world, following the idea that "the continents have a symbolic significance."⁴⁵

He also repeatedly asserts that, since the Jews consider themselves to be a chosen people, they are squarely opposed to Russian messianism, which is also an ideology of national exceptionalism. Another consistent opposition between Judaism and Russianness concerns the relation to territory. According to Dugin, life in the diaspora has desacralized the territories on which the Jews have lived for two millennia, and only the long-inaccessible land of Israel has kept its sacred character. Their supposed lack of emotion toward nature and their theological rejection of redemption by the earth—embodied by Jesus in Christianity—reveal

---

⁴² Aleksandr Panarin, *Pravoslavnaia tsivilizatsiia v global'nom mire* (Moscow, 2002), p. 406.

⁴³ Aleksandr Panarin, *Rossiia v tsiklakh mirovoi istorii* (Moscow, 1995), p. 173.

⁴⁴ Aleksandr Panarin, *Pravoslavnaia tsivilizatsiia*, p. 404.

⁴⁵ Aleksandr Dugin, *Misterii Evrazii*, republished in *Absoliutnaia rodina* (Moscow, 1999), p. 575.

their incompatibility with the Eurasian idea, for which territory is laden with meaning, as well as with Russian identity, marked by the cult of the nurturing soil. According to Dugin, the famous Jewish nomadism allegedly finds its most sophisticated expression in the trade character of the British Empire and the US unipolar domination.[46]

Outside of so-called neo-Eurasianist circles, a conjoint interest in territory and the cosmos has also emerged among other nationalist movements. Aleksandr Prokhanov, for example, one of the main names of the Russian nationalism since the 1970s, and the editor-in-chief of the weekly newspaper *Zavtra* (one of the centers of production of nationalist discourse with a Communist sensibility), has also availed himself of Cosmist assumptions in order to legitimize Russia as an empire. Prokhanov asserts that there can be no coincidence that Fyodorov and Vernadskii senior were both born in Russia, not to mention the fact that the first inhabited space flight took off from Russia, which is supposedly the exact meeting point between the earth and the sky. In a text with a telling title, *Kosmizm-leninism* [Cosmism-Leninism], published in 2010, he discusses the junction between the Bolshevik Revolution, the industrial successes of Stalinism, and Cosmism: For him, due to its industrializing obsession, Leninism availed itself of the works of Fyodorov, Vernadskii, Tsiolkovskii, and Chizhevskii insofar as it sought to "overcome death, anthropy, to ensure victory over thermodynamics, to create an immortal paradisiacal humanity," and its key issue was precisely the "Russian cosmic mission," which is in turn linked to the traditional messianism of the Russian people and its imperial nature.[47]

A similar schema is at work with Evgenii Troitskii (born in 1928), the founder and president of the Association for the Complex Study of the Russian Nation, or AKIRN (from the Russian *Assotsiatsiia po kompleksnomu izucheniiu russkoi natsii*). Troitskii presents himself as a great conciliator of various doctrinal movements, and offers a synthesis of pan-Slavism, Eurasianism, Cosmism, "Slavic socialism," and racialism. He has managed a very close collaboration with the Ministry of Nationalities and Regional Policy in the 1990s and has campaigned for two decades for a law to declare that Russia is the homeland of ethnic Russians and for abolishing the federal status of the country.[48] Troitskii has developed a modernized version of Cosmism, and works closely with the charity Fund of the *Mir* Space Station, the museum of aviation and astronautic history, and the Slavic

---

[46] Aleksandr Dugin, "Apokalipsis stikhii," *Elementy* 8 (1997): 56.
[47] Aleksandr Prokhanov, "Kosmizm-leninism," *Pravda* 16/857, April 21, 2010, http://www.zavtra.ru/cgi/veil/data/zavtra/10/857/11.html
[48] Galina Zvereva, "Diskurs gosudarstvennoi natsii v sovremennoi Rossii," in Marlène Laruelle (ed.), *Sovremennye interpretatsii russkogo natsionalizma* (Moscow, 2008), pp. 15–80.

international union of aviation and astronautics (*Slavaviakosmos*), whose aim is to "give to the Slavic states back their former leadership role in the control of the aerial and cosmic space."[49] His Cosmist texts combine several classic features of contemporary Russian nationalism, such as a feeling of nostalgia for the Soviet regime, since he claims that the control of the cosmos permitted Russian to establish itself on an equal footing with the United States; a vision of the human history marked by the dialectic materialism, since this history is divided into developmental stages (traditional, industrial, postindustrial, informational, then noospheric); and a form of "cosmos-ecology" that would show, through the experiments made in the *Mir* space station, how to live in harmony with nature.

AKIRN states that Russia is the only country to have understood the intimate link between humankind's spatial progress and its spiritual quest: Russians supposedly have a unique and prophetic Cosmic conscience whose character expresses itself both in the religious and scientific fields.[50] The association has therefore militated for the canonization of Yuri Gagarin, in order to accentuate the association between religion and technological progress.[51] Troitskii considers that Russian territorial immensity reveals the nature of the Russian soul, but also opens up the way to the conquest of extraterrestrial worlds, hence the importance given to maintaining a specific Russian science of space. He thereby takes up the notions espoused by Fyodorov, who considered that the territorial success of the Russian Empire, its huge advances into Asia—won without encountering much resistance—was the heralding sign of its destiny to conquer spaces of another nature, those of the cosmos.[52]

Conclusion

In Russia, the topic of empire is intrinsically linked to the traditional messianism inspired by Orthodoxy and the myth of Moscow as the Third Rome: Russia is

---

[49] From the former webpage of the association, http://www.novosti-kosmonavtiki.ru/content/numbers/195/42.shtml

[50] See Evgenii Troitskii (ed.), *Istoriko-metodologicheskie aspekty izucheniia russkoi (pravoslavno-slavianskoi) tsivilizatsii* (Moscow, 1994); Evgenii Troitskii, *Russkaia etnopolitologiia i natsional'naia ideia* (Moscow, 2006); Evgenii Troitskii (ed.), *Slavianstvo v usloviiakh globalizatsii i informatsionnoi voiny* (Moscow, 2002); Evgenii Troitskii, *Opora na sobstvennye sily i neokolonializm. Russko-slavianskii vzgliad* (Moscow, 1999); Evgenii Troitskii, *Russkii narod v poiskakh pravdy i organizovannosti (988–1996)* (Moscow, 1996).

[51] Evgenii Troitskii (ed.), *Russkaia ideia, slavianskii kosmizm i stantsiia Mir* (Kaluga, 2000), p. 23.

[52] Nikolai Fyodorov, "Filosofiia obshchego dela," in *Russkii kosmizm*, p. 70.

destined to bear a universalist message—whether religious or socialist—to the rest of the world and to announce the way to reconcile humanity above and beyond its divisions, an old biblical theme on life after Babel. The projection of a self without borders can take on various political or spiritual forms, and have as its object the territories of earth as well as of space. This religious-based messianism is thus in close interaction with theories that legitimate the empire as the natural expansion of Russia into Asia and Europe, as a Eurasian state without any natural internal borders, unifying very diverse populations under its embrace. To this is added the missing link of the cosmos: The geographical immensity of the Russian Empire implies a spatial destiny, since space is only the higher degree of territorial expansion on earth. This cosmos is conceived simultaneously in terms of technological mastery, in accordance thus with the industrializing obsessions of the Soviet Union, and of access to the divine, in agreement thus with the reflections of Orthodox theology about canonical territory and the kingdom of the heavens. In this way, it is possible to draw a parallel between the horizontal expanse of Russia and its ability to fly, in a concrete way, in space, or in an allegorical way, that is toward God. As Evgenii Troitskii contended, "our vast territory is a passage toward the celestial space."[53] Russia thus enjoys a large range of philosophical interpretations of empire, and intellectuals of nationalist sensibility have often worked on the imperial as a notion by offering new, decentering perspectives on the role of space in the so-called Russian destiny.

---

[53] "Nash prostor sluzhit perekhodom k prostoru nebesnogo prostranstva", in Troitskii's *Russkaia ideia*, p. 22.

PART II
Spatial Science and Geographical Knowledge

CHAPTER 4

The Mapping of Illiberal Modernity: Spatial Science, Ideology and the State in Early Twentieth-century Russia

Nick Baron

In this chapter I offer some reflections on the reconceptualization of Russian space and spatial development in the first half of the twentieth century. In particular, I focus on two scholars, D.M. Mendeleev and his disciple E.E. Sviatlovskii, who, in the late imperial and early Soviet periods respectively, sought to identify and map the forms and dynamics of Russian spatial change and to promote a rational, empirical, evolutionary approach to spatial planning and policymaking based on scientific method. In outlining their ideas and practice in the context of the spatial thinking of their time, and in tracing the rise and fall of their influence on state planning and policy, I hope to shed some light on the interactions of Russian science and government and the interrelations of culture and ideology, as well as on competing philosophies and visions of space and conflicting views of how space was to be analysed, apprehended, accounted for and acted upon.

Mendeleev and the Modernization of Imperial Space

At the end of the nineteenth century Dmitrii Mendeleev, having already won world renown for his achievements in chemistry, turned his attention to matters of Russian economic development and territorial planning.[1] In a series of

---

*   Research for this chapter was supported in part by a British Academy Small Grant (Ref. 50074, 'Spatial Planning in Russia and Germany, 1890s to 1945: A Transnational Study of Science, Ideology, Politics and Practice'), as well as by research leave and a travel bursary awarded by the Dean of the Faculty of Arts, University of Nottingham.

[1]   The best biographies of Mendeleev, among many, are Michael D. Gordin, *A Well-ordered Thing: Dmitrii Mendeleev and the Shadow of the Periodic Table* (New York, 2004); M. Belen'kii, *Mendeleev* (Moscow, 2010). See also M.N. Mladenstev and V.E. Tishchenko, *Dmitrii*

writings, addressed to government, industry and the general educated public, he now strove to remap Russian imperial territory as a modern rational space that could serve as a framework for the nation's balanced, self-sufficient economic, social, and cultural modernization.[2]

Mendeleev's efforts to understand Russian space and establish priorities for tsarist spatial planning were grounded in the same Enlightenment faith in scientific rigour, reason, and objectivity that informed all his undertakings, coupled with a deeply conservative, state-centred nationalism, faith in autocracy and belief in the crucial role of experts in government.[3] First, I shall briefly

---

Ivanovich Mendeleev, ego zhizn' i deiatel'nost' (Moscow, 1938); N. Figurovskii, *D.I. Mendeleev* (Moscow, 1961; revised edn 1983); Mladenstev and Tishchenko, *Dmitrii Ivanovich Mendeleev, ego zhizn' i deiatel 'nost'*: *universitetskii period, 1861–1890* (Moscow, 1993); and Nathan M. Brooks, 'Mendeleev, Dmitrii Ivanovich', in Noretta Koertge (ed.), *New Dictionary of Scientific Biography* (New York, 2008), vol. 5, pp. 105–10. There is no specialized scholarship in English on Mendeleev's geographical thinking, and little published work on his economic activities and political engagement. See Alexander Vucinich, 'Mendeleev's Views on Science and Society', *Isis* 58/3 (1967): 342–51. For unpublished work, see Beverly Almgren, 'Mendeleev: The Third Service, 1834–1882', Ph.D. dissertation (Brown University, 1968); Francis Stackenwalt, 'The Thought and Work of Dmitrii Ivanovich Mendeleev on the Industrialization of Russia, 1867–1907', Ph.D. dissertation (University of Illinois at Urbana, 1976); Mark Butorac, 'From the Other Oil Field: Mendeleev, the West and the Russian Oil Industry', Ph.D. dissertation (McGill University, 2001). For Soviet views of Mendeleev's economic analysis, see esp, G.Ts. Gurvich, *Ekonomicheskie vzgliady D.I. Mendeleeva* (Leningrad, 1951). For post-Soviet Russian accounts, see esp. P.V. Dziubenko, *D.I. Mendeleev i tamozhennyi tarif. Tamozhenno-tarifnaia politika v nauchnom nasledii D.I. Mendeleeva: Uroki dlia Rossii* (Moscow, 2003). See also works on specific topics referenced in subsequent notes.

[2] For this research I have used the standard Soviet edition of Mendeleev's collected works: D.I. Mendeleev, *Sochineniia* (25 vols, Leningrad, 1934–1936), especially vols 18–20 (1950), vols 21 and 23 (1952), and vol. 24 (1954). The major economic writings are anthologized in Mendeleev, *Problemy ekonomicheskogo raxvittia Rossii* (Moscow, 1960). These, however, are purgated texts, and need to be cross-referenced with pre- and post-Soviet editions when available. Two major post-Soviet collections of his economic writings are: Mendeleev, *S dumoiu o blage rossiiskom. Izbrannye ekonomicheskie proizvedeniia*, ed. S.V. Kazantsev (Novosibirsk, 1991) and Mendeleev, *Granits poznaniiu predvitet' nevozmozhno*, ed. Iu.I. Solov'ev (Moscow, 1991). Of particular value for study of Mendeleev's economic, political and cultural views is the reissue of his penultimate work, first published in 1905 and largely suppressed in the Soviet period, *Zavetnye mysli. Polnoe izdanie (vpervye posle 1905g.)* (Moscow, 1995). The principal statement of his spatial thinking is *K' poznaniiu Rossii* (St Petersburg, 1906).

[3] For discussion of Mendeleev's rationalism and faith in scientific method (most publicly exhibited in his denunciation of spiritualism), see Gordin, *A Well-ordered Thing*, Chapter 4, and of his political convictions and engagement with government, ibid., Chapter 6. Mendeleev's clearest political statement is the chapter 'Zhelatel'noe dlia blaga Rossii ustroistvo pravitel'stva', in *Zavetnye mysli*, pp. 324–405.

discuss Mendeleev's positivist understanding of space in the context of early twentieth-century Russian spatial thinking, and, second, his recommendations and prescriptions to government for spatial policymaking.

Mendeleev's vision of Russian space stretching across both the European and Asian continents was not of one a Romantic landscape of inchoate and unchanging nature, boundless, empty, and awaiting the intervention of human agency. Rather, he perceived a unified political-economic territory, formed through centuries of interaction between nature and society, coherently yet fluidly structured by innate, evolving constellations of centres and peripheries.[4] In other words, Mendeleev undertstood the Russian Empire as a particular historical formation – in one text he characterized it as an 'historical organism' – possessed of its own immanent rationality and self-ordering dynamic.[5] Correspondingly, he conceived of historical change as law-governed and amenable to rational understanding: 'the laws of geometry and history', he wrote, 'are equally natural.'[6]

His conception of Russia's Eurasian empire as an evolving spatial form and his vision of its potential transformation were shaped by his perceptions of contemporary processes as well as his beliefs about the nation's developmental needs. After centuries of territorial expansion in fits and starts, Russia's launch of a state-sponsored strategy of economic modernization at the end of late nineteenth century – involving rapid industrial growth and urbanization, the construction of new transport and communications networks, and the generation of mass population resettlements – had unleashed spatial change of unprecedented scale and momentum.[7] Between 1871 and 1916 over 9 million peasants, mostly from

---

[4] Born in Tobol'sk, Siberia, Mendeleev considered himself an 'Asiatic'; see Mendeleev (1884), 'O vozbuzhdenii promyshlennogo razvitiia v Rossii', in *Sochineniia* (Moscow, 1950), vol. 20, p. 75. On the context of Mendeleev's vision of Asiatic Russia as part of a unified imperial space, see Mark Bassin, 'Russia between Europe and Asia: The Ideological Construction of Geographical Space', *Slavic Review* 50/1 (1991): 1–17, and Bassin, *Imperial Visions: Nationalist Imagination and Geographical Expansion in the Russian Far East, 1840–1865* (Cambridge, 1999).

[5] Mendeleev, 'O vozbuzhdenii promyshlennogo razvitiia v Rossii', p. 79. A universal spatial dynamic that he claimed to perceive was the striving of nations toward 'the formation of large state units instead of small ones'; see Mendeleev (1897), 'Osnovy fabrichno-zavodskoi promyshlennosti. Toplivo', in *S dumoiu o blage rossiiskom*, pp. 46, 154 (n. 59).

[6] Mendeleev, 'Pis'ma a zavodakh. Pis'mo vtoroe', in *Problemy ekonomicheskogo raxvittia Rossii*, p. 235.

[7] For overviews of late imperial Russia's economic modernization, see Theodore H. von Laue, *Sergei Witte and the Industrialization of Russia* (New York and London, 1963); Peter Gatrell, *The Tsarist Economy, 1850–1917* (London, 1986); W.E. Mosse, *Economic History of Russia, 1856–1914* (London, 1996). For transport construction and resettlement, see Steven Marks, *Road to Power: The Trans-Siberian Railroad and the Colonization of Asian Russia, 1850–1917* (Ithaca, NY, 1991).

central European Russia and Ukraine, migrated within imperial territory, the majority to Siberia, the Kazakh steppe, and the Far East.[8] Within a few decades the centre's relationship to its periphery was radically transformed. New developmental visions coupled with new technological and administrative possibilities opened up new perspectives for overcoming the challenges of spatial scale, diversity, and distance, and for assimilating peripheral territories and exploiting their resources. In Russia, as elsewhere, science, culture, and philosophy, as well as government, grappled with these changes, manifesting an acute obsession with space as a problem to be solved, with its measurement and representation, with its reconfiguration and regulation, and with its metaphysical qualities.[9]

Two examples from Russian philosophy will suffice to demonstrate the urgent rethinking of space that formed the contemporary intellectual context of Mendeleev's positivist investigations and pragmatic interventions. On the one hand, Vladimir Lenin was seeking to make sense of space in terms of historical materialism: 'Are space and time real or ideal?' he asked in 1908. 'Do our relative conceptions of space and time approximate to objectively real forms of being? Or are they only products of developing, organizing, harmonizing, etc. human thoughts?'[10] As a Marxist, his answer was that time and space were empirical dimensions of objective experience that equated to material structures. Those who believed that they were mere conventions or abstractions of thought he condemned as idealists whose position was irreconcilable with the scientific account of historical progress.[11] Space, in Lenin's view, was an element of the material base of human society, not of its superstructure, and it therefore independently conditioned and constrained – though did not determine – human thought and action.[12]

---

[8] Figures from Willard Sunderland, 'The "Colonization Question": Visions of Colonization in Late Imperial Russia', *Jahrbücher für Geschichte Osteuropas* n.s. 48/2 (2000): 213. Solely in 1895–98 an estimated 3,930,000 migrants travelled to Siberia; see Donald W. Treadgold, *The Great Siberian Migration: Government and Peasant in Resettlement from Emancipation to the First World War* (Princeton, NJ, 1957), p. 147. See also Nikolaus Poppe, 'The Economic and Cultural Development of Siberia', in George Katkov et al., (eds), *Russia Enters the Twentieth Century* (London, 1973), pp. 138–51.

[9] Stephen Kern, *The Culture of Time and Space, 1880–1918* (Cambridge, MA, 1986).

[10] V.I. Lenin, 'Materializm i Empiriokrititsizm. Kriticheskie zametki ob odnoi reaktsionnoi filosofii', in *Polnoe Sobranie Sochinenii*. 5th edn (Moscow, 1961), vol. 18, p. 182.

[11] Lenin's principal target of criticism was A. Bogdanov, a fellow Bolshevik who sought to integrate contemporary philosophical innovations into Marxist thought. See George Katkov, 'Lenin as Philosopher', in Leonard Shapiro and Peter Reddaway (eds), *Lenin. The Man, the Theorist, the Leader; a Reappraisal* (London, 1967), pp. 72–85.

[12] On Russian Marxist debates on environmental determinism, see Mark Bassin, 'Geographical Determinism in Fin-de-siècle Marxism. Georgii Plekhanov and the Environmental Basis of Russian History', *Annals of the Association of American Geographers*

The novelist Andrei Bely, on the other hand, reflecting on the relationship between physical space and its cultural conceptualisation, denied the primacy of material reality over its symbolic incarnation:

> Petersburg not only seems to appear to us, but actually manifests itself – on maps: in the form of two small circles, one set inside the other, with a black dot in the centre; and from this very mathematical point, which has no dimension, it proclaims forcefully that it exists: from here, from this very point surges and swarms the printed book; from this invisible point speeds the official circular.[13]

For Bely, the spatial idea, here reified in a cartographic icon, possesses its own productive agency: the geometric point constitutes a source of energy that not only calls into being the imperial capital itself (which 'actually manifests itself – on maps'), but generates the empire's manifold spaces that radiate out like force fields around it – Russia's cultural space, within which the book 'surges and swarms', and its administrative space, through which the memorandum 'speeds'. Here the spatial idea takes precedence over real space, place, or territory. Enough to think a city or unified nation into existence, and it shall materialize. Later it will become clear how these pre-revolutionary metaphysical controversies related to debates in the first Soviet decade about the nature, scope, and purpose of planning.

Mendeleev was a resolute, self-proclaimed realist.[14] Since, in his view, Russian imperial territorial expansion had now reached its natural or political limits, the Russian government needed to embark on the coordinated and consistent planning of interior space, grounded in the rational analysis and precise plotting of the empire's innate, objective spatiotemporal configuration.[15] It was the role of state-sponsored scientific and technical experts (like himself) to understand and reveal the empire's latent spatial structures and forces, and, by weighing and evaluating both the constraints they imposed and the possibilities they afforded,

---

82/1 (1992): 3–22, and Richard Peet's and John Chappell's responses in *Annals* 83/1 (1993): 156–66.

[13] Andrei Bely, *Petersburg,* trans. David McDuff (London, 1995), p. 2.

[14] Mendeleev placed realism in-between idealism and materialism, both of which he felt were outdated orientations, tainted by preconception, prejudice and tendencies to extremism, and which produced violence, revolution and antagonism to other social groups and races. Realism, conversely, he believed to be commonsensical and tolerant. Optimistically, he considered that the Russian people, 'occupying the geographical heart of the old world', were naturally disposed to realism. *Zavetnye mysli*, pp. 5–6. For a subtle discussion of Mendeleev's philosophical outlook, see Vucinich, 'Mendeleev's Views on Science and Society'.

[15] Mendeleev (1882), 'Ob usloviiakh razvitiia zavodskogo dela v Rossii', in *Problemy ekonomicheskogo razvitiia Rossiia*, p. 138 and *passim.*

to propose new political, administrative, and economic frameworks to capture and channel the empire's spatial energies for the sake of its future prosperity.[16]

In his published texts, in correspondence with government officials and in public pronouncements, Mendeleev set out a number of interrelated priorities for imperial spatial planning. For one thing, it was vital to create a nationwide transport network to bind together disparate and distant areas, enabling an optimal territorial division of labour, in which some regions would be producers of raw materials, others centres of industrial processing and others predominantly centres of consumption.[17] 'The north will trade with the south of Russia', he declared in 1882 in a speech to industrialists, 'just as the south [will trade] with the north and the east with the west.'[18] The tsarist state needed also to invest in the exploration and assimilation of new territories rich in resources, in particular the Far North and Far East; this would then generate funding for their own regional growth as well as for national development.[19] Mendeleev called on the government to accelerate industrial construction in the Donets coal basin and the oil-producing regions of the Caucasus, to permit the domestic energy sector to reap profits from refining and processing products as well as extracting them from the ground. He hoped that industrial expansion could be realized through home-grown scientific and technological innovation rather than greater foreign investment.[20] Indeed,

---

[16] Mendeleev's faith in the role of scientists and technical specialists runs throughout his economic and spatial writings. Trotsky called this 'scientific-technical optimism' the defining core of Mendeleev's worldview, pitting him against both agrarian reactionaries and populists: 'Mendeleev believed that man could vanquish all forces of nature', see Lev Trotskii, 'D.I. Mendeleev i marksizm', speech delivered on 17 September 1925 to the 4th Mendeleev Congress of Pure and Applied Chemistry, in *Sochineniia* (Moscow and Leningrad, 1927), vol. 21. *Kul'tura perekhodnogo perioda*, pp. 268–90, available at: http://www.magister.msk.ru/library/trotsky/trotl961.htm (accessed 18 April 2012). For interactions among experts, industrialists, and government, see Thomas Owen, 'The Russian Industrial Society and Tsarist Economic Policy, 1867–1905', *Journal of Economic History* 45/3 (1985): 587–606.

[17] Mendeleev (1882), 'Ob usloviiakh razvitiia zavodskogo dela v Rossii', pp. 138–44 and *passim*.

[18] Ibid., pp. 141–2.

[19] Mendeleev's writings on the Arctic are collected in *Nauchnyi arkhiv. Osvoenie krainego Severa. Tom 1.Vysokie shiroty severnogo ledovitogo okeana* (Moscow and Leningrad, 1960), with an extensive editorial introduction. See also Mendeleev (1879), 'Ob issledovanii okrain Rossii', in *Problemy ekonomicheskogo razvitiia Rossiia*, pp. 102–3; and Beverly S. Almgren, 'D.I. Mendeleev and Siberia', *Ambix* 45/2 (1998): 50–66.

[20] See Mendeleev's writings in *Problemy ekonomicheskogo razvitiia Rossiia*, pp. 359–522. Secondary sources include Butorac, 'From the Other Oil Field'; T.S. Kudriatseva and M.E. Shekhter, *D.I. Mendeleev i ugol'naia promyshlennost'* (Moscow, 1952); and V.I. Parkhomenko, *D.I. Mendeleev i russkoe neftianoe delo* (Moscow, 1957).

Mendeleev's patriotism and pragmatism logically gave rise to a strong faith in protectionism. The Russian government, in his view, should focus equally on stimulating national economic development, in particular through a programme of factory construction, which he saw as the driving force of all economic, social, and cultural modernization, and on defending it by establishing tariff barriers against external competition and the debasement of prices.[21]

Mendeleev also preached the necessity of building a coherent and integrated system of territorial regions, which he saw as vital for the correct organization of the empire's huge landmass. During the eighteenth century the Russian Empire had undergone a series of administrative-territorial reconfigurations, designed principally to strengthen central state control over the periphery as well as to effect a more rational distribution of population.[22] In the mid-nineteenth century Konstantin Arsen'ev had developed a new scheme of regionalization, based on statistical analysis of the spatial distribution of natural resources, population and economic activity.[23] Although Arsen'ev's project attracted much attention, it was never implemented. In 1898, Mendeleev elaborated a new scheme for Russia's economic regionalisation, based on his own analysis of the distribution of forces of production and centres of consumption, as well as existing and required transport links (see Figure 4.1).[24] His design was empirical insofar as it took

---

[21] Factory construction as the basic means of modernization is the leitmotif of all his economic work (see n. 2). Specifically on protectionism, see Mendeleev (1892), 'Tolkovyi tarif, ili issledovanie o razvitii promyshlennoi Rossii v sviazi s ee obshchim tamozhennym tarifom 1891 g.', in *Sochineniia* (Moscow, 1950), vol. 19, and Mendeleev (1890), 'Materialy dlia peresmotra obshchago tamozhennago tarifa Rossiiskoi Imperii po Evropeiskoi torgovli', in *Sochineniia* (Moscow, 1950), vol. 17. See also Dziubenko, *D.I. Mendeleev i tamozhennyi tarif;* and Vincent Barnett, 'Catalysing Growth?: Mendeleev and the 1891 Tariff', *Research in the History of Economic Thought and Methodology* 22-A (2004): 123–44.

[22] A.N. Khmelev, 'Istoriia administrativno-territorial'nogo deleniia Rossii. Opyt vvedeniia i isuzhenie voprosa', unpublished MS, undated (early 1920s) in the State Archive of the Russian Federation (Gosudarstvennyi arkhiv Rossiiskoi Federatsii; henceforth, GARF), f. 6984, op. 1, d. 217, p. 127. See also the historical essays in G.M. Krzhizhanovskii (ed.), *Voprosy ekonomicheskogo raionirovaniia SSSR. Sbornik materialov i statei (1917–1929 gg.)* (Moscow, 1957).

[23] Konstantin Arsen'ev, *Statisticheskie ocherki Rossii* (St Petersburg, 1848). See Susan Smith-Peter, 'Defining the Russian People: Konstantin Arsen'ev and Russian Statistics before 1861', *History of Science* 45/1 (2007): 47–64.

[24] Mendeleev (1896), 'Fabrichno-zavodskaia promyshlennost' i torgovlia Rossii', in *Sochineniia*, (Leningrad, 1952), vol. 21, pp. 173–249; Mendeleev (1897), 'Osnovy fabrichno-zavodskoi promyshlennosti. Toplivo', pp. 42–5 and *passim*. This regionalization scheme is discussed at length in T.M. Kalashnikova, *Ekonomicheskoe raionirovanie* (Moscow, 1982), pp. 87–9, including map. See also O.V. Gritsai, G.V. Ioffe and A.I. Treivish, *Tsentr i periferiia v regional'nom razvitii* (Moscow, 1991), pp. 19–22.

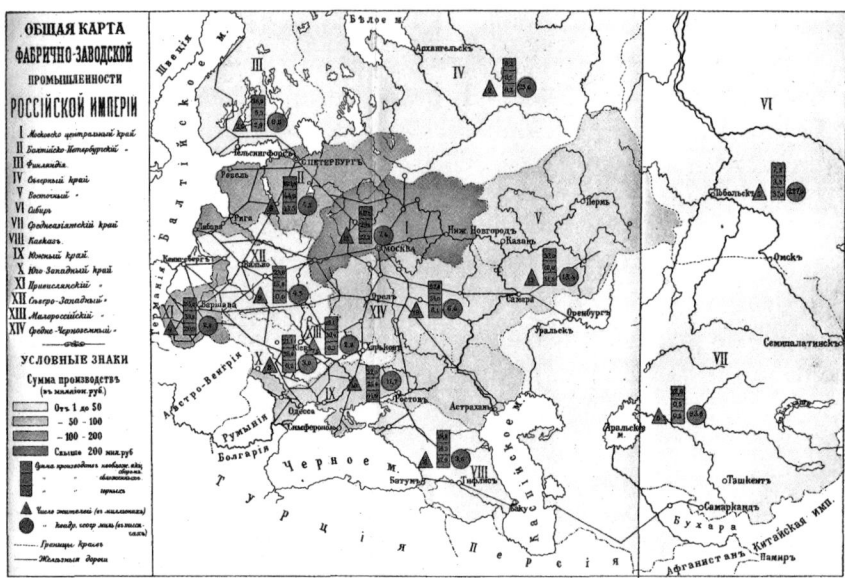

Figure 4.1 General map of factory industry of the Russian Empire, 1896.
Source: Mendeleev, *Fabrichno-zavodskaia promyshlennost' i torgovlia Rossii* (St Petersburg, 1896).

account of historical and actual circumstances, but it was also visionary – albeit within modest parameters – and instrumental: it strove not only to apprehend the vectors of spatial change but also to adjust their trajectories to facilitate and expedite the rationalisation of imperial space.

As noted above, Mendeleev's vision of Russian space and spatial evolution hinged on the significance of central points. A crucial stage in the planning of Russia's spatial configuration was therefore to identify the empire's demographic, economic, and other centres at various moments in time and to plot their historical trajectories. Mendeleev's approach, resting on theories of 'social physics' popular in America and Europe at that time, presupposed that central points, which were objectively existing entities even if they could be identified only statistically, exerted gravitational pull on their surrounding space, creating force fields or natural hinterlands around them that organized the corresponding phenomena in space.[25] These active multiple centralities, taking different forms and

---

[25] The American economist Henry Charles Carey first popularized 'social physics' in the mid-nineteenth century (although the notion that human society was subject to physical forces and laws had appeared earlier in work by Auguste Comte and other sociologists). See William M. McKinney, 'Carey, Spencer and Modern Geography', *The Professional Geographer* 20/2 (1968): 103–6; Clark Glymour, 'Social Science and Social Physics', *Behavioural* Science

materializing at different scales, could be used to define optimal administrative-territorial divisions. Eventually, as economies evolved and populations migrated, the accompanying displacement of their centres of gravity would disrupt existing regional formations and necessitate administrative-territorial reform. In this way, Mendeleev elevated to objective status the notion of centrality, long a mythic-spiritual principle of Russian (and other) culture, and since the early nineteenth century a focus of social scientific interest in Europe and North America.[26] In his view, the determination of centres and their movements was both the basis of rational spatial planning and the principal mechanism of its realization.

In 1906, the year before his death, Mendeleev summed up his spatial thinking in a short work titled *K' poznaniiu Rossii* [Towards a Knowledge of Russia]. In this, he elaborated a new cartographic projection which he thought would enable the viewer better to apprehend the extent and unity of Russian space, its regional structure and the interrelationships between natural features, administrative divisions, and major points of settlement (see Figure 4.2).[27] The orientation of the map was designed to stress the Eurasian character of Russian space and to communicate Mendeleev's belief in Russia's mission to 'overcome the thousand-year divide between Asia and Europe, to reconcile and unify two distinct worlds', and to find a balance between the West's 'progressive, yet haughty and inconsistent .. individualism' and the Orient's 'submissive, even benighted and grovelling, but still solid unity between state and society'.[28]

In this work Mendeleev also described methods for identifying the territorial centres of individual localities, regions, and the empire as a whole. For small

---

28/2 (1983): 126–34; I. Bernard Cohen, *Interactions: Some Contacts between the Natural Sciences and the Social Sciences* (Cambridge, MA, 1994), pp. 15–35. Russian geographer, geodesist and cartographer A.A. Tillo first introduced the study of centralities to Russian spatial analysis; see A.A. Tillo, 'Raspredelenie tsentrov materikov na poverkhnosti zemnogo shara', *Izvestiia Russkogo Geograficheskogo Obshchestva* 23 (1887): 750–53.

[26] On traditional Russian conceptions of space, see the contributions of Sergei Medvedev and Elena Hellberg-Hirn in Jeremy Smith (ed.), *Beyond the Limits: The Concept of Space in Russian History and Culture* (Helsinki, 1999). See also Mikhail Epstein, 'Russo-Soviet Topoi', in Evgeny Dobrenko and Eric Naiman (eds), *The Landscape of Stalinism: The Art and Ideology of Soviet Space* (Seattle and London, 2003), pp. 277–306. For the history of the centre–periphery concept, in both myth and science, see Jean Gottmann (ed.), *Centre and Periphery: Spatial Variation in Politics* (Beverly Hills, CA, 1980). For a Soviet view of the origins of centrality, see M.D. Akhundov, *Kontseptsii prostranstva i vremeni: istoki, evoliutsiia, perspektivy* (Moscow, 1982).

[27] Mendeleev, *K' poznaniiu Rossii*, pp. 143–57. The map and its projection are discussed in N.N. Belonin, 'D.I. Mendeleev kak kartograf', *Naukovy Zapiski* 7/8, *Trudy Naukovo-Doslidnogo Institutu Geografii* 2 (1942): 223–3.

[28] Mendeleev, *K' poznaniiu Rossii*, p. 146.

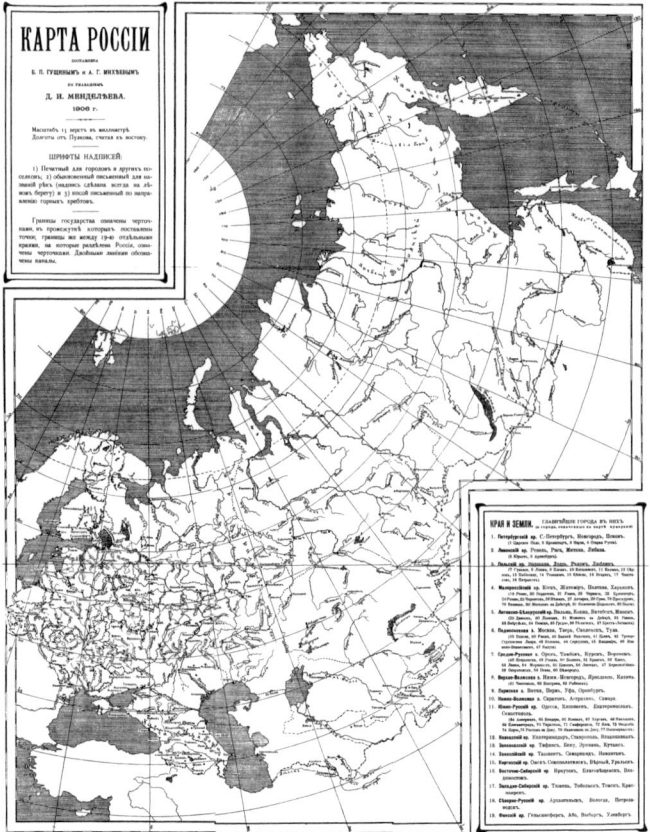

Figure 4.2   Map of Russia. Compiled by V.P. Gushchnyi and A.G. Mikh'evyi on the instructions of D.I. Mendeleev, 1906.

Source: Mendeleev, *K' poznaniiu Rossii* (St Petersburg, 1906).

areas, this could be accomplished by hanging a cut-out of a map of the territory from a thread attached in sequence to several points along its edges, and each time tracing in pencil a line representing the vertical continuation of the thread across the paper until three or more of these plumb lines intersected: this point of intersection would be the centre of the surface. The surface centres of larger areas, maps of which would suffer distortion, and the centres of which would in fact be located under the earth's surface, could be found by mathematical calculation.[29] He then used historical demographic data to trace the trajectory

---

[29]   Ibid., pp. 124–5.

of Russia's territorial and population centres of gravity from the inception of the modern state to the present time, thereby to determine the 'natural' vectors of the empire's spatial change. These vectors, he stated, pointed to a general movement of settlement and economic activity eastward and southward.[30] According to his calculations, the territorial centre of the Russian Empire currently lay somewhere between the rivers Ob' and Enisei in central Siberia, almost on the Arctic Circle. However, this point, lying in the middle of the icy northern tundra, could not in his view correspond to the optimal population centre, so he adjusted the 'centre of population suitable for settlement' several degrees to the south-west, to the boundary of Tobols'k and Tomsk regions, just to the north of Omsk. It was approximately toward that point, he asserted, that the current population centre – which, by analysing the 1897 imperial census data, he located in Tambov region, a couple of hundred miles south-east of Moscow – should move, if the process of demographic redistribution were correctly left to pursue its evolutionary course.[31]

In stressing the necessity of spatial evolution, Mendeleev decried any attempt by 'power' to 'leap forward' in history or to violate the 'laws of historical necessity'.[32] The spatial development of the Russian Empire, in his conception, was a continuous dialogue and incremental, reciprocal rapprochement between Russian nature – that is, the objective-material world – and Russian society – that is, the world of scientific ideas and expertise, supported by educated public opinion, in alliance with the realm of politics, embodied in the enlightened absolute authority of the tsar, his government, and civil service. It was not only the role but the duty of the Russian autocracy to direct development, but its interventions should be informed by expert scientific analysis of evolutionary processes, and not rule but sensitively steer nature along its course: 'the maturing historical organism demands a conscious relation to its development if abnormalities, diseases and random factors are not desired.'[33]

For one thing, the Russian imperial state should ensure that administrative procedures and practices were rationalized and systematized across its territory.

---

[30] Ibid., p. 131.

[31] Ibid., pp. 140–42. Immigrant German geographer and ethnographer Gustav-Fedor Pauli had already noted in 1862 that 'the centre of gravity of the Empire moves daily farther to the east and south-east. The district of Orenburg and the governments of Saratov, Samara, and Caucasus are receiving a powerful impetus. It is toward these regions that voluntary and forced colonization is directed', in Théodore de Pauly, *Description ethnographique des peuples de la Russie* (St Petersburg, 1862), p. 7.

[32] Mendeleev, *K' poznaniiu Rossii*, pp. 131–2.

[33] Mendeleev (1884), 'O vozbuzhdenii promyshlennogo razvitiia v Rossii', p. 81. On the role of the monarchy, see *Zavetnye mysli*, p. 327.

As a first and important step, Mendeleev sought to establish nationwide standards for weights and measures, and instituted a central supervisory board and network of local bureaus. The purpose of these agencies, as a recent biographer has written, was to 'inspect the trade and industrial measures in each region, enforce local standards, and thus correlate and standardize the Empire'.[34] The Russian government should also act against foreign influence, whether this be western capitalism or socialist and communist ideas of revolutionary transformation (which he termed 'calamitous utopias').[35] Both transnational free markets and socialism, in Mendeleev's view, posed a mortal threat to the empire and should be resisted, the one by tariffs and internal investment, the other by the exercise of strong government.

Mendeleev proselytized his approach to Russian spatial reconfiguration and territorial development passionately and indefatigably, and found supporters among those 'enlightened bureaucrats' of late tsarism who also believed in the necessity of Russia's modernization.[36] He developed a close acquaintanceship with Sergei Witte during the latter's tenure of the post of Minister of Finance between 1892 and 1903.[37] Reportedly, they fell out during the 1905 Revolution because Mendeleev believed that his friend, by now promoted to Prime Minister, had betrayed the autocracy by surrendering some of the tsar's absolute power to pacify the rebels and satisfy liberal demands.[38] As noted, Mendeleev played an important role in lobbying for the 1891 Tariff and for the establishment in 1893 of a Chief Board of Weights and Measures, of which he became the first director. Both his scholarly work and his strenuous efforts to ensure its practical application informed the planning and development of policy concerning industrialization, transport construction, and population resettlement, although both political opposition and a perennial lack of funds meant that, to his frustration, many of his proposals and initiatives were never implemented.

---

[34] Gordin, *A Well-ordered Thing*, p. 168. See also Gordin, 'Measure of All the Russias: Metrology and Governance in the Russian Empire', *Kritika* 4/4 (2003): 783–815; Gordin, 'Making Newtons: Mendeleev, Metrology and the Chemical Ether', *Ambix* 45/2 (1998): 96–115; and Nathan M. Brooks, 'Mendeleev and Metrology', *Ambix* 45/2 (1998): 116–28.

[35] Mendeleev, *K' poznaniiu Rossii*, p. 98.

[36] I borrow the term from Bruce Lincoln, *Nikolai Miliutin: An Enlightened Russian Bureaucrat* (Newtonwille, MA, 1977) and Lincoln, *In the Vanguard of Reform: Russia's Enlightened Bureaucrats, 1825–1861* (DeKalb, IL, 1982).

[37] Dziubenko, *D.I. Mendeleev i tamozhennyi tarif*, pp. 223–9 and *passim*.

[38] Gordin, *A Well-ordered Thing*, pp. 233–4.

Centrography and Early Soviet Spatial Planning

The Russian preoccupation with the challenges and opportunities of space, and the struggle for discursive primacy between objectivist and idealist spatial conceptions, intensified after 1917 under the new Soviet regime. Spatial reconstruction became an inseparable part of the revolutionary project. One of the first acts of the new government was to ordain the territorial emancipation of the people. The 'Decree on Borders' of January 1918 permitted each locality to secede from any administrative-territorial unit into which it had been 'forcibly incorporated' under tsarist power, and 'to group itself around those natural centres towards which they feel gravitation'.[39] This presupposed that local populations shared an intuitive sense of the forces immanent in space, which might, for example, pull villagers toward one market centre rather than another, according to natural conditions, social, cultural, or kinship affiliations, transport infrastructures and facilities, and perceived economic or other benefits weighed against potential costs. Spatial democracy, however, brought about territorial chaos. The Soviet central authorities endeavoured to put a halt to spontaneous changes in boundaries.[40] In early 1920 the government undertook an audit of the territorial reconfigurations that had taken place, but found the situation still confused and in flux.[41] Soon after, the regime launched its own top-down process of comprehensive regionalization, substituting for the popular enactment of collective rational choice a drawn-out process of central administrative deliberation and political decision-making informed by spatial analysis performed by economists, geographers, statisticians, historians, ethnographers and linguists, and special pleading on the part of existing territorial authorities and economic and ethnonational interests both in the centre and the regions.[42]

---

[39] Explanatory circular on the decree of the Council of People's Commissars (Sovnarkom) 'On the Changing of Borders' of 27 January 1918, dated 11 May 1918, in GARF, f. 5677, op. 2, d. 2, l. 20.

[40] Sovnarkom decree, 15 July 1919, stipulating that border changes required the authorization of the Russian People's Commissariat for Internal Affairs (NKVD), in GARF f. 5677, op. 2, d. 2, l. 23.

[41] Circular of All-Russian Central Executive Committee (VTsIK), 30 April 1920, in GARF, f. 5677, op. 2, d. 2, l. 27.

[42] Data on popular spatial perceptions and behaviour were still collected for analysis; see Nick Baron, 'Nature, Nationalism and Revolutionary Regionalism: Constructing Soviet Karelia, 1920–1923', *Journal of Historical Geography* 33/3 (July 2007): 565–95. See also Jeremy Smith, 'Delimiting National Space: The Ethnographical Principle in the Administrative Division of the RSFSR and USSR, 1918–1925', in Smith, *Beyond the Limits*, pp. 241–58; and Francine Hirsch, 'Towards an Empire of Nations: Border-making and the Formation of Soviet National Identities', *The Russian Review* 59/2 (2000): 201–26.

Henceforth, the Bolshevik state regarded spatial planning and policy as its own prerogative and a key administrative and political concern. Indeed, the narrative of Soviet state-building can be read as an account of the progressive consolidation of the regime's control over all forms of spatial knowledge, representation and practice, of its striving initially to apprehend and regulate the forces inherent in space, later to overpower and transform space.

In the 1920s Soviet post-revolutionary thinking assigned primacy to objective space, the real, lived space of experience and abstract mathematical space, in accordance with Marxist-Leninist materialist doctrine. Through social science and artistic experimentation, Soviet culture strove to understand the innate constitution of space, identify its dynamics and triangulate its expanse, better to remodel it and redirect its energies toward the socialist reconstruction of humanity and nature.[43]

The specialists in economics, statistics, and geography working on regionalization, their outlook shaped more by their technical education and experience under tsarism than by revolutionary ideology or avant-garde culture, sought out theories and models that would help them to make sense of the data they were collecting on each area's resources and requirements, its structures, forces, and flows, and to infer policy recommendations. In particular, they were drawn to the work of German scholars Johann Heinrich von Thünen, who studied agricultural land use, and Alfred Weber, whose writings on industrial location were praised by Lenin and championed by the leading Soviet economist Eugen Varga.[44] Both Germans had developed normative spatial models that

---

[43] On the Bolshevik culture of space, see, for example, Richard Stites, *Revolutionary Dreams: Utopian Vision and Experimental Life in the Russian Revolution* (Oxford and New York, 1989); Katerina Clark, *Petersburg: Crucible of Cultural Revolution* (Cambridge, MA, 1995); Emma Widdis, *Visions of a New Land: Soviet Film from the Revolution to the Second World War* (New Haven and London, 2003). On Constructivist engagement with spatial theory and practice, see, for example, Aleksandr Rodchenko, *Inventarnaia Prostranstvo*, ed. Peter Noever (Vienna, 2006). On parallels between artistic Constructivism and post-revolutionary Soviet geodesy, see Nick Baron, 'Prostranstva Utopii: geodeziia, kartografiia i visual'naia kultura v SSSR, 1918-1953 gg.', in Iu.A. Vedenin and O.A. Lavrenova, (eds), *Geografiia iskusstva. Sbornik Statei, Vypusk 5* (Moscow, 2009), pp. 7-38.

[44] Von Thünen's *Der isolierte Staat in Beziehung auf Landwirtschaft und Nationalökonomie* (1826) had been published in a Russian translation in 1857. Alfred Weber's *Über den Standort der Industrie* (1909) was well known in Russia since its first publication, but did not appear in Russian until 1926: A. Veber, *Teoriia razmeshcheniia promyslennosti*, abr. and trans. N.V. Morozov, foreword by Nikolai Baranskii (Leningrad and Moscow, 1926). On the Soviet reception of Weber's work, see 'Veber, Al'fred', in *Bol'shaia sovetskaia entsiklopediia*, 1st edn (Moscow, 1928), vol. 9, pp. 123–4 and Richard Bräu, 'Zum Erscheinen und zur Rezeption von Alfred Webers Werk "Über den Standort der Industrien"

could serve as a basis of prescription as well as description, which made them all the more valuable to old-regime experts in the service of a new state that held that 'science is utilitarian from the social-historical point of view'.[45]

Mendeleev was tainted by his outspoken nationalist and pro-monarchist beliefs, as well as by his empiricism, and was treated with ambivalence: 'his materialism was wrapped up in conservatism', proclaimed Lev Trotskii.[46] Some of the old-regime experts working in the administration nevertheless continued to propound and develop his ideas on spatial analysis and regional organization. Chief among these was V.P. Weinberg, who had adopted Mendeleev's methods in the pre-war period and published on the historical movement of population and territorial centres.[47] A newcomer to Mendeleev's centrographical work was Evgenii Sviatlovskii (born 1890), who had studied law before the Revolution but under the Soviet regime turned his attention to statistics, the history of economic ideas, and industrial geography. Sviatlovskii started reading Mendeleev's economic and geographical work in 1919 and soon became an ardent devotee and publicist of his outlook and methods.[48]

In August 1922 Sviatlovskii gave a lecture titled 'On Centrographical Method' to the Statistical Division of the Russian Geographical Society. A summary of the talk was then circulated to all regional statistical bureaus. Sviatlovskii described in detail Mendeleev's techniques for identifying economic, industrial, and

---

(1909) 1926 in der Sowjetunion – eine wissenschaftshistorische Recherche', unpublished paper presented at Alfred Weber Institut für Sozial- und Staatswissenschaften, 19 January 1995 (revised January 1998).

[45] For a critical discussion of the von Thünen and Weber models, see Trevor Barnes, 'Envisioning Economic Geography: Three Men and Their Figures', *Geographische Zeitschrift* 86/2 (1998): 94–105. The quotation is from Lev Trotskii, 'D.I. Mendeleev i marksizm'.

[46] Lev Trotskii, 'D.I. Mendeleev i marksizm'. Trotskii condemned Mendeleev's empiricism and reactionary politics while claiming to find dialectical materialism in his analytical methods. For an extended Soviet attempt to co-opt Mendeleev as a proto-socialist in his philosophical and economic thought, while deploring his 'utter naivety' concerning government and politics, see P.P. Ionidi, *Mirovozrenie D.I. Mendeleeva* (Moscow, 1959); quotation from p. 112.

[47] V.P. Weinberg, 'Polozheniia tsentra poverkhnosti Rossii ot nachala kniazhestva Moskovskogo do nastoiashchego vremeni', *Izvestiia Russkogo Geograficheskogo Obshchestva* 51/6 (1915): 365–84; and Weinberg, 'Polozheniia tsentra naselennosti Rossii s 1613 po 1913 g.', ibid., pp. 385–408. For a brief discussion of Weinberg and other pre-revolutionary centrographers, see P.M. Polian, 'Ocherk istorii Russkoi tsentrografii', in S.B. Lavrov and B.B. Rodoman (eds), *Geografiia i khoziaistvo. Vyp. 3. Tsentrograficheskii metod v ekonomicheskoi geografii* (Leningrad, 1989), pp. 21–4.

[48] For a short, sympathetic biographical sketch by his son, see G.E. Sviatlovskii, 'Pamiati E.E. Sviatlovskogo', in Lavrov and Rodoman, *Geografiia i khoziaistvo*, pp. 6–8.

demographic centres. He noted that, although some economists and geographers 'condescended' to this work, it had been gaining currency in recent years among regionalization specialists in the Soviet State Planning Commission (Gosplan) and in regional planning offices. Properly used, the centrographical method could serve as a 'scientific basis for regionalization', permitting planners to identify the multiple centres – areal, demographic, economic, etc. – of territorial units and to locate each area's optimal 'centre of centres'. He warned, however, that the centrographical method did not explain the long-term dynamics that it traced or permit the prediction of future trends. In other words, the method could represent a series of synchronic points, but could offer little insight into the causes of change, which was invariably over-determined, and therefore no absolute foundation for extrapolating future transformations.[49]

Fifteen years later, writing with regard to the movement of population centres, Sviatlovskii maintained the same view:

> Of course, the direction and volume of the streams of migration during any period are the resultant of highly complex interrelated sets of factors. This resultant, however intricate the causal factors, is expressed by the centrographical method in the motion of a single point. Caution should be observed, however, in using this motion as a basis of prediction. If the same causal factors continue to operate, it forms a valid basis for prediction. If marked changes take place, however, such as war, pestilence, commercial development, and change in form of government, its reliability as a predictive instrument is lessened, if not destroyed.[50]

Despite centrography's resolute empiricism and its professed inability to accommodate the events and processes – revolution, nationalization, civil war, social upheaval, famine – that the Soviet Union had experienced since its birth, and although the early Soviet literature on regionalization rarely alludes explicitly to this method, the theorization and practice of boundary-drawing during the first 12 years of the communist system were influenced by its attention to centrality as the key organizing principle of space and by its scientific, inductive approach to spatial analysis and planning.[51] But from the start these principles generated controversy, even among specialists. Already in 1924, the Chief of Gosplan's

---

[49] The summary, undated, of Sviatlovskii's talk of 17 August 1922 is preserved among the documents of the VTsIK Administrative Commission, which was responsible for regionalization, in GARF, f. 5677, op. 3, d. 394, ll. 24–30.

[50] E.E. Sviatlovskii, with the collaboration of Walter Crosby Eells, 'The Centrographical Method and Regional Analysis', *The Geographical Review* 27/2 (1937): 244.

[51] On the theorization and role of centrality in regionalization, see Baron, 'Nature, Nationalism and Revolutionary Regionalism'.

Regionalization Committee, I.G. Aleksandrov, a professional engineer and not a Communist Party member, asserted that 'regional construction should be not only of an objective-analytical, but also of a teleological character'.[52]

Similar debates were taking place in mid-decade within Gosplan with regard to the character of economic and industrial planning. The empiricism of the centrographical method accorded with the thinking of one group of economists who argued that existing material circumstances and trends should provide a 'genetic' foundation for the compilation of plans – in the words of one historian, 'plan as description rather than plan as intention'.[53] Another commentator has written that, according to this view, the function of a planning agency was 'to study the economic forces around it and to provide the responsive instruments through which the "laws" and tendencies immanent in those forces could be put into operation and be given a smooth and frictionless effect'.[54] This is reminiscent of Mendeleev's 'conscious relation' of government to natural evolution. Other Gosplan economists, however, believed that plans should be more prescriptive than descriptive, and that planners should subordinate reality, perceived or predicted, to outcomes desired: as senior Gosplan official S.G. Strumilin declared in 1927, 'not prediction, but targets and advance directives are the central focus of any plan'.[55] For the time being, neither the genetic nor the teleological approach to planning prevailed, and the economists, statisticians, and geographers involved in this work sought to balance the two methods, to reconcile the realms of the real and the ideal, the objectively apprehended and the envisioned.

In 1926 Sviatlovskii took up the suggestion of the eminent geographer V.P. Semenov-Tian-Shanskii, to establish a Centrographical Laboratory under the auspices of the Section of Statistics of the Russian Geographical Society in Leningrad.[56] The new institution was named in honour of D.I. Mendeleev, whose widow attended its opening session and whose son participated in its work,

---

[52] I.G. Aleksandrov, 'Osnovy khoziaistvennogo raionirovanie SSSR', in G.M. Krzhizhanovskii (ed.), *Voprosy ekonomicheskogo raionirovaniia SSSR. Sbornik materialov i statei (1917–1929 gg.)* (Moscow, 1957), p. 214.

[53] Peter Rutland, *The Myth of the Plan: Lessons of Soviet Planning Experience* (London and Melbourne, 1985), p. 78.

[54] Maurice Dobb, *Soviet Economic Development since 1917* (London, 1948), p. 329.

[55] Cited in E.H. Carr and R.W. Davies, *A History of Soviet Russia: Foundations of a Planned Economy, 1926–1929* (London, 1969), vol. 1, p. 840. See also Eugène Zaleski, *Planning for Economic Growth in the Soviet Union, 1918–1932* (Chapel Hill, NC, 1971); and Alexander Baykov, *The Development of the Soviet Economic System: An Essay on the Experience of Planning in the USSR* (Cambridge, 1946).

[56] V.P. Semenov-Tian-Shanskii, *To, chto proshlo. Tom 2, 1917–1942* (Moscow, 2009), p. 194.

and had the declared purpose of developing and propagating the late scholar's ideas and methods of spatial planning. Sviatlovskii had grand ambitions for the centrographical method. It would not only lend theoretical weight and practical support to Soviet evolutionary planning in the short term, but it should aspire, he later wrote, to become 'a world language of economic geography ... a common language of scholarship'.[57] 'Geoeconomic synthesis', Sviatlovskii declared in a report to the International Geographical Union in Warsaw in 1934, 'can embrace the entire economic domain in a complete and profound manner.'[58] As we shall see, this report would prove to be fatal for centrographical methods, institutions and practitioners in the Soviet Union.

A Soviet geographer in the 1950s recalled Sviatlovskii as a 'true fanatic for centrography' and a 'gifted polemicist' with 'a great talent for persuasion'.[59] A sceptical American geographer of the same period wrote that the centrographers had been a 'noisy and active group'.[60] Thanks to Sviatlovskii's enthusiasm and energy, during the second half of the 1920s the centrographical method attracted increased attention from planners and scholars: of 45 papers presented in the Statistical Section of the Russian Geographical Society between 1926 and 1929, no fewer than 22 were concerned with theoretical aspects of centrography or its practical application, and another 16 dealt with questions of regional economic and demographic development.[61]

Sviatlovskii's proselytizing activities prompted numerous organisations in the later 1920s to commission centrographical studies to aid in planning. In the spring of 1929, for example, Gosplan's Section for Regionalization contracted the laboratory to compile a map representing the movement of various demographic and economic centres of gravity from the mid-nineteenth century to the present (see Figures 4.3 and 4.4). We noted above that in 1906 Mendeleev had predicted, basing his analysis on the 1897 census, that the centre of Russian population would shift toward the east, from Tambov region toward Omsk, in the context of the general historical movement of economic and demographic centres eastward

---

[57] E.E. Swiatlowsky, 'Die zentrographische Methode und ihre Entwicklung in Theorie und Praxis', *Allgemeines Statistisches Archiv* 24 (1934/1935): 24.

[58] E. Sviatlovsky, 'Méthodes centrographiques. Résumé du rapport au Congrès International de Géographie, 1934', *Résumés des communications* (Warsaw, 1934), p. 137, cited in Philip W. Porter, 'What is the point of Minimum Aggregate Travel?', *Annals of the Association of American Geographers* 53/2 (1963): 224.

[59] O.A. Konstantinov, 'Ekonomicheskaia geografiia v Geograficheskom Obshchestve za sorok let Sovetskoi vlasti', *Geograficheskii sbornik* 11 (1957): 138.

[60] Thomas M. Poulsen, 'Centrography in Russian Geography', *Annals of the Association of American Geographers* 49/3 (1959): 326–7.

[61] Konstantinov, 'Ekonomicheskaia geografiia', p. 134.

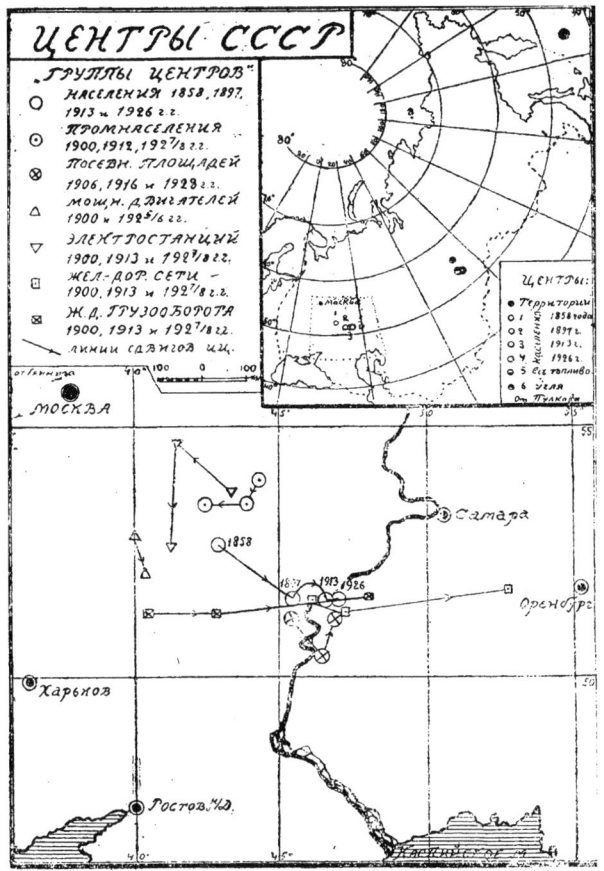

Figure 4.3   Economic centres of the USSR and their movements.
Source: E.E. Sviatlovskii (ed.), *Tsentrograficheskaia laboratoriia im. D.I. Mendeleeva k piatnadtsatiletiiu Oktiabria (1917–1932). Tsentrografiia I* (Leningrad, 1933).

and southward. In the event, the opening of the Trans-Siberian Railway in 1896 had directed vast numbers of peasant migrants toward the eastern territories of the empire, apparently vindicating Mendeleev's forecast. According to calculations in 1929 by Sviatlovskii and Weinberg (for Soviet territory), the Russian population centre had crossed the river Volga near Saratov in about 1912 and thereafter maintained its eastward movement on a vector parallel with, though from the 1920s lagging behind, the centres of the railway system and freight turnover. However, Sviatlovskii noted, Siberian pre-revolutionary colonization had been predominantly agrarian; his analysis demonstrated that, in opposition to the aggregate shift in population, the centre of the industrial population had moved since the mid-nineteenth century in a westerly direction toward the Central Industrial Region.[62] By implication, Gosplan might seek to correct or reverse this divergence through greater investment in the industrial development of eastern and southern regions. Industrial investment in the east indeed became a significant dimension of the early five-year plans since this (together with the industrial development of the north, undertaken principally with forced labour) accorded with the regime's strategic and political priorities.[63]

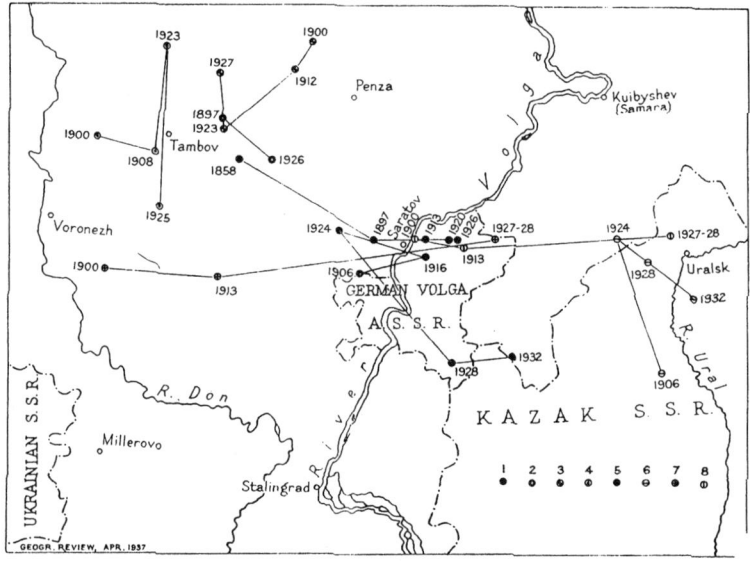

FIG. 4—Centrogram showing trends in the Union of Soviet Socialist Republics as revealed by movements of centers for various years from 1858 to 1932. Key: centers of 1, total population; 2, literate population; 3, persons engaged in industry; 4, horsepower in industry; 5, acreage under crop; 6, cattle; 7, railway system; 8, freight shipments by rail.

Figure 4.4 Movements of centres of Russia and Soviet Union, 1858–1932.
Source: E.E. Sviatlovskii, with Walter Crosby Eells, 'The Centrographical Method and Regional Analysis', *The Geographical Review* 27/2 (1937).

---

[62] E.E. Sviatlovskii (ed.), *Tsentrograficheskaia laboratoriia im. D.I. Mendeleeva k piatnadtsatiletiiu Oktiabria (1917–1932). Tsentrografiia. I* (Leningrad, 1933), pp. 3, 12–13.

[63] For the spatial priorities of the early five-year plans, see R.S. Livshits, *Ocherki po razmeshcheniiu promyshlennosti SSSR* (Moscow, 1954), pp. 123–33; and R.W. Davies, *Crisis and Progress in the Soviet Economy, 1931–1933* (London, 1996), pp. 485–90.

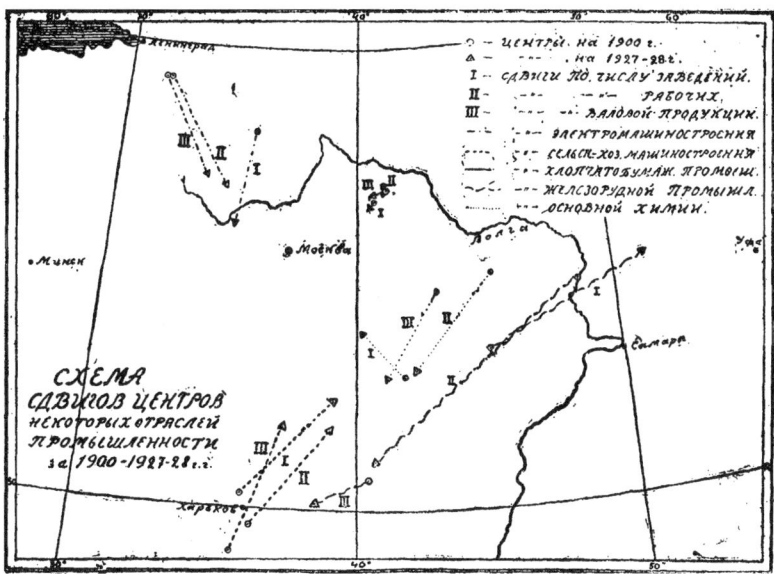

Figure 4.5 Diagram of the movements of several industries, 1900–1927.
Source: Sviatlovskii, *Tsentrograficheskaia laboratoriia*.

In 1929–30 Sviatlovskii's Centrographical Laboratory also worked on behalf of the Institute for Industrial-Economic Research attached to the Supreme Council for the National Economy (Vesenkha). The director of this institute was Nikolai Bukharin, who had recently been removed from leading positions in the Politburo, Communist International, and the central party newspaper *Pravda* for alleged 'rightist deviations'. The commission entailed compiling and mapping data on shifts in the centres of gravity of various industries, calculated according to the distribution of factories, gross output, and workers, since the turn of the century. The resulting map (see Figure 4.5) showed rather random motion in all indicators. For several industries, the centres of gravity of their total number of factories, their workforce, and their gross output were moving in different directions (this was particularly noticeable in the case of the iron-ore sector, whose enterprises were seen to be gravitating swiftly towards the cold north-east while its aggregate workforce migrated even more briskly toward the sunnier south-west). These crude illustrations of statistical generalizations, of course, offered a visually striking but almost meaningless snapshot of two moments in time, and certainly did not reveal any true vectors, either natural or ordained by state policy. That the centrographers refused to offer more than speculative explanations of their findings (which, in the case of iron ore, for example, were most likely due to the large number of factories under construction in 1927/28 in the east that had not yet recruited a full workforce or started producing) must only have added to the frustration of the economists and planners striving to translate the data into practical policy prescriptions.

In another job for Bukharin's institute, the centrographers applied their analysis to the territorial section of the First Five-Year Plan, plotting how the centres of different industries would move according to the distribution of capital investment envisaged in the plan.[64] The resulting map (Figure 4.6) graphically illustrated a substantial shift in industrial activity eastward and, in all branches but paper and cardboard manufacturing, a tendency toward the south as well. Encompassing a shorter period than the other centrographical analyses, and explicitly addressing envisaged outcomes rather than putative trends, these data have greater cogency - which is to say, they are as cogent as the plan itself was coherent or feasible, which it was not.[65]

Then, in 1930, the People's Commissariat of Transport commissioned statisticians in the Economics Faculty of the Leningrad Polytechnic Institute to carry out a study of grain transport using centrographical methods and to present policy proposals. Based on analysis of freight data, the report recommended that, in order to observe the correct location of its centre of gravity, grain cultivation should be maximized in the existing principal production regions in European Russia, minimized or eliminated in the main regions of consumption, and in Siberia limited solely to the volume required for the region's own needs. These were not timely conclusions in view of the Soviet political leadership's recent pronouncements on the massive expansion of agricultural production in the north and east. Furious denunciations of the centrographical method and its proponents ensued in central newspapers, specialist journals, and academic publications.[66] Soon afterward, Gosplan cancelled the First All-Union Centrographical Conference scheduled for that year.[67]

---

[64] Sviatlovskii (ed.), *Tsentrograficheskaia laboratoriia*, pp. 4, 7–14.

[65] On chaotic planning and plan chaos, see Nick Baron, 'Stalinist Planning as Political Practice: Control and Repression on the Soviet Periphery, 1935–38', *Europe-Asia Studies* 56/3 (2004): 439–62.

[66] Konstantinov, 'Ekonomicheskaia geografiia', pp. 138–9. The Polytechnic Institute published its findings and recommendations in *Bor'ba raionov za proizvodstvo khleba* (Moscow, 1930). For an attack on the 'errors' of centrography, and this work in particular, see the essay by Leningrad State University geographer M. Bogdanchikov, 'Zadachi ekonomicheskoi geografii na sovremennom etape', in *Na metodologicheskom fronte geografii i ekonomicheskoi geografii* (Leningrad, 1932), pp. 5–26.

[67] Sviatlovskii (ed.), *Tsentrograficheskaia laboratoriia*, p. 4. Sviatlovskii does not, of course, explain the reason for this last-minute cancellation.

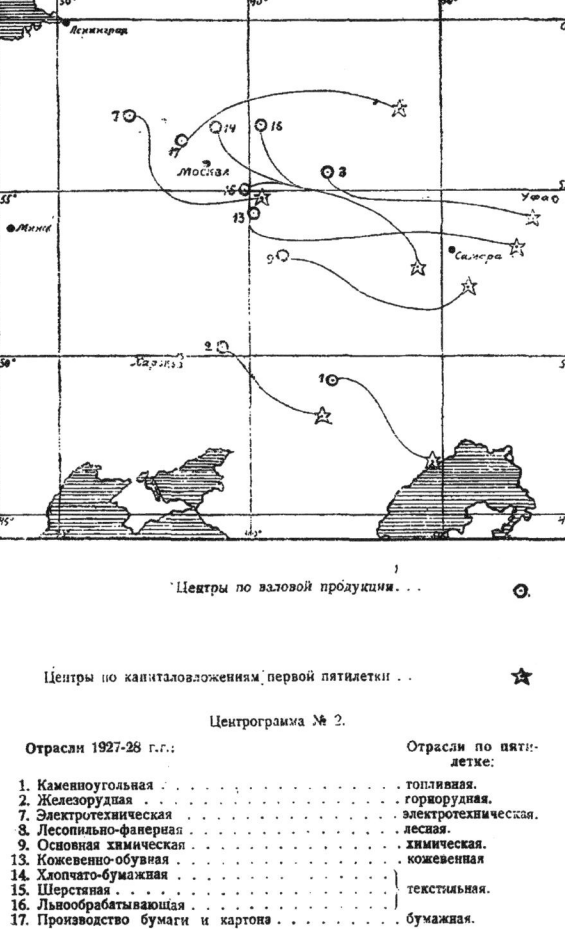

Figure 4.6   Centres of gross output, 1927/28, and of capital investment in the First Five-Year Plan.

Source: Sviatlovskii, *Tsentrograficheskaia laboratoriia*.

With the intensification and acceleration of Soviet industrialization at the end of 1920s, Sviatlovskii's empirical, evolutionary approach to spatial and economic planning was fast falling out of favour. Like others working in economic geography, Sviatlovskii and the centrographers had to steer between accusations of being proponents of Plekhanov's 'vulgar materialism', decried as mechanistic environmental determinism, or practitioners of Bukharin's 'ideographic' and 'descriptive' method, denigrated for ignoring the fact that 'there is no science that only describes a phenomenon without revealing its internal relations, its law-governed nature'.[68] Also at this time, the spatial theories of von Thünen and Alfred Weber – bolder, more coherently delineated, more internally consistent, and more influential than centrography, but sharing some of its conceptual and methodological tenets – were vilified as attempts 'to construct an abstract system of laws defining industrial location ... ignoring the influence of socio-economic conditions and the contradictions of capitalism ... and serving the cause of embellishing capitalist reality'.[69] Among Gosplan specialists, those who advocated teleological planning now found their approach in alignment with the Stalinist regime's determination to modernize rapidly and ruthlessly.[70] Those who advocated gradualism and genetic planning, and whose ideas were most in sympathy with centrographical principles, were accused of ideological deviation. Many were dismissed, and some found themselves on trial accused of economic sabotage and counter-revolution.[71]

During the 1930s Stalinist discourse elevated teleology to the guiding principle of spatial planning, and the idea of space to pre-eminence over its material reality. Thus, the compilers of a physical-geographical map of the Soviet Union for primary schools were instructed to 'exclude the term "desert zone" as in the USSR there are no deserts which cannot be developed'.[72] Although some of the goals of Stalinist planning accorded with Mendeleev's recommendations and the Soviet centrographers's spatial analyses – the role of extensive transport construction as a means of effecting a national division of labour; the importance of regional development; the need to reinforce the long-term shift in economic and demographic centres of gravity toward the east; the imperative to explore and assimilate the Far North and Far East – their methods could not have been more different. Whereas Mendeleev and the centrographers strove to establish a dialogue between society and nature, Stalinism sought by force of political will to vanquish the landscape and overwhelm space, to recreate both nature and

---

[68] V. Motylev, 'Ekonomicheskaia geografiia', in *Bol'shaia Sovetskaia Entsiklopediia*, 1st edn (Moscow, 1933), vol. 63, p. 246. For a closely-argued Stalinist assault on 'bourgeois' spatial theories, see Livshits, *Ocherki po razmeshcheniiu promyshlennosti SSSR*, pp. 49–55.

[69] Motylev, 'Ekonomicheskaia geografiia', p. 248.

[70] Rutland, *The Myth of the Plan*, Chapter 3.

[71] See, for example, Naum Jasny, *Soviet Economists of the Twenties: Names to be Remembered* (Cambridge, 1972), especially Part II 'The Trial'; and Jasny, 'A Soviet Planner – V.G. Groman', *Russian Review* 13/1 (1954): 52–8.

[72] Editorial Board of the State Cartographic Trust, Protocol 10, 4 February 1934, 'O karte SSSR fizicheskoi dlia nachal'noi shkoly, masshtaba 1:1.5m', Russian State Archive of the Economy (Rossiiskii Gosudarstvennyi Arkhiv Ekonomi, RGAE), f. 8223, op. 1, d. 167, l. 13.

society according to its own ideological vision.[73] In the event, the Stalinist mode of modernization created regional economies that were massively unbalanced, interdependent on one other, and wholly in thrall to an economically inefficient but politically all-powerful centralized system of resource allocation, reliant on labour redistributions effected through the prison camp system and mass deportations.[74]

Sviatlovskii strove to defend centrography against its enemies. In 1930 he formed an advisory council to the Centrographical Laboratory and recruited to its membership a number of eminent academics and specialists. He then publicized their testimonials on the laboratory's 'wholly appropriate' work for the First Five-Year Plan (Strumilin), its 'undoubted utility' (Shokal'skii), and its honest efforts to reform its earlier 'mechanistic approach' into a 'dialectical method' (Komarov).[75] In this context, a 'dialectical method' meant one that was not timidly synchronic, empirical, and analytical but which revealed socio-economic causation, took greater account of political and ideological factors in generating historical change, and could inform and provide scientific justification for policy decisions.

As Sviatlovskii's erstwhile patrons and supporters in Gosplan and Vesenkha were being purged and, not infrequently, arrested and sent to forced labour camps, the centrographers found themselves with fewer commissions or opportunities to publish in Soviet journals.[76] Sviatlovskii's response was to seek publicity abroad. In 1934 an article by Sviatlovskii on centrography appeared in the German Statistical Society's official journal, a publication that, if knowingly selected, was particularly ill-chosen, being, as one historian has written, 'a virtual

---

[73] Dobrenko and Naiman (eds), *The Landscape of Stalinism*; Widdis, *Visions of a New Land*, esp. Chapter 6.

[74] Nick Baron, *Soviet Karelia: Planning, Politics and Terror in Stalin's Russia, 1920–1939* (London, 2007).

[75] Sviatlovskii (ed.), *Tsentrograficheskaia laboratoriia*, p. 6. At this time S.G. Strumilin, a long-time advocate of teleological planning, was Chair of Gosplan, V.L. Komarov was Vice-President of the Soviet Academy of Sciences, and Iu.M. Shokal'skii was Honorary President of the State Geographical Society. Others on the council included economist G.M. Krzhizhanovskii, geographer V.P. Semenov-Tian-Shanskii, and I.D. Mendeleev, the chemist's son.

[76] Most centrographical publications after 1930–31 were preoccupied with defending the method against criticism, rather than developing new ideas or undertaking new analytical work. See the bibliography of published and unpublished works in Sviatlovskii (ed.), *Tsentrograficheskaia laboratoriia*, pp. 28–38, published in 1933 by the Centrographical Laboratory's patron the State Geographical Society; and the bibliography in Lavrov and Rodoman, *Geografiia i khoziaistvo*, pp. 137–9.

roadmap to the desires of Nazi statistical hierarchy'.[77] Other articles later in the same issue dealt with 'race statistics' and the ideological and political role of the discipline in the new Reich.[78] Sviatlovskii here strove to recast centrography in a heroic – one might say Nietzschean – mould, appropriate to the Stalinist cult of the leader, as well as to the journal in which it was published. The twentieth century, he wrote, was a 'space-consuming age', in which the idea of spatial distribution had the same significance as that of historical development or evolution in the nineteenth century. Although Mendeleev (whose 'bright flame over the years has almost become extinguished') and others had initiated the study of space, he continued, the new science still awaited its statesmen and scholars of genius who could overcome the challenge of 'overpowering and organizing space'.[79] Needless to say, the article contained no reference to Marxist ideology (though it does mention Hegel and Darwin) or to the socialist aspects and aims of Soviet planning. Centrographical space, as presented here, is rational, abstract, and ostensibly apolitical.

The same year, Sviatlovskii decided to take advantage of the Congress of the International Geographical Union in Warsaw to promote his discipline abroad and to rebut the attacks on his discipline at home. The Soviet government, however, permitted none of the Leningrad centrographers to attend the Warsaw congress in person. Sviatlovskii therefore submitted his report to the conference organizers to be delivered in his absence. In the final lines of his text, he characterized and refuted what he regarded as misconceived criticism of his methods:

> These problems of the real value [of centrography] cannot be discredited by the claims of some critics who try to characterize centrography as a form of mathematical-political-economy ... These criticisms envisage centrography as being identical with equilibrium theory, the politics of imperialism, the principles of the school of Weber, etc.[80]

---

[77] Swiatlowsky, 'Die zentrographische Methode', pp. 21–40. On *Allgemeines Statistisches Archiv*, see Edwin Black, *IBM and the Holocaust: The Strategic Alliance between Nazi Germany and America's Most Powerful Corporation* (Rockville, MD, 2009), p. 48.

[78] Karl Keller, 'Zur Frage der Rassenstatistik', *Allgemeines Statistisches Archiv* 24 (1934/35): 129–42; Johannes Müller, 'Die Stellung der Statistik in neuen Reich', ibid., pp. 241–50; Friedrich Zahn, 'Vom Wirtschaftswert des Menschen als Gegenstand der Statistik', ibid., pp. 461–4.

[79] Swiatlowsky, 'Die zentrographische Methode', pp. 21, 22.

[80] E. Sviatlovsky, 'La centrographie', *Comptes rendus du Congrès international de géographie* (Warsaw, 1934), vol. 3, p. 379, cited in Porter, 'What is the point of Minimum Aggregate Travel?', p. 225.

Unsurprisingly, Sviatlovskii's report and his tactics for publicizing it infuriated the authorities. The publication of his article in Germany doubtless did nothing to help his cause. Closure of the Centrographical Laboratory had been under discussion in the State Geographical Society since mid-1933, but it was finally shut down in December 1934, its method denounced as a 'bourgeois movement in economic geography'.[81]

In May 1935 the deputy head of the Leningrad regional political police sent a top-secret memorandum to the city's Communist Party leadership in which he noted that the centrographers, by submitting their materials to the Warsaw congress the previous year 'over the heads of the Soviet delegation', had caused 'considerable political complications'. Supposedly, 'the Soviet delegates [had] refused to present the centrographers' materials, and so a report was put together on the basis of these materials and delivered by Polish geographers, who were official members of the fascist party'. He further suspected that, following the closure of their institute, the centrographers were now attempting to regroup, under the protection of senior academic figures such as Academician Strumilin and Nikolai Bukharin, and to 'create a new centre [*sic*], reportedly in Moscow'. The police chief recommended that a network of agents and informers be established to study the 'counter-revolutionary activity' of the centrographers, as well as to investigate several prominent Leningrad geographers (including V.P. Semenov-Tian-Shanskii) who were accused of affiliations with the German school of geopolitics.[82] Relatively few of these scholars were arrested in subsequent years, but their work was disrupted and suppressed. After closure of the Centrographical Laboratory, Sviatlovskii became the Geographical Society's librarian. He died in 1942 during the Leningrad blockade.[83]

In 1957 a Soviet geographer surveying the development of Soviet economic geography reached the following verdict on Sviatlovskii and centrography: 'We

---

[81] Konstantinov, 'Ekonomicheskaia geografiia', pp. 138–9. Quotation from A. Danilov, 'Tsentrografiia', in *Bol'shaia Sovetskaia Entsiklopediia*, 1st edn (Moscow, 1934), vol. 60, pp. 586–7. Sviatlovskii continued to publicize his work abroad for a while. The *New York Times* in 1935 published a full-page feature on the Centrographical Laboratory (incorrectly locating it in Moscow), noting its role in the 1931 Gosplan Conference on Scientific Planning Work and the 1932 Conference for the Geographical Distribution of Industry, convened during the compilation of the Second Five-Year Plan, and its work to propose measures to develop railway networks, relocate industry, and shift populations to ensure the optimal coincidence of transport, industrial, and settlement centres, *New York Times*, 16 June 1935, Section X1, p. 18.

[82] Deputy Chief of the Administration of the People's Commissariat of the Interior for Leningrad Region Nikolaev to Leningrad Obkom Biuro, 7 May 1935, reproduced in Semenov-Tian-Shanskii. *To, chto proshlo*, p. 456.

[83] Konstantinov, 'Ekonomicheskaia geografiia', p. 139.

can only regret that he dedicated his vast knowledge, his inexhaustible energy, and his organizational talent to such a fruitless activity, which not only brought no benefit to the construction of socialism in the USSR, but, as we now see, even brought it harm.'[84] Centrography resurfaced in the mid-1960s, as the Soviet government deliberated over new economic reforms and geographers turned increasingly to quantitative methods to resolve questions of spatial form and territorial planning. By the 1980s it had regained some credibility among academics, though it played no role in practical planning.[85]

Conclusion

This chapter has attempted to read Mendeleev's theories and methods, and their promotion and application by Sviatlovskii and the early Soviet school of centrographers, in terms of a projection of Russian identity grounded in scientific rationalism, technological expertise, social reformism, territorial integration, and state power. Both Mendeleev and the centrographers propounded an empirical-materialistic conception of a unified and integrated Russian or Soviet space that took little or no account of the physical, ethnic, or cultural particularities of different areas. Populations, industries and territorial boundaries were to be mapped and remapped according to shifting centralities reconstructed and plotted statistically. Development was neither predestined nor predetermined but a function of vectors inferred by experts from empirical observation and analysis. The past was the only guide to the future.

Mendeleev's rejection of teleological and eschatological notions of Russian spatial identity and evolution was not, however, rooted in a liberal view of progress. He supported the tsarist autocracy as a force for political stability and sociocultural continuity, as sponsor of science, individual enterprise and capitalist industrial development and as protector of Russian national interests (via tariffs) in the face of the threat of globalizing economic and political forces. Similarly, early Soviet proponents of his methods of spatial analysis accepted the Bolshevik regime as guarantor of order and arbiter of rational, self-sufficient development.

Democracy played no role in their scientific rationalizations or prescriptions for practice. Mendeleev preached economic but not political freedom for Russia. While he believed that a state-regulated market at home was a precondition of

---

[84] Ibid., p. 134.
[85] For late Soviet centrographical studies, see Lavrov and Rodoman, *Geografiia i khoziaistvo*.

development, he was convinced that international free trade would destroy his country's chance to modernize and prosper. The Soviet centrographers laboured in a system that not only severely constrained the exercise of any autonomous choice, but denied the natural right to freedom, on grounds both of ideology and power politics. State interests took precedence over social aspirations. Spatial forms and forces were subordinated to political will. If in the 1920s Soviet spatial science had some room for manoeuvre, in the 1930s the centrographers found that their empirical, rational methods and evolutionary conception of spatial change could no longer be reconciled with Stalin's revolution from above, which undertook forcefully to transform nature in accordance with the regime's vision and in defiance of historical trends. Physical geography, the realm of the real and material, and spatial science, with its abstract yet no less objective gravitational centres and force fields, were overwhelmed by symbolic space, the idealist landscape of metaphor and imagination.

It is no surprise that Mendeleev's concept of Russia's evolutionary modernization, sponsored, supervised, and protected by a strong rational state, driven by the ideas and innovations of loyal cultural, scientific, and industrial elites, has attracted renewed interest among scholars and bureaucrats in post-communist Russia. He is lauded as an economic visionary, whose analyses of late nineteenth-century international trade relations and domestic modernization strategies offer crucial lessons for understanding contemporary globalization and for 'the development and implementation by the state of a scientifically grounded industrial policy' aimed at ensuring Russia's economic integrity and security.[86] Russian nationalists eulogize him as a proponent of a powerful Russian state and autocratic monarchy, an adherent of Orthodox Christianity, and a fighter against 'cosmopolitan' views of science, political economy, and government, impelled by 'fervent and active patriotism [and] a national world-view'.[87] One contemporary Russian historian highlights Mendeleev's belief that all policy 'must be national and proceed from an examination of the concept of "Russia", revealing the specificities of the historical development and character of the Russian people'.[88] His framing of Russia's national space as Eurasian and

---

[86] Dziubenko, *D.I. Mendeleev i tamozhennyi tarif*, esp. pp. 260–64. Also I.A. Kozikov, 'Proekt modernizatsii Rossii D.I. Mendeleeva', *Sotsial'no-gumanitarnye znaniia* 5 (2009): 235-55.

[87] M.F. Antonov, 'Mendeleev – Chlen Soiuza russkogo naroda', available at: http://www.hrono.ru/biograf/bio_m/mendeleev_di.php (accessed 18 April 2012). See also Antonov, 'Genii russkoi ekonomicheskoi mysli', *Molodaia gvardiia* 3 (2000): 5-44. In fact, there is no evidence that Mendeleev was a member of the extreme right-wing Union of the Russian People in 1905–6, see Belen'kii, *Mendeleev*, pp. 301–2.

[88] Antonov, 'Mendeleev – Chlen Soiuza russkogo naroda'.

his interest in international relations have qualified him as an early geopolitical thinker.[89] 'One forms the impression', writes another commentator, 'that someone from the modern pseudo-Russian [*rossiianskikh*] democrats has carefully read [Mendeleev's work] in order to do everything the other way around'.[90]

This widespread promotion of Mendeleev's political and economic ideas, and his image as a 'national prophet', have shaped popular attitudes. In the Russian government's 2008 competition to identify the greatest Russians in history, a panel of expert judges, including senior church, political, cultural, and academic leaders, ranked him fourth, and in the public poll he garnered over 300,000 votes, placing him ninth, above Ivan the Terrible, Catherine the Great, and Alexander II.[91] To many in contemporary Russia, a country still struggling to formulate a coherent strategy of economic modernization, to balance state power with the interests of society, to integrate its vast and diverse territory, and to find its place in the world, Mendeleev's century-old vision of illiberal modernity seems still to offer a solution.

---

[89] E.S. Andreev, 'Osnovnye etapy razvitiia otechestvennoi geopoliticheskoi mysli', *Vlast'* 4 (2010): 146–7.

[90] Vladimir Boiarintsev, *Evreiskie i Russkie uchenye. Mify i real'nost'* (Moscow, 2001), p. 146.

[91] 'Imia Rossii. Istoricheskii Vybor 2008'. In the panel's ranking, Mendeleev was beaten by Aleksandrs Nevskii and Pushkin (joint first), Suvorov and Stolypin. Even if the Russian authorities manipulated the popular vote to ensure that Stalin did not win (he came third after Nevskii and Stolypin), this probably did not greatly affect Mendeleev's ninth rank: http://www.nameofrussia.ru (accessed 18 April 2012).

CHAPTER 5

Regionalization, Imperial Legacy, and the Soviet Geographical Tradition

Marina Loskutova

The collapse of the Soviet Union brought about a major paradigm change in Western scholarship concerned with Russian and Soviet history, as it dramatically highlighted the role of non-Russian ethnic groups within the Soviet state and the Russian Empire. For the last 20 years historians have been engaged in a lively debate about Soviet national policies and the interplay of national/imperial identities under Soviet rule. Much less attention, however, has been given to the spatial dimension in the making of the Soviet state. The Soviet administrative-territorial framework, as it emerged in the 1920s, was a compromise between the so-called economic and national, or ethnographic, models of spatial organization. Both visions were backed by competing expert communities that helped the regime in formulating its distinctive approach to territorial reorganization. One of these groups, the community of ethnographers and anthropologists, has recently become an object of close scrutiny by historians,[1] while we still poorly understand the academic tradition that was a principal source of expertise for the rival mode of administrative-territorial rearrangement—the Russian geographical tradition.

One of the most conspicuous features of the Soviet geographical tradition was its binary structure—a sharply drawn division into two uneven parts, physical geography and economic geography, with a striking omission of political and cultural geography. This peculiarity of Soviet geographical research in its heyday was evident for Western observers who believed it was one of the major obstacles for its reception in the West.[2] Soviet geographers, for their part, were

---

[1] Francine Hirsch, *Empire of Nations: Ethnographic Knowledge and the Making of the Soviet Union* (Ithaca, NY, 2005).

[2] David Hooson, "Some Recent Developments in the Content and Theory of Soviet Geography," *Annals of the Association of American Geographers* 49 (1959): 73–82; R.A. French, "Geography and Geographers in the Soviet Union," *The Geographical Journal* 127/2 (1961): 159–65.

also sometimes uneasy about the internal split of their field, and occasionally tried to bridge the gap between the "two geographies."[3] Yet, the rift endured even after the collapse of the Soviet Union and is still visible today in the institutional infrastructure of geographical research. Most Western observers assumed it was the trait acquired by Russian geography in the Soviet period, or more precisely, in the late 1920s–early 1930s. Its causes have been commonly identified with the impact of the orthodox Marxist–Leninist ideology and the Stalinist "revolution from above." While the former insisted on a rigid dichotomy between physical and social phenomena governed by different laws, the Stalinist industrialization harnessed geography to immediate, applied tasks, thus reinforcing centrifugal tendencies within the geographical profession. Physical geographers were engaged in exploration of natural resources, and therefore gravitated toward geology and geophysics, while economic geographers were preoccupied with economic planning and the location of new industries—a mission that prompted their closer association with economists. Finally, the mass purges of the late 1920s–30s might also have been a factor that contributed to a disproportionate growth of physical geography in the Soviet Union, since the latter field was probably seen as a safer option, less exposed to ideological campaigns and controversies.[4]

Another significant trait of the Soviet geographical approach that was duly noted by foreign commentators was its unremitting interest in regionalization—the task of identifying, mapping and describing regional variations within the country's territory, in terms of its nature and economy.[5] Unlike the former characteristic, the latter feature has usually been viewed favourably by Western scientists, some of whom even call for an integration of the Soviet approach to regions and landscapes to the body of anglophone research in this area.[6] The origins of this peculiar focus on regions and regional divisions are not clear for both Russian and foreign observers. Remarkably, they are rarely attributed to the Soviet era: Most observers emphasize a strong pre-revolutionary tradition of regional studies in Russian geography dating back to the eighteenth century.

---

[3] David Hooson, "Methodological Clashes in Moscow, 1962," *Annals of the Association of American Geographers* 52 (1962): 469–75. Nikolai N. Baranskii, *Moya zhizn' v ekonomgeografii* (Moscow, 2001).

[4] Hooson, "Some Recent Developments," pp. 73–82; Denis J.B. Shaw and Jonathan D. Oldfield, "Landscape Science: A Russian Geographical Tradition," *Annals of the Association of American Geographers* 97/1 (2007): 111–26.

[5] Hooson, "Some Recent Developments"; David Hooson, "The Development of Geography in Pre-Soviet Russia," *Annals of Association of American Geographers* 58/2 (1968): 250–72; Shaw and Oldfield, "Landscape Science."

[6] Shaw and Oldfield, "Landscape Science."

The purpose of this chapter is to re-examine the provenance of these two elements in the Soviet geography. While its peculiar focus on regional divisions may in fact be a feature of a few other traditions of geographical research, it is still important to explore its origins, linked, as I will argue, to its imperial legacy. In particular, I will concentrate on the role of particular sites, particular local settings where two distinctively spatial approaches to imperial diversity were, arguably, first articulated in Russia. As historians of science have increasingly demonstrated over recent years, scientific enterprise is always embedded in local environments that shape the production, transmission, and reception of knowledge.[7] By concentrating on those places that served as meeting grounds for certain groups of specialists, provided forums for their debates and oriented scholars toward particular types of research, while effectively excluding other voices from discussion, I hope to contribute to a growing corpus of research on the "geographies of scientific knowledge."

Although some Russian eighteenth-century explorers are occasionally credited with a particular interest in regional geography and regionalization, it is an early nineteenth-century statistician Konstantin Arsen'ev (1789–1865) who is conventionally portrayed as the man who laid the foundations for regionalization as a scientific enterprise.[8] Indeed, in his *Brief General Geography* (1818–19) Arsen'ev did partition the European part of the Russian Empire into ten regions or "spaces" [*prostranstva*] in order to stress the diversity of their climate, soils, and vegetation. Arsen'ev's approach evidently impressed his contemporaries with its boldness: The statistician dared to ignore established administrative divisions and "usurped the right to partition lands"—the right that his opponents reserved exclusively to the state.[9] After publication, the book provoked harsh criticism in the press; nevertheless, it soon became one of the most popular geography textbooks in Russia and in the next few decades those authors who wished to contribute to a rapidly growing body of popular reading, and to school manuals on geography, felt obliged to provide some scheme of regional divisions within the empire.[10]

---

[7] David N. Livingstone, *Putting Science in Its Place: Geographies of Scientific Knowledge* (Chicago, 2003); Diarmid A. Finnegan, "The Spatial Turn: Geographical Approaches, in the History of Science," *Journal of the History of Biology* 41 (2008): 369–88.

[8] Evgenii N. Pertsik, *K.I. Arsen'ev i ego raboty po raionirovaniyu Rossii* (Moscow, 1960); Nikolai P. Nikitin, "Dorevolyutsionnaya ekonomicheskaya geografiya", in Nikolai N. Baranskii (ed.), *Ekonomicheskaya geografiya v SSSR. Istoriya i sovremennoe razvitie* (Moscow, 1965), pp. 9–53; Nailya Tagirova, "Mapping the Empire's Economic Regions from the Nineteenth to the Early Twentieth Century," in Jane Burbank, Mark von Hagen, and Anatoliy Remnev (eds.), *Russian Empire: Space, People, Power, 1700–1930* (Bloomington, IN, 2007), pp. 125–38.

[9] Cited in Pertsik, *K.I. Arsen'ev*, p. 37.

[10] Pertsik, *K.I. Arsen'ev*, pp. 35–9.

Two important clarifications must be made at this point, however. Arsen'ev's conservative opponents were certainly correct in emphasizing the arbitrary character of his regionalizing enterprise. While he claimed that his (or any other) scheme had to be based on natural factors, it was only a programmatic statement, and neither in Arsen'ev's early works, nor later, would a reader find explanations as to why he drew the boundaries between the regions the way he did. In fact, in 1848, in the *Statistical Outline of Russia* he substantially revised his approach and offered a different vision, which probably reflected changing patterns of settlement, migration flows, and economic development.[11] This time he also extensively discussed the distinctive character of his "spaces." His reasoning was evidently affected by history and the ethno-cultural identities of the population, since he always distinguished between "the Baltic space," "the Carpathian space," "the low space" on the western fringes of the empire, the historic core of the country (composed of several "spaces"), "the Ural space," and "the steppe space" to the east, even if he preferred to dwell on their nature and the population's employment. Yet crucially, even his mid-nineteenth-century scheme lacked precise procedures or criteria that would justify his divisions.

Arsen'ev's career developed mainly within the czarist civil service, where for a long time (1835–53) he administered the statistical division at the Ministry of the Interior. His understanding of imperial diversity and regional distinctions within the empire must have been influenced by a rapidly expanding collection of statistical data that had been accumulated by the ministry from the 1830s. Significantly, the next milestone in the tradition of regionalizing schemes was laid by a man who in some ways inherited Arsen'ev's position both in the Ministry of Interior and the Russian Geographical Society (RGS). Petr Semenov-Tian-Shanskii (1827–1914), a famous explorer of Central Asia, for many years served as a vice-president of the RGS and at the same time chaired the Central Statistical Committee (CSC) at the Ministry of the Interior (1864–97). In this way, he effectively presided over Russian statistics, as a branch of the czarist civil service. His position at the ministry and the RGS gave him sufficient authority and credibility to "partition" the empire into a number of regions in order to process a growing mass of local statistical data and to mediate between them and the empire as a whole. His first move was to reject major administrative divisions as the matrix for the arrangement of statistical data: Their arbitrary, "unnatural" character made them useless for analytical purposes. In his early map of regional divisions that Semenov proposed in 1871 in the *Statistical Chronicle of the Russian Empire*[12] he disregarded borders between provinces [*guberniya*],

---

[11] Konstantin I. Arsen'ev, *Statisticheskie ocherki Rossii* (St. Petersburg, 1848).
[12] *Statisticheskii vremennik Rossiiskoi imperii* 2/1 (1871).

and opted instead for smaller administrative units [*uyezd*], as the basic elements of his scheme. Later, however, pragmatic considerations evidently forced him to return to a more conventional scheme. A new version of his scheme, presented in the *Statistics of Landed Property*,[13] was based on provinces and their borders. The scheme proved to be very influential among the upper echelons of the Russian civil service: Its other branches, such as the Ministry of State Domains, the Ministry of Trade and Manufacturing, and the Ministry of Finance, adopted it as the basis for accumulation of their own statistical data.

It can be argued that for Semenov his scheme of regional divisions was something more than a convenient device for handling vast amount of local data; it provided him with a matrix for understanding and representing the diversity of the Russian Empire, its nature, culture, and history. In 1881–1901, under the aegis of the RGS, Semenov compiled, edited, and published a luxurious multivolume book series, the *Picturesque Russia*.[14] Its aim was to provide a general reader with a detailed description of the whole country, and Semenov's map of regional divisions was used as the organizing principle: Each of its 12 volumes was devoted to a particular region, its history, monuments, and places of interest, its customs and habits. To achieve his goal, Semenov assembled a big team of prominent journalists, historians, ethnographers, and explorers. Most of them, however, were more interested in local places and their occupants, than in considering larger spatial units, or regions.

This was particularly the case with those authors who wrote about the historic core of the empire populated mostly by ethnic Russians. On the other hand, the volumes on the western or southern borderlands had a potential for representing these territories, respectively, as a national or a colonial space. It was only Semenov who tried to understand and represent these territories as regions with their own distinctive identities; in essays written for the series he sought to demonstrate the unity of their constitutive elements, visible to a perceptive observer, to establish causal connections among their landscapes, history, the patterns of human settlement and housing. In this way, he certainly made a major contribution to the regionalizing tradition in Russian geography, and this was duly acknowledged by subsequent generations of scholars. Yet he was given credit for his scheme of regional divisions, and not for his analytical regional descriptions. In the 1880s regionalizing enterprise was still a matter of personal interest for Semenov; other

---

[13] *Statistika pozemel'noi sobstvennosti i naselennykh mest Evropeyskoi Rossii* (St. Petersburg, 1880–85).

[14] Pyotr P. Semenov (ed.), *Zhivopisnaya Rossiya: Otechestvo nashe v ego zemel'nom, istoricheskom, plemennom, ekonomicheskom i bytovom znachenii* (12 vols., St. Petersburg; Moscow, 1881–1901).

contributors to his series, however, seemed unreceptive to his concept of a region as a holistic entity, an intermediate space between a locality and the empire.

Things dramatically changed, however, in the 1890s, and the change first took place in an institutional milieu different from the CSC and the RGS. In 1896 a statistician, Aleksei Fortunatov (1856–1925), published in the *Transactions of the Free Economic Society* his paper "On the Question of Agricultural Regions in Russia."[15] It was the first paper in which the regionalization enterprise, or the task of identifying regions within the empire, was posed as a research problem.

Fortunatov's paper showed his remarkable familiarity with natural sciences, particularly with the advances made by Russian scholars in botany, soil science, and climatology in the two preceding decades. Before him, Arsen'ev could only argue for the importance of climate and soil for regionalization, but he could not substantiate his position, as he had no reliable information on their spatial variability. Both fields remained virtually unexplored in his time. Semenov, apparently, was more concerned with other factors and did not closely follow research in these areas, most likely because these studies had been carried out by people with little or no connection to the institutions where he was in command, the RGS and the CSC. Unlike these statisticians before him, Fortunatov explicitly called on his colleagues to take into account the data produced by a group of naturalists associated primarily with the St. Petersburg University and led by Vasilii Dokuchaev (1846–1903)—an eminent Russian soil scientist and one of the founders of pedology on a world scale.

Fortunatov's article opened up a stream of publications that addressed the regionalization problem. These papers were written by two distinctive groups of scholars: by Dokuchaev's colleagues and students, who identified themselves with botany, soil science, and meteorology, and by a new generation of statisticians, most of whom, like Fortunatov, had experience of working for local elected authorities, the *zemstva*. Despite their different academic backgrounds, the naturalists and statisticians proved to be equally interested in debating the regional distinctions of the country and they actively exchanged their visions. The statisticians, in particular, were receptive to ideas that were advanced by the naturalists.

The Soviet geographical tradition, at least from the late 1940s, always emphasized its debt to Vasilii Dokuchaev—an eminent Russian soil scientist

---

[15] Aleksei Fortunatov, "K voprosu o sel'skokhozyaistvennykh raionakh v Rossii," *Trudy Imperatorskogo Vol'nogo Ekonomicheskogo Obshchestva* 5 (1896): 1–12, 2nd pagination; on Fortunatov, see Nikolai P. Nikitin, "A.F. Fortunatov," in Baranskii, *Ekonomicheskaya geografiya v SSSR*, pp. 405–10.

and one of the founders of this discipline. Soviet physical geographers, in particular, referred to his works as the source of their interest in regions and regionalization; while in economic geography he was mentioned only in passing, as a figure who "greatly influenced" Fortunatov and other "founding fathers" of the discipline, yet the nature of this influence remained unspecified. More recently, however, the role of Dokuchaev in the making of the Soviet tradition in physical geography has been questioned.[16] Soviet physical geographers began to quote him much later than their key concepts had been first articulated in the 1910s–20s. Dokuchaev's influence, as the argument goes, was a kind of "invented tradition" that crystalized in the late 1940s. In those gloomy years of the struggle against "cosmopolitanism," his figure provided an impeccable Russian pedigree for a discipline that otherwise would have been tarred by its close association with the German geographical tradition, at least in its early days.

It seems, however, that the recent revisionist perspective has exceeded its plausible limits. The influence of some of Dokuchaev's ideas on leading Soviet physical geographers has already been reasserted elsewhere.[17] Here I would like to shift the stress and emphasize not so much the influence of Dokuchaev and his ideas as the impact of the encounter between two groups of professionals, and the role of the milieu in which the debates took place. As I will argue, it was the debates at the FES between the statisticians and naturalists when regionalization first emerged as the key problem that shaped not only Soviet physical geography but a number of related disciplines. At the same time, it was these debates that prefigured a binary structure of the Russian geographical tradition to the detriment of cultural and political geography.

Cadastral Surveys

It is well known that Dokuchaev first articulated his pioneering approach to soils in the 1880s—the decade when he was actively engaged in fieldwork, in the Nizhnii Novgorod (1882–86) and then the Poltava (1888–90) provinces. In the course of these projects Dokuchaev formulated his concept of soils as a natural phenomenon in its own right (and not a mere derivative of a geological formation) formed by a unique combination of climate, vegetation, relief, and time. For our purposes, it is important to stress that Dokuchaev considered soil as a key component linking organic and inorganic nature in such a way that

---

[16] Nikolai M. Dronin, *Evolyutsiya landshaftnoi kontseptsii v russkoi i sovetskoi fizicheskoi geografii (1900-e–1950-e gg.)* (Moscow, 1999).

[17] Shaw and Oldfield, "Landscape Science."

no component can be properly understood in isolation from others. His vision suggested, among other things, that a scientist could expect strong correlations between these factors. The concept prompted Dokuchaev (a geologist by training) to develop close ties with specialists in related fields, particularly with botanists from the St. Petersburg University who proved to be very receptive to his ideas. Dokuchaev's expeditions of the 1880s were not solitary trips: They were team projects carried out by students and junior faculty members of the St. Petersburg University under Dokuchaev's supervision.[18] While Dokuchaev and his students from the chair of geology were interested in identifying and analyzing soil types, a group of young botanists tried to explore potential links between vegetation and soils. All these studies had a strong spatial dimension: Dokuchaev and his associates were looking not just for soil types but for zones or regions with distinctive ensemble of constitutive elements—soils, climate, underlying geological formations, relief, and vegetation.

To a certain extent their approach was influenced by the very pragmatic objectives of these two expeditions that were funded by local authorities (the *zemstva*). Dokuchaev and his team were hired to carry out a cadastral survey; they were expected to assess the value of land in these provinces and to work out guidelines for levying taxes on land. Therefore from the start, the scientists were expected not only to establish soil typology (which could be further translated into a tax scale) but to identify these types on the ground and map them.

However, the task of working out the scientific basis for assessing the value of land in these two provinces proved to be much more difficult than Dokuchaev initially assumed. Two cadastral expeditions yielded an extraordinarily rich analysis of soils and vegetation, yet the data produced by Dokuchaev and his team could not be easily translated into explicit guidelines on levying the land tax. When Dokuchaev completed his survey in the Nizhnii Novgorod province, local *zemstva* had to hire a different group of experts, the statisticians, led by Nikolai Annenskii (1843–1912), who spent another four years to do the required job (1887–90).

The role of *zemstvo* cadastral surveys in the making of a new professional group—the *zemstvo* statisticians, different in their background, value system, and ideology from the personnel of the CSC and other branches of the czarist

---

[18] Catherine Evtuhov, "The Roots of Dokuchaev's Scientific Contributions: Cadastral Soil Mapping and Agro-Environmental Issues," in Benno P. Warkentin (ed.), *Footprints in the Soil* (Amsterdam and Oxford, 2006), pp. 125–48; Anastasiya A. Fedotova, "Botaniki v Nizhegorodskoi ekspeditsii V.V. Dokuchaeva: 'starye' territorii, novye zadachi," *Istoriko-biologicheskie issledovaniya / Studies in the History of Biology* 2/4 (2010): 66–83.

administration, has already been analyzed elsewhere.[19] For our purpose it is important to recapitulate that, by the 1890s, their experience of cadastral surveys, as well as their ideological commitments prompted this group of professionals to emphasize the importance of local social factors in measuring and assessing land values. When *zemstvo* statisticians began to see a peculiar logic of peasant subsistent economy, as distinct from profit-oriented market production, they increasingly stressed the gap not only between an average market price of land (or an average income the land generated) and its "real" value but also between the latter and the quality of soil. As they argued, the real value of land could be established only when actual practices of land utilization were taken into account. While asserting their position on land assessment, *zemstvo* statisticians opposed not only various branches of the czarist administration, they had to challenge the authority of Dokuchaev and his team of naturalists. Both groups of specialists frequented the same place—the Free Economic Society (FES) in St. Petersburg, the oldest learned society in Russia. The FES first provided them with an institutional home (soil scientists established their commission within the society in 1888, while statisticians formed their commission in 1894), and very soon it also became a principal forum for their debates, waged both at its sessions and on the pages of its *Transactions*.

In 1893–94 the issue of *zemstvo* cadastral surveys, their underlying conceptual assumptions, methodology, and practical arrangements, came to the foreground, as the Russian government introduced a new tax statute of June 8, 1893, while a year later the Ministry of Finance supplemented it with more detailed guidelines on *zemstvo* taxation (June 4, 1894).[20] The new legislation was meant to streamline local taxation, which since the reform of 1864 had been delegated to *zemstva*. The 1864 legislative framework for *zemstvo* institutions left many important questions relevant for local taxation to the discretion of local authorities. Among other things, it empowered *zemstva* to carry out cadastral surveys but it did not prescribe tax rates or methods of assessing land. As a result, in the 1870s–80s *zemstvo* taxes varied greatly even within a

---

[19] Alessandro Stanziani, "Statisticiens, *zemstva* et état dans la Russie des années 1880," *Cahiers du monde russe et soviétique* 32/4 (1991): 445–67; Martine Mespoulet, "Statisticiens des *zemstva*: Formation d'une nouvelle profession intellectuelle en Russie dans la période prérévolutionnaire (1880–1917). Le cas de Saratov," *Cahiers du monde russe* 40/4 (1999): 573–624; Martine Mespoulet, "Une lutte pour l'autonomie professionnelle: être statisticien dans une région au début des années 1920," *Le Mouvement social* 196 (2001): 63–88; David W. Darrow, "The Politics of Numbers: Zemstvo Land Assessment and the Conceptualization of Russia's Rural Economy," *Russian Review* 59/1 (2000): 52–75.

[20] For details, see Darrow, "The Politics of Numbers."

province, while the methods of assessing land were even more dissimilar. Most *zemstva* were slow in conducting cadastral surveys; they either taxed land at a flat rate or adopted the redemption payments (part of the 1861 abolition of serfdom) as the basis for assessing land value. The 1893–94 legislation was meant to bring some order into a chaotic state of local taxation and to speed up the making of cadastral surveys by making them an obligatory part of local land tax assessment.

The emerging professional group of *zemstvo* statisticians met the new tax statute with considerable enthusiasm, as it seemed to secure its institutional basis: from now on all *zemstva* needed statistical data for tax assessment—in other words, they needed professionals to compile them. The FES, which had already acted as an informal coordinating and advisory board for local authorities of a liberal leaning, seized an opportunity to enhance its own position and announced its intention to work out technical guidelines on *zemstvo* cadastral surveys. Yet the very first discussion of the issue at the FES demonstrated: *zemstvo* statisticians were not the only group that claimed to be the experts in this field.

By 1893 a group of naturalists around Dokuchaev had accumulated substantial experience in this field. Moreover, a devastating drought and resulting famine in 1892 had already brought them to the foreground of public and governmental attention, as leading experts on environmental factors in agricultural production. Dokuchaev and his fellow naturalists shared with *zemstvo* statisticians their sense of civic duty, their commitment to work out a rational, more equitable system of taxation at a local level.

Both groups evidently considered *zemstvo* cadastral surveys as a means to achieve larger social and academic goals. The statisticians hoped to understand the internal operation and logic of peasant society, its "natural economy" (presumably matching local environment); the naturalists aspired to work out a "natural," scientific classification of soils and vegetation that would contribute to agricultural improvement by suggesting optimal selection of crops, their rotation, the timing of planting and harvesting, and so on. In other words, they assumed that agricultural, or economic, regions either already coincided or would eventually coincide with natural zones or regions. In fact, some of Dokuchaev's students believed they could demonstrate homology between the two phenomena.

Nikolai Sibirtsev (1860–1900) was the only member of the Nizhnii Novgorod expedition who remained in the province when Dokuchaev announced the completion of his project. For several years he was employed by the local *zemstvo* board: He assisted Annenskii and other statisticians in carrying out the economic survey of the province, acted as a curator at a local natural history museum, which had been founded in the course of the Dokuchaev expedition, and took an active part in organizing food relief during the famine of 1892. Sibirtsev's experience of working with *zemstvo* statisticians convinced him that "natural" regions, as identified by Dokuchaev and his team, coincided with patterns of economic exploitation of land and other natural resources, as uncovered by statistical research. He was confident that all economic variables, studied by Annenskii and his group, such as yields, types of corn, methods of land cultivation, were dependent on soils.[21]

The statisticians, on their part, did not dispute the assumption about a strong correlation between natural phenomena and economic variables. However, they had important reservations: The "natural economy" of the peasants was not a mere function of environmental factors; it was the key issue to be explored in order to advance agriculture and ensure social equity. The statisticians were alarmed by Dokuchaev's expansionism and his insistence on the primacy of the naturalists' methods in cadastral surveys. In Dokuchaev's opinion, cadastral surveys were to be carried out in two stages: At the first one a province was to be explored by naturalists (botanists and soil scientists), invited for the purpose from a nearby university; at the second stage the task of economic survey could be left to statisticians who would bring some local knowledge into the picture.[22] For naturalists, the second stage was clearly subordinate and rather trivial, as compared to the first one.[23]

The statisticians immediately sensed that Dokuchaev and his colleagues were undermining their own professional status. Statistics was a science with its own methods of research that required special training. While they did not question the credibility or practical relevance of soil science for agriculture, they challenged the feasibility of Dokuchaev's recommendations on cadastral surveys. His two-stage method was extremely expensive and therefore hardly affordable for most *zemstva*, while his soil types and maps of natural regions were not automatically

---

[21] Nikolai M. Sibirtsev, "O trekhverstnoi pochvennoi karte," *Trudy Imperatorskogo Vol'nogo Ekonomicheskogo Obshchestva* 2/5 (1893): 125–35.

[22] Vasilii V. Dokuchaev, *K voprosu o pereotsenke zemel' Evropeiskoi i Aziatskoi Rossii, s klassifikatsiei pochv* (Moscow, 1898).

[23] "Soedinennye zasedaniya Pochvennoi i Statisticheskoi komissii 1–3 marta 1895 g.," *Trudy Imperatorskogo Vol'nogo Ekonomicheskogo Obshchestva* 5 (1895): 110–80; Vasilii E. Vazar, "Pochvennaya karta Chernigovskoi gubernii v svyazi s voprosom o statisticheskom issledovanii pochv," *Trudy Imperatorskogo Vol'nogo Ekonomicheskogo Obshchestva* 1/2 (1895): 143–51; A.N. Kotel'nikov, "K voprosu ob organizatsii statistiki naseleniya v Rossii," *Trudy Imperatorskogo Vol'nogo Ekonomicheskogo Obshchestva* 2/5 (1895): 135–8; Dmitrii I. Rikhter, "Zamechaniya na pochvenno-otsenochnyi proekt V.V. Dokuchaeva," *Trudy Imperatorskogo Vol'nogo Ekonomicheskogo Obshchestva* 1/1 (1898): 42–59 2nd pagination.

convertible into a tax scale. On the other hand, some statisticians believed that the application of statistical methods of inquiry (questionnaires and interviews with local residents) could ultimately yield reliable soil maps as well.[24]

Essentially, both groups defended their own professional expertise, while questioning the credibility or practicability of methods advocated by their opponents. Yet, despite a bitter controversy over cadastral surveys, the encounter between the two groups stimulated an exchange of ideas. In 1894–95 the Soil and Statistical Commissions held a series of joint meetings at the FES, debating the merits and disadvantages of their approaches.

Dokuchaev was absent at most of these meetings, as in 1892 he accepted the directorship at the New Alexandria Institute of Agriculture and Forestry in Russian Poland (in Pulawy near Lublin) where he established the first chair in soil science in the Russian Empire. As the head of a new school he had an opportunity to offer faculty positions to his students and associates. Thus, he hired Sibirtsev, who had not been happy with his *zemstvo*-funded job in Nizhnii Novgorod, and was keen to move to a place where he could resume his research on soils. Dokuchaev also offered the chair of statistics at his institute to Aleksei Fortunatov, who had just lost his job in Moscow, with the closure of the Petrovskaya Agricultural Academy—an important center of statistical research in the 1870s–80s that provided trained cadres for *zemstvos*. Fortunatov moved to New Alexandria, where he worked till 1899. Thus, in the 1890s the New Alexandria Institute emerged as another important center, apart from the FES in St. Petersburg, that brought together naturalists of the Dokuchaev school and *zemstvo* statisticians.

In his 1896 paper Fortunatov raised the debates between the two professional communities onto a new plane by shifting attention from cadastral surveys and their methods to a research agenda. For both groups of scholars, cadastral surveys offered more than funding opportunities; they reframed their vision by prompting naturalists, as well as statisticians, to focus on spatial distribution of phenomena. Now Fortunatov explicitly called both communities to identify agricultural regions in the empire based on a combination of natural and social factors. Within the next few years both communities came up with their response.

An Encounter between Naturalists and Statisticians in the 1890s

Already in 1896 a botanist, Gavriil Tanfil'ev (1857–1928)—a former member of the Dokuchaev's research team who was by that time employed by the Ministry of Agriculture and who also acted as the secretary of the FES Soil Commission—

---

[24] Vazar, "Pochvennaya karta."

presented at the FES meeting his own contribution, the *Physical-Geographic Regions of the European Russia*.[25] Two years later Dmitrii Rikhter (1848–1919)—the man who in 1894 had established the Statistical Commission of the FES, served as its secretary, and would later act as a secretary of the FES—presented a paper, "An Experiment in Partitioning European Russia into Regions on the Basis of Their Natural and Economic Traits."[26] Later, in 1903, at a FES meeting a former *zemstvo* statistician from the Poltava province, Nikolai Kulyabka-Koretskii (1846–1931), who in 1897–1900 also served as the FES secretary, read a paper on "Grain Producing Regions of the European Russia and Western Siberia."[27]

In his 1896 paper Fortunatov did not only pose the problem of regionalization; he also sketched the history of attempts to identify regions within the Russian Empire that had been made from the early nineteenth century. Thus, he was the first to point to Arsen'ev and Petr Semenov-Tian-Shanskii as the pioneers in this field. Their studies, however, were of little interest for those naturalists who responded to Fortunatov. In his work Tanfil'ev referred to the mid-nineteenth-century botanists Trautfetter and Beketov (his mentor at the St. Petersburg University), whose data on plant geography he used in order to work out his own scheme of regional divisions. Trautfetter and Beketov, however, were interested in classic botanical geography: They mapped frontiers beyond which certain species of plants could not be found in nature. Unlike them Tanfil'ev was interested not so much in the distribution area of a particular species—he studied vegetation and plant communities, as determined by their environment, or more precisely by soils.[28] The assumption about a strong correlation between soils and vegetation shaped the direction of botanical research that was carried out in the course of the Dokuchaev's expeditions to Nizhnii Novgorod and Poltava. Pragmatically, botanists hoped that, when the correlations were uncovered, vegetation could be used as a good indicator of underlying soil types (and thus the costs of surveying would be more affordable). Conceptually, however, the same assumption could be easily extended to encompass not only natural but also

---

[25] Gavriil I. Tanfil'ev, "Fiziko-geograficheskie oblasti Evropeiskoi Rossii," *Trudy Imperatorskogo Vol'nogo Ekonomicheskogo Obshchestva* 1 (1897): 1–30 2nd pagination.

[26] Dmitrii I. Rikhter, "Opyt razdeleniya Evropeiskoi Rossii na raiony po estestvennym i ekonomicheskim priznakam," *Trudy Imperatorskogo Vol'nogo Ekonomicheskogo Obshchestva* 4 (1898): 46–91 2nd pagination. On Rikhter, see Gavriil D. Rikhter, "D.I. Rikhter," in Baranskii, *Ekonomicheskaya geografiya v SSSR*. pp. 411–18.

[27] Nikolai G. Kulyabka-Koretskii, "Raiony khlebnoi proizvoditel'nosti Evropeiskoi Rossii i Zapadnoi Sibiri," *Trudy Imperatorskogo Vol'nogo Ekonomicheskogo Obshchestva* 4–5 (1903): 40–84.

[28] Fedotova, "Botaniki v Nizhegorodskoi ekspeditsii."

social and economic factors: Domestic plants, and crops in particular, followed the same patterns as wild ones, while agricultural practices were determined by dominant crops. Therefore, in his 1897 paper, Tanfil'ev explicitly tried to demonstrate that distinctive patterns of agricultural production in the empire (or its European part) were fairly compatible with his "natural regions"; he also expected that further research in both fields, statistics and natural history, would eventually not only clarify his scheme of regional divisions but also make the two types of regions even better adjusted to each other.

However, for any unbiased reader his own map seemed radically different from those that had been proposed by statisticians. For Tanfil'ev, as for any Russian nineteenth-century naturalist, the major line of division was between the north and the south, the steppe and the forest. This way of "reading" the imperial space originated, probably, in Anton Friedrich Büsching's Neue Erdbeschreibung (1754; Russian translation 1766),[29] which for the first time suggested a threefold latitudinal division of the empire. Büsching's scheme was adopted by many Russian geographic textbooks of the early nineteenth century, as well as by some governmental agencies, particularly those that were concerned with agriculture, such as the Ministry of State Domains. Tanfil'ev elaborated and refined this approach: He identified three distinctive subzones, or "belts," in the north, two belts in the south, plus he singled out the Aral–Caspian Desert and the southern coast of the Crimean peninsula, as independent zones of the same order as the forest and the steppe zones. Longitudinal divisions were much less pronounced on his map, while they had been clearly legible on the maps produced by the statistical tradition. Subsequently, Tanfil'ev refined his map in his Main Traits of Russian Vegetation (1903),[30] yet his basic preconceptions remained unaltered there.

Dmitrii Rikhter immediately seized an opportunity opened by Tanfil'ev's paper and attempted to integrate his scheme into his own research. Although he paid a lip-service to climate and ethnicity, his own model was based on four factors: 1) soils (or rather soils and vegetation, as explicated by Tanfil'ev); 2) patterns of land use (here he distinguished between forest, pasture, arable land, and wasteland); 3) population density; and 4) industry versus agriculture as the primary occupation. His choice of variables was obviously dictated by the logic of cadastral surveys, although he never explicitly acknowledged the influence of their agenda on his reasoning. Tanfil'ev had already hinted a likely causal link between soils and dominant types of crops produced in a particular region or zone. Rikhter picked up the thread and explored further connections

[29] Nikitin, "Dorevolyutsionnaya ekonomicheskaya geografiya."
[30] Gavriil I. Tanfil'ev, *Glavneishie cherty rastitel'nosti Rossii* (St. Petersburg, 1903).

between environment and economy. His scheme of regional divisions in many ways followed the conventional statistical approach that had been advanced by Semenov-Tian-Shanskii. The crucial difference was in not in his map but in its rationale: he explicitly excluded history, ethnicity or culture from consideration—a move that enabled him, among other things, to group the Volyn' province in Western Ukraine together with Lithuanian provinces.

Unlike Rikhter, Kulyabka-Koretskii narrowed down his focus of research by concentrating on dominant types of grain that he tried to relate to environmental factors, such as soils and wild vegetation. In this way, he constructed a slightly different map of economic regions. Yet, essentially, his contribution reinforced the tendency that had already been visible in the work of Fortunatov and Rikhter—to dispense with the human element in his understanding of the spatial diversity of the empire by focusing on land and its products.

Finally, in 1904 a group of St. Petersburg naturalists and statisticians published a Festschrift that celebrated the 50th anniversary of a prominent Russian agrostologist, Ivan Stebut. The major theme of the volume was regionalization. Three leading articles were written by Fortunatov,[31] Rikhter,[32] and a meteorologist, Petr Brounov (1853–1927),[33] while Tanfil'ev also contributed a paper on smaller regions that could be identified in the Black Sea coastal area of the Caucasus. Essentially, Rikhter and Fortunatov provided summaries of research that had already been done in this field by statisticians, botanists, and soil scientists. A really innovative piece of research was contributed by Brounov who had not previously taken part in the debates, presumably because in the early 1890s he was away from St. Petersburg.

Unlike Dokuchaev, Tanfil'ev or even Sibirtsev, Brounov has never been referred to by subsequent generations of Soviet physical geographers as a man who contributed to the advancement of their discipline, presumably because in the twentieth century a conceptual and institutional distance between meteorology and physical geography was much greater than between physical geography and plant geography. Yet in the early 1900s he was the only geography professor who was involved in the regionalization debates. Like Dokuchaev,

---

[31] Aleksei F. Fortunatov, "K geografii preobladayushchikh yarovykh posevov," *Sovremennye voprosy russkogo sel'skogo khozyaistva* (St. Petersburg, 1904), pp. 3–19 2nd pagination.

[32] Dmitrii I. Rikhter, "Popytki razdeleniya Rossii na raiony po estestvennoistoricheskim i ekonomicheskim priznakam," *Sovremennye voprosy russkogo sel'skogo khozyaistva* (St. Petersburg, 1904), pp. 49–78 2nd pagination.

[33] Pyotr I. Brounov, "K voprosu o geograficheskikh raionakh Evropeiskoi Rossii," *Sovremennye voprosy russkogo sel'skogo khozyaistva* (St. Petersburg, 1904), pp. 23–45 2nd pagination.

Tanfil'ev and Sibirtsev, Brounov was a graduate of the St. Petersburg University. In 1882–87 he taught physical geography there, while later on, in the 1890s, he moved to Kiev, where he got a full professorship at the St. Vladimir University. In Kiev he also established a regional network of agricultural meteorological stations funded by local *zemstva*. In 1897 he returned to the capital to take up a position at the Ministry of Agriculture and State Domains: He was offered the chance to lead its Meteorological Bureau, which had just been established.[34]

Brounov certainly did not belong to the group of botanists and soil scientists around Dokuchaev, whose approach was shaped by the *zemstvo* cadastral surveys of the 1880s, yet from the early decades of the nineteenth century climate had always been considered an important factor for agriculture, plant geography, or local economy. From the 1840s the Ministry of State Domains— the leading governmental agency for agricultural research that also sponsored Dokuchaev's research on soils—had promoted meteorological observations and research on climate and its local variations. From the 1880s and particularly from the 1890s *zemstvo* boards stepped in and began to establish their own meteorological stations. Brounov's professional career reflected these trends and his contribution to the regionalization debate indicated that it had begun to expand beyond the initial circle of people who were in one way or in other involved in *zemstvo* cadastral surveys.

Brounov's intervention was important because he was the first professional meteorologist to step into the debate: Before him statisticians, botanists, and soil scientists often mentioned climate as a very important element in a postulated unity of environmental and economic factors, yet they failed to explore this matter in any detailed way. Brounov was the first scientist who attempted to establish correlations among weather maps produced by the Main Physical Observatory at St. Petersburg, Dokuchaev's soil maps, Tanfil'ev's vegetation maps, and maps of dominant grain crops, as they had been worked out by Fortunatov and Kulyabka-Koretskii. In this way, Brounov attempted to construct a truly synthetic map of regional variety that would encompass both environmental and economic variables.

A major feature of his own scheme was its cardinal north–south division that corresponded to the maximal atmospheric pressure: the line run through Kishinev, Khar'kov, Saratov, Ural'sk, and further eastward along the 50th parallel. Within the northern and the southern parts the scientist identified a few subzones, or belts, in a manner very similar to the scheme proposed by Tanfil'ev. Remarkably, in the south Brounov refused to see any significant

---

[34] For his biography, see Semyon A. Maksimov, *P.I. Brounov—osnovopolozhnik sel'skokhozyaistvennoi meteorologii* (Leningrad, 1952).

variations between the western and the eastern fringes of European Russia (i.e. between the Ukraine and Bessarabia, on one hand, and the Low Volga and the South Urals, on the other). He was more cautious with the northern part, where he acknowledged a certain distinctiveness of the region westward from the Riga meridian, with its milder "European" climate and vegetation. It is hard to judge if his own personal experience of living and working in Kiev made him particularly reluctant to accept any specificity of the Ukrainian provinces: In stressing the importance of latitudinal divisions he certainly followed Tanfil'ev, Sibirtsev, and other naturalists of the Dokuchaev's circle, yet compared to them he was much more assertive about the synthetic nature of his model, in which economy was a function of nature, not an independent variable.

Regionalization in the Early Decades of the Twentieth Century

Later on, in the early decades of the twentieth century, the problem of regionalization remained in the focus of statistical research. Significantly, the New Alexandria Institute remained an important center for this type of inquiry. Aleksandr Skvortsov (1848–1914), a statistician who taught at the New Alexandria Institute from the early 1880s, first offered his own vision in 1901 when he published a paper on "The Principles of Dividing Territory into Agricultural Regions," while his seminal book *The Economic Regions of European Russia* was published posthumously by the Ministry of Agriculture in 1914.[35] Essentially, Skvortsov elaborated the ideas that had been first advanced by Fortunatov, Rikhter, and Kulyabka-Koretskii. Like them, Skvortsov was interested in integrating the ever-expanding data supplied by the natural sciences with economic data. However, the range of economic variables remained limited in his research to those factors that had been singled out by Rikhter. Increasing sensitivity to local variations in geology, climate, soils, vegetation, population density, dominant types of land use, and so on, led the scholar to increase the number of regions he identified within the European part of the empire.

A younger generation of statisticians, however, began to question the assumptions that shaped the vision of Skvortsov, Rikhter, and Fortunatov. In 1911 a graduate of the New Alexandria Institute, Aleksandr Chelintsev, openly challenged his former mentors, when he presented his paper on economic regions at the twelfth congress of Russian naturalists and physicians in Moscow in December 1909 – January 1910, at the same meeting where Skvortsov presented his own paper on the problem. A year later Chelintsev published a

---

[35] Aleksandr I. Skvortsov, *Khozyaistvennye raiony Evropeiskoi Rossii* (St. Petersburg, 1914).

book on *Agricultural Regions of European Russia as the Stages of Agricultural Evolution*.[36] Economic factors that Chelintsev selected for his analysis remained essentially the same as those that had been identified by Fortunatov and Rikhter in the 1890s: population density, its proportion occupied in industry as opposed to agricultural employment, dominant crops, grain yields and grain prices, the distribution of space by types of land use, and so on. Chelintsev, however, insisted on the autonomy of agricultural practices from environmental conditions, and at this point his arguments were very similar to those that had been advanced by statisticians in the early 1890s, when they asserted their own methods of research against Dokuchaev and his team in the debates about the best way of conducting cadastral surveys. Yet, unlike them, the younger scholar was interested not only in spatial but also in a temporal dimension: In his model agricultural regions had a propensity for development; they evolved following the same economic laws from most primitive forms of land exploitation to the most advanced ones. Chelintsev's refusal to take into account environmental factors resulted in a scheme that bore a greater resemblance to the older regional maps, as they had been proposed by Semenov-Tian-Shanskii. The western frontiers of the empire with its distinctive political, cultural, and religious traditions retained their unity and particularity on the Chelintsev's map, even if these factors were never explicitly acknowledged by the economist.

At the same time, Tanfil'ev and Brounov continued working on the problem of regional divisions, as seen from the perspective of the natural sciences. It is important to stress that in this period they began to occupy two important positions in Russian universities directly related to the field of geography. In 1900 Brounov resumed his teaching at the St. Petersburg University where he was offered a full professorship at the chair of geography, anthropology, and ethnography, while in 1905 Tanfil'ev was appointed as the chair of geography at the Novorossiiskii University in Odessa. In Khar'kov the chair of geography was occupied by Andrei Krasnov (1862–1914)—another graduate of St. Petersburg University and a former student of Dokuchaev, who had taken part in his expeditions to the Nizhnii Novgorod and Poltava province. His own research on plant geography had also been informed by the agenda that he and his fellow botanists had earlier formulated in the course of the cadastral surveys of the 1880s.

However, the chair of geography, anthropology, and ethnography at the Moscow University was evidently not a part of this network. An undisputed leader of Moscow geographers, Professor Dmitrii Anuchin (1843–1923) had an amazing range of research interests, from zoology and limnology to ethnography

---

[36] Aleksandr N. Chelintsev, *Sel'skokhozyaistvennye raiony Evropeiskoi Rossii kak stadii sel'skokhozyaistvennoi evolyutsii i kul'turnyi uroven' sel'skogo khozyaistva v nikh* (St. Petersburg, 1911).

and archaeology, yet he was in no way related to agricultural research or *zemstvo* cadastral surveys.[37] Perhaps for this reason he had never contributed to soil science, meteorology, plant geography, or economic statistics. Some of his students, however, who were interested in physical geography, did follow the debates at the FES in St. Petersburg.[38] Later on, one of these students, Aleksandr Kruber (1871–1941) suggested his own scheme of regional divisions.[39] He elaborated and improved the regionalizing models that had been advanced by Brounov, Sibirtsev and Tanfil'ev, and even introduced new variables, such as geological formations and relief. However, his real innovation was in his theoretical framework. He directly linked regionalization with the very definition of geography, as an independent field of knowledge. In this way, his paper on natural regions of Russia became the manifesto of a new geography in Russia: a discipline that studied the spatial relations of elements on the Earth and in this way identified holistic units, or "landscapes."[40] Characteristically, despite his training under Anuchin, Kruber explicitly abstained from introducing human elements into his model: He excused himself on the grounds that the primitive state of the Russian economy did not leave room for any substantial human influence upon the environment. Most likely, however, Kruber's perspective was shaped by the state of research in this field: Unlike the statisticians affiliated with the FES and the New Alexandria Institute, the Moscow anthropologists had not been interested in exploring potential correlations between their data and the maps produced by the St. Petersburg soil scientists, meteorologists, or plant geographers.

After Kruber, two students of Anuchin, Aleksandr Borzov (1874–1939) and Lev Berg (1876–1950), recapitulated and substantiated his concept of geography as a discipline with the primary objective of the identification of natural regions,

---

[37] Vasilii A. Esakov, *Geografiya v Moskovskom universitete: Ocherki organizatsii, prepodavaniya, razvitiya geograficheskoi mysli (do 1917 g.)* (Moscow, 1983); Tatyana D. Solovei, "Institutsionalizatsiya nauki v Moskovskom universitete (Zhizn' i trudy D.N. Anuchina v kontekste epokhi)," *Vestnik Moskovskogo universiteta, seriya 8: istoriya* 6 (2003): 3–38; *Marina Mogil'ner, Homo imperii. Istoriya fizicheskoi antropologii v Rossii (konets XIX – nachalo XX v.)* (Moscow, 2008); Yurii G. Simonov, *Isoriya geografii v Moskovskom universitete: sobytiya i lyudi*, 2 vols.; vol. 1.: *Nachala universitetskoi geografii: Anuchinskii etap v ee razvitii, pervye geografy-professionaly v Moskovskom universitete* (Moscow, 2008)..

[38] Aleksandr Kruber, "Opyt razdeleniya Evropeiskoi Rossii na raiony," *Zemlevedenie* 3–4 (1898): 175–84.

[39] Aleksandr Kruber, "Fiziko-geograficheskie oblasti Evropeiskoi Rossii," *Zemlevedenie* 14/3–4 (1907): 163–220.

[40] Nataliya G. Sukhova, *Razvitie predstavlenii o prirodnom territorial'nom komplekse v russkoi geografii* (Leningrad, 1981); Dronin, *Evolyutsiya landshaftnoi kontseptsii.*

or "landscapes."[41] Their theoretical framework was certainly influenced by the German school of geography, and Alfred Hettner in particular. However, their understanding of regional variations in the Russian Empire was strongly informed by the works produced by the St. Petersburg naturalists. In other words, by 1914 we can distinguish only one center of geographical research where an alternative approach to regional variability in the empire was pursued. It was the RGS where Veniamin Semenov-Tian-Shanskii, a son of Petr Semenov-Tian-Shanskii, presented his own ideas that he also elaborated in a series of publications.[42] Semenov was in no way related to *zemstvo* cadastral surveys or the Ministry of Agriculture—he was employed by the CSC and then by the Ministry of Finance, while his academic pursuits gravitated toward human geography and political geography.[43] He was particularly interested in migration and colonization flows, and their dependency on physical geography, especially on geomorphology—all these problems were of little concern for the Dokuchaev school and for statisticians associated with the FES and provincial *zemstva*.

Regionalization and Soviet Geography

World War I and the 1917 Revolution dramatically altered the institutional landscape of science in the Russian Empire. Among other things, they destroyed or damaged established networks of scholars and drained financial and human resources available to universities, the Academy of Sciences, and especially to learned societies such as the FES and the RGS. At the same time, the war opened up new opportunities for collaboration between the government and those scientists who knew how to adjust their own research interests to the war effort.

In 1915, with the establishment of the Commission for the Study of the Natural Productive Forces of Russia (KEPS), funded by the War and Naval ministries and affiliated with the Academy of Sciences, Russian naturalists of the

---

[41] Lev S. Berg, "Opyt razdeleniya Sibiri i Turkestana na landshaftnye i morfologicheskie oblasti," *Sbornik v chest' 70–letiya D.N. Anuchina* (Moscow, 1913), pp. 117–51; for details, see Sukhova, *Razvitie predstavlenii* and Dronin, *Evolyutsiya landshaftnoi kontseptsii*.

[42] *Torgovlya i promyshlennost' Rossii po raionam: 1* (St. Petersburg, 1900); Veniamin P. Semenov-Tyan-Shanskii, *O mogushchestvennom territorial'nom vladenii primenitel'no k Rossii: ocherk po politicheskoi geografii* (St. Petersburg, 1915); Veniamin P. Semenov-Tyan-Shanskii, *Tipy mestnostei Evropeyskoi Rossii i Kavkaza: ocherk po fizicheskoi geografii v svyazi s antropogeografiei* (St. Petersburg, 1915).

[43] Pavel M. Polyan, *Veniamin Petrovich Semenov-Tyan-Shanskii, 1870–1949* (Moscow, 1989); Veniamin P. Semenov-Tyan-Shanskii, *To, chto proshlo* (2 vols., Moscow, 2009).

Dokuchaev school got a new institutional platform for research,[44] even if two leading Russian plant geographers, who had been most influential in the earlier decades, were not among their ranks. Tanfil'ev was in Odessa, while Krasnov died in December 1914 in Tiflis (Tbilisi). At the same time, Veniamin Semenov-Tian-Shanskii joined KEPS where he tried to promote his own research agenda: He was active at a Committee for the Description of Russia by Region, which was established within KEPS at least by 1919. Another member of the same committee was Lev Berg, a former student of Anuchin, who first moved to Petrograd in 1903, oscillated between Moscow and Petrograd in the war years and finally settled in Petrograd in 1917. A second major center of geographical research that emerged in Petrograd in 1916–17 was the Geographical Institute that was staffed by the same group of people who were active at the KEPS Committee for the Description of Russia by Region.[45]

Even before the end of the civil war, regionalization, of course, ceased to be a matter of a mere academic interest and became one of the top issues on the political agenda of the early Soviet state when it began to delimit its administrative borders. Geographers and specialists in other branches of natural sciences, who had been working at KEPS, did provide consultations to the VTsIK Administrative Commission and the Gosplan Regionalization Commission—the principal agencies of the Soviet government that advocated the concept of a federation organized exclusively along administrative-economic lines, as opposed to ethno-territorial units.[46] Certainly, the history of interaction between geographers and the Soviet planning agencies in the period of the regionalization debate needs further exploration. For the moment it is important to stress the Gosplan approach to administrative-territorial regionalization was steeped in the pre-revolutionary tradition of research, as it developed in the 1890s–1900s, prompted by *zemstvo* cadastral surveys.

Further on, in the 1930s–50s, two leading figures of Soviet geography, Aleksandr Grigor'ev and Lev Berg, made their personal contribution to research in this field. Berg has already been mentioned as the person who was instrumental for rearticulating the Dokuchaev school approach in such a way that it would become the language of the new geography as an academic discipline. Grigor'ev started his career in the KEPS Committee for the Description of Russia by Region. The third "great man" of the Soviet geography of the Stalinist period, Aleksandr

---

[44] Anatolii V. Kol'tsov, *Sozdanie i deyatel'nost' Komissii po izucheniyu estestvennykh proizvoditel'nykh sil Rossii* (St. Petersburg, 1999).

[45] Semenov-Tyan-Shanskii, *To, chto proshlo*.

[46] Konstantin D. Egorov (ed.), *Raionirovanie SSSR: Sbornik materialov po raionirovaniyu s 1917 po 1925 gg.* (Moscow and Leningrad, 1926); Petr M. Alampiev, *Ekonomicheskoe raionirovanie SSSR* (Moscow, 1959): Hirsch, *Empire of Nations*, pp. 70–87.

Baranskii, had no personal connection to the pre-revolutionary debates between naturalists and statisticians. Yet it was he who particularly encouraged historical research on Russian statistics of the eighteenth–nineteenth centuries: It would not be exaggeration to say that most key publications in this field appeared in the Soviet Union in the late 1940s–60s under his supervision.

It has recently been argued that the territorial continuity of continental empires had a profound implication for earth sciences, as they advanced in these countries: Internal divisions between the metropole and its colonies were far less explicit, and more ambiguous, in the Russian or Habsburg empires than in the British or French oceanic empires. Therefore, continental empires "had an imperative to map and continually remap the empires' internal boundaries, social and natural"—these were the sources of their regionalization projects.[47]

In the case of the Russian Empire, we should also stress a long-standing frustration of the czarist state over its perceived inability to "penetrate undergoverned provinces." Cadastral surveys, therefore, were a matter of particular importance: They were not so much a means to establish and assert property rights on land, as an instrument intended to make the land and its inhabitants "legible" to the state and to assert its own authority over them. In the post-Emancipation epoch, provincial *zemstva* adopted the same vision of cadastral surveys as a technology of power, a way to introduce rational scientific management that would eventually make local administration more efficient than the centralized bureaucratic machine of the czarist state.[48] The high-priority status and broad objectives of cadastral surveys explain their unusual role in the history of quite a number of academic disciplines in the Russian context, as Russian scholars were quick to perceive opportunities that cadastral surveys opened for them. The history of Dokuchaev's expeditions seems to be the most spectacular case, yet it was by no means exceptional: The early history of meteorological and soil research in Russia is strongly linked to cadastral surveys that were carried out by the Ministry of State Domains in the 1840s–50s. The impact that cadastral surveys exercised on the conceptual field of natural sciences in Russia, their research agenda, terminology, and so forth, has recently been highlighted by some historians of science.[49] The "archaeology" of Soviet geography seems to support the argument for the importance of the nineteenth-century cadastral surveys and, more generally, of the inventorying efforts of central and local administration directed at land and the ways of its exploitation.

---

[47] Deborah R. Coen, "Imperial Climatographies from Tyrol to Turkestan," *Osiris* 26/1 (2011): 45–65.

[48] Aleksei E. Karimov, *Dokuda topor i sokha khodili: Ocherki istorii zemel'nogo i lesnogo kadastra v Rossii XVI – nachala XX v.* (Moscow, 2007).

[49] Fedotova, "Botaniki v Nizhegorodskoi ekspeditsii."

PART III
Political and Cultural Economy of the (Post)-Soviet Space

CHAPTER 6

The Controlled Space of Socialist Internationalism and its Transgression: COMECON Energy Projects between 1970 and 1990[1]

Ulrich Best

In recent years there has been a renewed interest in Eastern Germany, but also other countries of the former Soviet bloc, in a remarkable venture in the history of the socialist states: a number of joint pipeline building projects in the Soviet Union that brought together workers from the COMECON in the USSR. One possible question we could ask about these projects therefore relates to the politics of memory implied in the recent interest.[2] However, the project is also interesting for the insights it allows into the construction of socialist space and, due to its international scope, also of the international system. In this chapter I would like to analyze how the regulation of the everyday life on these building sites was related to wider transformations. These transformations—toward a more flexible territorial arrangement of sovereignty, of production, and of social control—did not take place in the socialist states. However, the contradictions that enforced these changes in the Western states were evident in the socialist states as well—particularly in a project of such international scope as the pipeline construction. In the following, I will first briefly outline the transformations of the territorial system in the 1970s, then introduce the pipeline project, and finally, in the third part, discuss the regulation of everyday life on the building sites. In this chapter I focus on the workers from the GDR, using contemporary publications as well as documents from the federal archives and the Trassenmuseum [pipeline museum] in Deutzen.

---

[1] Previous versions of this paper have been presented at the Aleksanteri Institute, Helsinki, at the AAASS meeting in Boston in 2009, and at a workshop in Bologna.
[2] See for example Hajo Obuchoff, Lutz Wabnitz & Frank Michael Wagner (eds.), *Die Trasse. Ein Jahrhundertbau in Bildern und Geschichten (*Berlin, 2012).

Three Transformations

Three interlinked transformations of territoriality can be traced in the 1970s. I will only briefly outline these three transformations as they are relevant to my case study here. The start of the Cold War is closely linked to the coining of the term "containment." Containment, as George Kennan defined it in 1947[3], meant that attempts by the Soviet Union to gain influence beyond its borders were to be opposed by the US. Although as a principle guiding US foreign policy, it was soon supplemented and partly replaced by other doctrines, the main tenet of containment was the delineation of clear borders between states, ideologies, and zones of influence. Containment was linked to a concept of the state as container: territory, rule, and culture limited by clear borders. Furthermore, in this approach, a spilling over of communist ideology or political influence beyond the borders of the container was presented as a threat—or, more exactly, as a threat to the other "containers."[4]

There was, however, a further structure to these container-states: They were ordered into two super-containers, divided in Europe by the Iron Curtain. Internally, these super-containers were ordered hierarchically, with the US and the Soviet Union as the ideological and military leaders of the respective containers. The underlying idea of containment was therefore not only that the individual states were presented as containers, but also that the international system was effectively containerized. The doctrine of containment can be linked with the Westphalian system of states, which has generally a similar underlying idea: that a state is characterized by exclusive territorial sovereignty. Already in the 1970s, however, critics pointed out that Western Europe was moving towards a post-Westphalian order: Sovereignty was partially referred to different scales, to the European Economic Community and to the regions.[5] At the same time, the container was increasingly breached in the course of East–West negotiations consequent to the West German *Ostpolitik* and the Conference on Security and Cooperation in Europe (CSCE). Although the Soviet Union viewed the results of the CSCE negotiations as an affirmation of the container principle, it could also be read as part of a breakdown of barriers. The 1970s presented a change in the drawing of boundaries in the international system—a move toward cooperation and negotiation, away from confrontation.

---

[3] X, "The Sources of Soviet Conduct", *Foreign Affairs*, July 1947: 566–582.

[4] Paul A. Chilton, *Security Metaphors: Cold War Discourse from Containment to Common House* (New York, Berne, and Frankfurt am Main, 1996).

[5] Hedley Bull, *The Anarchical Society: A Study of Order in World Politics* (London, 1977).

Using a different theoretical approach, the Westphalian system (and the container concept) can be interpreted as being linked with a specific construction and maintenance of social order. The territoriality of government and the territorial state is a prime example of what Foucault called the disciplinary society. In his analyses of the construction of normality and deviation, Foucault drew on not only micro-processes such as the organization of a prison but also larger-scale issues such as geopolitics. For Foucault, disciplinary space is characterized by "implantations, distributions, demarcations, control of territories and organizations of domains."[6] In his analysis of the control measures taken against the plague, Foucault describes how a system of strict spatial order and a strictly segmented hierarchical space were imposed on individuals—and used as the means of control:

> This enclosed, segmented space, observed at every point, in which the individuals are inserted in a fixed place, in which the slightest movements are supervised, in which all events are recorded, in which an uninterrupted work of writing links the centre and periphery, in which power is exercised without division, according to a continuous hierarchical figure, in which each individual is constantly located, examined and distributed among the living beings, the sick and the dead—all this constitutes a compact model of the disciplinary mechanism.[7]

Foucault's concept of the disciplinary society connects the different scales: The territoriality of the state (in the Westphalian model) corresponds to the spatial control of the citizens. In a disciplinary society, control works through space. However, building on Foucault, Gilles Deleuze argued in 1990 that the disciplinary society was slowly being replaced by a different mechanism—the society of control, where control is no longer through space, but through the individual. Deleuze located the beginning of the transformation after World War II.[8] The society of control is characterized by a constant monitoring of the individual and the individual's will to constant self-improvement, flexibility and mobility. The clear distribution of sovereignty (and its link with territoriality) was replaced by a mixed constitution, in which borders are supposed to be open

---

[6] Michel Foucault, "Questions on Geography," in *Power/Knowledge: Selected Interviews and Other Writings, 1972–1977*, trans. Colin Gordon (New York, 1980), p. 77 (here referring to geopolitics). For an overview of Foucault's rare considerations of the Soviet Union, see also Jan Plamper, "Foucault's Gulag," *Kritika* 3/2 (2002): 255–80.

[7] Michel Foucault, *Discipline and Punish: The Birth of the Prison* (New York, 1977), p. 197.

[8] Gilles Deleuze, "Postscript on the Societies of Control," *October* 59 (1992): 3–7 (first published in 1990).

or (at least) more porous, and containers replaced by a space of negotiations. Yurchak has taken up Foucault's notion of governmentality to describe the changes in subject-formation in the post-Soviet world, using similar concepts to Deleuze.[9]

These two related concepts of a transition of territorial concepts after World War II can be linked to a third concept that offers a third perspective on this transition. In the organization of the economy, production, and work, the Fordism / post-Fordism divide is often placed at roughly the same time, using similar concepts. While Fordism had entailed large-scale mass production for an undifferentiated mass consumer, post-Fordism meant the manufacture of specialized products for differentiated groups. Production was increasingly shifted away from single large factories into geographically dispersed, international networks of different suppliers. Workers were increasingly called upon to be as flexible as the production process—mobile, small entrepreneurs.[10] This third perspective can provide an illustration of some of the aspects Deleuze referred to as the society of control.

These three transformations—the territorial system, the social ordering, and the mode of production—went hand in hand in postwar Western Europe. And all three concepts were developed using the example of Western states. There is very little consideration of the socialist systems in the theories of these transformations of the 1970s. However, some points can already be made here. The COMECON was meant to provide a framework for political and economic cooperation, but was rather limited in its range. The mobility of workers was equally limited. Nevertheless, internationalism was a governing ideology of the socialist system, and examples of it were proudly displayed. In the following, I will attempt to explore these contradictions using the example of international building sites in the Soviet Union.

Energy Projects in the COMECON

In the 1960s energy projects had moved to the forefront of cooperation in the COMECON and had become symbols of socialist internationalism. Infrastructures in socialism, not unlike those in Western systems, are often

---

[9] Alexei Yurchak, "Entrepreneurial governmentality in post-socialist Russia. A cultural investigation of business practices," in: Victoria E. Bonell and Thomas B Gold, (eds.), The New Entrepreneurs of Europe and Asia. (New York, 2002): 278–323.

[10] Bob Jessop, "The Regulation Approach, Governance, and Post-Fordism: Alternative Perspectives on Economic and Political Change?" *Economy and Society* 24/3 (1995): 307–33.

symbolically over-determined. Well-known examples are not only the German motorways, but also dams and irrigation systems[11] or the building of the Soviet Belomor (White Sea – Baltic Sea) Canal.[12] They were meant to convey modernity, the control of nature and the territory of the state, as well as the ability of state leaders. The same applied to the energy networks of the COMECON. The primary function of these energy networks was, of course, the power supply of the different populations and later the export of energy to Western Europe. Beginning in the 1950s, a network of international electricity lines was established. Later, in the late 1950s and the 1960s, the Druzhba oil pipeline was the most important international energy project of the COMECON. Finally, toward the end of the 1960s, in the course of the conversion of the energy industry to natural gas, the building of international natural gas pipelines was begun. The pipelines transported gas from the deposits in the Soviet Union, particularly in Western Siberia, to the western member-states of the COMECON, usually through Ukraine and Czechoslovakia. From 1964 to 1973 the building of the Bratstvo pipeline into Czechoslovakia and of a transit pipeline to the GDR, to Austria and the Federal Republic of Germany (FRG) took place. This pipeline also transported natural gas to Italy. It was an international project, and one that transcended the boundaries of the systems, but it was not yet built as a fully cooperative project of the socialist states—on Soviet territory it was built by Soviet, and in Czechoslovakia by Czech and Slovak workers. In 1974 the building of the Soyuz Pipeline began (also called the "Orenburg Pipeline"), and was finished in 1978. The pipeline was built as cooperative project—that is, work brigades from the individual countries were assigned sections in the Soviet Union, with gas deliveries as payment to the different countries. The next project of this kind began in 1982, when further export pipelines were built on the territory of the USSR, in particular to export gas to Western Europe (the Progres, Urengoy Uzhgorod, and Yamburg pipelines). After the collapse of the socialist regime, the remaining contractual obligations

---

[11] Maria Kaika, "Dams as Symbols of Modernization: The Urbanization of Nature between Geographical Imagination and Materiality," *Annals of the Association of American Geographers* 96/2 (2006): 276–301; Eric Swyngedouw, "Modernity and Hybridity: Nature, *Regeneracionismo*, and the Production of the Spanish Waterscape, 1890–1930," *Annals of the Association of American Geographers* 89/3 (1999): 443–65; Olaf Briese, "Symbolische Siege. Die Talsperren und ihr Double," *Zeitschrift für Geschichtswissenschaft* 51/6 (2003): 510–36.

[12] Cynthia A. Ruder, *Making History for Stalin: The Story of the Belomor Canal* (Gainesville, FL, 1998).

of the states were fulfilled by the successor states.¹³ As suggested above, these building projects were strongly over-determined, starting with their symbolic names—*Progres*, *Druzhba* [Friendship], *Soyuz* [Union]. In all of the involved socialist states, special supplements and reports in the newspapers were regularly published, the workers were honoured, and during the first project international celebrations took place on the building sites. The pipelines were celebrated as evidence of socialist internationalism and of the common future.

In addition, a change in how such projects were represented was evident from the 1950s to the 1970s. The representation of the first projects (such as the Druzhba oil pipeline) portrayed them as a project of the reconstruction of the socialist national economies after the war, which was to be achieved with the support of the USSR. The pipeline was also represented as a pipeline "against capitalism," as an example of international cooperation without exploitation. In the later projects of the late 1970s and 1980s, this was changed. Since the export of natural gas to Western Europe had become the main driving force of the projects, the pipelines were represented as pipelines for "peace in Europe," thus as an example of the overcoming of Eastern –Western bloc borders and the cooperation of the West with the Eastern European states. When, in the early 1980s, the Reagan Administration tried to undermine the cooperation, the project also contributed to the formulation of a joint position of the participating West European states. Julie Katzman argues that it also contributed to the emergence of a West-European geopolitical consciousness that was different and autonomous from the US perspective.¹⁴

There are therefore a number of aspects that link the pipeline projects with the transformations of the international system I sketched above. The context of East–West cooperation and the overcoming of boundaries are clear—at least as far as the geopolitical divide of the bloc confrontation is concerned. Second, the project was also linked to socialist internationalism—the transcending of boundaries within the socialist system. This aspect is, however, more ambiguous and this I will turn to in the following section. The third aspect, the transformation of the mode of production, is also relevant to the pipeline projects. The projects were part of an attempt to shift the socialist economies into a more international framework. Socialist economists at the time described

---

¹³ Margarita M. Balmaceda, "Der Weg in die Abhängigkeit. Ostmitteleuropa am Energietropf der UdSSR," *Osteuropa* 54/9–10 (2004): 162–79; Klaus Gestwa and Johannes Grützmacher, "Infrastrukturen," in Stefan Plaggenborg (ed.), *Handbuch der Geschichte Rußlands. Band 5: 1945–1991. Vom Ende des Zweiten Weltkriegs bis zum Zusammenbruch der Sowjetunion* (Stuttgart, 2003), pp. 1089–152.

¹⁴ Julie E. Katzman, "The Euro-Siberian Gas Pipeline Row: A Study in Community Development," *Millennium—Journal of International Studies* 17/1 (1988): 25–41.

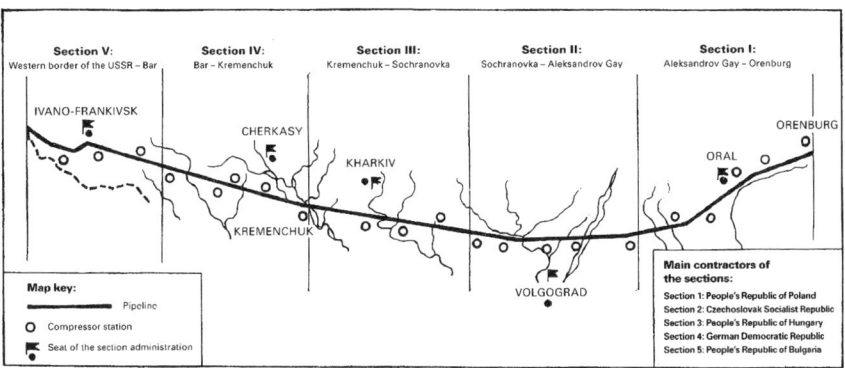

Figure 6.1　Plan of the Sojuz project (1974–1978), with national subdivisions (I–V: Poland, CSSR, Hungary, GDR, Bulgaria).
Source: Bohumil Lehár *Rada vzájemné hospodářské pomoci: sborník dokumentů o vývoji a činnosti RVHP (1978–1983)* (Prague, 1984), p. 192.

this as the transition to an intensive reproduction of the economy, from an era of extensive reproduction.[15] This transition was interlinked with a change in the image of the ideal socialist worker. Initially, the propaganda around the projects centered on the traditional male worker—big machines, the taming of nature, and so on. In the later years, however, it became more difficult to present this as a model. The socialist economies and societies had moved toward greater inclusion of women, production was at least aiming to become more flexible, and the new leading technologies in the socialist systems were now electronics, nuclear power, and high-tech, meaning that the new model worker was no longer the pipeline welder with dirty boots and a big machine, but the lab-coated specialist.[16]

The central contradiction in the building projects, however, was the relation between the promise of a transgression of boundaries and the attempt to uphold a strictly disciplinary model of rule. The individual sections of the building sites were organized in a way that each country had a headquarters in its section but maintained several building sites. The work consisted not

---

[15]　See for example Zdeněk Šedivý and Marian Sling, "Improvement of the Economic Mechanism and the Transition to Intensive Development", in: *Eastern European Economics*, 25/3 (1987): 50-62.

[16]　Ulrich Best, "Arbeit, Internationalismus und Energie. Zukunftsvisionen in den Gaspipelineprojekten des RGW", in: Martin Schulze Wessel, Christiane Brenner (eds), *Zukunftsvorstellungen und staatliche Planung im Sozialismus: die Tschechoslowakei im ostmitteleuropäischen Kontext*, (München, 2010): 137-147.

only of pipeline construction, but also comprised compressor stations as well as further objects, among them residential buildings and buildings with social or cultural functions. Depending on the exact location and character of the work, the conditions on the building sites, the individual brigades, and, above all, the building phases could be very different. Some were in close proximity to villages or cities, partly even in cities; others again (particularly in the later projects in the Perm area) were located far away from any larger community. The workers who constructed the pipeline route (the so-called "linear part"), were often mobile—that is, they commuted to the respective site and returned to spend the night in the camp. Not all workers were builders—there were also functionaries responsible for administration, cultural affairs, cooks, and so on. Although a clear surplus of males prevailed, there were not exclusively men on the building sites. The conditions of the building site camps were also different—in principle, the workers lived in mobile housing units, which together formed a camp (usually without a fence). The motivation for the workers to go to the Soviet Union was primarily a material one. The pipeline workers received wage subsidies, which made hard-to-get goods accessible. Beyond that, they were awarded privileges in the GDR, for example with regard to housing or education.[17]

The attraction of the pipeline project to the workers—as I have tried to illustrate with a few points—was that it challenged the bounded spaces of the socialist states. The project was part of the envisioned "socialist future" of internationalism, but at the same time merged into the present geopolitical landscape. The building sites were national places beyond the national territory, which they extended into the international arena. They were international, gave access to goods beyond the normal restrictions in the national states, but nevertheless were representations of national territories. At the same time, the privileges linked the building sites back to the national territory, because they could only be realized there. On a larger scale, they represented the contradiction between socialist cooperation and increasing export orientation toward. In the following section, I will turn to an analysis of the construction of the everyday life on these building sites and how it tied national delineations, international encounters, and the contradiction between a disciplinary system and the promise of the transgression of boundaries.

---

[17] See Freie Deutsche Jugend, *Fragen und Antworten zum Zentralen Jugendobjekt "Erdgastrasse"* (Berlin, 1986).

Regulating Socialist Space

In order to examine some hypotheses concerning the construction of socialist space, I will now first analyze the construction of deviation, standardization, and Otherness, starting with the selection of the workers, to the control of the interaction with other "national" brigades and to the perception of Soviet society. The selection of the workers took place in several steps.[18] Generally, the recruitment and selection of workers for jobs in the USSR was the task of the home companies. In the later building phases, people were also recruited straight out of military service. In the later phases, even applications from the workers themselves became possible.

After a worker was selected by the company, a check by the secret police was carried out. Approximately 30 percent of the selected workers were not deemed suitable by the Stasi agencies—reasons were often that people had contacts with the West (through their family), that they had displayed small political deviations, or that they were unsuitable for "moral" reasons (homosexuality, promiscuity). Thus, there were already two stages of selection in place—one by the enterprises regarding skills, the second by the state security regarding "political" aspects. Both stages were normalizing. The first line of selection excluded those with low qualifications. The second stage, the moral examination, took place in the background and was also usually spatially organized—enquiries were made, for example, into how the person was regarded in his/her neighborhood. The main goal of these examinations was the strict control of access to the building sites, which formed both a showcase for the nation and a space beyond the nation. The building-site crews were meant to be a perfected selection—a better GDR, in which unwanted persons (and their unwanted morals) should not exist. Those that were selected were then sent on a preparatory course, which included further technical training, language training, and, above all, "the political-ideological operational preparation."[19]

After this selection, access to the "Other space" of the building sites was granted. The journey to the building sites was strictly controlled—there were prescribed routes, prescribed arrival stations, and special trains only for the workers from the GDR. After the arrival, encounters or the avoidance of encounters with the Soviet population and with representatives of the other national building sites became the focus of control. These encounters were to take place particularly in the context of organized meetings. There were friendship

---

[18] See BArch DY 24 9345.

[19] BArch DY 24 9345, "Ordnung für die Auswahl und Delegierung," p. 5 ("Order for the selection and delegation").

treaties between the building site organization, the Freie Deutsche Jugend (FDJ), and the local Komsomol.[20] Encounters were strictly orchestrated and planned. This strict regulation was, on the one hand, meant to keep intact the control of the workers, with the workers tied to their national spaces and their building sites forming mini-containers of the nation. On the other hand, it served to maintain the hierarchy of the socialist system, with the Soviet Union at the top as the most developed socialist state, helping other nations, and with the other nations learning from the Soviet Union. Nevertheless, encounters could not be prevented—and these encounters often proved to be detrimental to the hierarchical order of the socialist states. One building-site manager wrote in a monthly report:

> Many friends are disappointed that they did not find what they were told in the training courses. For example, in meetings with production workers from Soviet companies, our friends saw that Soviet work methods, such as Slobin, Bassow, etc., were unknown. Questions of productivity, industrial safety, and the role of women in production are different here in Ukraine than with us.[21]

"Slobin" and "Bassow" were work practices that the GDR workers had been taught as new methods that were state-of the-art in the Soviet Union. There were other contradictions. Even when meetings took place within the official framework, the contradiction between the allegedly most progressive socialist society and the GDR became obvious. This is evident in a quote from another such report:

> The material conditions for our pipeline workers are very good and exceed many FDJ delegates' expectations. This concerns the accommodation, the food supply, and also the remuneration. Among the Soviet comrades there are divided opinions over our building-site accommodations, which are not comparable with the building site accommodations in the Soviet Union. [...] While a proportion of the Soviet comrades hold the opinion that our camp corresponds to a building site of communism, others are of the opinion that many Soviet citizens do not live as comfortably as the pipeline workers of the GDR.[22]

This quote shows the other side of the relationship: The hierarchical order in which the Soviet Union was held to be more advanced than the GDR was also shaken on the Soviet side by such encounters. A third factor affected this hierarchization:

---

[20] BArch DY 24 – 20203, DY24 – 17043.
[21] BArch DY24 – 16993, monthly report August, 26.8.1975.
[22] BArch DY24 – 11222, information about some problems, 3.2.1976.

> Additionally, there are some unclarities with some friends concerning ideological problems, particularly the valuation of work and life as well as the economic policy of the Soviet Union. This is expressed in such opinions as: [...] The machines and equipment from the NSW [non-socialist economic area] are much better than the Soviet machines. The demand to work with such machines is great. [...] What are we supposed to learn from the USSR? They ought to be learning from us.[23]

Here some further aspects of the building sites become clear. On the one hand, they highlight their function as a window on the West, as a transgression of the system's borders. On the other hand, there emerged a criticism of the hierarchical order of socialist space.

A further important aspect of the disciplinary order of the Soviet area was that not only did the GDR not want their workers to have too many contacts with the Soviet population, but this was also the case for the Soviet administrations: Workers from the GDR were not wanted in the cities and the militia proceeded against them. "Due to the strict rules of the militia in Bar such questions arose: How do we want to arrange the friendship? Does the militia want to isolate us from Soviet people?" asked a site manager in one report.[24] In other sites (Perm in this case), the militia strictly inhibited any movement outside the camp:

> There are no operationally significant occurrences so far. Any infringement of discipline is punished with immediate return to the GDR. Contact with Soviet citizens is not very close. Furthermore, it is forbidden to leave a small designated area of a few kilometers. The obedience to these rules is strictly controlled by the Soviet militia.[25]

A further report shows the close control of the building sites. It lists the special occurrences of the month, among them traffic accidents, thefts, and, in addition, "offences against the Soviet laws and standards by building-site members" (twice) and "substantial disturbances of socialist living together within the residential and leisure area of the camp as well as during arrival and departure" (three times). These offences were often offences against access and movement prohibitions. Moreover, the report lists a "physical attack against

---

[23] BArch DY24 – 16993, monthly report November, 1.12.1975.
[24] Ibid.
[25] BstU, MfS, BV Karl-Marx-Stadt, IM-file XIV 18/82, "Christian Schulze," p. 100, 30.10.86

members of the security group by Soviet citizens." The full description of this event is as follows:

> In the course of their service as members of the security group at the location Talnoe, they were abused and the leader of the group was violently attacked by Soviet citizens, who were in the camp without authorization. He suffered medium to severe bodily injuries and is in stationary treatment. Despite intensive efforts by the militia, it has not as yet been possible to determine the identity of the perpetrators.[26]

The GDR building sites formed a disciplinary space in themselves. Not only were infringements of all kinds logged, but both the crossing of the boundary from the inside outward, and entrance into the site by outsiders, were discouraged. The security personnel performed, on the one hand, the function of a border patrol and, on the other, the control of the interior and its inhabitants. At another camp, a "security collective" had been formed in order to control the workers:

> The FDJ in Krementschug formed a security collective; it achieved an improvement in the order and discipline of the colleagues in the city. [...] The political-ideological work, qualification courses, and the cultural programme have to further strengthen the development of socialist personalities and to influence the behavior of our workers in the Soviet Union. So far, 20 colleagues had to begin the journey home due to infringements of discipline, damage to the reputation of the GDR, and incorrect behaviour in public.[27]

The security collective at this location had yet another function: the control of the GDR workers outside of their "own area"—in the Soviet city. The reputation of the GDR depended on the correct behaviour of the workers in the Soviet public space, which could be guaranteed only by the education of "socialist personalities." This led to a further normalization process that took place on the building sites themselves—a third selection, as it were, in which unwanted elements were sent back to the GDR. The control did not cease upon the return of workers to the GDR. An informer reported one worker as having said:

> The work was fun, too, but the things I experienced there during this time, how we were being exploited, nobody can imagine that. We girls were only called "Fritz whores," and the boys were not allowed to be seen elsewhere, or they would be attacked and knifed. We were not allowed to go anywhere else, because we

---

[26] BArch DY24 – 16993, report of the director of building site, 27.1.1978.
[27] BArch DY34 – 25150, report of the large-scale building site, 10.11.1975.

were not supposed to see how the people live. German–Soviet friendship is over for me, just like the SED [Socialist Unity Party of Germany]; I'll resign there, too. It really opened my eyes there, how we were being lied to by everyone.[28]

The consequences of this report to the worker are unclear, but it demonstrates that the pipeline workers were still subjected to considerable surveillance back in the GDR. The international building sites in the Soviet Union can exemplify some of the contradictions of the regulation of socialist space both in their wider geopolitical relevance and in the micro-geopolitics of the international system. Spatial segmentation, a spatial hierarchization, the control of access, movement, and encounter are the central elements of this spatial order that I have discussed. Normalization, monitoring, and selection are the techniques that affected the "population" of the building sites. The building sites were at the same time outside and inside the spatial order—they made it possible to transgress the borders of the GDR, but functioned as part of the GDR at the same time, as a reflection and reinforcement of the disciplinary regime of the state. They were embedded into a hierarchical space in which the Soviet Union represented the most advanced socialist society and in which the building sites were meant to offer a bridge, the possibility of encounter. At the same time, they offered a view of the world beyond socialism, of Western technology and hard currency, that questioned the existing hierarchy of socialist space. However, the building sites were not beyond the system. They were linked with the system of the GDR in numerous ways. They offered only a limited transgression. Thus they also had the function of supporting the system and, moreover, demonstrated the potential of a different method of control that did not rely on the prohibition of movement but on the regulation of transgression, the integration of prescribed transgression into the workings of control. This was, however, impossible to implement within the framework of a disciplinary society. It would have required a society of control, in Deleuze's terms.

Conclusion: International Building Sites and the International System in the 1970s

In the introduction to this chapter I outlined the three transformations that are associated with the 1970s: the emergence of a post-Westphalian order in Europe, the rise of post-disciplinary modes of control, and the flexibilization of production. All three are relevant for the case study I have presented, although

---

[28] BstU, MfS, HA XVIII 1827, Bd 2, 1974–1978, Bericht 12.9.1978.

my focus has been on the connection between the territorial system of the socialist states and their disciplinary regimes. The pipeline building projects were—at the the level of the Eastern–Western bloc boundaries—linked with the *Ostpolitik*, the process of negotiations and rapprochement in Europe. On the one hand, this took the form of closer economic cooperation, the exchange of natural gas from the Soviet Union against hard currency from the Western countries, along with some equipment and the rare participation of Western experts in the construction projects. On the other hand, the pipeline projects were also connected with a closer coordination of the policies of Western European countries in opposition to the policy of the US. Both these aspects translate as a challenge to bloc boundaries and the international order that questioned the role of the United States in Western Europe.

On the building sites themselves and in the socialist states, the projects were tied into the ideology of internationalism and the hierarchical construction of socialist space. They replicated the national segmentation of this space and its disciplinary regime. However, and more importantly, the building sites offered a challenge to both this segmentation and the disciplinary regime. They demonstrated that the hierarchies could not be sustained, that the borders could not be effectively controlled, and that the normalization of the population could be successful only to a certain degree.

This case study demonstrates that the contradictions not only in the national, but also the international ,systems of the socialist states were already apparent in the 1970s. It seems that the socialist systems were unable to shift to a different regime of territoriality and control—the shift that began in the Western countries in the 1970s did not take place in the socialist systems. It is precisely the failure of the socialist system to cope with the challenges of mobility, flexibility, and international exchange that allows a clearer evaluation of the transformations that took place in the Western countries from the 1970s—and that transformed the socialist states after 1989.

CHAPTER 7

The Rearrangement of the Post-Soviet Space and the Representation of Russia as a Eurasian Bridge

Katri Pynnöniemi

Introduction

The phrase "post-Soviet space" is often used to denote a specific geographical area—countries and territories that were part of the former Soviet Union. In this chapter, however, I offer a slightly different reading of the term "post-Soviet space." Rather than focusing on ethnic, cultural, and national borders that differentiate Russia from what used to be the Soviet Union, the political aspect is sought in what is actually the functional component of the Russian/Soviet territory: the infrastructure network.

The infrastructure network—the road and rail linkages, oil and gas pipelines, and the electricity network—form the backbone of the Russian economy, and constitute the residue of a particular political order in space. In this sense, the post-Soviet space is understood as an assemblage—a nested space that carries within it the incompleteness of the Soviet modernization project but also the potential for renewal. The analysis of the infrastructure policies in contemporary Russia is a form of "decentering" as understood in this volume. It focuses on the "decomposition" of the order built into the infrastructures, an order that is understood as an inherently unstable and ambiguous one.

Metaphors related to building and construction became central to the 1990s political discourse in outlining change in the post-Soviet Russia. With the emphasis on international competitiveness and the active role of the country in global politics, the previous vocabulary was replaced in the 2000s by a new set of "code words" such as "transparency," "market," and "international transport corridor." The last term was coined in the Russian discussion to refer to the main transport arteries of the country. The term emerged in connection with the talks on the development of the so-called pan-European transport corridors between the EU and Russia. These corridors were designed by the EU to spur infrastructure investments and other horizontal measures on the "pan-European level," and particularly in those countries that would later become the new EU member states.¹ It soon became quite clear that this framework was too narrow for Russia to accept and it duly redefined the corridor concept to better fit its interests.

From the viewpoint of Russia, transport and infrastructure development is the conjunction point of three major processes: the fragmentation of the post-Soviet space, the integration of Russia into the global markets and the EU, and the reorganization of Russian polity. In other words, actualized in the "international transport corridor" concept is a transition from the planned economy and infrastructure system designed for those purposes to one that is feasible in the conditions of the market economy and globalization.

Thus, the Baikal–Amur Railroad, the road between Moscow and Vladivostok, and the high-speed train between St. Petersburg and Moscow transcend simple distinctions of Soviet versus post-Soviet space. What was once built as a monument to Soviet power is currently viewed as a means for Russia to engage in the global economy.² The prevailing idea is that by activating the potential that already exists, largely the infrastructures inherited from the Soviet era, Russia will be able not only to spur economic growth, but also to regain its position in the former Soviet space.

Yet, at the same time, the degradation of the Russian infrastructure base undermines the very integrity of Russia's economic space, to say nothing of the country's ability to project its power in what used to be the Soviet space.³ In fact, the economic growth during the last decade did not bring substantial change to the country's infrastructure network, although thoroughfares in major cities have been upgraded. Moreover, the failure to reinforce Russia's role as a transit

---

¹ The concept "pan-European transport corridor" refers to ten priority directions agreed at the EU level in the mid-1990s. After the EU eastern enlargement, this framework was largely replaced by the intra-EU focus on the trans-European network development. At the EU–Russia level, cooperation continues in the context of five "international transport axes" that integrate the transport infrastructures belonging to the EU and Russia. See the detailed discussion on Russia's response to the pan-European transport policy in Katri Pynnöniemi, *New Road, New Life, New Russia: International Transport Corridors at the Conjunction of Geography and Politics in Russia* (Tampere, 2008).

² See the discussion on the Baikal–Amur Railroad project and the principles of Soviet infrastructure planning in Katri Pynnöniemi, "In Celebration of Monumentalism: Transport Modernization in Russia," in Markku Kangaspuro and Jeremy Smith (eds.), *Modernization in Russia since 1900* (Helsinki, 2006): pp. 124–49.

³ See further discussion on the degradation of Russia's infrastructure base in Katri Pynnöniemi, *The Political Constraints on Russia's Economic Development: The Visionary Zeal of Technological Modernization and Its Critics* (Helsinki, 2010).

bridge between Europe and Asia is jeopardizing the traditional image of the country as the rightful heir to Eurasia. The aim of this chapter is to elaborate on current Russian thinking on (transport) infrastructure development. The article analyzes arguments put forward in support of Russia's "transit power" vis-à-vis its neighbors and the state-forming function of the infrastructure network in Putin's Russia.

Space and Transport

The Power over Space

The historian J.N. Westwood summarized the problem of transport in Russia in the following way: It is "a consequence of the geographic feature of Russia, the union of an enormous territorial expanse into a single economy."[4] The paradox depicted in this formulation is that "an enormous territorial expanse" does not readily transform into "a single economy" nor into a coherent sovereign space. However, the official discourse in Russia addresses ambiguities involved in the building of a "united transport system" as *temporal obstacles* that can be done away with by improving the system of governance. As this is a permanent feature of the Czarist, Soviet, and subsequent Russian discussion on transport and infrastructure modernization, it also provides a convenient starting point for studying the way in which the "international transport corridor" concept *figures* against the *background* of existing policies and the purported constellation of geography and politics in Russia. That is, the background refers to the burden of enormous space and the challenges and promises of its effective governance.

In the advertisement for one of Russia's biggest forwarding companies, the DVTG group, Russia is envisioned as a bridge between Asia and Europe (Figure 7.1). The advertisement says: "Whatever your cargo. Wherever its destination." The territory of Russia is portrayed as a blue sky and the stars in the sky are the company's freight centers. The freight centers, rather than the thin dotted line marking the border, constitute the interface between local/global and inside/outside of Russia. Europe, Russia, and China are locations in the space of the global capital markets. Moscow, which is often represented as the nexus of the Russian space, is, in this image, just one of the stars. The yellow figure against the blue background represents an "international transport corridor," and the arrow signifies the main direction of the freight traffic, from Asia to Europe. The figure of the corridor is, in fact, a *service* offered by the company. It is the company that

---

[4] J.N. Westwood, *Soviet Railways to Russian Railways* (New York, 2002), p. 79.

Figure 7.1   Advertisement for the DVTG Group.
Source: Rossiiskaya Gazeta, March 23, 2005.

makes travelling through Russia fast, reliable, and safe. Thus, it is the yellow figure delineating the corridor rather than the blue background that is highlighted.

In the analytical sense, the shift from the foreground, namely the yellow "figure" of the corridor, to the background of the blue "sky," denotes a shift in the purposive order of the Russian space. The foreground—the figure of the corridor—is a constellation of the Russian space formed in accordance with the principle of *competitiveness* in the global markets. The blue background to the figure, however, signifies the *unity of power of the sovereign territory*. In this picture, two versions of spatiality (the "space of flows"[5])—global networking and sovereign territoriality—are not seen a priori as mutually exclusive but rather as the two coexistent, spatial domains of politics.

In the federal government discourse on transport corridors, the relationship between the delineated corridor and the blue background is reversed. What is emphasized is the unity of the transport and political space in contrast to the practice of delineating space into specific "corridors." The image of "Moscow—a port of five oceans" captures what can be regarded as the background vision of the Soviet/Russian space.

---

[5]   According to Manuel Castells, the order of flows owes its logic to temporal fluctuations—the flux of events, stock-exchange and currency rates, and other entities that "can be bought and sold but which you cannot drop on your foot," Originally this refers to *The Economist* magazine's definition of "services." See Manuel Castells, *The Information Age: Economy, Society and Culture. Vol. 1: The Rise of the Network Society* (Oxford, 1996). See also John G. Ruggie, "Territoriality and Beyond: Problematizing Modernity in International Relations," *International Organization* 47/1 (1993): 142.

Figure 7.2   Moscow—a port of five oceans.
Source: USSR in Construction 8 (1932) [*Construction* was a Soviet illustrated monthly, published in Russian, English, German, and French].

In order to understand what the shift between the foreground and the background entails, we may start with the notion of a "united transport system" [*Edinaya Transportnaya Sistema*, ETS]. This captures what is regarded as an essential feature of Russian space and the state policy on transport and infrastructure modernization. The use of the notion can be traced back to the 1930s, while the systematic study of the subject started in the 1950s. The establishment of the Institute of Complex Transport Problems signaled that problems concerning the "united transport system" were to be prioritized.[6] The three main attributes of

---

[6]   V.G. Galaburdy et al. (eds.), *Edinaya transportnaya sistema* (Moscow, 1996), pp. 14–15.

the ETS are: the coherence or unity [*tselostnost'*] of the infrastructure network, the hierarchy [*ierarhichnost'*] of the different modes of transport, and, lastly, the synthesis[7] [*vzaimoproniknovenie* or *sintez*] of the operation of the system as a whole.[8] With the emphasis on *tselostnost'*, meaning integrity and unity but also in a more diffuse sense something that is untouched, the arrangement of space that it is subject to calls for effective governance and "taming."

The Space of Flows Circumventing Eurasia

The story of a video recorder produced in South Korea and its journey to Vladivostok in Russia pinpoints the existence of imagined and real interfaces between the foreground and the background—between global and local, space and place, state and markets.

The major transshipment route is a detour circumventing Eurasia proper. In the first phase of the journey the video recorder is shipped on a huge container ship via the Suez Canal to a major European port. From there, a container bound for Vladivostok continues the journey first to Finland, where it is either stored awaiting further delivery or immediately carried on a truck to Russia. At the Finnish–Russian border the truck will, in all probability, get stuck in a queue waiting to cross the border into Russia.[9] After perhaps a two-day delay at the border, the truck continues on its way to Moscow where the part of the cargo destined for Vladivostok is transferred to the train on which it continues its journey further eastward.

In a variation on the theme, the container carrying the video recorder is shipped from South Korea to the port of Vladivostok, from where it continues by special express train across Russia to Finland, is stored for a while in Finland and then

---

[7] In current international usage, the equivalent term for synthesis would be multi-modality, which means carriage of goods by two or more modes of transport, irrespective of the types of freight, within a single transport chain.

[8] Galaburdy et al., *Edinaya transportnaya sistema*, p. 15.

[9] The long lines of trucks crossing the Finnish–Russian border emerged around the mid-1990s and extended for just a couple of kilometers at first. In September 2006 the queue, which during the previous couple of years had normally been from 10 to 15 kilometers in length, stretched all the way to Hamina (about 40 kilometers from the border). The lengthening queue is in large part due to increased traffic, especially new cars that are transported via Finland to Russia. By the end of 2006 the authorities in Finland agreed on several emergency measures that would improve road safety along the route from Hamina to the border. Similar problems with road transport are encountered at both the Lithuanian–Latvian and Latvian–Russian borders. See, for example, Christer Pursiainen, *Russia between Integration and Protectionism: International Road Transport, Ports, and the Forestry Sector* (Stockholm, 2007).

carried back by truck to Russia. In specialist jargon, this practice is referred to as "artificial transit." This type of freight traffic virtually came to a halt at the beginning of 2006 after the sharp increase in transit tariffs along the Trans-Siberian Railway.[10] Perhaps the most straightforward and least time-consuming version of the story is the one where a shuttle-trader goes to South Korea, buys a video recorder from a shop or on the black market, and then carries it back home to Vladivostok.[11]

The narrative about the video recorder's journey from South Korea to Vladivostok illuminates the different domains of "interaction capacity"[12] from sovereign territoriality, marked by the multiple crossings over the state border, to a more diffuse sense of global interaction practices embodied in the practice of shuttle-trading. But it should be noted that the demarcation line between state/private or official/unofficial spheres is not as clear as it might seem. The practice of rerouting high-value consumer goods bound for Russia through Finland proved to be profitable for those willing to pursue gray tax schemes.[13] The lack of specialized cargo-handling infrastructure and storage space, coupled with the availability of such services in Finland, made this route attractive to shippers. Ultimately, the fact that trucks destined for Russia through Finland were standing in line for days rather than for hours is a symptom of the "incompleteness" of Russia's transformation, in this case the non-implementation into practice of reforms in the sphere of customs administration.

The narrative also points to the difference in the dynamics of infrastructure development in Russia compared to Finland, or to Europe in general. In the 1990s only 1 to 2 percent of cargo transport handled by the Russian railways was carried in containers. Even as late as 1999 only a handful of Russian transshipment stations were equipped to handle larger containers. Moreover, during a significant part of the Soviet era, containers had "disappeared" en route, ending up in new locations and put to new uses; for example as garages,

---

[10] *Kommersant* June 9, 2004; see also Simon-Erik Ollus and Heli Simola, *Russia in the Finnish Economy* (Helsinki, 2006).
[11] The story of the video recorder was told by an adviser of the Minister of Transport of the RF, the Chairman of the supervisory board of the EuroAsian Logistics Association, Rashad Guseinov, in an interview for the TV channel RBK on October 27, 2005. See Rashad Guseinov, "Logistic Market of Russia Today and Tomorrow," *Round Table at the 23nd German Logistics Congress, Berlin, October 18–20, 2006.*
[12] Barry Buzan, Charles Jones, and Richard Little, *The Logic of Anarchy: Neorealism to Structural Realism. New Directions in World Politics* (New York, 1993), p. 72.
[13] For more on tax avoidance and customs practices at the Finnish–Russian border, see Ollus and Simola, *Russia in the Finnish Economy*.

mushroom plantations, bathhouses, and so on.[14] The stacks of abandoned containers are not, however, a feature that is unique to the former Soviet landscape. As Marc Levinson notes, discarded containers litter landscapes around the world, creating environmental problems, while the possibility of their "non-conventional" use in terrorist activities or, as is often the case, in transporting illegal immigrants, makes this otherwise very "functional" invention a matter of national and human insecurity.[15]

Notwithstanding the difference in the technology used in freight handling in Russia, the growth of containerization has been rapid in recent years. In Russia, the volume of containers used in transshipments tripled between 1998 and 2005 from 0.5 million TEU to 1.7 million TEU annually. The Russian container market has grown approximately tenfold from 2000 to 2010 and this trend is expected to continue in the future. However, the projected capacity of Russian ports to handle containers (20 million TEU) will not exceed the current capacity of the world's largest container port in Singapore.[16] The special container services that run between the major cities in Russia and between, for example, Moscow and Berlin ("East Wind"), and, in particular, between Russia's Far Eastern ports of Nahodka and Vladivostok and the Finnish or Belarusian border, have been developed during the 2000s.[17] The shipping container story suggests that a relatively minor change in the sphere of technology may have far-reaching consequences, creating the "ground" required for the emergence of a new global domain of political and economic action.

Infrastructure and State-forming

The views presented at the All-Russian Scientific-Practical Conference "The Transport of Russia at the Turn of the Century," held in December 1999, sum up what later became the state policy on infrastructure modernization.

---

[14] The Soviet railways were heavy users of containers but these were smaller than the current standard used in international cargo transportation. Westwood, *Soviet Railways to Russian Railways*, pp. 121–3.

[15] Cited in Witold Rybczynski, "Shipping News," *The New York Review of Books* 53/13 (2006): 9–11.

[16] Guseinov, "Logistic Market of Russia Today and Tomorrow"; Generalov, Sergei, "Investments into Russian Logistics and Transportation Industry," *Round Table at the 23nd German Logistics Congress, Berlin, October 18–20, 2006*; *Izvestiya*, January 26, 2004.

[17] In 2005 there were 3,542 container block trains that carried 323,300 TEU. Petr Baskakov, "JSC Russian Railways as an Integrator of Transport Services in the Markets of Europe and Asia," *Round Table at the 23rd German Logistics Congress, Berlin, October 18–20, 2006*.

The conference was the first major event organized in the 1990s that focused entirely on transport problems. Later it was specifically given the status of a "foundational moment" in the creation of the "ideological basis" for a policy on transport infrastructure modernization. This conforms to the general perception of change in the spectrum of Russian political life during autumn 1999 and especially after President Yeltsin's resignation on New Year's Eve 1999.[18]

Speaking in front of nearly six thousand *transportnikov* [transport workers], Vladimir Putin, the still relatively unknown Prime Minister, seized the opportunity and formulated the main tasks of the government in the sphere of transport. The point of departure was the realization that the current infrastructure system was obsolete. During the previous decade nothing, or almost nothing, had changed when it came to the speed of passenger and cargo transportation and its organization, Putin argued. Second, precedence had to be given to the development of the national machine-building industry that would also function as a catalyst for the development of a real sector of the national economy. And, third, the development of the transport sphere had to be closely linked with developments taking place in the world economy and in the economy of Russia.[19]

What was required was an improvement in the quality of the transport system. However, the throughput and capacity of the system were no longer sufficient quality indicators. "The transport system also has to be economically feasible, comfortable, and safe for people and the environment," Putin emphasized. "International experience shows," continued Putin, "that the solution of these tasks requires completely new approaches [to transportation]: the application of new information-administrative systems, the principles of logistics, and the integration of transportation with industrial technologies."[20] He also said:

> Therefore the Government also supports the technological modernization of transport, and reforming the administrative system in such a way that it is directed at the future and synchronized with the development of the Russian and world economy. It goes without saying that transport should stay one step ahead of the other sectors of the economy in the future. This is the only way to provide Russia

---

[18] *Rossiiskaya Gazeta*, May 27, 2003; Sergei Frank, "Ob itogah raboty transportnogo kompleksa v 1999 godu," speech at the Collegium of the Ministry of Transport of Russia, February 16, .2000; *Transport Rossii*, December 6–12, 1999; *Transport Rossii*, December 27–31,.1999; Lilia Shevtsova, *Putin's Russia* (Washington, DC, 2005), pp. 41–43; Richard Sakwa, *Putin: Russia's Choice* (London, 2004).

[19] Vladimir Putin, "Rabotat' na perspektivu," speech at the All-Russian Scientific-Practical Conference "Transport of Russia at the Turn of the Century," Moscow, December 6, 1999, published in *Transport Rossii*, December 13–19 1999.

[20] Ibid.

with a competitive advantage in the world markets and to allow us to execute the major economic and, dare I say, state and state-forming [*obshchegosudarstvenno-obrazuyushchuyu*] function of transport.[21]

The rearrangement [*obustroistvo*] of the existing infrastructures would be a required catalyst to achieve stronger economic growth and improve Russia's competitiveness in the international markets. In addition, the infrastructure development was regarded as a mechanism for the preservation of the integrity of Russia's economic-political space:

> A uniform [*edinoe*] economic space, the integrity of our statehood [*gosudarstvennosti*], and the defense and safety of the country rests on and functions to a large extent because of the stability and reliability of your work, especially in such remote regions as trans-Baikalia, and the Far East where people also live, and have taken stock of the problems the country has faced in recent years. Your work is important not only for the state as a whole, but also for each individual. People wish to be assured that they will not be cut off from the historical center of Russia, will be protected against possible threats, and integrated into the uniform economic and cultural life of the country.[22]

Later, in his annual address to the Federal Assembly in 2004, President Putin returned to the same issue and defined the transport sector modernization as one of the key tasks to be tackled in the near future:[23]

> Today, the poor condition and low density of the road network, oil pipelines, gas-transport system and the infrastructure of the power industry places serious restrictions on the development of the Russian economy [...]. At the same time, a modern, well-developed transport infrastructure will be capable of turning Russia's geographical features into a real competitive advantage for the country. What needs to be done to achieve this? Above all, we need to unite the economic centers of the country, to provide economic subjects with unhindered access to regional and international markets, and at the same time provide infrastructure services of a world standard.[24]

---

[21] Ibid.

[22] Ibid.

[23] Vladimir Putin, address to the Federal Assembly of the RF, Moscow, the Kremlin, May 26, 2004. URL: http://www.kremlin.ru/eng/text/speeches/2004/05/26/1309_type70029_71650.shtml. Accessed July 14, 2007.

[24] Ibid.

To emphasize that the modernization of the country's transport infrastructure was not on the agenda merely with the aim of reaching a target figure—the doubling of GDP within a ten-year period—Putin added:

> I would say that the development of infrastructure is more than an economic task. Solving it will not just directly affect the state of affairs in the economy, but ensure the unity of the country as a whole—whether people feel they are citizens of a united, large nation, and whether they can make use of its advantages.[25]

These few lines encapsulate what the main government programs on transport infrastructure modernization—the Modernization of the Transport System 2002–2010 and the Transport Strategy of the Russian Federation—seek to accomplish. The long-term strategy of the Government of the Russian Federation, as outlined in these two federal-level programs, is aimed at enhancing the coherence of the country and the competitiveness of Russia in the transit of goods and people between Europe and Asia.[26]

Furthermore, the Russian government considers transport to be the most important component of a productive infrastructure, and its continued development to be a priority of the state.[27] The possibility of "private investment" in the transport branch has not been ruled out provided that those investments fulfill the objectives of the definite plans elaborated on by the government. The particular reference points of Putin's speech in 2004 were the Strategy for the Development of Transport, and the subsequent Transport Strategy of the Russian Federation, which had been elaborated on the year before by a special commission.[28] At that time, the "international transport corridor"

---

[25] Ibid., emphasis added, cf. Vladimir Putin, speech at the meeting of the State Council of the RF, the Kremlin, Moscow October 29, 2003. http://www.kremlin.ru/appears/2003/10/29/1555_type63378_54670.shtml (accessed May 13, 2005). Note that no emphasis has been added to the quote.

[26] Government of the RF, Postanovlenie Pravitel'stva RF N848 "O federal'noi tselevoi programme 'Modernizatsiya transportnoi sistemy Rossii (2002–2010),'" May 12, 2001, URL: http://www.mintrans.ru/Pressa/N_848.htm. Accessed December 12, .2001; Government of the RF, Press release N663, September 7, 2000, "Osnovnie napravlenie formirovaniya i razvitiya mezhdunarodnyh transportnyh koridorov na territorii RF," URL: http://www.government.ru/data/news_text.html?he_id=103&news_id=1032 (accessed December 3, 2001).

[27] B. Eijbergen et al., *Russia: The Transport Sector*, World Bank Policy Note, 2006, p. 1; Government of Russia, "Modernizatsiya transportnoi sistemy Rossii (2002–2010)."

[28] Pynnöniemi, "In Celebration of Monumentalism."

concept provided a solution to tie together the requirements of *competition* in the sphere of international transit transport, the *control* of the execution of the development plans, and the *coherence* of Russia's economic space.

Eurasian Transit Power

The narrative of the video recorder's journey from South Korea to Vladivostok brings to the fore Russia's weak capability to establish itself as a major trade route between Europe and Asia. This aspect is, however, omitted in the geopolitical envisioning of Russia as the heir to Eurasia. In the Modernization of the Transport System of Russia Federal Target Program (approved in December 2001) this latter idea is expressed as follows: "Since Russia comprises 30 percent of the territory of the Eurasian continent and has a well-developed transport system, it is objectively a natural bridge providing a set of transit connections in this direction."[29]

Improving Russia's competitiveness in comparison with the alternative routes required the implementation of "market principles" in every sphere of transportation, argued Transport Minister Nikolai Tsakh[30] at the joint meeting of the Ministry of Transport and the Ministry of Railways held in February 1998.[31] The process of changing the transport legislation in accordance with the requirements of a market economy and the opening up of Russia to international markets effectively started in the mid-1990s and this process continues today. The current transport legislation is a mixture of Soviet laws and the new codes [*kodeks*], regulations [*ustav*], as well as decisions [*postanovlenie*] issued by the federal government or different ministries.

One of the problems from the Russian point of view, as argued by deputy Prime Minister Vladimir Bulgak in 1997, was that the domestic freight operators were not ready to face the growing foreign competition. Speaking on the same occasion as Minister Tsakh, Bulgak characterized the role of the transport ministry as an "initiator of decisions" on the new form of administration in the transport sphere. "What kind of transport service market do we have today?" was his rhetorical question, to which he replied by saying: "We do not know." While the responsible federal agencies worked "with their

---

[29] Mintrans, *Federal'naya tselevaya programma modernizatsiya transportnoi sistemy Rossii (2002–2010 gody), Podprogramma Mezhdunarodnye transportnye koridory*, December 5, 2001 (Moscow, 2001), p. 13. URL: http://www.mintrans.ru/pressa/FZP/FZP_VV.htm?lvl=2 (accessed December 12, 2001).

[30] Minister of Transport of Russia from January 12, 1996 until February 28, 1998.

[31] *Rossiiskaya Gazeta*, February 11, 1998.

tail between their legs," domestic transport markets as well as the former post-Soviet transport system were lost to foreign competitors. This was unacceptable and required "operational decisions" in support of the national freight operators and forwarders. According to Bulgak, these decisions ought to be directed at *the elaboration of a market-based system of administering the economy*. But the market, he added, was only an addition to the head, not something that should replace it.[32]

The idea of markets as an *addition* to what was considered *a rational state policy* aptly captures the general lines of reasoning. In this framework, it was logical to argue that national transport operators should be protected from foreign competition by "legal means." What is more, as was unanimously agreed at the joint Collegium meeting of the Ministry of Transport and the Ministry of Railways, the development of a united transport system would be impossible if the problems that the national forwarders faced were not solved by providing them with "legislative defense" [*pravovoi zashchiti*]. In this connection in particular, the need to formulate a law on "strategic cargo and cargoes with a double meaning" was expressed. Only by these means would the state be able "to reserve a considerable part of export volumes for the national forwarders."[33]

In fact, this was a plausible remedy to argue for because, in accordance with the law On the Government of the Russian Federation issued in 1997, the government agencies are obligated to protect the interests of the domestic producers of goods and services.[34] An "interdepartmental commission" was established with the express purpose of overseeing the implementation of this policy objective, although, according to Bulgak, it had not succeeded in its mission to improve the competitiveness of Russian companies. "We have a commission for competitiveness, but a lack of competitiveness," he noted and called for further activation of the work of the commission.[35]

Even though working methods and commissions have changed over the years, the basic position has remained largely the same. Speaking at the Center for Strategic Development in Moscow in March 2000, Transport Minister Sergei Frank[36] stated that the "sacred responsibility of the state" is to protect

---

[32] V.B. Bulgak, "Rynok diktuet novye resheniya," speech at the enlarged meeting of the Collegium of the Ministry of Transport of RF, *Transport Rossii* 2 (1998): 2.

[33] *Transport Rossii* 7 (1998): 2.

[34] Nadeshda Salischeva, "Main Institutions of the Russian Administrative Law in the Sphere of the Administration of Economy," in Juha Tolonen and Boris Topornin (eds.), *Legal Foundations of Russian Economy* (Helsinki, 2000), p. 95.

[35] *Transport Rossii* 7 (1998): 2; *Transport Rossii* 2 (1998):.1.

[36] Minister of Transport of Russia from April 30, 1998 until February 2004.

and to put in order [*obustroistvo*] the transit corridors, and also to "define the conditions of their use for 'our' transport operators and for the 'others'".[37]

Clearly, the benefits that we mentioned make the transit market an arena of active rivalry. And the main characters here are not only, and not so much, the transport companies, but the governments and interstate alliances.[38]

In the *fight for transit flows*, the main instruments comprise the national legislation, tax subsidies, and direct state funding as well as international agreements. Using the example of the Traceca project, Minister Frank argued that everywhere else, unlike in Russia, the fight for transit was regarded as a subject of active state involvement. "Last, but not least," the minister argued, "transit is the correct means, as we used to say, "to strengthen friendship and good neighborhood relations" and, to use more contemporary wording, to increase the international standing of the transit country. "When a country permanently directs its cargo transport through our territory or is our partner in exploiting a transit corridor, the political leadership of the country will hardly wish to complicate relations with us on trivialities."[39] To achieve the objective— to make Russia a "strong transit country" —the minister proposed that the transit freight flows be included in the list of the state's "strategic priorities."[40]

As a "logical next step," Minister Frank argued that the state should elaborate on the official propaganda in support of Russian transit corridors and antipropaganda against competing corridor proposals. This would require "systemic support" from the MID (Ministry of Foreign Affairs), special services (FSB and others), state media, and the education system (elementary schools and schools for transport specialists). For example, maps of international transport corridors

---

[37] The practice of granting special customs privileges by presidential edict for certain commodities or particular agencies is yet another example of similar reasoning. In the early 1990s customs benefits had become a much-favored form of income because it was virtually impossible to control their actual amount or utilization.

[38] Sergei Frank,, "Ob itogah raboty transportnogo kompleksa v 1999 godu," speech at the Collegium of the Ministry of Transport of Russia, Moscow, Russia, February 16, 2000. URL: http://www.mintrans.ru/pressa/doklad_000216htm (accessed December 3, 2001); Sergei Frank, "Realizatsiya tranzitnogo potentsiala dlya stimulirovaniya ekonomicheskogo razvitiya i novogo geopoliticheskogo pozitsionirovaniya Rossii," speech at the Seminar "Modernization of the Economy". Centre for Strategic Development, Moscow, Russia, March 14, 2000. URL: http://www.mintrans.ru/pressa/doklad_000314.htm (accessed December 3, 2001).

[39] Frank, "Ob itogah raboty." For the same argumentation, see also Frank, "Realizatsiya tranzitnogo potentsiala" and Sergei Frank, speech at the second International Euro-Asian Transport Conference, St. Petersburg, Russia, September 12, 2000. URL: http://www.mintrans.ru/pressa/doklad_000912.htm (accessed 12 March, 2001).

[40] Frank, "Realizatsiya tranzitnogo potentsiala."

should be incorporated in the atlases used in elementary schools.⁴¹ In more concrete terms, the development of transit should be considered when drafting the legislation in the transport sector, although no special law or laws would be required to stimulate transit, Frank argued.⁴²

The envisioned "systemic support" for Russian transport corridors materialized in what was termed "Transport Diplomacy," which was introduced to the public in January 2006. The Ministry of Foreign Affairs of Russia and the OAO Russian Railways subsequently signed a cooperation agreement that, according to press releases from the Ministry, "reflects the growing role of transport diplomacy in our foreign policy activities." The Ministry offered its "information and legal expertise" for the purpose of "joint elaboration of large-scale and long-term projects" that the Russian Railways had undertaken. In response to claims that this would be a sign of Russia using its economic leverage in a negative way, Foreign Minister Sergei Lavrov stated that:

> The opportune use of a state's economic advantages in foreign policy is neither extraordinary nor unusual. On the contrary, a normal state in its right mind has to use its advantages, whether economic or otherwise, in order to pursue its foreign policy in the interests of its security, its economic development, and the improvement of its people's standard of living.⁴³

It can be said that the concept of Transport Diplomacy brought together previous lines of reasoning from 1997 onward on the "foreign transport policy" of Russia. The three International Euro-Asian Transport Conferences organized in St. Petersburg in 1998, 2000, and 2003 served as venues for the communication of Russian interests to international audiences with regard to the development of *Russian international transport corridors*.⁴⁴ It goes without saying that the language used in this context was considerably different from that used in the

---

⁴¹ Ibid.

⁴² Frank, "Realizatsiya tranzitnogo potentsiala."

⁴³ Ministry of Foreign Affairs of the RF 2006, transcript of remarks and reply to a media question by Russian Minister of Foreign Affairs Sergei Lavrov after signing a cooperation agreement between the Foreign Ministry and OAO Russian Railways, Moscow, January 19, 2006. URL: www.mid.ru (accessed January 25, 2006); *Edinaya Lenta Novostei*, January 20, 2006 15:22 MSK, "Vladimir Iakunin: podpisannoe segodnia soglashenie o sotrudnichestve mezhdu OAO 'RZhD' i MID RF iavliaetsya v vysshei stepenii aktual'nym," URL: http://www.rzd.ru/agency/pnews.html?pnews_id=39668&he_id=652.

⁴⁴ Declaration 1998. Declaration of the International Euro-Asian Conference on Transport, St. Petersburg, Russia, May 12–13, 1998; Declaration 2000. Declaration of the Second International Euro-Asian Conference on Transport. St. Petersburg, Russia,

domestic discussion on transport corridors. Instead of envisioning Russia as a "bridge" and the development of "international transport corridors" as a fight over control of that bridge, a new interpretation was offered, namely a vision of the development of Russian international transport corridors as "interfaces" between Europe and Asia.

The second International Euro-Asian Transport Conference in September 2000 took place just five days after the government meeting where the "international transport corridor" concept was officially included in the federal transport policy glossary.[45] Addressing an international audience, Minister Frank emphasized that Russia was not entering the transit transport markets as an "aggressive competitor" but as a "partner that offers transit services for the needs of the new century." Russia was also willing to cooperate "as an equal" with those countries that saw it first and foremost as a competitor in "a fight [*bor'be*] for transport flows." "This approach," concluded Frank, "can be considered constructive from the viewpoint of priorities of integration and stabilization."[46] Later in the same speech Minister Frank referred again to unspecified "foreign partners" who, during recent years, had come to the conclusion that:

> Russia as a country is a dead end, its communications are routes intended for the export of minerals and the import of finished products to the Russian market. Today, along with oil and metals, Russia offers the world community a new national product, namely the export of transit services. We are ready to produce and sell this product on mutually beneficial terms with our foreign partners.[47]

Couched in language befitting an international seminar, the idea of "transit service" repeats the general point made earlier by Minister Frank at the government session. The "Geographical location of Russia," said Frank, "and the level of development of its transport infrastructure" offers a solution to the problem of how to create an optimal *interface* [*interfeisom*] between Europe and

---

September 12–13, 2000; Declaration 2003. Declaration of the Third International Euro-Asian Conference on Transport, St. Petersburg, Russia, September 11–12, 2003.

[45] Government of the RF, "Osnovnie napravlenie formirovaniya i razvitiya mezhdunarodnyh transportnyh koridorov na territorii RF."

[46] Sergei Frank, "Razvitie mezhdunarodnyh transportnyh koridorov na territorii RF," speech at the meeting of the government of the RF, Moscow, Russia, September 7, 2000. http://www.mintrans.ru/pressa/doklad_000907.htm (accessed 3.12.2001).

[47] Frank, "Razvitie mezhdunarodnyh"; Sergei Frank, speech at the Second International Euro-Asian Transport Conference, St. Petersburg, Russia, September 12, 2000. URL: http://www.mintrans.ru/pressa/doklad_000912.htm (accessed December 3, .2001).

Asia.[48] The use of the loan word "interface" widens the scope of the solution. The development of international transit corridors in the territory of Russia is approached not only in the abstract terms of "geopolitical rivalry" but is also seen in the context of "circulation of power through space." The latter pattern of argumentation results in different kinds of actions from those envisioned in the context of "geopolitical rivalry."

The task, as suggested by Minister Frank at the St. Petersburg conference, is to create "software" that is adjusted to manage transit flows effectively. In this way, Russia will become more than just a point of conjunction between Europe and Asia. The elaboration and active development of the international transit corridors in the territory of Russia is expected to bolster the federal (and regional) budget, steer foreign and domestic investments toward the modernization of the required infrastructure, and, all in all, act as a catalyst for regional economic development. Achieving these aims would require the formation of a coherent transport space, in terms of the transport and administrative-legislative "infrastructure."[49]

Conclusion

The positive vision of the "bridge" and its negative counterpart, the "dead end," mirrors the traditional way of positioning Russia between Europe and Asia. The picturing of the transport puzzle in this way reiterates the Eurasianist and classical geopolitical understanding of *Russia–Eurasia*. But, contrary to Eurasianist thinking, Russia is not envisioned as something exceptional, quite the contrary. What is emphasized here is Russia's aspiration to be similar to other transit hubs found elsewhere on the globe. Picturing Russia as an "international transport corridor" (the yellow figure in the foreground of the DVTG advertisement; Figure 7.1), is an argument in favor of greater "harmonization" and "transparency" of the transport business in line with international norms and rules.

On the other hand, the infrastructure development mindset during the Soviet period, and since, has been fixed by an image of Moscow as a "port of five oceans." In this regard, the country's infrastructures are imagined as

[48] Frank, "Razvitie mezhdunarodnyh."
[49] Center for Strategic Research, "Tranzitnyi potentsial, kak faktor stimulirovanija ekonomicheskogo razvitija i novogo geopoliticheskogo pozitsionirovanija Rossii," Moscow, March 14, 2000. Proceedings of a seminar held at the Center for Strategic Research. URL: http://www.mintrans.ru/pressa/Tranzit.htm. (accessed March 20, 2000); Frank, speech at the Second International Euro-Asian Transport Conference; Frank, "Razvitie mezhdunarodnyh."

a centrifugal element that helps to tie the country and regions adjacent to it together. In this game of competition [*konkurentsiya*], the "international transport corridors" are considered as a means of "fighting for" the transit flows rerouted through the Russian territory. The price in this game is the international recognition of Russia as a great Eurasian (transport) power [*derzhava*]. In actual fact, however, a mere 1 percent of the trade flows between Asia and Europe runs through Russia at present. What is more, a substantial proportion of Russian imports (originating from Asia) are carried via distribution centers in Europe to Russia.

Set against this background, the "pan-European transport corridor" concept becomes in the Russian discourse a synonym for the metaphor of the "dead end." Thus, instead of using a term that carries a negative connotation in the Russian discursive context, it is replaced with the concept of "international transport corridor." By inventing the new term "international transport corridor," Russia has sought to accommodate the vocabulary used in the EU context to fit more neatly into its internal and external policies. Although conceptually the move from "pan-European" to "international" transport corridors is a parallel move, in practical terms it is a way of distancing Russia from the EU's discursive context. Whereas the EU discourse on corridors focuses on integration and the straightening-out of the previously isolated regions, the Russian debate is outlined in terms of dislocation and the physical disintegration of the country's infrastructure space.

CHAPTER 8

Debating Soviet Imperialism in Contemporary Poland: On the Polish Uses of Postcolonial Theory and Their Contexts

Tomasz Zarycki

Introduction

As it appears, the view of the Soviet Union as an empire, in particular a colonial empire, was not particularly popular in contemporary Polish political and intellectual discourses, at least until recently. In this chapter I will point out a number of reasons for which the "imperial" view of the Soviet Union and a "postcolonial" reading of Poland in the communist period have been often questioned or simply ignored until the second part of the first decade of the twenty-first century. Given the growing global interest in postcolonial theory in the past two decades and, in particular, the growing number of its applications to post-communist societies, one could expect that Poland would be one of the leading centers of intellectual debate on post-communism and postcolonialism. The country appears, however, to be a latecomer to the debate, joining it after a crucial transformation of its political scene, which took place after 2005. Once the "post-communist cleavage," which divided the political scene on the basis of attitude toward the communist past, had been replaced by the cleavage emerging from the differences in attitudes toward the West, postcolonial theory, as it will be demonstrated below, appeared to gain popularity in intellectual, political, and media discourses. Paradoxically, the growing recognition of the dependence of Poland on the West resulting from this transformation effected in the same way a rise of interest in postcolonial readings of the dependence of Poland on Moscow. This mechanism seems to confirm the complex nature of Poland's position in Europe and the historically intertwined character of its dependencies and perceptions of its western and eastern neighbors. The discussion in the present chapter also attempts to illustrate the role of the political and geopolitical context of the uses of postcolonial theory.

Resistance to Theories of Empire and Colonialism

One cannot claim that postcolonial theory has been well known in Poland to date; nevertheless, some of the classic works identified with this tradition were published in Poland relatively early. For example, Edward Said's seminal *Orientalism* (1978) was translated into Polish in 1991, just after the fall of communism.[1] However, at that time it didn't evoke any considerable debate. Nor did it induce debate with reference to the situation in post-communist Poland. Frantz Fanon's *The Wretched of the Earth* was published in Polish even earlier—in 1985.[2] The communist censorship most probably considered its publication as politically beneficial, given that postcolonial theory was clearly aimed against Western imperial powers. Similarly, the study of dependency theory in its various forms was allowed in the communist period, as long as interpretations didn't suggest that some kind of dependency might exist between the Soviet Union and its "satellites." In fact, neither postcolonial theory nor dependency theory was used to interpret relations inside the Soviet bloc. During the communist period, from time to time the opposition disseminated publications presenting the Soviet Union as a colonial empire, but most such publications were authored by foreigners.[3] They did not, however, have a wider resonance in oppositional discourse. Early references to "postcolonial" theory appeared in political discourse at the moment of the fall of communism, in particular in the camp of anticommunist radicals.[4] But this did not have much impact on the political or intellectual debates.

In order to interpret this late and restricted use of postcolonial theory in Poland, let me briefly sketch out the background of the political logic behind the debates on Soviet and Russian domination in post-communist Poland. The most important structure of the political scene of that period, in particular until 2005, was the so-called post-communist cleavage, known also as the post- vs. anticommunist axis or the left–right cleavage.[5] It had its roots in the late communist period, when a strong opposition to the system emerged, and it continued to structure the political and intellectual fields for several years after the fall of communism. Its interpretation may be very different depending on the point of view we assume.

---

[1] E.W. Said, *Orientalizm* (Warsaw, 1991).

[2] Frantz Fanon, *Wyklęty lud ziemi* (Warsaw, 1985).

[3] Alain Besançon, "Imperium sowieckie i panowanie sowieckie," in Jakub Karpiński and Irena Lasota (eds.), *Imperium Sowieckie* (New York, 1988), pp. 7–18.

[4] Michał Drozdek, *Istota sporu CENTRUM kontra ROAD* (Warsaw, 1990).

[5] Tomasz Zarycki, "Politics in the Periphery: Political Cleavages in Poland Interpreted in Their Historical and International Context," *Europe-Asia Studies* 52/5 (2000): 851–73.

Looking from the (post)-communist side, it could be defined as an internal Polish conflict, one related to the attitude toward the communist/socialist revolution as a Polish national manifestation of a universal phenomenon. Lipset and Rokkan have envisaged such a type of cleavage, which was defined by the attitude toward the Bolshevik Revolution.[6] It was proposed as a supplement to their four classic cleavage types (state vs. church, center vs. periphery, urban vs. rural, and class conflict). The anticommunist look at the same cleavage tends to see it in an international perspective, as an effect of Soviet expansion. Thus, the Bolshevik Revolution would not be seen as a universal phenomenon similar to national or industrial revolutions, but rather as a local, Russian one. Communism in this perspective is interpreted as a new form of Russian imperial ideology imposed on its provinces. In this context the "post-communist cleavage" in Poland, viewed as a periphery of the Soviet Empire, could be seen as a center–periphery type of cleavage in the Lipset–Rokkan typology. As in several other cases of such center–periphery cleavages described by Rokkan, it has the Catholic Church as an ally of the peripheral (in this case Polish anticommunist) camp.[7] Such an international reading of the "post-communist cleavage" in Poland, which would be compatible with a view of the Soviet Union as a colonial empire is, however, not common even in the anticommunist camp. Nevertheless, most of the references to postcolonial theory relating it to the Soviet domination over Poland can be attributed to those who are somehow linked to anticommunists identity. On the other hand, the post-communists, relabeled as social democrats in 1990, were very clearly opposed to the idea of looking at the former Soviet Union as a colonial empire. Such a vision would imply questioning their patriotism or even Polishness by defining them as a former comprador elite and, currently, a postcolonial elite or even as members of the former wider Soviet establishment. This is why they always prefer to interpret the communist period, in particular its final years, using terms like "an unequal partnership," rather than talking of a colonial type of dependence.

The absence of colonizers on Polish land, that is, the Soviets in this case, is one of the arguments used against applications of postcolonial theory to Poland in the communist period. This seems to be a questionable thesis in particular in reference to the Stalinist period, when numerous Soviet citizens occupied top positions in the Polish military, security services, and other parts of the state

---

[6] Seymor M. Lipset and Stein Rokkan, *Party Systems and Voter Alignments. Cross-national Perspectives* (New York, 1967).

[7] Stein Rokkan, "Territories, Centres, and Peripheries: Toward a Geoethnic-Geoeconomic-Geopolitical Model of Differentiation within Western Europe," in Jean Gottmann (ed.), *Centre and Periphery: Spatial Variations in Politics* (Beverly Hills, CA and London, 1980), pp. 163–204.

apparatus. Soviet military presence in Poland, in fact, lasted until 1993. The colony of "Soviet advisers," both civil and military, was quite visible in Warsaw until 1989, with its numerous elite apartment and office buildings, schools, bookstores, and other institutions. At the same time, the Soviet soldiers could often be seen on the streets of many towns in western Poland. Quite naturally, the former leaders of the Polish United Workers Party, as the communist party of Poland was officially called, currently tend to underplay their own and their country's dependence on Moscow, in particular the role of "Soviet advisors" working in Polish institutions. For example, General Wojciech Jaruzelski, the former leader of communist Poland, who still actively participates in public life, continues to emphasize his alleged autonomy from the Kremlin. Even his decision to introduce the so-called "marital law" on December 13, 1981 is still presented by him as his own sovereign act and, of course, as a successful act of saving Poland from Soviet invasion. Jaruzelski occasionally goes as far as to present himself as an active opponent of the Kremlin leaders. Moreover, in reference to the last years of his rule, Jaruzelski suggests that he had been able to influence Gorbachev's perestroika. This supposedly happened by presenting liberal reforms in Poland as a model, which inspired the Soviet leader to speed up his own reform.[8] Thus, Jaruzelski and his former colleagues from the communist party leadership, as well as their followers who formed the core of the Democratic Left Alliance (Sojusz Lewicy Demokratycznej, SLD), oppose any "colonial" interpretations of the communist period. They consider such interpretations as offensive given their self-image as patriotic leaders of "socialist," but sovereign, Poland. On the other, the anticommunist side of the political spectrum, vison of the Soviet Union as a colonial empire was usually acceptable. However, such labels, as have already been mentioned, were never very popular—neither in political nor academic discourse. There are several possible explanations of this reluctance to view the Soviet Union's hegemony over Poland in colonial terms, even by the anticommunist camp.

One major reason behind this tendency seems to lie in the common aversion of envisioning Poland as a peripheral country. Poland in the mainstream narrative of its history is imagined as an active actor on the political scene with the ability to control not only its own destiny but also an ability to influence developments in the entirety of Central and Eastern Europe. Poland is thus currently presented, for example, as the key actor that triggered the process of the fall of communism. Its agency is seen first of all in numerous outbursts of

---

[8] "Interview with Gen. Wojciech Jaruzelski," (undated) Parallel History Project on NATO and the Warsaw Pact, Oral History Interviews with Polish Generals http://www.php.isn.ethz.ch/collections/colltopic.cfm?lng=en&id=20671&navinfo=15708

unrest and active protest against communist power, in particular in the years 1956, 1970, 1980, 1988, and others. A key role is in particular assigned to the Solidarity movement. Early examples of its allegedly crucial impact on the region include the first Solidarity congress in 1981 and its appeal to the working people of Central and Eastern Europe. Among other manifestations of anticommunists' activities, such events are quoted as resistance to martial law, constructive negotiations with communists, round-table talks, and a resulting peaceful revolution that set an example with the appointment of the first noncommunist government in Central and Eastern Europe in 1989. At the same time, the dominant narrative of the Polish political and intellectual elite assumes the need to demonstrate that Poland belongs to the Western European core or at least a determination to be part of it. Poland, much like its political and intellectual leaders (irrespective of what orientation they seem to maintain), may not agree to be assigned a place in the European periphery, or in any periphery in fact. This widely shared geopolitical imperative seems to strongly influence academic discourse, discouraging interpretations that may be seen as implying the peripheral status of Poland. In other words, concerns about the self-image of Poland produced for Western audiences make looking at Poland as a colony, or a periphery in general, difficult.

The mythical image of Poland as an engine of anticommunist revolution in Europe, with its emblematic story of workers and intellectuals combining their forces under the leadership of Lech Wałęsa in the Gdańsk shipyard during the great strikes of 1980, is accompanied by another important narrative. It is the narrative of Poland as a suffering victim, a fundamental element of the modern Polish national identity whose roots lie in the classical writing of the Polish nineteenth-century Romantic poets. In modern times, its key manifestations are the narratives of the destruction of Poland by Nazi Germany and by the Soviet Union in 1939 with the Katyń Massacre, Stalinist-period atrocities, and other crimes and cruelties of the communist regime in Poland. Apparently, this Polish self-image of a "Christ of nations" more or less fits with the model of the Soviet Union as a colonial empire with Poland as its colony. Nevertheless, the Polish stereotypical understanding of the notion of "colony" appears not to be fully compatible with this mythical concept of Polish victimhood. One has to emphasize that, from the moment of its very inception with Adam Mickiewicz's writings, the concept has had a very strong messianic element borrowed from the Jewish biblical tradition.[9] Thus, Poland in this narrative, even when

---

9   Zdzisław Krasnodębski, "Adam Mickiewicz' politische Theologie," in Zdzisław Krasnodębski and Stefan Garsztecki (eds.), *Sendung und Dichtung: Adam Mickiewicz in Europa* (Hamburg, 2002), pp. 33–58.

suffering, makes conscious choices and confronts its torturers with dignity and courage. Moreover, it is through this conscious suffering that Poland, according to the master narrative of "Christ of nations," is influencing the external world, changing it morally and, in effect, also politically.[10] A good example of a recent incarnation of this idea was Pope John Paul II's call for an active Polish role in the revival of Christianity in Western Europe.

These and other Polish myths, while changing in form (in particular undergoing secularization), seem still to permeate the mainstream discourse of Polish national identity and shape the way Poland's image directed toward the external world is constructed. While liberals and conservatives may differ regarding the particular content and importance assigned to these myths, their main figures and political implications remain stable. In particular, most of the actors on the contemporary Polish political scene seem to share the assumption that anticommunist forces were an important actor on the international political stage.

An interesting example of this tendency to assign Poland a particular agency in the international scene, even in the communist period, is the popularity of the so-called Giedroyć Doctrine. Jerzy Giedroyć was the editor-in-chief of the Paris-based *Kultura* monthly. The novel vision of Poland's eastern policy, which his milieu advocated from the 1960s, involved unconditional recognition of the eastern border of Poland and support for the independence of Belarus, Lithuania, and Ukraine.[11] It is considered today to be the cornerstone of contemporary Polish foreign policy. Despite its rejection of the prewar Polish aspirations to retain political control over at least part of the region, the project is still considered as neocolonial in some milieus in Russia or Ukraine, as one that is aimed at restricting the ability of Russia to influence the countries in question by making them fully independent. While the "Giedroyć Doctrine" was an idea of minor importance in the communist period—it could even be considered to have been extremely unrealistic and obscure at that time—after 1989 it not only assumed a central role in the legitimization of Poland's foreign policy but also influenced the way the communist period was reviewed. In particular, the Polish anticommunist opposition, seen through the figure of Giedroyć, now appears to have been an independent actor on the international political scene. One could, of course, remember that the Polish government in exile existed in

---

[10] Andrzej Walicki, *Philosophy and Romantic Nationalism: The Case of Poland* (Oxford and New York, 1982).

[11] Janusz Korek, "In the Face of the West and the East—The Formation of the Identity of the Polish Intelligentsia after the End of World War II," in Janusz Korek (ed.), *From Sovietology to Postcoloniality: Poland and Ukraine in the Postcolonial Perspective* (Stockholm, 2007), pp. 229–69.

London during the entire communist period. However, after it ceased to be recognized by the Western powers in 1945 it was never portrayed as a significant actor on the international scene. In contrast, the role of Giedoryć and his circle is currently presented in the mainstream discourse as much more significant than that of the London government. Even former communist leaders, such as Aleksander Kwaśniewski, claim to have been under *Kultura*'s influence in the late communist period. Thus, Poland's role in the late communist period is redefined today by the valuation of the role of Giedroyć. His supposed agency, although delayed in time, is at odds with the role of the passive Soviet colony. Even if communist Poland was controlled by the Soviets, the émigré community is now presented as having been able to influence international relations. When Poland became the first state to recognize the independence of Ukraine or the active participation of Poles in the 2004 Orange Revolution can be seen, according to this interpretative logic, as delayed effects of Giedroyć's thinking. At the same time, General Jaruzelski was able to claim in 2003 that his decision to introduce martial law in 1981 paved the road to the democratization of Poland and eventually to accession to the European Union.[12]

The assumption that seems to lie behind these reevaluations of Poland's history rejecting its colonial status in the communist era is the view that colonized states are passive and devoid of agency. Colonial states seem to be identified first of all with "black" African nations perceived as submissive victims of their "white" superior masters. Their suffering appears as meaningless and their cultural inferiority is obvious. Such simplified, but nevertheless dominant, interpretations of colonization are hard to reconcile with the mainstream discourse of Polish historiography in which Poles are imagined as active agents of change; external influences on their fate are in most cases marginalized. The way the fall of communism is presented today (as an outcome of the activities of Polish anticommunists), Polish courage and determination is incompatible with the image of a postcolonial state created, as is often considered "artificially," by former European empires. The victory of Solidarity in many such Polish interpretations brought about not only the democratization of Poland but also prompted the process of liberation of Central and Eastern Europe from the Soviet yoke. In other words, while Poland is imagined mostly as a dependent country in many periods of its history, it is nevertheless never presented as a passive or non-European nation. At the same time, the rejection of any "colonial" status, as it is understood in Poland, seems to emphasize passivity and non-Europeanness.

---

[12] Wojciech Jaruzelski, "Towarzysze, głosujcie 'za'. Z Wojciechem Jaruzelskim rozmawiał Jarosław Kurski," *Gazeta Wyborcza*, May 30, 2003, p. 16.

Poland and Russia

Another important reason for the rejection of the colonial and postcolonial interpretations of the relations between Poland and the Soviet Union is the widespread and historically rooted conviction of the cultural superiority of Poland over its eastern neighbors—and Russia—in particular. Moreover, the status of a fully European nation is usually assigned to Poland as part of Western Europe, a trait from which its agency is also derived. Russia, on the other hand, is imagined as not fully European, and, for this reason, inferior and in some sense passive, especially as far as the transfer of ideas and innovations is concerned. Classical colonial theories are read at the same time as implying the cultural superiority of the metropolis. Several analysts suggest that Poland's submission by the Soviet Union, and earlier the Russian Empire, may be seen as an exceptional type of colonial dependence where the periphery appears to have a higher cultural status than the center. Dariusz Skórczewski asked, in such context, for the development of a specific theory of Soviet colonialism, which in his view had its peculiar traits and makes it different from the Western European model. Its specificity in particular lies in the fact that the classic model of relations (civilized metropolis vs. barbarian empire) does not work here and Russian imperialism should be seen as "regressive" in contrast to "progressive" Western imperialisms.[13] A similar attempt at defining the specific traits of Russian colonialism was also made by Ewa Domańska.[14] She sees them in particular in the context of national rather than race issues. Another specificity is that after the fall of the Western empires their colonies often retained the former political and educational system, while in the case of Russian colonialism most of the traces of the colonial past are usually carefully removed.

In most cases, however, the colonial type of interpretation seems to be rejected for the above-mentioned reason: a fear of recognition of the cultural and, in effect, also the moral superiority of Russia over Poland. At the same time, images of Russia as a barbarian, backward and non-Western empire seem to lie at the heart of Polish self-image. As I have argued elsewhere, one of the main mechanisms behind imagining Russia as an inferior evil empire may be seen in the Polish inferiority complex towards the West, or more generally an extreme concern about Poland's perception in the West. Another factor to be taken into account is the particular role of the intelligentsia in Poland—its identity and

---

[13] Dariusz Skórczewski, "Dla czego Polska powinna upomnieć się o swoją postkolonialność?," *Znak* 628 (2007): 145–53.

[14] Ewa Domańska, "Obrazy PRL w perspektywie postkolonialnej. Studium przypadku," in Krzysztof Brzechczyn (ed.), *Obrazy PRL. Konceptualizacja realnego socjalizmu w Polsce* (Poznań, 2008), pp. 167–86, esp. p. 168.

ideals. They can be theoretically described as defining a particular role of cultural capital in Poland's internal social hierarchies as well as a key asset used by Poles in their relations with foreign partners.[15] Cultural capital is used as a key factor to compensate Poland's weaknesses as far as the economic and political spheres are concerned. In other words, Polish elites tend to construct their self-images as members of the European high society, as fully Westernized, culturally equal partners of Western elites, even if they come from a poorer and weaker country of Central and Eastern Europe. Russia in this narrative is imagined as not fully European, as a country that makes anyone associated with it look less European, less civilized, and less "cultured." As I would argue, this basic assumption of the inferiority of Russia (in all its political incarnations, including, of course, the Soviet Union) may explain a considerable part of the current uses and interpretations of the period of Soviet domination over Poland. In general, what Poland and, in particular, its elites are trying to communicate to the West is that they have nothing in common with Russia, which they consider non-European. At the same time, associations with barbarian, backward Russian influences are used as a stigma in discourses directed against external and internal opponents of the Polish elite. This imperative also makes use of interpretations of the past that assume deeper interactions between Poles and Russians and are problematic form the point of view of the dominant standards of political correctness.

One of the manifestations of the above-described tendency is the current and past silencing of the history of Polish–Russian political and intellectual interactions.[16] First of all, the history of Russian influences on Polish political and cultural life is almost absent from mainstream academic and political discourse. A good example is the so-called "period of partitions." It should be remembered that Poland ceased to exist as a state in 1795 and was divided among Austria, Prussia, and Russia. Borders between these countries were decided at the Congress of Vienna in 1815 and lasted almost a hundred years—until the outbreak of the World War I. During that period the three parts of the Polish space developed in completely different social, economic, and political frameworks. The long-term effects of that separate development during the nineteenth century are still visible in several dimensions of Polish social and economic geography.[17] The way in which

---

[15] Tomasz Zarycki, "The Power of the Intelligentsia: The Rywin Affair and the Challenge of Applying the Concept of Cultural Capital to Analyze Poland's Elites," *Theory and Society* 38/6 (2009): 613–48.

[16] Janusz Tazbir, "O czym się pisać nie godziło," *Gazeta Wyborcza*, December 27, 2003, pp. 16–17.

[17] Tomasz Zarycki, "The Persistence of the Borders on the Territory of Poland," in Olga Brednikova and Victor Voronkov (eds.), *Nomadic Borders / Кочующие Границы. Proceedings of the seminar held in Narva, November, 13–15.1998* (St. Petersburg, 1999), pp. 141–5.

this historical heritage has influenced current cultural, political, and economic developments, in particular in the regions, is still controversial. Interpretations of the role of history, and in particular the historical role of the three former empires in shaping contemporary regional identities, are often discussed when Polish election results are announced. This is because the electoral geography of the country remains strongly influenced by nineteenth-century borders. When one looks at the dominant narratives in these interpretations of the role of history, Russian influences are always presented in darker hues than Austrian and Prussian influences, which are currently considered as at least partly beneficial.[18] The Russian presence in Polish lands during the nineteenth century is blamed, among other things, for the current economic underdevelopment of those lands as well as for a low civic culture. The history of positive economic developments in these territories,[19] or the widespread fascination with Russian culture found among Poles,[20] is usually silenced. The numerous Poles who had successful careers in the Russian Empire and their impact on Russian culture or politics are very rarely mentioned. The same phenomenon could be observed in reference to the Soviet period. The study of Moscow's influences in different spheres of life in communist Poland is not a popular subject. While some historical studies in this field are being published by the Institute for National Remembrance (IPN), set up by the anticommunist government in 1999, the institute itself is often criticized for its obsessive and politically motivated digging into the "dirty past." For this reason the post-communist left (SLD party) systematically calls for the disbanding of the IPN. Thus, Soviet influences on Polish culture or academia are usually marginalized and, if mentioned at all, are usually presented as unsuccessful and their traces, if any, as having been eliminated a long time ago. At the same time, accusations of being "Sovietized" or "Russified" are used as terms of abuse and are aimed at political enemies or groups considered as backward or reactionary. Use of these terms is in most cases not at all related to any in-depth analysis or to a given person's or group's involvement in Polish–Soviet/Russian interactions. Typically, a "Homo-Sovieticus" mentality is assigned to those considered as not very resourceful or smart in different ways. What is intriguing in this context is that even clear Polish influences on Soviet cultural

---

[18] Tomasz Zarycki, "History and Regional Development: A Controversy over the 'Right' Interpretation of the Role of History in the Development of the Polish Regions," *Geoforum* 38 (2007): 485–93.

[19] Jacek Kochanowicz, "Polish Kingdom: Periphery as a Leader," Paper prepared for the XIV International Economic History Congress in Helsinki, Finland, August 21–25, 2006.

[20] Marian Zdziechowski, *Wpływy rosyjskie na duszę polską* (Cracow, 1920).

and intellectual life, which could be otherwise seen as a source of Polish pride, are rarely discussed in contemporary Poland.

This is particularly the case with the phenomenon of Poland's intermediary role in cultural contacts between the Soviet Union and the West. The apex of this phenomenon might be said to have been in the 1960s and 1970s when the Soviet intelligentsia were learning Polish in great numbers. Polish books, magazines, or music disks were in high demand in all major Soviet cities, primarily because they gave access to Western culture. Western books were often accessible only in Polish translations, and Polish magazines were the only publications in the Soviet Union where photographs of Western stars of popular culture could be seen. Products of Polish popular and high culture were themselves perceived as more Western and desirable. This phenomenon, despite the fact that it seems to fit well with Poland's self-image as superior to Russia in cultural terms, is almost forgotten in contemporary Poland. At the same time, most Polish artists, intellectuals, and academics rarely, and, in most cases, only with embarrassment, recall their visits to the Soviet Union and cooperation with Soviet institutions or personalities other than anticommunist dissidents. Interestingly, this tendency could be noted even in the communist period. Paradoxically, the presence of Soviet or Russian culture in Polish cultural productions was also considerably restricted. Although Soviet cultural products were widely disseminated and stories of Polish–Soviet friendship and cooperation aggressively pushed, Soviet themes in Polish TV productions, films (in particular comedies), and novels were almost taboo after the Stalinist period.[21] The main motive behind this policy was probably a fear of producing images that suggested the Polish leadership were Soviet puppets or, in other words, images of Poland as a colony of the Soviet Union. One of the best examples of this tendency was the TV series *Życie na gorąco*, first shown in 1979. Its main hero was an agent of the Polish communist secret services who is working undercover as a journalist while tracking down members of a Nazi organization of war criminals in different parts of the world. Although the series was produced with the clear political motive of improving the image of the Polish security services and was even partly filmed in the Soviet Crimea (which doubled as South America), no Soviet-based storyline or personage appears in any of the nine episodes. At the same time, the brave Polish spy cooperates as an equal partner with CIA agents and works hand in hand with police officers from several Western countries.

---

21 Piotr Zwierzchowski, "Obraz Rosjan w kinie PRL," in Konrad Rokicki and Sławomir Stępień (eds.), *W objęciach Wielkiego Brata: Sowieci w Polsce, 1944–1993* (Warsaw, 2009), pp. 275–92.

In the context of a long history of rejection of any cultural or political links with Russia and Russians, even the status as Russia's victim can be considered difficult to accept in contemporary Poland. This is probably one of the reasons why Ewa Thompson's *Imperial Knowledge: Russian Literature and Colonialism*, first published in English but translated into Polish the same year (2000), has not met with particular interest in Poland. Thompson proposed looking at Russian and Soviet classic literature through the postcolonial lens. Poland, in such a perspective, appears as a typical colonial territory with its native voices muted or heard only through intermediaries. Thompson's book was discussed, in particular, in conservative milieus. However, even there, it didn't attract as much interest as one might expect from such an innovative work. Thompson herself pointed to the fact that Polish conservatives discount her book just as they reject any discussion of postcolonial theory, which they see as Marxist and thus illegitimate.[22] One could note in this context that Marxist theory, which Thompson herself avoided in her book, is still largely ignored in Polish academia. Among other reasons, this is due to its perception as Soviet or Russian. Similar arguments to explain the lack of interest in postcolonial theory in Poland have been presented by David Moore. He points out two main reasons for a lack of interest in postcolonial theory in post-communist Europe. Firstly, he identifies claims to be "European" with the side of the "white" population of the former Soviet Union. Secondly, he identifies a compensatory behavior—a cult of the glorious, powerful past that is typically found in Central and East European nations, which is usually considered incompatible with the status of a colony.[23]

Rise of Interest in Postcolonial Theory after 2005

Interestingly, analyzing Poland's peripheral location in any setup is often considered as harmful to Polish national interests, as such views may be used by "the enemies" of Poland as an argument for its marginalization. Thus, mainstream discourses of the transformation period envisage Poland as "returning to Europe," where its place has always been, while a recognition of a postcolonial character of Poland may imply its in some way deficient European status and is thus avoided. Moreover, looking at Poland as peripheral in relation to the West may imply a more or less critical attitude toward the latter, which is a very risky attitude

---

[22] Ewa Thompson, "Postkolonialne refleksje," *Porównania* 5 (2008): 113–26.
[23] David Chioni Moore, "Is the Post- in Postcolonial the Post- in Post-Soviet? Toward a Global Postcolonial Critique," *PMLA* 116/1 (2001): 111–28.

given the context of Poland's political scene and the extreme politicization of the issue of Poland's stance toward the West, in particular Western Europe. It was in 2005, when the Polish political scene underwent a considerable transformation, that there was, debatably, a change in its main point of reference, from Soviet Union as former metropolis to the West as the new center. In 2004 Poland joined the European Union, and soon thereafter the post-communist coalition of the SLD and the Polish Peasants' Party (Polskie Stronnictwo Ludowe, PSL) lost their majority in the parliament to two right-wing parties—the liberal Civic Platform (Platforma Obywatelska, PO) and the conservative Law and Justice (Prawo i Sprawiedliwość, PiS). They soon become the main antagonists on the political scene. Debates about the communist past and the role of the former communist leadership, which defined the key political cleavage in the previous period, gave way to debates about the place of Poland in the European Union. The key role of the West as Poland's "significant other" was of course evident much earlier, in particular in the economic or symbolic sphere. However, it was only in 2005 when the political scene appeared to be dominated by the cleavage defined directly by the attitude toward the West, and no longer by the so-called "post-communist cleavage" defined through its different evaluation of the communist past. In these circumstances, postcolonial theory began to appear as a much more appealing political narrative than it had in the past. Interestingly, its uses, especially those that reference dependence on the Soviet Union, were concentrated on one side of the newly reorganized political spectrum, namely in the Euroskeptic, conservative camp.

In such a context, a series of articles by Ewa Thompson published between 2005 and 2007 attracted more interest. In her articles, which appeared in Polish in the *Europa* magazine, a supplement to the *Dziennik* daily, Thompson referred to Poland as suffering from postcolonial syndrome, revealing many of the classic symptoms described by postcolonial authors. They included, in her view, pessimism (among others the invention of "necessary fictions"), lack of confidence, and resentment. Thompson argued that the Soviet Union was the colonial empire that had subdued Poland and it was mostly under Soviet domination that Poland and its elites lost their self-confidence and ability to autonomously define Poland's national interests. The period of the nineteenth-century partition of the country was also mentioned by Thompson as a time of colonization, while a truly independent Poland was, for her, represented mostly by the Polish–Lithuanian Commonwealth of the sixteenth and seventeenth centuries. It was that period, she argued, that should serve as a point of reference for the reconstruction of Poland's new identity and self-confidence. Interestingly,

Thompson called the West a "surrogate hegemon."[24] As she suggested, the current elites of Poland, both post-communists and liberals, have not been able to overcome their "postcolonial mentality," which had developed in the communist period and was now shaping attitudes of the Polish elites toward the West. Thus, Poland appears to be in a state of "enslavement" by the West, but this situation, as Thompson suggests, is, to a large extent, an effect of the voluntary choice of the elite conditioned by its colonial mentality inherited from the period of Soviet colonization. One could probably summarize this interpretation as the thesis that the Polish elite is in a state of mental colonization by the nonexistent Soviet Empire and, therefore, acting in symbolic self-submission to the West. These interpretations offered by Thompson have had a considerable impact on Polish political discourse. They have been, in particular, picked up by conservative politicians including the leader of PiS, Jarosław Kaczyński, who started to talk about the "postcolonial mentality" of his opponents. At the same time, Thompson overtly supported Kaczynski's government. This tendency, let me stress, started to gather momentum only around 2007. At that time we could talk about the entrance of elements of postcolonial theory into mainstream political discourse in Poland.[25]

A similar position toward the application of postcolonial theory was assumed by Dariusz Skórczewski, a professor at the Catholic Lublin University. While sharing many of the conservatives' views, he criticized what he considered to be an inadequate interest in postcolonial theory in Poland. In his view, this could provide the language that would allow Poles to communicate their concerns and sensibilities to Western audiences.[26] Skórczewski refers to the Polish experiences of suffering at the hands of Soviet Russia, or more generally communism, which most Poles consider to be not fully recognized by the West. Skórczewski suggests that the West is not ready to accept a Central–Eastern (and first of all Polish) critical view of Russia because Poles are unable to articulate such a view in an adequate theoretical language. He applauded Thompson's *Imperial Knowledge* for presenting the Central European critical perspective on Russia in a theoretical language of Western academia. At the same time, Skórczewski claimed that the criticism Thompson's work encountered in the West is a symptom of the

---

[24] Ewa Thompson, "Said a sprawa polska. Przeciwko kulturowej bezsilności peryferii," *Europa*, June 29, 2005, p. 11.

[25] For a recent example of references to postcolonial theory by Jarosław Kaczyński, see, for example, PAP, "Kaczyński: Możemy odrzucić system postkolonialny. Potrzeba referendum," *Polska The Times*, March 30, 2012, p. 2.

[26] Dariusz Skórczewski, "Modern Polish Literature: Through a Postcolonial Lens— The Case of Paweł Huelle's Castorp," *Sarmatian Review* 26/3 (2006): 12–29.

status enjoyed by Russian and Soviet cultures in Western academia.[27] It is much higher than the standing of Central European cultures and results in a spread of positive images of the Soviet and Russian Empires in the West. As Skórczeski argued, the Soviet Union is still often perceived as the advocate of colonized peoples/nations and analyzing it as a colonial empire is difficult to accept for many Western academics[28].

In effect, the field of postcolonial theory is seen by Skórczewski as a battlefield between Poland and other Central European nations and Russians. Its main arena is Western academia while its outcomes can be observed on bookshelves of Western academic bookstores. As Skórczewski argues, Poles and other Central Europeans are losing that battle to Russians, views of whom are much better represented in mainstream Western academic discourse. The debate on Russian internal colonialism initiated by Alexander Etkind is seen by Skórczewski as one of the recent arenas of the above-mentioned Central European–Russian battle inside the field of postcolonial studies. Let us remember that Etkind proposed to reinterpret the notion of "internal colonization" introduced by Michael Hechter in his study of centre–periphery relations in Great Britain. As Etkind argued, English internal colonization was different from the case of the Russian Empire, which was colonization of a "geographically and ethnically internal population subject to economic exploitation while resisting cultural assimilation."[29] In the Russian case, according to Etkind, "the heartland regions of the country were exploited more than peripheral regions" and "typical colonial endeavors were directed not overseas but rather at the people in the homeland." Moreover, Etkind drew a comparison with the nineteenth-century *narodnichestvo* movement among the Russian intelligentsia, which idealized the peasantry (usually translated into English as "Populism" or "Western Orientalism") and which supposedly also produced "amalgams of fear, guilt, pride, and curiosity in areas as divergent as ethnography, fiction and terrorism." Thus the 1917 Revolution becomes, according to Etkind, a narrative of a colonial people—the Russian *narod*—taking power from their colonizers—the country's political and educated elite. This view is unacceptable to Skórczewski who sees in it a reincarnation of the old myth of "the innocently suffering Russia," which removes from Russia

---

[27] For a review of Thompson's work, see, for example, Steven Cassedy, "Review of Imperial Knowledge: Russian Literature and Colonialism by Ewa M. Thompson," *Slavic Review* 60/4 (2001): 880.

[28] Dariusz Skórczewski, "Modern Polish Literature."

[29] Alexander Etkind, "Internal Colonization and Russian Cultural History," *Ulbandus* 7 (2003): 17–25. See also Alexander Etkind, *Internal Colonization: Russia's Imperial Experience* (Cambridge, 2011).

responsibility for its colonial conquests and brutal oppression of its colonies. Similar criticism toward Etkind's application of "internal colonialism" has been voiced by Andrzej Nowak.[30] As Nowak argues, Russians can be perceived as victims of communism, as a "captive nation," but this should not be allowed to overshadow the status of its main benefactors and their responsibility for the Bolshevik Revolution and imposing communism on other nations across the world. Nowak is thus warning that recognizing the Russian nation as a victim of the Soviet regime may absolve it from the responsibility for its crimes, which will be partly transferred to the true victims of communism—nations of the Central Europe that never endorsed the Bolshevik Revolution—and which is another incarnation of an aggressive Russian imperialism and colonialism. One could note that the 1919–1921 Polish–Soviet War was similar in one important aspect to the Polish uprisings of 1831 and 1863. In both cases, the Russian/Bolshevik side was offering the Polish peasants liberation from slavery (in particular serfdom) under "Polish lords." During these occasions, the Polish peasants appeared to be divided, but in particular in 1919 a majority of them did not support the "emancipatory" option offered from the east and sided with Polish nationalism, which presented itself as a bulwark against the "Bolshevik barbarians." Thus, as we can see, the same conflict can be imagined as a universal class conflict from the point of view of the Russian/Soviet center, while in peripheries like Poland it assumes the nature of a national liberation fight. In the same way, debates regarding the application of postcolonial theory may differ in their implications. In Russia, as Etkind's writings seem to exemplify, they tend be seen as more abstract, referring mostly to interpretation of the nature of class structure of the Russian and Soviet Empires. At the same time, in peripheral countries like Poland or Ukraine the very same issues are viewed rather as manifestations of tensions between Russian and Central European nationalisms.

This seems to be also visible in the example of Ukraine, where one finds specific patterns of use of postcolonial theory. Interpretations of Ukraine as a postcolonial state in which Russia is defined as a colonial empire, are much more common than in Poland.[31] Ewa Thompson, when comparing Polish and Ukrainian uses of postcolonial theory, applauds Ukrainian determination to point openly to Russia as the imperial hegemon. Polish intellectuals, in her opinion, appear too

---

[30] Andrzej Nowak, *History and Geopolitics: A Contest for Eastern Europe* (Warsaw, 2008).
[31] Taras Kuzio, "History, Memory and Nation Building in the Post-Soviet Colonial Space," *Nationalities Papers* 30/2 (2002): 241–64; Mykola Riabchuk, "Culture and Cultural Politics in Ukraine: A Post-colonial Perspective," in Taras Kuzio and Paul J. D'Anieri (eds.), *Dilemmas of State-led Nation Building in Ukraine* (Westport, CT, 2002), pp. 47–70.

timid, too much concerned about Western opinion. In effect, they are losing the battle regarding the postcolonial field both to Russians and Ukrainians. Thompson seems to suggest that Poland may be considered what Rokkan called an "interface periphery," that is a territory under overlapping Western and Russian/Soviet influences. While the status of an interface periphery is usually considered privileged, as it allows for the opportunity to play on contradictions between competing centers, Thompson sees it rather as a constraint. Another reason for Polish inability to clearly voice national interest in the language of postcolonial theory is, according to Thompson, the duality of Poland's status as a nation that can be considered as being in the past both a colonizer and colonized. Here Thompson seems to refer to the above-mentioned problem of Poland's agency seen as an important asset in self-image. Ukrainians or Lithuanians, as Thompson argues, don't have such problems and are ready to admit their peripheral status *tout court*, even when this status may be seen as minimizing their agency. The Polish inability to choose between the role of a passive victim and autonomous actor is, in other words, one of the basic problems in the application of postcolonial theory for interpreting its history. As Maria Janion[32] has pointed out, Claire Cavanagh[33] and Maxim Waldstein[34] were among the first non-Polish authors to discuss the ambiguous position of Poland in the context of postcolonial theory. Cavanagh, in particular, called for the removal of the "white spots" in postcolonial studies, by which she meant the absence of studies on the Polish experience of being simultaneously an object and an agent of colonization.

Poland—Imperial Agent or Object?

Cavanagh's call is slowly finding resonance. Works assuming the role of Poland as a victim of Soviet or Russian colonization, on the one hand, and analyses of Polish colonial heritage and orientalist attitudes, on the other, started to emerge after 2000. Historians such as Andrzej Nowak[35] and sociologists

---

[32] Marian Janion, *Niesamowita słowiańszczyzna. Fantazmaty literatury* (Cracow, 2006).

[33] Claire Cavanagh, "Postcolonial Poland," *Common Knowledge* 10/1 (2004): 82–92.

[34] Maxim Kupovykh Waldstein, "Observing Imperium: A Postcolonial Reading of Ryszard Kapuscinski's Account of Soviet and Post-Soviet Russia," *Social Identities* 8/3 (2002): 481–99.

[35] Andrzej Nowak, "From Empire Builder to Empire Breaker, or There and Back Again: History and Memory of Poland's Role in Eastern European Politics," *Ab Imperio* 1 (2004): 255–89; Andrzej Nowak, "Between Imperial Temptation and Anti-imperial Function in East European Politics: Poland from the Eighteenth to Twenty-first Century," in Kimitaka

such as Jan Sowa[36] got involved in debates on whether the Polish–Lithuanian Commonwealth could be considered an empire. One could also mention, in this context, the inspiring interpretations of Ewa Domańska. Domańska sees the rarely used postcolonial perspective as an approach different from dominating paradigms of totalitarianism and post-communism. According to Domańska, these stereotypical approaches to Central and Eastern Europe force us to think along the lines promoted by Soviet ideologues, that is, they strengthen the impression that the communist ideology was the only factor defining the treatment of conquered states and nations, while, as Ewa Thompson argued, the leading role was played by nationalism, manifesting itself in the form of "internal European colonialism."[37] Following Thompson, Domańska considers the period of 1939–41 as the most spectacular colonial expansion in the entire history of Russia. She criticizes the Polish historiography for using notions like "vassal" or "satellite" rather than "colony" for the status of Poland in the communist era. One of the greatest successes of the Soviet Union, in her opinion, is the fact that it managed to turn our attention from Soviet/Russian colonialism to problems of communism and/or totalitarianism. In effect, then, aggressive nationalism is masked by turning attention to its internal victims—the suffering executors of imperial ideology. Russian literature, including works by such famous dissidents as Aleksandr Solzhenitsyn or Victor Suvorov, as Domańska argues, has shaped an image of Russia as a victim, both in the West and in Poland. This is an image of a country paying an enormous price for its conquests, oppressing and exploiting its own citizens more than those of the subjugated nations and states. Such images of the oppressed function in the framework of colonial meta-discourse, which includes in itself critical narratives, which, in turn, legitimize the domination of the center.

Domańska analyzes a short documentary film, *Festival of the Soviet Song in Zielona Góra* (1974), and how it has been received in the context of contemporary Polish popular culture. The Zielona Góra Festival was an annual musical contest for the best Polish interpreter of Soviet songs. From its establishment in 1965 until the end of communist Poland it was promoted in the media and, in effect, every adult citizen of communist Poland was more or less familiar with the festival. Each year, besides some well-known Polish singers, the festival hosted selected Soviet stars. The public included Poles but

---

Matsuzato (ed.), *Emerging Meso-areas in the Former Socialist Countries: Histories Revived or Improvised* (Hokkaido, 2005), pp. 247–84.

[36] Jan Sowa, *Fantomowe ciało króla: Peryferyjne zmagania z nowoczesną formą* (Cracow, 2011).

[37] Domańska, "Obrazy PRL."

also Soviet guests, in particular, representatives of the Soviet army and other Soviet personnel based in Poland. In the original footage from the 1974 event Domańska focuses on a Polish amateur artist playing a Russian song. The performance is, for Domańska, a manifestation of Homi Bhabha's concept of "mimicry"—losing one's own authenticity and being jammed between two cultures. The current uses of the documentary, which was included in a 2007 DVD featuring "the funniest moments of communist Poland," is interpreted by Domańska as a "comic turn." It is a transformation of the "noble ideals" of communism into the "funny everyday life of communist Poland" in which the "metonymic presence" of the colonizers reveals itself. According to Domańska, such recycling of communist-era documentaries reminds us about the "colonial past" and proves that something from the colonizers is still left in Poles. This is because Poles treat their past in the same way that the colonizers treated their own past after the Revolution. Russian communists mocked the aristocratic lifestyles, turning objects that had been of great importance for the aristocrats into grotesque items, which after the Revolution started to serve completely different purposes from those for which they had originally been made for. The effect of such linking of a "real tragedy" with its repetition as farce is a "comedy of doubles" typical of tragic farce. Domańska sees here an effect of camouflage as mentioned by Homi Bhabha in his discussion of mimicry. In her insistence on seeing Soviet communism as an ideology of Russian imperialism, Domańska seems to inscribe herself into a long Polish tradition of equating the Russian Empire with the Soviet Union.

In addition to analyses of Polish discourse on Russia and the Soviet Union, studies of the Polish myth of Kresy, or the "Eastern Borderland," started to emerge after 2007. Evocations of Kresy, a territory that was formerly the eastern provinces of Poland, usually involve images of a peaceful, multicultural rural land in which Polish culture is dominant. The Kresy discourse has been identified as a postimperial and highly orientalist narrative by Bogusław Bakuła.[38] Nevertheless, it is possible to find attempts at defending the Kresy myth even in the liberal camp. Janion points to the similarity of the Kresy myth to the American myth of the Wild West. Most of the interpretations of the Kresy discourse are, however, much less critical. This stream of scholarly discourse deals both with a history of Poland viewed as a colonial empire, and with the contemporary discourse on the historical heritage of the Kresy region, which can be seen as a virtual territory. Although it refers to a real area, encompassing most of present-day Belarus,

---

[38] Bogusław Bakuła, "Colonial and Postcolonial Aspects of Polish Discourse on Eastern 'Borderlands,'" in Janusz Korek (ed.), *From Sovietology to Postcoloniality: Poland and Ukraine from a Postcolonial Perspective* (Stockholm, 2007), pp. 41–57.

Lithuania, Latvia, and Ukraine, it is in fact a discourse detached from the contemporary developments in that region, instead reproducing Polish historical images of the territory. The French historian Daniel Beauvois, although he has never directly referred to postcolonial theory, is one of the staunchest critics of the Kresy myth.[39] For a long time he has asked for the abandonment of the Kresy discourse, calling it historically false and arguing that it is based on myths of the superiority of Polish culture over its Belarusian, Lithuanian, and Ukrainian counterparts. Aleksander Fiut fears that use of postcolonial theory may have the "hidden danger" of strengthening the identity of Poland as a victim, a suffering nation tortured by its enemies.[40] At the same time, Ewa Domańska sees the rise of the Kresy discourse in the post-communist period as one of the "postcolonial syndromes."[41] The Kresy nostalgia is, for her, a manifestation of a will to regain lost identity on the basis of mythical sources. In this way, the colony (in this case Poland as the former Russian colony) is copying imperialist patterns. She sees similar manifestations of Poland's lasting feelings of humiliation attached to the period of the nineteenth-century "partitions" as well as the Nazi and Soviet occupations.

Besides critical analyses of Polish discourses on the former eastern borderlands, there is also a stream of publications making use of the notion of "internal colonialization." It is most often used in reference to the region of Upper Silesia.[42] However, the internal colonialism of intelligentsia elites is also sometimes mentioned. Bohdan Jałowiecki has written, for example, about the domination of the Congress Kingdom's (that is the Russian part of Poland in the second part of the nineteenth century) intelligentsia and imposition of its symbolic system over the lower classes and remaining regions of Poland.[43] Michał Buchowski, professor of Poznań University, drawing on Alexander Etkind's work, accused the Polish liberal intelligentsia of internal orientalism directed towards the workers of the former state farms.[44] Buchowski has argued that the so-called "losers of the transformation" in Poland, irrespective of their location in geographical space, are often identified as "Easterners." Their supposed "Eastness" is mostly related to their post-communist mentality, best known under the

---

[39] Daniel Beauvois, "Mit 'kresów wschodnich' czyli jak mu położyć kres," in W. Wrzesiński (ed.), *Polskie mity polityczne XIX i XX wieku* (Wrocław, 1994), pp. 93–105.

[40] Aleksander Fiut, "Polonizacja? Kolonizacja?," *Teksty Drugie* 6 (2003): 150–56.

[41] Domańska, "Obrazy PRL."

[42] Maria Szmeja, *Niemcy? Polacy? Ślązacy!* (Cracow, 2000).

[43] Bohdan Jałowiecki, "Przestrzeń historyczna, regionalizm, regionalizacja," in Bohdan Jałowiecki (ed.), *Oblicza polskich regionów* (Warsaw, 1996), pp. 19–88.

[44] Michał Buchowski, "The Specter of Orientalism in Europe: From Exotic Other to Stigmatized Brother," *Anthropological Quarterly* 79/3 (2006): 463–82.

label of "Homo Sovieticus." Any failure of these "orphans of communism" is, as Buchowski suggests, ascribed to their "oriental nature."⁴⁵

Postcolonial theory is also used occasionally in debates on the material heritage of the Soviet presence in Poland. Warsaw, which was redesigned by Stalinist urban planners as a new capital of communist Poland, has been the main arena for these debates. Discussions over the fate of the Palace of Culture and Science, originally named after Joseph Stalin—the famous "gift from the Soviet people"—are an excellent manifestation of ambiguous attitudes toward the Soviet heritage and its postcolonial interpretations. The Moscow-style skyscraper remains the highest building in Warsaw and dominates the city landscape, despite the recent emergence of a number of tall modern buildings in its vicinity. After the fall of communism, the Palace of Culture became an object of heated debates between those calling for its removal and those defending its place in the city center. The latter party has won so far—the Palace remains in place. The opponents of the Palace often made references to the Alexander Nevsky Orthodox Cathedral in Warsaw built by the Russians in the last years of their presence in Warsaw before World War I. The huge structure located in what is called today the Piłsudski Square (formerly known as Saxon Square and, in the communist period, the Victory Square), had been an object of equally emotional debate just after Poland regained its independence in 1918. After a few years the cathedral was demolished in 1926 as a symbol of Russian domination over Poland. Today the "Russianness" of the Palace of Culture is a problem even for its supporters, and, as some of them admit, they don't like it when Western tourists compare it to Moscow's skyscrapers and are excited by its Russian character. Let us quote some of the arguments of opponents of the presence of the Palace in the city center. Jeremi Królikowski, a professor at the Warsaw University of Life Sciences (SGGW), interpreted the victory of the proponents of the Palace within the framework of postcolonial interpretations. As he argued,

> imperial and totalitarian policy had succeeded. A characteristic of a province of an empire is not only a lack of sovereignty in production of forms but also a lack of sovereignty in their interpretation. [...] Affinity between Russification, Communization and Bolshevization of space is striking, when analyzing the "Letters from Russia" by the marquis de Custine. In his notes one finds almost

---

⁴⁵ Buchowski, "The Specter of Orientalism," p. 475.

everyday remarks on the architecture and urban setting of St. Petersburg, which taken together appear to be an excellent essay on the poetics of a socialist city.[46]

Królikowski concludes that after the regaining of independence in 1918 Russification, encountered opposition, while after the regaining of independence in 1989 the heritage of socialism in the realm of architecture did not suffer from any harm; quite the opposite, it enjoyed higher status than works from earlier or later periods. Thus, for Królikowski "from opposition toward Russification we moved to acceptance of the totalitarian heritage. These metamorphoses are results of moving from elite nihilism to total nihilism."

To adapt the Palace to the new realities, the name of Joseph Stalin on its front has been hidden with a metal sheet and other inscriptions referring to its being a "gift from the Soviet people to the Polish nation" have been removed. More importantly, a huge clock has been installed at its top in 2000 in order to improve the image of the Palace as a functional element in the landscape of the city. Still, debates continue, and in particular the discussion concerning the development of the area around the building. On the one hand, there are the supporters of the erection of several new skyscrapers, which would "hide" the palace, reducing its visual domination. On the other hand, there are those who want the central role of the Palace to remain intact, applauding its esthetic, functional, and historical role and denying any negative connotation.

Interestingly, the attitudes towards the Palace do not necessarily follow the logic of the political division between the liberals and the conservatives. Filmmaker Andrzej Wajda, one of the most ardent critics of the Law and Justice (PiS) party claims to be personally offended by the Palace's presence. As Agata Lisiak reports, Wajda, in an open letter published in Poland's biggest daily *Gazeta Wyborcza*, mockingly called the Palace "the temple of Joseph Stalin" and reminded readers that "works of architecture are the most important symbols of what the sovereigns want to tell their subordinates."[47] Wajda demanded "more courage" and added that the Palace "has to disappear among other high-rise buildings so that, surrounded by them, it is no longer a symbol of those gruesome times, but rather an example of 1950s Soviet architecture astray on the Vistula." As Lisiak notes, the new Warsaw skyline, crowded with

---

[46] Jeremi Królikowski, "Metamorfozy polityki imperialnej – od soboru na placu Saskim do Pałacu Kultury i Nauki," in Dariusz Konstantynów and Piotr Paszkiewicz (eds.), *Kultura i polityka. Wpływ polityki rusyfikcji na kulturę zachodnich rubieży Imperium Rosyjskiego (1772–1915)* (Warsaw, 1994), pp. 273–79, esp. p. 277.

[47] Andrzej Wajda, "Świątynia Józefa Stalina czy zabytek sowieckiej architektury z lat 50.?," *Gazeta.pl Warszawa*, May 6, 2008. http://wiadomosci.gazeta.pl/Wiadomosci/1,80269,5194903.html

skyscrapers as envisioned by the filmmaker, would resemble Manhattan and not "the village of Warszawa with Joseph Stalin's church." Also, the Minister of Foreign Affairs from the Civic Platform government, Radek Sikorski, "would like the Polish capital to look like New York City and suggests the Palace be razed and replaced with an enormous lawn with a pond in the middle and a Warsaw version of Central Park."[48] Lisiak concluded that the desire to get rid of the Palace of Culture and Science is mostly motivated by two factors: first, embarrassment at, and in turn the rejection of, the Soviet-imposed heritage; second, by the aspiration to transform Warsaw into a Western(-like) metropolis. Thus, she sees Poland's problems with its Soviet heritage as a result of an overlay of Western and Russian influences. On that basis, she defines her notion of the (post)colonial Central European city as

> a city whose politics, culture, society, and economy have been shaped by two centers of power: the former colonizer, whose influence remains visible predominantly in architecture, infrastructure, social relations, and mentalities, and the current colonizer, whose impact extends over virtually all spheres of urban life.

It is "characterized by political, cultural, social, and economic tensions resulting from the condition of being postcolonial and colonial at the same time; the intensity of the tensions is proportional to the differences between the former colonizer and the present colonizer."[49]

Conclusion: The Interplay between Eastern and Western Dependencies

As it seems, the above-discussed reluctance to use postcolonial theory in Poland could be interpreted by the effect of the cross-cutting influences and heritage of Soviet/Russian and Western domination. One could note that the emerging interpretations in this field could be broadly classified into two types. The first type would be defined by the perception of Soviet/Russian domination read as colonization as the primary source of Poland's current problems. From such a point of view, Polish problems in dealing with Western domination, as has been suggested by Ewa Thompson, have their roots in unresolved issues related

---

[48] Agata Anna Lisiak, "Disposable and Usable Pasts in Central European Cities," *Culture Unbound. Journal of Current Cultural Research* 1 (2009): 431–52, esp. p. 439.
[49] Agata A. Lisiak, "The Making of (Post)colonial Cities in Central Europe," *CLCWeb: Comparative Literature and Culture* 12/1 (2010).

to Soviet colonialism. In the same way, the Kresy orientalist discourse, as Ewa Domańska has suggested, would be interpreted, first of all, as a delayed reaction to Soviet occupation. On the other hand, we have a number of interpreters who tend to view Western domination over Poland also as a form of colonization and as the primary source of Poland's current problems and inability to deal with the heritage of the communism. Such a point of view is very clearly represented by Maria Janion who links the Polish perception of Russia as inferior to the widely spread conviction of the inferiority of Slavic culture and civilization in general. This conviction, in Janion's view, is an effect of the colonization of Poland and other Slavic countries by the West. In fact, Janion sees the entire history of Polish statehood as a history of colonization starting in at least the tenth century. The adoption of Christianity by Poland, which took place in 996, as Janion insists, was not entirely voluntary. It was mainly accepted under the pressure of military incursions from the West, principally those of the Germans of the Holy Roman Empire, who used the slogans of Christianization and the battle against the infidels. Janion argues that the pre-Christian Slavic heritage was eradicated by Catholic institutions in Poland in a much more radical way than, for example, in Ireland, where a much larger part of pre-Christian traditions have been preserved. However, for Janion this is not only the problem of a lack of interest among medieval monks in Poland in documenting pre-Christian culture, but also the problem of a current low interest in this culture. Janion, in particular, contrasts the prestige of Slavic mythology in Polish lands with that of Celtic mythology in Irish lands. As she argues, the low status of Slavic mythology and the relative ignorance of Poles about its traditions are partially an effect of the Eastern European inferiority complex. In Janion's opinion, prevailing negative stereotypes of the Slavic peoples that include their low level of civilization, lack of technical and organizational capabilities, laziness, melancholy, and so forth have been largely constructed by German historiography and assimilated in turn by Poles themselves.[50] This way of interpreting Polish attitudes toward Russia and the Soviet Union is also developed by Katarzyna Barańska and Claudia Snochowska-Gonzalez in their interpretation of the well-known novel *Wojna polsko-ruska pod flagą biało-czerwoną* by Dorota Masłowska . Masłowska, whose book has been translated into English under the title *Snow White and Russian Red*, is seemingly dealing with the Polish superiority complex over the "Russian" east. Barańska and Snochowska-Gonzalez argue, however, that in fact no Russian personage appears in Masłowska's novel, while the figure of "Rusek," as Russians and other East Slavs are called contemptuously in Poland,

---

[50] Maria Janion, "Polska między Wschodem a Zachodem," *Teksty Drugie* 6 (2003): 131–49.

is part of Polish identity—the internal, inferior, alter-ego of every Pole. Thus, the "Polish–Russian war" that Masłowska writes about is not a war with Russia or with Russians but a war with the Polish inferiority complex resulting from Western domination/colonization; one resulting from the inability to cope with Poles' own "Russianness" or "Easternness."

In any case, questions of Poland's past and present dependence from Russia and the West are closely intertwined. The argument presented in this chapter may lead us to a conclusion that the recent surge in interest in postcolonial theory both in academic and political discourse also illustrates the above-mentioned connection. While the main impulse comes from the process of transformation of the political scene under Western influence, it has been the heritage of Soviet domination over Poland that has become the main arena for the application of postcolonial theory's vocabulary.

PART IV
Representing Empire:
Media, Art, Literature

CHAPTER 9

Playing Games with Empire: Finnish Political Imaginaries on the Early Soviet State

Anni Kangas

This chapter analyses the ways in which the imperial frame of interpretation was imposed on the early Soviet state by Finnish political cartoonists during the beginning of the interwar period (1918–26). The chapter engages with the notion of empire while recognizing that the analytical usefulness of the concept has been challenged in International Relations and related disciplines. On the one hand, insights that emerge from transhistorical analyses of empires have been recognized to be so abstract that they could equally well apply to other political formations, such as large states. On the other hand, analysing politics through the frame of empire often has a normative dimension; to say that a political unit is imperial is to impose a specific, often pejorative, frame on the phenomenon under analysis. In Russian studies, attempts to interpret the early Soviet state though the imperial frame have also been challenged. Mark Beissinger, for example, argues that 'the temptation to read empire forward from Tsarist Russia and backward from the Soviet collapse ... confounds the difference between the colonial state and the aggressively modern state'.[1]

This chapter argues for the continued importance of empire as a category of practice.[2] As Beissinger notes, 'there is something quite powerful and distinctive about empire as a political concept ... that is not captured by any other terms in our analytical vocabulary'.[3] The fact that empire is a fruitful but at the same time analytically problematic concept calls for an interpretive understanding of empire: The focus of this chapter is on the ways in which meanings related to the notion of empire functioned as a practical category of politics in a

---

[1] Mark Beissinger, 'Soviet Empire as "Family Resemblance"', *Slavic Review* 65/2 (2006): 296.

[2] Cf. Rogers Brubaker and Frederick Cooper, 'Beyond Identity', *Theory and Society* 29/1 (2000): 1–47.

[3] Beissinger, 'Soviet Empire', p. 297.

specific empirical setting. It probes the important role that language-games of empire played in attempts to a forge a new relationship with Soviet Russia and the Soviet Union in the newly independent Finland. The research materials comprise political cartoons that were published in magazines representing various political views.

The early years of the interwar period (1918–26) provide a particularly interesting setting for an analysis of the functioning of the language-game of empire. In the beginning of the period, Finland ceased to be an autonomous Grand Duchy within the Russian Empire. Following the Bolshevik decision to acknowledge the Finnish Senate's declaration of independence, Finland became an independent state. The question of what constitutes an empire goes to the very heart of this sequence of events as the independence of Finland was enabled by Soviet leadership's projection of itself as a post-imperial form of power. The Bolshevik government's recognition of Finnish independence formed part of the Soviet state's attempt to convince its citizens and the world alike that, unlike its predecessor, it was not an imperial political unit. Nevertheless, in the political practices analysed here the nascent Soviet state was construed as an empire-like formation. The Finns were quite fast to impose the imperial frame on the former metropolitan country despite its self-definition as the 'world's first post-imperial state'.[4] Language-games of empire were frequently deployed in Finnish political practices geared at establishing a new modus vivendi with the eastern neighbour.

The chapter is based on a set of ideas that have been presented in the context of the 'practice' or 'pragmatist turn' in social sciences.[5] To study political practices is to focus on the ways in which political agents seek to come to terms with challenges that the world throws up.[6] This involves activating language-games – in this case imperial language-games. I use the notion of a language-game in this context to point out that regardless of the variety of ways in which the cartoons presented here actualize the notion of empire, they are nevertheless connected to one another by family resemblances. There is no essential quality that would necessarily be common to all of these games, but they remain united by overlapping and criss-crossing similarities and cohere around the notion of empire.[7] I further suggest that language-games are made up of symbols that comprise historically sedimented condensations of meaning that may act as repositories of cultural

---

[4] Terry Martin cit. Beissinger, 'Soviet Empire', p. 296.

[5] For example: Karin Knorr Cetina, Theodore R. Schatzki and Eike von Savigny (eds), *The Practice Turn in Contemporary Theory* (London, 2000).

[6] Anni Kangas, 'Beyond Russophobia: A Practice-based Interpretation of Finnish–Russian/Soviet Relations', *Cooperation & Conflict* 46/1 (2011): 40–59.

[7] Ludwig Wittgenstein, *Philosophical Investigations* (Oxford, 2001), § 51–4; cf. Beissinger, 'Soviet Empire', p. 297.

memory, and that undergo variation as they are actualized in particular contexts.⁸ Arguably, political cartoons provide a particularly fruitful illustration of the way in which attempts to come to terms with challenging situations activate such archaic symbols and, through them, imperial language-games.

National Liberation and Imperial Invasion

An apt illustration of the language-game of empire is provided by Eetu Isto's well-known painting *The Attack* [*Hyökkäys*] dating from 1899 (Figure 9.1). The original painting was a comment on the so-called Russification measures that can be interpreted as a specific kind of imperial act: an attempt to reconcile the geographical space of the empire with the cultural-historical features of Russia.⁹ The painting avails itself of the symbols of the maiden and the double-headed eagle to put forward an argument on the attempt to homogenize the empire, to eliminate competing sovereignties, and to standardize administration.

The maiden is quite clearly meant to represent the Finnish nation and the eagle the Russian administration.¹⁰ A conflict between the two is at the heart of the painting. The double-headed eagle is depicted attacking the pure and innocent maiden. She is shown protecting herself with the book of law that stands for the Finnish constitution. The reference to the constitution establishes a link to the Finnish imperial experience whereby Finland had been an autonomous unit within the Russian Empire for almost 100 years: when Finland became a part of the Russian Empire in 1809, Alexander I had promised to guarantee its autonomy on the basis of institutions and fundamental laws that had been established during the rule of Sweden. The emperor's argument was that Finland was thus elevated among the nations of Europe [*placée désormais au rang des nations*].¹¹ This suggests that in the Finnish nineteenth-century imperial experience, nationhood and empire were not mutually exclusive but had rather a symbiotic relationship. The Russification measures of the late nineteenth

---

⁸ Yuri M. Lotman, *Universe of the Mind: A Semiotic Theory of Culture* (Bloomington, IN, 1990).

⁹ Mark Bassin, 'Russia between Europe and Asia: The Ideological Construction of Geographical Space', *Slavic Review* 50/1 (1991): 1–17.

¹⁰ See also Mika Aaltola, 'Agile Small State Agency: Heuristic Plays and Flexible National Identity Markers in Finnish Foreign Policy', *Nationalities Papers* 39/2 (2011): 257–76.

¹¹ For example: Matti Klinge, *Keisarin Suomi* (Espoo, 1997), pp. 16–19, 24–5; Raoul Palmgren, *Suuri linja Arwidssonista vallankumouksellisiin sosialisteihin: kansallisia tutkielmia* (Helsinki, 1948).

Figure 9.1 Eetu Isto, *The Attack [Hyökkäys]*, 1899, Finnish National Museum, Helsinki.

and early twentieth century were perceived to threaten this situation and the favourable status of the Grand Duchy within the empire.

The painting draws on the idea of Finland as a female body. Anthropologist Mary Douglas has argued that the human body can provide a suitable model for any bounded system.[12] Conventionally, female figures are used to symbolize national political units[13] and are often associated with ideals of virtue.[14] In the case of Isto's painting, the primary significance of the bounded female body is in the way it points to the Finnish political unit and its secondary significance lies in the ideals associated with the female figure (autonomy, integrity,

---

[12] Mary Douglas, *Purity and Danger* (London, 2002), p. 116.
[13] Marina Warner, *Monuments and Maidens: Allegory of the Female Form* (London, 1996).
[14] Richard S. Wortman, *Scenarios of Power: Myth and Ceremony in Russian Monarchy*, Vol. 1: *From Peter the Great to the Death of Nicholas I* (Princeton, NJ, 1995), p. 16.

wholeness). But the symbol of maiden also embodies another narrative that suggests that, due to internal weakness or external pressure, such ideal qualities may be lost. On the level of political practices, representations of weak and oppressed territories as female figures draw on this narrative, as exemplified by the imagery of the princess and the city of Silene rescued by St George.[15] Arguably, the tension embodied in female figures forms a key element of an imperial language-game: it calls to mind integrity and wholeness as well as conquest, domination and submission.

A cartoon published in the magazine *Tuulispää* in the summer of 1918 shows how the symbols of this imperial language-game underwent variation as they were actualized to come to terms with changing political circumstances (Figure 9.2). The drawing obviously mimics Isto's painting to issue an interpretation of another event, the Finnish Civil War fought in the spring of 1918. Playing with the language-game enables the cartoonist to suggest that the Civil War was not a struggle between the Finnish Reds and Whites but rather an attempted conquest.

The 'Russian' eagle now carries the features of Oskari Tokoi and Akilles Manner, leaders of the Finnish Reds, who had migrated to Moscow after the Finnish Civil War. These small alterations serve to turn the cartoon into an apology for the violence of the Civil War. It suggests that the victory of the Reds in the Civil War would have been a violation against Finland's self-determination and would have eventually meant the country's reintegration into the 'Soviet empire'. If the maiden – in spatial terms – refers to the nation as a bounded political unit, then the Russian eagle signifies outreach, expansion and omnipresence. Such a story exists in a condensed form in the symbol of the double-headed eagle, which was adopted and appropriated from the Holy Roman and Byzantine Empires by Ivan III – an act that concurred with the emergence of the conception of Moscow as the Third Rome.[16] In this 'Roman' understanding, the empire stands for universalism, for a single, infinite world domain.[17] In addition to the fact that the eagle had been appropriated from a former imperial formation, imperial omnipresence is iconically embodied in the double-headed figure: its two heads seem to enable the bird to simultaneously observe and govern both the east and the west. Both Isto's painting and the *Tuulispää* cartoon thus evoke language-games of empire in the sense that they build on the juxtaposition between bounded space and limitless geography.

---

[15] Wortman, *Scenarios*, p. 16.
[16] Wortman, *Scenarios*, p. 25.
[17] Anthony Pagden, *Lords of All the World: Ideologies of Empire in Spain, Britain, and France, c. 1500–c. 1800* (New Haven, CT, 1995), pp. 26–8.

Figure 9.2 'The failed "attack" of Kullervo Akilles Manner and Oskar Tokoi' [*Kullervo Akilles Mannerin ja Oskari Tokoin epäonnistunut hyökkäys*] (extract).

Source: *Tuulispää* 24–5 (June 1918).

In addition to the symbol of eagle, attempts to make sense of the changing character of Soviet Russia and the USSR during the early interwar period frequently avail themselves of other symbols that enforce the interpretation of Russia as an empire. One among these is the Orthodox Church, which is also linked to the idea of the Christian Empire, the thought of Russia as the Third Rome and the heritage of the Byzantine emperor as the defender of Orthodoxy.[18]

The cartoon in Figure 9.3 was published in the magazine *Ampiainen* in May 1919. Around this time, the Russian Whites had appealed to the Finnish government for help in the fight against the Bolsheviks. The cartoon opposes participation in the war. Its argument revolves around the symbols of eagle and church. Here as well, the eagle is used to call to mind imperial expansion,

---

[18] Wortman, *Scenarios*, p. 6.

Playing Games with Empire: Finnish Political Imaginaries on the Early Soviet State 225

Figure 9.3   'Russian friends of the fatherland in cooperation' [*Venäläiset isänmaanystävät yhteistyössä*].
Source: *Tuulispää* 24–5 (June 1918).

but its facial features now indexically connect the bird to the Russian Whites. This yields an argument that their victory in the Russian Civil War would have resulted in the swift reintegration of Finland into the Russian Empire. The Orthodox Church and the gallows in the background enforce this argument as they conjure up an idea of Russia as an imperial political formation and of empires as internally repressive political formations, as a form of governing that usurps the autonomous nation.[19]

The lion of the cartoon stands for the Finnish state. Its iconic features tell the animal apart from a victim of usurpation: he seems upright, straight-backed and free. The drawing signals Finland's independent status, a triumph over the past and

---

[19] Cf. Ronald Grigor Suny, 'The Empire Strikes Out: Imperial Russia, "National" Identity and Theories of Empire', in Ronald Grigor Suny and Terry Martin (eds), *A State of Nations: Empire and Nation-Making in the Age of Lenin and Stalin* (New York, 2001), p. 23; see also Beissinger, 'Soviet Empire', p. 299.

a rejection of the previous status of Finland as a constituent element of the Russian imperial constellation. This idea is strengthened by the fact that a river represents the Finnish–Russian/Soviet border. As a feature of physical geography, the river adds to the idea that the independence of Finland was a natural condition. On this basis, the drawing emerges as a celebration of Finland's independent status.

Empire as a Legitimate Form of Control

As the Finns attempted to make sense of the changing character of the former metropolitan country, they did not always juxtapose the 'natural' condition of independent statehood to violent and brutal imperial conquest. The so-called *Pax Russica* interpretation that looks positively to the experience of Finland as a part of the Russian Empire also continues to crop up in discussions over the early Soviet state. The experiential basis for this interpretation is provided in the fact that the change in the status of Finland from a part of Sweden to a Russian Grand Duchy in 1809 was followed by a peaceful period of more than 100 years. During the Swedish reign the population had suffered from clashes between the Swedish and Russian forces on its territory. Had Finland remained part of the Swedish Empire, this interpretation suggests, it would have become a marginalized part of the larger whole and would have been less well-off both materially and culturally.[20]

The *Pax Russica* interpretation provides a historical frame of interpretation that was variously actualized in attempts to make sense of the early Soviet state. The drawing in Figure 9.4 was published in the conservative Swedish-language magazine *Fyren* in 1920. It is intended as a criticism against the ruling political factions of Finland who, willing to negotiate a peace with the Bolsheviks, had decided not to take part in the Russian Whites' invasion against St Petersburg (Petrograd). The bark shoes of the maiden offer an indexical hint; they call to mind certain Finnish-speaking sections who were opposing the participation. The maiden together with a Russian deserter are hiding from the battle behind a rock, suggesting cowardice. By contrast, the representatives of the Russian Whites are depicted as heroic characters. The juxtaposition of cowardice and heroism is bolstered by the caption that avails itself of chivalric imagery: 'Knight and the deserters'. The idea of the heroism of the Russian Empire thus goes to the

---

[20] Osmo Apunen and Helena Rytövuori, 'Ideas of "Survival" and "Progress" in the Finnish Foreign Policy Tradition', *Journal of Peace Research* 19/1 (1982): pp. 65–6; Henrik Meinander, *Suomen historia: linjat, rakenteet, käännekohdat* (Helsinki, 2006), pp. 93–119.

Figure 9.4　'Knight and deserters, or The last bastion of humanity crumbling' [*Riddare och desertörer eller mänsklighetens sista front bröts*].
Source: *Fyren* 9–10 (1920).

very heart of the cartoon, which condemns the Finnish government's decision to avoid involvement in the Russian Civil War.

The drawing revolves around a conservative theme through its depiction of the Russian Whites as an embodiment of civilized and heroic conduct. The cartoon longs for Finland's former position within the old, aristocratic Russia, thus actualizing a language-game that sees empire as a legitimate form of control. It is conservative in the sense of seeing in the restored Russian Empire not a usurper of nations but a guarantee against the revolutionary forces of the time. In a written commentary published in *Fyren* in 1921, the role of a vanguard is explicitly assigned to the Russian Empire '[which] for hundreds of years stood as an unfaltering bulwark on the border between Europe and Asia, protecting with its body the Christian civilization against the barbarism of the East'.[21] An interpretation that sees rule imposed from the outside on a native population as a possibility for overcoming the latter's backwardness resonates with Russian

---

[21]　'Vem har mördat Rysslands tsarer?', *Fyren* 8–9 (1921).

Figure 9.5   'Overview of the year 1925' [*Katsaus vuoteen 1925*].
Source: *Tuisku* 20–21 (December 1925).

discourses: 'in the eighteenth and nineteenth centuries, the myth of the ruler as conqueror was used to express the monarchy's bringing to Russia the benefits of civilization and progress, and the ruler was portrayed as a selfless hero who saved Russia from despotism and ruin'.[22] Furthermore, instead of being framed in national terms, the *Pax Russica* interpretation is organized here around a class-based interpretation of the benefits of empire.

A communist magazine, *Tuisku*, also actualized the idea of benefits associated with being a neighbour of (Soviet) Russia and also used class as a key criterion of political differentiation (Figure 9.5), but did so with very different aims from the previous cartoon. The symbol of the apple tree communicates an idea of the Soviet Union as an ideal kind of society. On the pages of *Tuisku* this interpretation does not relate to Russia's past as an aristocratic empire but rather to its future as a post-imperial power, a civic multinational state able to transcend oppression in the name of class solidarity.[23]

---

[22]   Suny, 'Empire Strikes Out', p. 35; see also Wortman, *Scenarios*, pp. 6, 23.
[23]   Cf. Beissinger, 'Soviet Empire', p. 295.

Unlike cartoons that actualize symbols of boundedness and protection to celebrate Finland's 'natural' partition from the Russian Empire, this drawing problematizes the new situation in which Finland was administratively separated from Russia. More specifically, the malevolent-seeming male figure at the border stands for the Finnish passport authorities who had been given the right to deny passports to labour activists and their families wishing to migrate to the USSR. Resonating with the communist creed to abolish the state, in this cartoon the boundary between Finland and the USSR does not appear natural but rather somewhat artificial as it cuts across a road leading from one place to another.

During the interwar period, the interpretation that viewed the empire as a legitimate form of political authority continued to form part of the practices of the Finnish political imaginary but was regarded with increasing criticism. In a cartoon published in *Kurikka* in September 1926 the statue of Alexander II is being removed from the Helsinki Senate Square to communicate the enthusiasm of certain right-wing activist groups to get rid of everything that evoked the status of Finland as a constituent member of the Russian Empire and to establish the Finnish nation as the sole source of authority and target of loyalty (Figure 9.6). On the pages of *Kurikka*, which was a publication of the Finnish Social Democrats, this policy is treated with gentle irony; a set of symbols standing for the imperial past, the possibility of a harmonious relationship and common interests between Finland and Russia – a friendly bear and a palm leaf symbolizing peace – are packed in a wheelbarrow together with the Russian emperor's statue.

The Form of Foreign Rule

While sameness forms an important part of national language-games, difference is a key element in imperial language-games. The relationship of the metropolitan country to the constituent parts of the empire is commonly marked by ethnic difference or geographical separation.[24] Richard Wortman has argued that during the fifteenth–late nineteenth centuries the foreign origin of Russian rulers was emphasized in order to enforce their separation from the ruled population. The rulers' foreignness was then thought of as a positive factor: it was argued to indicate superiority while nativeness denoted inferiority. A foreign background was expected to elevate rulers above their subjects and to give parity with other monarchs.[25] The definition of imperial rule as characteristically foreign also forms part of Finnish interwar political debates, but as a target of criticism: the

[24] For example: Suny, 'Empire Strikes Out', p. 25.
[25] Wortman, *Scenarios*, pp. 5–6, 22.

Figure 9.6   'Union of independence and Alexander II' [*Itsenäisyysliitto ja Aleksanteri II*].

Source: *Kurikka* 36 (September 1926).

alien, non-native character of the rulers is evoked to represent the empire as an illegitimate form of power.

In the drawing published in *Tuulispää* as a comment on the fifth anniversary of the Bolshevik Revolution in 1922 (Figure 9.7) the difference between the rulers and the ruled is taken up to condemn the Soviet polity. The idea of the Soviet state as an alien imposition, and thus as an illegitimate political formation, was aimed at the Finnish admirers of the USSR. They are represented by a family standing behind a veil of fog as if unable to see the true character of the Soviet Union. It is possible to identify at least three motifs of imperial language-games in this cartoon. Firstly, the drawing plays with the notion of difference between the rulers and the ruled; notably, it does not speak to Russian imperial tendencies but rather suggests that the Russian people are being colonized by alien rulers. To this end, it actualizes the motif of racial difference that yields an anti-Semitic argument pointing to the Jewish background of the Communist Party elite. Secondly, the idea of empires as internally repressive political formations is conveyed by picturing the giant of Russia as a prisoner, which enforces an argument about the immorality of empire

Playing Games with Empire: Finnish Political Imaginaries on the Early Soviet State 231

Figure 9.7   'The fifth anniversary jubilee of communism in Russia' [*Kommunismin viisivuotisriemujuhla Venäjällä*].
Source: *Tuulispää* 44 (November 1922).

and provides a visual shorthand for the idea that Soviet rule is not based on the consent of the governed. And, thirdly, the drawing turns on the motif of imperial succession since it draws an analogy between the Tsarist empire and Bolshevik policies: the word 'communism' seems to have been merely glued over the word 'Tsarism' on the stone attached to the leg of the gigantic male figure standing for the Russian people [*Wenäjän kansa*].

Imperial Succession

In early 1918 *Fyren* published a drawing which describes the transfer of political authority from Russia to Finland in terms of a coronation scene (Figure 9.8).

Figure 9.8   *Nya Fyren*, New Year's Issue (January 1918), untitled cover art (extract).

At first glance, the drawing appears as a celebration of Finland's newly gained independence from the Russian Empire. Its point, nevertheless, is to elaborate on the perplexing situation of Finland having 'gained freedom from Russia with the help of Russians'.[26]

The idea of independence together with the norm of sovereignty is embodied in the symbol of the Phrygian cap that Lenin is about to place on the head of the Finnish maiden. The symbol has its origins in the French Revolution.

---

[26]   Juhani Aho, *Hajamietteitä kapinaviikoilta* (Porvoo, 1918), p. 54.

It stores up meanings related to the principle of national self-determination, also propagated by the Bolsheviks. In order to grasp the point of the cartoon, we must note the way in which the cartoonist activates imperial language-games, playing with at least three motifs that cohere around the notion of empire. Firstly, the vertical composition of the Finnish maiden and Lenin is suggestive of two political units in a hierarchical, inequitable relationship and thus of the idea of imperial power unencumbered by any other authority. Secondly, Lenin's clothing motivates an interpretation that is tied to the language-game of imperial succession: if one scratches the surface, the drawing hints, one will find in Lenin a representative of Russian imperial tendencies. The ermine cape with its royal connotations quite directly calls to mind the Russian emperor. Thirdly, Lenin is wearing the outfit of a Russian peasant man (kulak) underneath the cape. The clothing functions as a powerful 'mnemonic device'[27] directing attention to attempts to homogenize the imperial space by standardizing administration, eliminating competing sovereignties, and reducing cultural and linguistic differences within the imperial space. During the Russification periods (1899–1905 and 1908–17), the symbol of a bearded man in a traditional Russian peasant outfit had appeared in Finnish cartoons to symbolize the Great Russian chauvinism that was held responsible for the oppressive policies of Russian administration.[28] By activating such historically sedimented symbols, the drawing develops into an argument that the Bolshevik decision to grant Finland its independent status was a malevolent move. Appearances notwithstanding, the drawing suggests, the 'gift' given to the Finns by the Bolsheviks was a Trojan horse.

The language-game of imperial succession is often intertwined with that of Russia's imperial tendencies. The fact that Russia was 'inclined' to commit imperial deeds was perceived as a problem for the newly gained Finnish independence. The Agrarian Party's Santeri Alkio argued that

> from our experience thus far we know that there is no party in Russia, no matter what the colour, that would not regard the Finnish independence with deep bitterness and would not think of reconquering the country. If Russia once again becomes a great power, destroying Finland will be one of its primary goals.[29]

---

[27] Lotman, *Universe of the Mind*, p. 110.

[28] Kari Immonen, *Ryssästä saa puhua... Neuvostoliitto suomalaisessa julkisuudessa ja kirjat julkisuuden muotona 1918–1939* (Keuruu, 1987); Johanna Valenius, *Undressing the Maid: Gender, Sexuality and the Body in the Construction of the Finnish Nation* (Helsinki, 2004).

[29] Santeri Alkio, *Talonpoika ja Suomen vapaus* (Vaasa, 1922), p. 50.

Figure 9.9   'A Finnish communist in Moscow' [*Suomalainen kommunisti Moskovassa*].

Source: Kurikka, March 1922.

The proposition in both the *Fyren* drawing and Alkio's written argument is that the Bolshevik decision to grant Finland independent status was a cunning move intended to ensure the country's future integration into the Soviet polity. This argument comes into focus when the Russian Empire and the nascent Soviet state are assimilated through the motif of inherent imperial impulses and reflexes.

Frequently, the language-game of imperial succession was evoked to counter the self-presentation of the Soviet state as a post-imperial political unit. The cartoon in Figure 9.9 was published by *Kurikka* in March 1922. Similarly to the coronation cartoon above, the point of this drawing revolves around an analogy between Lenin and the Russian emperors. The genuflecting figure stands for Finland calling to mind the motif of subjugation, conquest and inequality. Here, Lenin is depicted as a decadent figure, which is a forceful way of challenging the interpretation of the Soviet state as a progressive political formation. A spiked mace in Lenin's hand together with luxurious Cuban cigars and vintage wine suggest that Soviet Russia was no different from the conservative and autocratic Romanov dynasty.

The cartoon provides a convenient illustration of the fact that imperial language games can be put to work in different ways in attempts to come to terms with topical political challenges. In this case, the challenge relates to a situation where the Finnish labour movement had split into two factions after the defeat of the Reds in the Civil War. The Social Democrats attempted to regain political legitimacy in 'White Finland' but the communists were for the most part forced to operate either underground or abroad. The *Kurikka* cartoon must be interpreted in the context of the Social Democrats' attempt to distinguish themselves from the communist faction. More specifically, it is related to rumours according to which the Finnish communist leaders living in Moscow had sent a circular letter urging Finnish workers to steal from their employers for the benefit of the Soviet regime. The link between the drawing and the rumours is confirmed by the caption: 'Here are some small things from Finland'. By turning to the language-game of imperial succession, the cartoonist has crafted a powerful message about the illegitimacy of such demands of loyalty.

Unconstrained Power

A connection between political cartoons and imperial language-games is established by the figures of bears or giants. These symbols are not unique to the Finnish political imaginary or to the interwar period. The bear is a well-known metonym for Russia, and this association can be put to work broadly: on the one hand, it is a visual shorthand referring to wildness, to something that is close to nature and the animal realm;[30] on the other hand, it has been used to symbolize Russia's might, especially in its dealings with foreigners.[31] If the eagle stands for Russia or the Soviet Union in the sense of Weberian *Herrschaft* [authority, administrative rule], then the bear represents its *Macht* [unconstrained, wilful power].[32] That is, bears and giants link up to a wider discussion on the legitimacy or illegitimacy of power relations. The drawing in Figure 9.10 featuring the

---

[30] Jane Costlow, '"For the Bear to Come to Your Threshold": Human–Bear Encounters in Late Imperial Russian Writing', in Jane Costlow and Amy Nelson (eds), *Other Animals: Beyond the Human in Russian Culture and History* (Pittsburgh, PA, 2010).

[31] Hope B. Werness, *The Continuum Encyclopedia of Animal Symbolism in Art* (New York, 2004), p. 33.

[32] Max Weber, *Economy and Society: An Outline of Interpretative Sociology* (Berkeley, CA, 1978), p. 53; Osmo Apunen, 'Beauty and the Beast: Semiotic Perspectives on the

Figure 9.10   'The fate of small nations' [*Pienten kansain kohtalo*].
Source: Tuulispää, June 1920.

Russian bear was published in *Tuulispää* in June 1920. It shows an aggressive bear forcing its will on smaller political units and thus directs attention to the problem of the unconstrained and arbitrary exercise of power.

The drawing is a comment on Polish attempts to create a federation of Central and Eastern European countries, the ensuing Polish–Soviet War, and the British position on this. It shows John Bull – the personification of England – sitting high up in a tree and attempting to tame the aggressive Russian bear by throwing Poland into its jaws. The cartoon actualizes an imperial language-game through its elaboration on the character of Soviet power as non-authoritative *Macht* aggressively savouring smaller political units. The caption of the cartoon – 'The fate of small nations' – suggests that the drawing is intended as a more general argument about the character of Soviet Russia as

---

Formation of Finnish/Russian National Characters', Paper presented at the IV Pan-European IR Conference, Canterbury, 2001.

Playing Games with Empire: Finnish Political Imaginaries on the Early Soviet State 237

Figure 9.11   'The Bolsheviks and us' [*Bolschevikerna och vi*].
Source: *Hovnarren*, July 1919.

a danger to the existence of smaller states beyond the case of Poland. The skulls and the bones at the feet of the bear provide an additional visual shorthand for the idea of an existential threat.

Depicting Russia as a landlocked giant on a lookout for more living space provides another way to direct attention toward Russia's expansive tendencies.[33] The drawing in Figure 9.11 features the Russian giant in its comment on the suggestion that Finnish Reds imprisoned during the Finnish Civil War should be granted amnesty. Although this was a domestic Finnish political debate, an imperial language-game is crucial for its argument: soft-handedness with domestic Reds – represented by a man with a bomb – is argued to leave the door open for Russian expansion, the idea of which is embodied in the figure of a giant in a familiar kulak outfit. The weakness of the door hints that the border between independent Finland and its former metropolitan country was not yet

[33]   See also Immonen, *Ryssästä saa puhua*, pp. 38–46.

sufficiently strong. The argument of the cartoon targets the institutions of the Finnish state represented here by a soldier absorbed in reading a newspaper, but the drawing revolves around the idea of imperial expansiveness and the possibility of foreign rule. This serves to conceal the ideological motif of the Civil War behind a seemingly non-ideological warning of Finland's very existence being threatened.

Concluding Remarks

Finnish political cartoons depicting the early Soviet state are rich with symbols that are bound to imperial language-games. Despite the former metropolitan country's self-projection as a post-imperial state, the Finns often actualized an imperial frame of reference in attempts to come to terms with the changing character of the neighbouring polity. 'Empire' provided a frequently used but variably actualized way of relating to the Soviet power. It was connected with quite disparate policies and practices but, as variable as the games played with imperial symbols were, they remain united by Wittgensteinian family resemblances.[34] Such imperial characterizations of the eastern neighbour often formed part of political debates and struggles that were only indirectly associated with the Soviet polity but contributed toward the emergence of the outside view of the Soviet Union as an imperial political formation.

It seems legitimate to define the interwar period as a transitional period in Finnish imperial imaginings. If it had previously been possible to see empire as a legitimate form of control, in the newly independent Finland the imperial character of Russia and the Soviet state was increasingly seen as a violation of the 'natural' condition of national self-determination and norms of sovereignty. However, the 'pre-national' way of conceptualizing empires and national units in symbiotic relations did not disappear completely, although it became marginalized towards the end of the interwar period.[35] Similarly, although the early twenty-first century is formally post-imperial, the historically sedimented *Pax Russica* conception still crops up from time to time in political discussions over the significance of Russia's proximity to Finland, and one of its embodiments – the statue of Alexander II – continues to occupy a central spot on the Helsinki Senate Square. This highlights the fact that paying attention to the actual uses of imperial language-games helps decentralize the naturalness of contemporary relations of authority.

---

[34] See also Beissinger, 'Soviet Empire'.
[35] Anni Kangas, *The Knight, the Beast and the Treasure: A Semeiotic Inquiry into the Finnish Political Imaginary on Russia* (Tampere, 2007).

CHAPTER 10

Imperiia Re/Constructed: Narratives of Space and Nation in 1960s Soviet Russian Culture

Sanna Turoma

As every Soviet schoolboy and schoolgirl was made to memorize, the Soviet Union covered "one-sixth" of the earth's landmass. The concept of the "one-sixth" was worked into early Soviet popular imagination by Dziga Vertov's 1926 film *One-sixth of the World* [*Shestaia chast' mira*]. By the end of the 1960s the phrase had been popularized to such an extent that the poet Joseph Brodsky was able to use its ironic reversal, the "five-sixths," in reference to the world outside the Soviet Union, that is, the world out of his and his readers' reach.[1]

As the widespread use and popularity of "one-sixth" demonstrates, the vastness of Russia's geographical space offered powerful symbolism for narratives of empire, nation, and identity in the Soviet period. The importance and impact of space and spatial imaginings in the narratives the Soviet period produced was felt acutely in post-Soviet Russian intelligentsia's efforts to respond to the disintegration of the Soviet Union and the reduction of Soviet space it insinuated.[2] This chapter attempts to shed light on the origins of post-Soviet attitudes toward Soviet and Russian territory by discussing representations of geographical space in the post-Stalin period of the late 1950s and early 1960s.

---

[1] Joseph Brodsky (1940–96) is one of Russia's best-known late 20th-century poets. He emigrated from the Soviet Union in 1972, settled in the US, received the Nobel Prize for Literature in 1987, after which, in the perestroika years, his poetry began to appear in print in the Soviet Union. "The End of a Beautiful Era" (1969), the poem cited here, circulated among Brodsky's contemporaries as a *samizdat* poem (reproduced by hand). Here are the relevant lines in Brodsky's own English-language translation: "Either old Europe's map has been swiped by the gents in plain clothes, / or the famous five-sixths of remaining landmass has just lost / its poor infamous colleague, or a fairy casts spells over shabby / me, who knows – but I cannot escape from this place". Joseph Brodsky, *Collected Poems in English* (New York, 2000), p. 39.

[2] See, for instance, Marlène Laruelle's discussion of post-Soviet debates about Russian neo-Eurasianism and Russia as a Eurasian space in Chapter 3 of this volume.

This period—characterized by the liberalization of Khrushchev's "thaw"—shaped the worldviews of those Russians who in midlife, at the height of their careers and personal lives, were faced with the fall of the socialist system and the disintegration of the Soviet Union.[3] The 1960s was also a period when the "one-sixth" offered a multiethnic and multicultural space for Soviet tourists, travelers, and prospectors [*razvedchiki*] to explore. The dream of travel and the liberalization of travel practices informed Russian high and popular culture in many ways. Travel, tourism, and expeditions were a popular topic in Soviet film, literature, and lyric songs.

The questions this chapter poses concern cultural representations of Soviet territory: What were the symbolic meanings invested in Soviet geographical space, and what was the role of spatial and geographical imaginings in constructing a collective Soviet identity as well as individual subject positions in the late 1950s and 1960s? To answer these questions I will examine representations of Soviet geographical space in the context of ideological production and outside it. I analyze journalistic writing in the popular monthly *Around the World* [*Vokrug Sveta*], that is, writing controlled by official Soviet cultural institutions. To give a broader picture of spatial imaginings of this period, I also discuss literary texts by Russian-language metropolitan writers who were affiliated with dissenting cultural practices and often vacillated between official and unofficial cultural practices. These include Andrei Bitov's travelogue *Lessons of Armenia* [*Uroki Armenii*], Joseph Brodsky's poetry of the 1960s, and *The 60s: The World of the Soviet Man* [*60-e: mir sovetskogo cheloveka*], a study of 1960s Soviet culture written in the 1980s by Petr Vail and Aleksandr Genis. Born in 1949 and 1953 respectively, Vail and Genis refer to themselves as "the last children of the 'thaw.'" Emigrating in the 1970s, they became leading voices of the so-called third-wave Soviet emigration. Their book is used widely as a scholarly reference book, but I read it as a memoir. Using these materials as case studies, I will show how geographical imaginings of Soviet territory created narratives of space, nation, and empire and how these narratives articulated what I will call a Soviet identity on both the official and unofficial planes of Soviet culture. Through an analysis of these texts I seek to uncover the roots of the cultural authority that spatial imaginings have exercised on Russian-language intellectual formations and the endurance of the spatial identity these imaginings produced.

---

[3] Alexei Yurchak's study *Everything Was Forever, Until It Was No More* (Princeton, NJ, 2006) discusses the fall of the Soviet Union through the eyes of what he calls the "last Soviet generation," that is the generation whose formative years were shaped by the period of late socialism (1960s–80s). Yurchak's study includes Soviet citizens born during this period, whereas my focus is on the generation that came of age in the 1960s, the *shestidesiatniki* or "sixtiers," as they are sometimes referred to.

Around the World: Constructing a Soviet Spatial Identity

How was the geographical space of the Soviet Union imagined by those Soviet citizens who came of age at the end of the 1950s and early 1960s? To answer this question, it is instructive to look at the monthly *Vokrug sveta* [Around the World], which offered Soviet readership articles about geography, climate zones, natural history, and other related topics with ample illustrations and color photos.[4] *Around the World* was a popular journal especially among the educated urban population. It was considered ideologically less heavy-handed than most publications, and it offered knowledge of foreign countries at a time when most Soviet citizens could not travel abroad.

During Stalin's regime *Around the World* promoted domestic travel, and articles about foreign countries were scarce; when they appeared, they had a strong propaganda goal.[5] In the post-Stalin period stories and reportage about foreign countries became more regular, and their propaganda content was less prominent. The series titled "In the Countries of National Democracies," which ran in every issue of 1954, was replaced gradually by an increasing number of stories about Western European and other capitalist countries. In the 1960s there emerged also advertisements about trips to India and other Soviet-friendly countries. An advertisement for Sputnik, the "agency for international youth tourism," as it was officially called, was printed regularly on the back cover (Figure 10.1). However, the journal also continued to publish stories about the Soviet Union, and that coverage reflected with varying degree the Communist Party program and, during the Khrushchev period, his reforms.

The task of *Around the World* was to bring to Soviet readers not only the world around the Soviet Union but also the world within its borders. Its task was to participate in the construction of the Soviet country's spatial identity. In the January issue of 1954, which was the beginning of the Khrushchev period, an article titled "Winter and Summer (Observations on Our Climate)" captures the Soviet territory through a description of its varying climate conditions. In winter in the Verkhoyansk Range of Eastern Siberia the temperature can drop down to -70 ºC (-94 ºF) as the author Nikolai Mikhailov writes, while at the other end of the country, in Murmansk, the waterways stay unfrozen. In the summer the temperatures in Central Asia can go as high as 50° C (122° F), while on the same latitude in Primorye at the Sea of Japan boats sail in cold breeze

---

[4] The journal was established in 1861 and celebrated in 2011 its 150th anniversary: http://www.vokrugsveta.ru/ My discussion covers the journal's issues from 1954 to 1969.

[5] See Anne E. Gorsuch, "'There is no place like home': Soviet Tourism in Late Stalinism," *Slavic Review* 62/4 (Winter 2003): 760.

Figure 10.1 Advertisement for Sputnik, the Soviet travel agency for youth. The map shows Moscow as the center from which other Soviet cities and capitals of republics radiate. The thinner lines represent the network of roads interconnecting the other cities.

Source: Vokryg sveta [Around the World] 3 (1966).

and thick fog. "Our vast country," Mikhailov asserts patriotically, "contains such extremes."[6] In the next issue Mikhailov continues to map out Soviet territory

---

6   Nikolai Mikhailov, "Zima i leto (ocherki o nashem klimate)," *Vokrug sveta* 1 (1954): 18. Nikolai N. Mikhailov (1905–82) was the author of such patriotic accounts of Russia and the Soviet Union as *Our Country* (1945), *Over the Map of Fatherland* (1947), which won him the State Stalin Prize of 3rd degree, and *My Russia* (first volume titled *My Russia. Russian Expanses* came out in 1964), for which he received the Maxim Gorky USSR State Prize in 1966. His books were translated into many foreign languages, among them an

in an article titled "From Tundras to Subtropics." Again, the geographical and natural extremes of Soviet territory are depicted with patriotic underpinnings reinforced with the repetitious use of the phrase "our country" [*nasha strana*]. As the article on climate conditions concludes: "Our country is gigantic, and socialist construction opens up in front of us a great space to know, to transform and to benefit from its immense natural resources."[7]

Ten years later in 1964, with Stalin's memory overshadowed by Khrushchev's initiatives to modernize the country, this "socialist construction" was located in Siberia. The January issue of *Around the World* quotes Khrushchev's speech at the Communist Party Plenum of December 1963. The Soviet people, especially *komsomoltsy*, the Komsomol youth, were "to build numerous factories and plants on unspoiled places," and more specifically, they were to "clear out the Siberian jungles [*raschishchat debri sibirskie*]." This followed Khrushchev's "virgin land" campaign, the goal of which was to increase grain cultivation in large Siberian territories.[8] On the same page the editors launched what was to be a series of future articles under the heading "Parallels and Meridians of Heroic Deeds." These included reportages under the subheading "Great Journey to Chemistry." This, in turn, referred to Khrushchev's launch to develop Soviet chemical industry. The goal of "Big Chemistry" [*Bolshaia khimiia*] was to provide new chemical technology for the production of consumer commodities and fertilizers that would facilitate the needs of Soviet agriculture, an important area of Khrushchev's modernization project.

The coverage of Big Chemistry in the following issues of *Around the World*, and descriptions of other industrial constructions sites, represented Soviet territory as a space of technological, industrial, and agricultural progress, a space that was to be thoroughly exploited and modernized as well as peopled by Soviet citizens. The quotation from Khrushchev's call to "clear out the Siberian jungle" was paired with an article on Siberia titled "Toward the Morning Dawn." It starts by describing Siberia's geographical vastness and then moves on to depict the Soviet people who have come to occupy it:

> On airports, railway stations, on roads one meets people hurrying about with suitcases resembling chests, sacks that nearly cover the whole person, with light sports bags. These are geologists, drivers, mechanics, concrete-workers, bulldozer-engineers,

---

English edition titled *Glimpses of the U.S.S.R.: Its Economy and Geography* published by the Soviet publishing house Foreign Languages in Moscow in 1960.

[7] Mikhailov, "Zima i leto," p. 25.

[8] See Fiona Hill and Gaddy Clifford, *The Siberian Curse: How Communist Planners Left Russia Out in the Cold* (Washington, DC, 2003), p. 87.

travelers. If you ask any of them "Who are you?" they will speak for all when they answer (here people usually speak for all): "We are construction workers!"⁹

This passage demonstrates how Siberia was transformed on the pages of *Around the World* into Soviet space, that is, a rational modernized space occupied by active Soviet people controlling that space collectively to build a new post-Stalin Soviet country.

Alongside the narrative of modernization of Soviet space in *Around the World* there appeared articles, reportage, journalist diaries, fiction, and travel writing that approached the massive construction projects and expeditions from a less utilitarian viewpoint. In the series "Parallels and Meridians of Heroic Deeds," M. Denim captured the preparations for an oil expedition in Siberia in a short first-person narrative "Everything changed unexpectedly and all of a sudden...":

> The overcrowded airport is busy from dawn to darkness. [...] People arrive here from all corners of the country. People with diverse looks. Prospectors, suppliers, interns from the capital city universities. The restless age has driven them here, made their paths and fates cross. They converse in the dim lounge. Talk on the phone with their superiors. Wait to get a flight to the back of beyond. They argue, they sing, and they talk by themselves, dreaming.¹⁰

The image of the crowd, excited by the anticipation of the unknown, shifts the focus away from the structured, controlled, and public sphere of the socialist construction steered by the Communist Party, and redirects it to the less-controlled sphere of people on the move. Here the construction site has been replaced by the airport. The official Soviet space has been transformed into a space of travel, journey, and adventure. The collective effort makes way to a private experience.

On a yet more private note, a less enthusiastic look at the scene at the airport was given by the young Joseph Brodsky. In "I was waiting for a bus in the city of Irkutsk...," a 1962 poem written on a geological expedition, Brodsky's poetic thought moves from the bleak details of "water imprisoned in the tap" and "moldy snacks" at the airport restaurant, to the idea of escape from the Soviet Union. In the final four lines his experience of travel and sense of geography give rise to the poem's central paradox—the idea of the vastness of Soviet territory being a cul-de-sac for an individual inhabiting it: "Foreign land is related to homeland, / as space neighbors a dead end."¹¹

---

⁹ A. Vinogradov and L. Krivenko, "Navstrechu utrennei zare," *Vokrug sveta* 1 (1964): 6.
¹⁰ M. Denim, "Taezhnaia neft'," *Vokrug sveta* 5 (1964): 6.
¹¹ Joseph Brodsky, *Sobranie sochinenii* (St. Petersburg, 1997), vol. 2, p. 172.

The reverse of the official narrative of constructing, transforming, and modernizing the Soviet territory was, then, the unofficial story of domestic travel, free mobility, amateur geology, exploration, excitement, and the dream of freedom. In official publications, as was the case in M. Denim's article, these stories were framed in the official narrative of Soviet modernization. Outside the officialdom of Soviet cultural institutions, as was the case in Brodsky's *samizdat* poetry, this frame was not necessary. Writing about travel and exploration offered a discursive space for reflecting on the Soviet reality and the limits of individual freedom. But both the official and the unofficial imagination were equally nourished by the sense of adventure increasingly represented in *Around the World* by stories of space exploration. Also at this time Soviet *turizm* [tourism] featured more prominently in the journal. *Turizm* implied hiking, camping, sports, active outdoors living, but it also implied the increasing possibilities of domestic travel.[12] The March issue of the 1964 *Around the World* included *Marshrut* [Route], a few-pages-long section dedicated to tourists. The launch of the "tourist news" began with a quotation from the early Soviet leader Mikhail Kalinin—"Patriotism starts from a profound knowledge of one's country"—and was justified by the observation that "tourism has entered firmly into the life of Soviet youth, it has become one of the methods of communist education. [...] Hardly any other country in the world compares with our Fatherland, when it comes to touristic possibilities and variety of itineraries."[13] The geographical expanses of Soviet territory, and the variety of its climate and natural zones, are represented as exceptional and unique, and this uniqueness is invested with patriotic meanings that reinforce Soviet nation-building.

The construction of Soviet space within the frame of early socialist ideology has been well researched.[14] The urgency of spatial exploration and "the dash to the periphery" began in the 1920s. Besides an ideological frame, it also had a pragmatic goal. The revolutionary country was to overcome not only history but space; it had to survey, map, and explore its territory to create new routes and networks of communication and infrastructure, and to industrialize and electrify.[15] What was, essentially, a decentering impetus of the 1920s and early 1930s, had turned into a centrally governed and rigidly organized spatial

---

[12] On Soviet tourism, see Anne E. Gorsuch and Diane P. Koenker (eds.), *Turizm: The Russian and East European Tourist under Capitalism and Socialism* (Ithaca, NY, 2006).

[13] L. Gurvich, *Vokrug sveta* 3 (1964), p. 53.

[14] See the contributions to Evgeny Dobrenko and Eric Naiman (eds.), *The Landscape of Stalinism: The Art and Ideology of Soviet Space* (Seattle and London, 2003); Emma Widdis, *Visions of a New Land: Soviet Film from the Revolution to the Second World War* (New Haven, CT, 2003).

[15] Emma Widdis, "To Explore or Conquer? Mobile Perspectives on the Soviet Cultural Revolution," in Dobrenko and Naiman, *Landscape of Stalinism*, p. 220.

ideology by the mid-1930s. Emma Widdis has recently described this through two concepts central to Soviet discourse of the time: The exploration [*izuchenie* or *razvedka*] of the 1920s was gradually transformed into the Stalinist conquest or mastery of space [*osvoenie*].¹⁶ Stalinist spatial ideology presented a classical imperial structure of space with a center and the provinces spread out around it:

> The aesthetics of "conquest," or *osvoenie*, predominant during the "high" Stalinism from the mid-1930s onward pictured a space that was essentially static and hierarchically organized around a dominant center (Moscow) that extended radiant lines of influence. [...] It produced a vision of the Soviet territory as known and mapped, a vision in which relations between center (Moscow) and periphery provided the key axis. All roads led to and from a central, nodal point; the periphery was dependent upon center.¹⁷

The 1960s orientation toward periphery, and the imagery and terminology of exploration in *Around the World*, recalls the early Soviet period. In the official realm of Soviet life, the impetus and urge to explore was rationalized by the need for technological modernization. At the same time, the representation of exploration in official discourse was designed to reinforce the territorial unity of the vast country and its citizens. The construction of Soviet space, whether through reportage of Great Chemistry or through first-person accounts of Siberian expeditions, entailed the construction of Soviet identity in terms of spatial and geographical imagery. Exploration was about molding a unified Soviet identity. On the other hand, exploration was also understood as a freedom to go beyond the limits, to decenter Soviet space and culture, to de-Stalinize its centralized, imperial hierarchies. Nevertheless, these decentering journeys were usually written from a metropolitan viewpoint and, thus, they in fact not so much deconstructed as reconstructed a hierarchy of an imperial space. The advertisement for Sputnik with the roads radiating from Moscow captured the hierarchy of Soviet space that offered opportunities for travel and mobility, but structured the mobility according to an imperial hierarchy. And, then again, this hierarchy differed from the Stalinist one in which all roads led to Moscow, whereas here the main radii are interconnected by smaller roads.¹⁸ Even if thinner and thus less significant, these roads invoke an idea of a multidimensional, decentering imperial space, a similar spatiality as suggested by the unknown itineraries of exploration and expedition.

---

¹⁶ Ibid., p. 221.
¹⁷ Ibid.
¹⁸ Compare, for instance, the Stalinist image of "Moscow—a port of five oceans" discussed by Katri Pynnöniemi in Chapter 7 of this volume.

Brodsky in the Outskirts: Imaginary Empire

What linked writing within official cultural politics and writing outside it in the 1960s was the idea of the vastness of Soviet space. In both realms of cultural practices, the geographical magnitude of the country was understood as a point of identification, as something that all Soviet citizens shared, whether they were readers of the official Soviet publications or *samizdat* poetry. Even a poet such as Joseph Brodsky who did not aspire to speak for a unified Soviet identity communicated his own position within this spatial paradigm and the metropolitan or imperial hierarchy it produced.

Before his arrest and internment in 1964, Brodsky wrote poetry that reflected various forms of Soviet travel, geological expeditions, and voluntary flights to the Soviet south and the Baltic seafront. Mapping out Brodsky's trips and travels through the geographical points of references of his early 1960s poetry creates an imaginative space that covers a large part of the Soviet territory with Leningrad as its center and the following places as the outer regions: Yakutsk, Kazakhstan, Estonia, Moscow, the Karelian isthmus, Irkutsk, Tarusa, Baltiisk (Pillau), Kaliningrad, Pskov, and finally Norenskaia, the site of his internment in the Arkhangelsk region where he was exiled after sentenced for parasitism [*tuneiadstvo*] in 1964.

After the forced stay in Norenskaia, the poetic exploration of Soviet territory resumes with an increasing awareness of that territory as an "imperial" space.[19] Roman imperial culture and the Russian romantic era with its imperial imaginings formed the framework through which Brodsky imagined Soviet space and located himself in it. Brodsky's post-Norenskaia poetry includes such regions and cities as Sevastopol, Palanga, Moscow, Yalta, Kaliningrad, Koktebel, and Odessa.

In these late 1960s poems Brodsky's traveling subject was transformed from the young expeditionist into the post-exile, celebrated, and scandalous poet of the 1967 "Anno Domini." This is a thoroughly anthologized poem with a memorable first line: "The provinces are celebrating Christmas / The Governor-general's mansion is bedecked / with mistletoe [*Provintsiia spravliaet Rozhdestvo / Dvorets Namestnika uvit omeloi*]. What follows is a description of the Governor-general's ill-health and his wife's deceptive relationship with the Governor's secretary. The lyric subject identifies himself with the Governor-general and then turns to speak of himself in the first person:

> And I, a writer who has seen the world,
> who has crossed the equator on an ass,

---

[19] This passage is based on my research on Brodsky's poetry published in Sanna Turoma, *Brodsky Abroad: Empire, Tourism, Nostalgia* (Madison, NJ, 2010), pp. 26–44.

> look out of the window at the hills asleep
> and think about the identity of our woes:
> the Emperor won't see him [the Governor-general],
> I won't be
> seen by my son and Cynthia.... And we,
> we here shall perish.[20]

The lyric plot takes place in an imaginary Roman province. First identified with the Governor-general [*namestnik*] fallen out of Caesar's grace, and the speaker eventually comes forth as relating himself to Propertius, (in)famous among his contemporaries for provoking a scandalous image of a lyric subject and his relations with the non-reciprocating Cynthia, as Propertius calls the addressee of his love elegies and as Brodsky calls the spouse/mistress of his lyric subject.

At the end of the poem we find out where Brodsky locates the contemporary counterpart of the historical Roman province: It is Soviet Lithuania, identified at the end of the poem through the dating "January 1968, Palanga." The Roman province is transposed on the geographical hierarchies of the Soviet Union; references to imperial Rome are projected on Soviet spatial hierarchies. This is a metropolitan (i.e. Leningrad) Russian-language poet in a Soviet province (i.e. Lithuania).

The concept of empire emerges in Brodsky's works as one of the essences structuring his historical and geographical imagination, as well as his understanding of cultural signification.[21] His experience of the Soviet Union and his understanding of the country as an empire was crucial to his understanding of empire both as a historical fact and a metaphysical concept. In his creative imagination, empire was a cultural given that provided the conditions necessary for a civilization with its arts, philosophy, and moral order to develop, while it could also exhibit the "human negative potential." Despite Brodsky's use of Roman references to depict the absurdity or moral unruliness of the authoritarian Soviet state or his marginalized position within it, Brodsky never questioned the historical legitimacy of the Roman Empire, the significance of the imperial culture it produced, or the authority of its cultural heritage.

With his ardent advocacy of Roman writers and their poetic forms, and his saturated use of imperial Rome as the means of his intertextual poetics, Brodsky fixed the semantic groundwork of his poetic imagination on the archive of knowledge informing all European as well as Russian imperial discourses. This said, the view that Brodsky took of the empire in his imaginings

---

[20] Brodsky, *Collected Poems in English*, p. 6.
[21] For more on this, see Turoma, *Brodsky Abroad*, pp. 63–71.

of antiquity while still in the Soviet Union was a view from the provinces. As Petr Vail and Aleksandr Genis, two ardent commentators of Brodsky's works, point out, it was a view defiant of the imperial center. Ovid and Propertius, the two seminal figures for Brodsky's poetic self-fashioning, offered him a model for representing a poet's political—and, in the case of Propertius, also amatory—marginalization. Then again, the view from the provinces was still a view informed by Russian and Soviet metropolitan formations, by a Leningrad awareness of the cultural significance of Petersburg's imperial past. To strike the pose of the margins, Brodsky set his lyric subject in Lithuania or on the Black Sea shore, the borderlands of the Soviet and historical Russian Empire. He did not speak for the borderlands but incorporated them into his imaginary imperial space. Even if defiant of the imperial center, his poetic imagination did not decenter or deconstruct imperial spatiality but, rather, reinforced it through the refashioning of a poetic identity banished from the metropole.

Genis and Vail on Siberia: Empire and National Identity

Discussing Joseph Brodsky's significance for their generation of Soviet *samizdat* readers, Petr Vail and Aleksandr Genis suggest that Brodsky's use of *imperiia* [empire] as a metaphor for the Soviet Union—as in this thoroughly anthologized line, "empire is a country for fools"—reflected the use of the term as an expression of ideological opposition to the Soviet regime at the time.[22] According to Vail and Genis, the term was used as a synonym of "the absurd evil" of the Soviet regime among the post-Stalin generation of creative intelligentsia. The mythology of "Moscow the Third Rome," a medieval doctrine used to legitimize Muscovy's religious and political preeminence in the fifteenth century and re-evoked by some Slavophile thinkers in the nineteenth century, surfaced in the 1960s as a metaphor for the Kremlin's centralized authoritarian policies. The question Vail and Genis see as crucial for analyzing the Soviet 1960s is the transformation of the utopia of communism into the dystopia of empire: "The poetic vagueness of both terms [communism and empire], the ability of these metaphors to not so much describe a real historical process as to give it a wider, symbolic, mythological meaning—all this allows the 1960s to be turned into one question: How did communism again become an empire?"[23] In other words,

---

[22] This is the first line of Brodsky's often-quoted poem "Post aetatem nostra" (1970); see the Russian original in Joseph Brodsky, *Sobranie sochinenii* (St. Petersburg, 1997), vol. 2, p. 397.

[23] Petr Vail and Aleksandr Genis, *60-e: mir sovetskogo cheloveka* (Ann Arbor, MI, 1988), pp. 250–51, 260. Compare this with Mark Beissinger's observation that "The more

while the official Soviet ideology propagated the cold war concept of peaceful coexistence of communism with capitalism [*mirnoe sosushchestvovanie*], the token phrase of the Communist Party after the 1962 Cuban Crisis, there developed among the post-Stalin critical intellectuals an awareness of the Soviet Union as a totalitarian "empire," whose imperial/ist aspirations outside the country's borders were becoming more and more evident; the final signal of them being the invasion of Czechoslovakia in 1968.

But how do Vail and Genis, sensitive to the anti-imperial/ist and, at the same time, metaphorical meanings invested in the concept of empire in dissenting cultural practices, portray the geographical space this "empire" governed in their recollections of it? To answer this question, I will look at the chapter titled "Geography Instead of History. Siberia" in their memoir *The 60s: The World of the Soviet Man*.

According to Vail and Genis, every Russian [*rossiianin*] was "aware of the importance of the State," which covered "one-sixth of the earth" and "a whole one side of the globe, the North." However, the imaginative map the two writers create in their collective memoir renders a majority of the geographical magnitude curiously anonymous. A large part of the "empire" has no identity, nor language; it is an emptiness of nothing waiting for the Russian language articulations to give it a signification: "Somewhere there existed the absolutely definable France, England, Italy. But only Russia [*Rossiia*] was on one side bordered by civilization and on the other by endlessness."[24] What emerges from Vail and Genis's conjecture is a map with three geographical designations: "Civilization" on the left, "Russia" in the middle, and "Endlessness" on the right. The latter is then identified as Siberia, and the signification Vail and Genis give to it, is its role as the space where "*russkaia udal'*," the "reckless boldness" thought to be characteristically Russian, has traditionally been played out. In this historical conjecture the role of Siberia is, then, to reinforce Russia's self-identification with the wild and austere "North." At the same time, the distinction between Russia and Siberia remains: Unlike the parts of Russia that lie next to "civilization," Siberia is a space "not within the borders of the cultured world but outside it." Not that Siberia ever was, the authors are quick to contest, an "ordinary colony," it was an "abstraction," "a storehouse of space, an almost

---

one examines the variety of meanings attached to empire across history, the more one is tempted to conclude that the notion has always contained some metaphorical element, even in its original Roman usage." Mark Beissinger, "Soviet Empire as 'Family Resemblance,'" *Slavic Review* 65/2 (2006): 294.

[24] Vail and Genis, *60-e*, p. 69.

inexhaustible geographical repository. Siberia served not so much as a source of real profit, but as a spring of poetic metaphors."[25]

Vail and Genis fail to analyze the ideological or political underpinnings of the national symbolism and their own metaphors. Instead, they venture on to describe the Siberian contribution to the mythologies of Russian national identity. In this narrative, historical events recognized by historians as colonizing processes of military conquest, systematic scientific research (cartography and geology), commercial exploitation, and extensive Russification of indigenous peoples are romanticized as empire-building founded on individual men's heroic if "despairing bravery."[26] The concept of "North," disassociated now from Siberia and associated exclusively with the more "civilized" Russia is invested, then, with positive meanings signifying the Russian national character.

Vail and Genis's essayistic style is ironic, and the authorial irony is intensified when the text turns to concern the post-Stalin effort to transplant the construction of communism on the "virgin soil of Siberia." The aim of the irony is to expose the inefficiency of the Soviet enterprise and the disillusion it brought about. Its aim, however, is not to question the Soviet identity that the construction projects and exploration produced or the imperial attitudes they both implied and provoked. While Vail and Genis seem to ironically undermine the official narratives of Soviet space, they reconstruct an alternative narrative, the narrative of historically more legitimate and authentic Russian imperial space. And even within the ideology of Soviet space their position remains somewhat ambiguous: Instead of uncovering the official ideologies underlying the geographical mythology of the "one-sixth," which informed the patriotic discourses of the Soviet Union, Vail and Genis further mythologize it. They endorse it by representing it as a foundation for the coherent if somewhat naïve world-picture of the 1960s Soviet citizen, their idealized projection of their own generation, who emerge as the collective positive hero of the memoir. The ironic style of the two authors signals their dissident positions, but the authorial irony does not aim at deconstructing or even challenging Russian or Soviet myths of empire or imperial missions. Vail and Genis's nostalgic recapturing of the 1960s "mental landscape" reinforces the mythologies they set out to explore, while it also functions as a retrospective and nostalgic articulation of Soviet spatial identity.

---

[25] Ibid., p. 70.

[26] On the Russian expansion eastward, see J.L. Black, "Opening up Siberia: Russia's 'Window on the East,'" in Alan Wood (ed.), *The History of Siberia: From Russian Conquest to Revolution* (London, 1991), pp. 57–68.

Bitov in Armenia: National or Imperial Identity?

One of the popular forms of travel in the 1960s Soviet Union was the so-called *tvorcheskaia kommandirovka*, "artistic work assignment," practiced by members of the creative intelligentsia who were able to take advantage of official permissions and funds in arranging trips to places out of reach for most Soviet citizens.[27] This type of literary travel offered Soviet intellectuals a discursive space for reflecting on the Soviet Union and its realities while negotiating the borders of what was officially accepted.

It was on this kind of assignment that Andrei Bitov traveled to Armenia in 1967. The circumstances that led to the trip were typical of the period: After being declined a trip abroad (to Japan to join a Soviet–Japanese film production), Bitov was offered a trip to a non-Russian republic within the Soviet territory.[28] As a result of this trip, he wrote *Lessons of Armenia* [*Uroki Armenii*], which became popular among the Soviet intellectual youth of the time. (The English text appeared in *A Captive of the Caucasus* together with a later travel piece on Georgia titled *Georgian Album* [*Gruzinskii Al'bom*]).

The first three chapters of *Lessons of Armenia* are titled "Language Lesson," "History Lesson," and "Geography Lesson." In "Geography Lesson" the subchapter titled "Space" starts with the following passage:

> Space [*prostor*] is a national category. A necessary condition for the realization of a nation. When I look at the Soviet map, our scarlet bedsheet, I feel distance [*prostranstvo*]—enormous distance—but I still don't feel open space [*prostor*]. And if there's a little speck squeezed into a corner somewhere, like a tiny marsh (Estonia) or washtub (Armenia), how could you suspect it had any kind of space? Stand in the center and spin around on your heel, and your eye would demarcate all its boundaries. How could anyone live on a pocket handkerchief like that? Backed by distances so inconceivable, you shrug.[29]

The passages can be read as an ironic comment on the mythologies of Russia's geographical expanses [*prostor*], but, at the same time, Bitov seems to offer, in all earnestness, the idea of equating nation with space, that is, the idea that a nation is defined in spatial terms. This is an equation that draws on the classical

---

[27] See Irina H. Corten, *Vocabulary of Soviet Society and Culture: A Selected Guide to Russian Words, Idioms, and Expressions of the Post-Stalinist Era, 1953–1991* (Durham, NC, 1992), pp. 41, 148. See also Turoma, *Brodsky Abroad*, pp. 26–7.

[28] Bitov in Andrei Bitov, *A Captive of the Caucasus*, trans. Susan Brownsberger (New York, 1992), pp. 3–4.

[29] Bitov, *Captive*, p. 50.

understanding of a nationality and nation-state being based on shared territory. It echoes the Foucaultian concept of nation-centric space, where the flat surface of the map is covered by "boxes" of different size.[30] There is the "box" for Estonia and Armenia, and Estonian and Armenian nations defined by their respective "boxes," that is, territories.[31]

In what follows the author zooms in on one of the "specks," that is Armenia. He presents an account of a trip he made with his Armenian friends to the Charents Arch, a famous landmark named after a famous Armenian poet Yegishe Charents. This is an arch built on top of a hill, a place for viewing the Mount Ararat and the valley around it. The author describes how they ascend the hill and arrive at the arch:

> The arch on the summit grew nearer and at last blocked everything else. We got out [of the car]. I looked uncertainly at my friends. Why had we stopped? What was remarkable about this elephantine structure? 'The Charents Arch,' they told me. Silently they let me pass ahead.—I walked through the arch and exclaimed. My God, what space opened up! It blazed forth. Something within me lifted.[32]

In the following passages Bitov describes the view and the sensation it invokes in him. The contemplation of the sublime mountain scenery is interrupted by his Armenian friends' exclamations when they usher him to see Mount Ararat: "See? One minute's it's gone, the next you see it again." The author comments: "I strained to see it. Maybe I did, maybe I didn't. After all, I didn't know exactly what I was supposed to see." To his friends he confirms ecstatically that he can see the mountain. Happy with the visit, his friends turn back to leave the arch, and the author concludes: "A man's country is not too small for him if he just once feels its space [*prostor*]. How could he suspect the existence of borders, once he has seen this... 'Here I first saw the world,' people say of their homeland."[33] In other words, one of the "specks in the corner" has offered him a sensation of infinite space, and the lesson of Armenia that the author draws from this experience is that seemingly small spaces of small nations, "pocket handkerchiefs," can against his expectations offer a sense of open space. For his Armenian friends, as Bitov imagines it, this sense of space reinforces their sense of nationality, sense of belonging to a nation.

---

[30] Cf. "Introduction" to this volume, p. XX. Page number!!!

[31] In the Soviet context, the territorialization of nationality and ethnicity originated in the Stalin period. See Francine Hirsch, *Empire of Nations: Ethnographic Knowledge and the Making of the Soviet Union* (Ithaca, NY, 2005).

[32] Bitov, *Captive*, p. 51.

[33] Bitov, *Captive*, p. 53.

Bitov's observations of nation and space create a frame for his visit to the Charents Arch, but they also rouse a few questions. To begin with, Bitov's way of equating nation with space entails a hierarchy of nations. According to his reasoning, a nation's geographical size is directly related to its political and cultural significance: "a tiny marsh" and a "washtub," that is Estonia and Armenia, are referred to as "a little speck squeezed into a corner". But what, then, is the nation that makes them appear so small? From which viewpoint do Estonia and Armenia seem as "specks squeezed in the corner" and from which viewpoint does the author study the map? Whose point of view is the "*our* point of view" in the sentence that immediately follows the passage when Bitov writes: "And what foolish surprise takes you over, when you drive hour upon hour though a miniature (from our point of view) country, and there's no end or limit to it?"[34]

To answer these questions one should start by noting that throughout the travelogue Bitov keeps comparing Armenian language, culture, and people with Russian language, culture, and people. The trip is, in fact, as trips in travel writing often are, a pretext for the author to reflect on his own culture and his own cultural identity, in this case a Russian-language metropolitan identity. His authorial viewpoint is fixed in Leningrad, where, as he imagines, he can see from his window a "small Finnish birch tree." The "Finnish" here does not refer to Bitov's contemporary Finland but invokes a historical fact central to the cultural mythologies of St. Petersburg: Russia's historical capital was built by the Gulf of Finland on lands inhabited by Finns. Bitov's double vision combines the mythologies of the past with the Soviet present and produces an imaginative geography, which recalls the textual representation of Russia's imperial space put forth by Andrei Bely in his famous 1913 novel *Petersburg*. In the novel there is a passage where the narrator imagines Petersburg as the central "point" that "manifests itself on maps" and from which "surges and swarms the printed book; from this invisible point speeds the official circular."[35]

Just as Bely imagined Petersburg as the center of the literary and cultural production of the Russian Empire, Bitov, too, sets contemporary Leningrad as the central point of the Russian-language cultural production of the Soviet Union. In Bitov's contemporary Russia print culture "speeded" from several centers of Soviet territory, but his travel narrative establishes Lennigrad as the authoritative metropolitan center of Soviet cultural space. Bitov's viewpoint of Estonia and Armenia is a Russian-language Soviet metropolitan viewpoint fixed in the historical awareness of Russia's imperial past. The "Soviet map, our scarlet

---

[34] Bitov, *Captive*, p. 50 (italics ST).
[35] Andrei Bely, *Petersburg*, trans. David McDuff (London, 1995), p. 2. See also Nick Baron's commentary on Bitov in Chapter 4 of this volume.

bedsheet" is structured according to a classic imperial hierarchy where the author's metropolitan vantage point is defined by an imperial center (Leningrad/Petersburg) from where he surveys and comments on its outskirts: Estonia and Armenia.[36] Within the hierarchy of imperial space that Bitov's travelogue seems to rest on, Armenia and Estonia are represented as equally provincial in terms of the hierarchy of one vast Russian or Soviet space imagined from the bird's-eye-viewpoint of the author looking at the map.

Bitov's imaginative geography represents as much an imperial as a national space structured on the center–periphery axis. He comes to point at the fact that not only nations but also empires are defined in terms of space. With the reconstruction of this imagined imperial space, the author also reconstructs an imperial identity articulated in the "*our* point of view," that is, a Russian-language metropolitan viewpoint. But to return to the question I posed above: What is the nation that the space, or the lack of it, on the Soviet map should "give a form to"? Is it a "Russian nation," *rossiiskaia natsiia* or *russkaia natsiia*? Both are equally non-idiomatic in Russian, where the more common word used in this context is *narod*, "people," instead of *natsiia*, "nation". Or, since the Soviet map is mentioned, and the Soviet flag evoked ("our scarlet bedsheet"), is it a "Soviet nation," *sovetskaia natsiia*, that the space on the map gives form to? "Soviet nation," in turn, recalls the concept of "Soviet people," *sovetskii narod*, which in the official Soviet idiolect referred to the community of nations within the Soviet Union and was widely used in the 1960s and 1970s in popular ethnographic literature about the Soviet Union.[37] From this viewpoint one can argue that Bitov's travel narrative, no matter how ironic, invokes an idea of Soviet nationhood within the hierarchical imperial space it reconstructs.

Conclusions

Seeking explanations to the collapse of the Soviet Union, some scholars have argued that the Soviet leaders failed to build a uniform Soviet national identity.[38] To continue that thought, it seems to me that such identity was successfully constructed in Russian-language metropolitan formations, if not in

---

[36] Cf. Mary Louise Pratt's discussion of the "monarch-of-all-I-survey" trope and its many manifestations in European travel literature from the eighteenth century to the postwar period in *Imperial Eyes: Travel Writing and Transculturation* (London, 1994), pp. 201–27.

[37] See Hirsch, *Empire of Nations*, pp. 317–18.

[38] For the argument of Soviet leadership's failure in All-Union Soviet identity-building, see Ronald Suny and Terry Martin's "Introduction," in *A State of Nations: Empire and Nation-making in the Age of Lenin and Stalin* (Oxford, 2001), p. 9.

non-Russian or non-metropolitan societal and cultural practices, but it never became uniform or universal enough to stop other social, cultural, political or economic processes that eventually led to the disintegration of the Soviet Union. Nevertheless, this identity, articulated in terms of geographical and spatial imagery, exercised great cultural authority on the generation that came of age in the post-Stalin period. The forming of this identity within official cultural practices took place through similar spatial imaginings as was the case in unofficial cultural practices where identities and subject positions were markedly anti- or, at least, non-Soviet. Andrei Bitov's and Vail and Genis's narratives of space and nation as well as Joseph Brodsky's imperial imaginings articulated a Russian-language metropolitan identity embedded in Soviet spatial hierarchies that also informed and were partially produced by reportage and stories about the 1960s modernization of Soviet territory, the construction of Soviet space in the journal *Around the World*. The overlapping ambiguity of national and imperial symbolism in 1960s spatial imaginings demonstrates ultimately how national and imperial spatiality as discursive constructs and products of the imaginary constantly coexisted and crossed over each other's boundaries in the Soviet imperial situation.

Just how powerful the cultural authority of this spatial identity was is manifest in the nostalgic responses voiced by the Russian intelligentsia after the fall of the Soviet Union and the reduction of imperial space it insinuated. The Leningrad/Petersburg writer Viktor Krivulin (1944–2001) reflected ironically on this nostalgia in an article written for the third anniversary of Joseph Brodsky's death: "We all still sense our 'great and mighty' as something vast, powerfully seizing the 'one-sixth of the earth,' even if we are no longer citizens of the language that disappeared long since."[39] The "great and mighty" is a quotation from a poem by Ivan Turgenev, and it refers to the creative power of the Russian language—in this case, its power to govern the vast geographical expanses, which, in the post-Soviet situation that Krivulin was writing in, were no longer within its legitimate governance. The symbolic meaning of the language of empire, as Krivulin seems to be saying, unraveled with the disintegration of the space of empire, the "one-sixth of the earth." The symbolic meanings of the spatial identity articulated in that language, however, seem to linger on.

---

[39] Viktor Krivulin, "Zaveshchanie v zanaveshennom zerkale (K tretei godovshchine Iosifa Brodskogo)," *Novoe literaturnoe obozrenie* 37 (1999): 382.

CHAPTER 11

Picturing Infinity: Space Race and the Cosmic Landscape

Iina Kohonen

A Slash in the Sky

> Do you hear *Sputnik*'s voice? He is out there, in the void, in the middle of meteoric rain and cosmic radiation, in the world of secrets and eternal coldness, circling around our planet, around the continents and the oceans. And not only is he flying in these mysterious heights—he is also working and telling us what he sees and hears out there.[1]

One of the first published photographs of *Sputnik*, the first Earth-orbiting artificial satellite, was a faintly glowing line in the night sky (Figure 11.1). Taken with a long exposure time, the photograph illustrates the satellite's long path across the dark heavens. The line is like a cut, an incision in the celestial sphere. This image, or rather the idea behind this image, was one of the driving forces of the Soviet visual propaganda concerning the space race: Much of the Soviet cosmic propaganda drew from the idea of outer space's immensity and the rhetoric of conquest and exploration.

Flying, actual, potential, and dreamlike, has always implied more than a mechanism for overcoming gravity.[2] Right from the beginning Soviet society had been striving to find blank pages on maps, spaces "on which it could inscribe itself."[3] In the 1920s the project was electrification and construction of the railroad network. In the 1930s attention turned toward the ultimate north, the Arctic and into the ultimate deep—the underground, the pride of Stalinist Moscow. The prevailing tendencies of this time were hovering between conquest,

---

[1] L. Kachosvily, "Sputnik III Moskovan yllä," *Neuvostoliitto Tänään* 11–12 (1958): 19.

[2] Jyrki Siukonen, *Uplifted Spirits, Earthbound Machines: Studies on Artists and the Dream of Flight, 1900–1935* (Helsinki, 2001), p. 11.

[3] Eric Naiman, "Introduction," in Evgeny Dobrenko and Eric Naiman (eds.), *The Landscape of Stalinism: The Art and Ideology of Soviet Space* (Seattle, WA and London, 2003), p. xiv.

Figure 11.1 *Sputnik 1*.
Source: *Ongonyok* 1 (1958) (unknown photographer).

colonization, and exploration. It was in the late 1950s and 1960s that attention turned towards the skies and beyond. The triumph of the cosmos was treated as a victory over time and place and as transcendence of all earthly hardship. An idea of exploration and conquest united all these Soviet projects. Unknown space was transformed into known and mapped territory.[4]

During the 1950s and early 1960s the theme of space exploration was so widespread that it can be seen as a leitmotif of the whole cold war generation, in East and West alike. In Soviet Union this "cosmic enthusiasm" was utilized by the Khrushchevian propaganda machinery, deeply connected to the military industry and to the arms race. At the same time, it had roots in and connotations for utopian cosmic dreaming. The scientific optimism of the late 1950s describing a utopian vision of a future in outer space stands in poignant contrast to the disillusionment of later decades.

In the following, I will discuss how the idea of cosmic dimension and humankind's place in it has been represented visually. I will illustrate how the Soviet Union produced and projected its new cosmic scale through visual representations—that is, through the photographs and other illustrations

---

[4] Emma Widdis, "To Explore or to Conquer?: Mobile Perspectives on the Soviet Cultural Revolution," in Dobrenko and Naiman, *The Landscape of Stalinism*, ,pp. 219–40.

depicting the first cosmic triumphs. As a case example I will take the early Soviet Luna Program: the first three robotic spacecraft missions sent to the Moon by the Soviet Union in 1959. Via a massive media program and through a carefully selected repertoire of representations, outer space became a vital part of the Soviet landscape in the Khrushchev period. Photographs revealed raw unseen space transforming it into an imaginary map of the cosmic lunar landscape.[5] The basic argument of this chapter is that this cosmic imagery was, as a practice, very much imperial in nature. Via mapping and naming, outer space was included into Soviet territory.

The empirical material of this chapter consists of space-related photographs published in popular media in the Soviet Union during the first decade of the space age. In addition, I have studied the photographic collections of the Russian State Archive of Scientific and Technical Documents (RGANTD), located in Moscow.

Roots of the Cosmic Enthusiasm

> On that day, the fourth of October, when the world's first satellite—a Soviet one— was launched, man was allowed to feel like a resident of the Universe. For the first time he stepped over the threshold of the home where he was born and raised. That home is called the planet Earth.[6]

The obsession with the cosmic was not an invention of what we know as the space age. As an idea, "Russian Cosmism" [*Ruskii kozmizm*] can be traced as far back as nineteenth-century philosophy. The dream of space flight had enjoyed a long tradition in the Soviet Union. Such names as Vladimir Vernadskii, Aleksandr Chizhevskii, and Nikolai Fyodorov, all somewhat peculiar figures in the field of philosophy, can be connected to this ideology. Perhaps the best known of the supporters of Russian Cosmism is Konstantin Tsiolkovskii (1857–1935). "Mankind will not be bound to Earth forever" wrote this self-made rocket designer, space philosopher, writer, and teacher from the small provincial town of Kaluga. He was the first to connect the theories of Cosmism to more practical considerations of rocket technology, and many of his inventions were

---

[5] Ibid., p. 221. Widdis discusses the use of space in Stalinist discourse of Soviet territory. Her ideas about space are also applicable to Khrushchevian space exploration.

[6] B. Ljapunov, "Natshalo kosmitsheskoij ery," *Ogonyok* 41 (1958): 6–7.

later proved to work. Apart from his technological studies, he was also a devoted theorist of Cosmic philosophy and an enthusiastic reader of Jules Verne.[7]

Tsiolkovskii worked in isolation, unconnected to the scientific community; but a growing popularity of the idea of space travel was in the air. In the Soviet Union, as well as in Western Europe, the idea of interplanetary exploration caused a phenomenon in the 1920s that can rightfully be called a "space boom." Science-fiction literature flourished and the idea of space flight was taken seriously in an era when even electric lighting was a luxury. Flying machines real and imagined were, as Susan Buck-Morss puts it, "invested with transformative social meaning" and utopian impulses were tolerated and even supported by ruling powers. Interplanetary travel was a preferred form of social utopian expression.[8] Thus, when the space age finally dawned, Soviet culture already had visual imagery and concepts to understand the phenomenon. As Cathleen S. Lewis puts it:

> The space program artifacts reflected the hopeful imagery drawn from pre-Soviet, revolutionary and Stalinist culture that evoked optimism for the future. They also embodied a well-crafted message that tied cosmonauts and spaceflight to Soviet ideology. At once, they symbolized an abrupt break with and deep ties to the past.[9]

Scout of the Heavenly Depths

The cosmic dream was realized when *Sputnik* was launched by the Soviet Union on October 4, 1957—just a few weeks after the 100th birthday of Konstantin Tsiolkovskii. In the popular media *Sputnik* was frequently referred to as a "scout of the heavenly depths" [*razvedchik nebesnyh glubin*].[10] The choice of the word *razvedchik*, a scout, is an interesting one. The term refers to a military investigation

---

[7] Viktor Sytin, "Chelovek realnoj mechty," *Ogonyok* 38 (1957): 12–13; Michael Hagemeister, "The Conquest of Space and the Bliss of the Atoms: Konstantin Tsiolkovskii," in Eva Maurer et al. (eds.), *Soviet Space Culture: Cosmic Enthusiasm in Socialist Societies* (New York, 2011), pp. 27–41; Iina Kohonen, "The Space Race and Soviet Utopian Thinking," in David Bell and Martin Parker (eds.), *Space Travel and Culture: From* Apollo *to Space Tourism* (Oxford, 2009), pp. 114–31. See also Marlène Laruelle's contribution to this volume, esp. n. 4 on p. **XX**.

[8] Susan Buck-Morss, *Dreamworld and Catastrophe: The Passing of Mass Utopia in East and West* (Cambridge, 2000), p. 45; Alexander C.T. Geppert, "Space *Personae*: Cosmopolitan Networks of Peripheral Knowledge," *Journal of Modern European History* 2 (2008): 262–86.

[9] Cathleen S. Lewis, "The Red Stuff: A History of the Public and Material Culture of Early Human Spaceflight in the U.S.S.R," Ph. D. diss. History (George Washington University, 2008), p. 2.

[10] Sergei Vasilev, "Razvedtšikam nebesnyh glubin," *Pravda*, October 6, 1957, p. 1; S.N. Vernov, "Razvedka glubin kosmosa," *Ogonyok* 44 (1957): 5.

and had been in frequent use at the time of the First Five-Year Plan referring to the masses of people who were called upon to explore the vast Soviet territory. Geologists and cartographers mapped the terrain; virtually everybody—scientific experts as well as ordinary citizens—was encouraged to set off and discover the nation. As Emma Widdis has noted, it was through this *discovery* that the nation was to be transformed from a czarist empire into a socialist union. The entire Soviet space was to be remade and transformed.[11] The same process of transformation was put into action through depictions representing the early conquest of space. Outer space was to be discovered, mapped, and measured in order to make it a place. And as a place it could be monopolized and someday even, in a Tsiolkovskiian tone, perhaps inhabited. This was empire-making on a celestial scale.

Taking over the Moon: *Luna 1*—A New Dimension of Time and Space

Sputnik was perhaps just a scout, but the information that it gained was to be used by specialists. Soon after that, the Soviet space program entered into a next stage: The rockets were equipped with photo-correspondent's equipment. And the information this produced was to be published widely.

The process of "taking over outer space" was literally put into action soon after the first artificial Earth satellites. The Luna Program was a series of robotic spacecraft missions sent to the Moon and included 15 successful orbital flights or Moon surface landings (the failures were not reported). In what follows I will demonstrate how the first three Luna missions operated as imperial agents, literally acting as conquerors of the newly explored space.

Going to the Moon and the planets, first robotically, then with cosmonauts, had been Sergei Korolev's[12] prime objective, a dream so vivid that the first rocket launched toward the Moon was named *Mechta* ("Dream," later known as *Luna 1*).[13] On January 2, 1959 this first *Luna* probe was successfully launched in the Moon's direction. The spacecraft was a hermetically sealed sphere with external sensors to detect radiation and magnetic fields. The sphere included scientific and radio-technical instruments including a cosmic ray counter, a radio system used to determine the flight trajectory, and equipment for producing an artificial

---

[11] Emma Widdis, *Visions of a New Land: Soviet Film from the Revolution to the Second World War* (New Haven, CT and London, 2003), pp. 97–119.

[12] Sergei Korolev was in charge of Soviet space program but known to the public only under the pseudonym "Chief Designer." Korolev was publicly acknowledged as the man behind Soviet success in space only posthumously in January 1966; see *Ogonyok* 4 (1966).

[13] James J. Harford, "Korolev's Triple Play: *Sputniks* 1, 2, and 3," in Roger D. Launius (ed.), *Reconsidering* Sputnik. *Forty Years since the Soviet Satellite* (Amsterdam, 2000), pp. 141–2.

sodium cloud. Besides scientific equipment, also on board was a sphere made of 72 stainless-steel segments (the design was similar to a football) filled with liquid and an explosive charge. The sphere was meant to explode and spread the pentagonal pennants out across the surface of the Moon. Stamped on one side of each of these pennants was the launch date, while on the other side was the heraldic symbol of the Soviet Union.[14]

However, that impact never came. Owing to an error in navigation, on January 4, 1959, after 34 hours of flight, *Luna 1* missed the Moon by about 3,700 miles (6,000 km). The mission was a failure, but the Soviet media nonetheless turned the disappointment into a triumph. Ignoring the failure altogether, Nikita Khrushchev described the mission as if it was part of a long-term strategy.[15] *Luna 1* became the first-ever manmade object to reach the escape velocity of the Earth and, according to media propaganda, the Soviet Union had "succeeded in launching an artificial planet."[16]

Luna 2: To Conquer the Moon

The anticipated triumph came eight months later. *Luna 2*, almost an exact copy of *Luna 1*, was launched on September 12, 1959. At a distance of some 70,200 miles (113,000 km) from the Earth, a cloud of sodium gas was released by the spacecraft. This glowing orange trail of gas, with the brightness of a 4 to 5-magnitude star, allowed astronomers to track the spacecraft. The cloud received plenty of media attention and photographs of the "artificial comet created by Soviet scientists" were published in the media.[17]

On September 13 *Luna 2* became the first spacecraft to impact the surface of the Moon, crashing west of Mare Serenitatis. As did her older sister, *Luna 1*, this mission also carried pennants and medallions in it. Media depicted this memorabilia as well as the exact landing point carefully (Figure 11.2).[18] Three days after the impact, Khrushchev arrived in the US. It was the first official visit from a Soviet Secretary and this, alone, was something to boast about, but now Khrushchev was able to make most of it. On meeting Eisenhower, he offered him two replicas of the emblems and, with a grin on his face, said:

---

[14] Ibid., p. 142.

[15] It was 30 years before the Soviets admitted that *Luna 1* was actually meant to land on the Moon.

[16] V. Sharonov, "K solntsu! K zvezdam!," *Ogonyok* 3 (1959): 3.

[17] Yu Krylov, "Mezhplanetnaya trassa prolozhena...," *Ogonyok* 39 (1959): 6; A.G. Maselvich, "Skazka stala bylju!," *Ogonyok* 40 (1959): 8.

[18] *Ogonyok* 39 (1959); *Ogonyok* 40 (1959).

Figure 11.2 An artists interpretation of how *Luna 2* impacts the surface of the Moon.

Source: Ogonyok 40 (1959) (drawing by N. Denisovskii).

We have no doubt that the excellent scientists, engineers and workers of the United States of America who are engaged in the field of conquering the cosmos will also carry their pennant over the Moon. The Soviet pennant, as an old resident, will then welcome your pennant, and they will live there together in peace and friendship.[19]

---

[19]   William Taubman, *Khrushchev: The Man and His Era* (London, 2003), p. 419; Paolo Ulivi and David Harland, *Lunar Exploration: Human Pioneers and Robotic Surveyors* (Berlin, Heidelberg, and New York, 2004), p. 26.

In the Soviet Union, nobody seemed to remember that, just a little more than a year before, *Ogonyok* had boldly stated that "according to [Soviet] opinion, it is by no means desirable [contrary to the opinion of the US] to erect any national flags on the surface of the Moon. Our goal is a noble one: to expand mankind's understanding of the natural world without borders."[20]

Luna 3: Mapping and Naming the Moon

As is well known, the Moon rotates once as it orbits the Earth, allowing for the same side to always face the Earth. The far side remained a mystery to any earthbound observer. Only three weeks after the *Luna 2* mission, this mystery was revealed to humans. *Luna 3* was launched on October 4, 1959, the second anniversary of *Sputnik 1*. The spacecraft swung around the Moon and on October 7, at a distance of some 39,500 miles (63,500 km), photographed the far side. The technology was impressive: the film was automatically developed onboard, scanned by a television unit, and transmitted by radio back to Earth. Within 40 minutes the probe took a total of 29 photos, covering 70 percent of the far side.[21]

The first published photograph was a sensation and was widely published in both the Soviet and Western media (Figure 11.3). The photograph was a symmetrical square, so heavily retouched that it looked like a painting. The Moon was in the center of the photograph, light and a little fuzzy. *Ogonyok* published this sensational photo freshly on its first page.[22]

This version of the photograph looks tampered: There are marks, lines, and numbers drawn into it. The reason for this intrusion becomes understandable if we consider it from an imperial perspective. After the manipulation the photograph has ceased to be merely a celestial landscape; the markings have turned it into a more powerful tool: from a mere photograph into a *map*. The Moon was conquered: Via the map it had been transformed from something unknown into a known and mapped territory.

So, then, what kind of a map was this, this fuzzy black-and-white photograph published in *Ogonyok*? There were eight newly found, until then anonymous, celestial objects that were named in this map. The clearly defined dark area in the middle of the surface was named the Mare Moscoviense [Sea of Muscovy]. A more utopian name was given to the broad, shadowy area in the "southeastern"

---

[20] A. Blagonravov, "*Mechanics Illustrated* zajavljajet pravo na lunu," *Ogonyok* 29 (1957): 22.

[21] Harford, "Korolev's Triple Play," pp. 141–2; N.P. Barabashov (ed.), *Atlas of the Other Side of the Moon*,(Oxford, 1961).

[22] *Ogonyok* 45 (1959): 1.

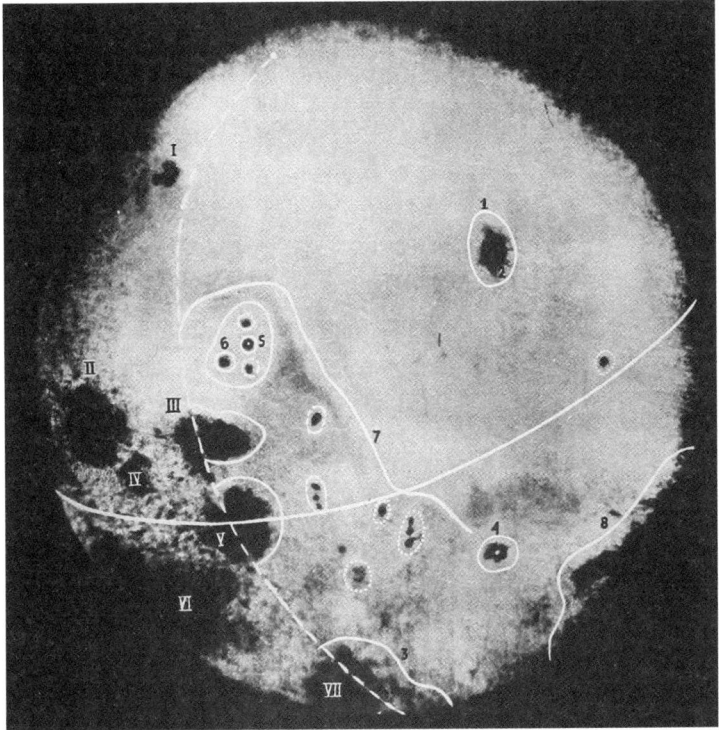

Figure 11.3 The far side of the Moon.
Source: Ogonyok 45 (1959) (photograph produced by the *Luna 3* probe).

corner: the Mare Desiderii [Sea of Dreams]. The surface is cut diagonally by the Montes Sovietici [Soviet mountain range].[23] In addition, craters were named for Mikhail Lomonosov, Frédéric Joliot-Curie, and Konstantin Tsiolkovskii as well as for his inspirational hero, Jules Verne—the two early dreamers of space had finally made it to the Moon's surface.

The naming was carried out by the USSR Academy of Sciences. Soon after the publication of this first crude "map," the academy published a more meticulous atlas of the Moon's far side, which included a catalogue of 500 notable features of the newly found landscape.[24] Among the toponyms were craters named for distinguished scientists, including Thomas Alva Edison, Giordano Bruno,

---

[23] Barabashov, *Atlas of the Other Side*; *Ogonyok* 45 (1959): 1.
[24] Barabashov, *Atlas of the Other Side*; Ewen A. Whitaker, *Mapping and Naming the Moon: A History of Lunar Cartography and Nomenclature* (Cambridge, 1999).

Heinrich Rudolf Hertz, Nikolai Lobachevskii, Louis Pasteur, Aleksandr Popov, Marie Skłodowska-Curie, James Maxwell, and Igor Kurchatov.[25] After some debate the International Astronomical Union confirmed these names.

The act of naming caused international controversy. Was there something provocative in the names? To name a large dark area as the Sea of Muscovy was not conventional—traditionally, ever since the seventeenth century, the seas of the Moon had been named after natural phenomena or emotional states. Moreover, to name the mountain range after the Soviet Union was not customary: historically, the mountains of other celestial bodies had been named after terrestrial mountains, not existing nation-states. Still, none of the names were exceptionally provocative—with perhaps the exception of Igor Kurchatov, who had been the leader of the Soviet nuclear weapons program since 1943, but even he, in his later years, had been devoting his work to the peaceful application of atomic physics.[26] And, in all probability, Aleksandr Popov was not considered as the "inventor of the radio," as he was in the Soviet Union. Still, it would be an overstatement to call any of the new names as something remarkably propagandistic, even in the context of the cold war. So, why the outrage? Why did the international community feel that it had been taken for a ride by the Soviet propaganda machinery?

In the course of history, every empire has used mapping and cartography as an instrument of legitimizing its territorial power: "As much as guns and warships, maps have been the weapons of imperialism."[27] Even before the birth of Socialist Realism, from the very first days after the Revolution, mapping had been an important vehicle of self-representation in the Soviet Union. Between 1917 and 1935 a vast mapmaking process took place in Soviet Russia. The creation of a coherent imaginary geography for the enormous boundless space of the Soviet Union was a vital task for the new regime, as it delineated the boundaries of power. Drawing the map of the new territory was a process of social and political consolidation. Mapmaking was not limited to cartography. It was a huge propaganda campaign involving the vast machinery of the Soviet cultural system.[28] Emma Widdis calls this an "obsessive process of self-representation."[29]

---

[25] Whitaker, *Mapping and Naming the Moon*, p. 156.

[26] Eugene Rabinovitch, "Igor Kurtchatov 1903–1960: An Introduction," *Bulletin of the Atomic Scientists: A Journal of Science and Public Affairs* (December 1967): 8–9.

[27] J.B. Harley, "Maps, Knowledge, and Power," in Denis Cosgrove and Stephen Daniels (eds.), *The Iconography of Landscape: Essays on the Symbolic Representation, Design and Use of Past Environments* (Cambridge, 1989), pp. 277–312; James C. Scott, *Seeing Like a State: How Certain Schemes to Improve the Human Condition Have Failed* (New Haven, 1998), p. 87.

[28] Widdis, "To Explore or to Conquer?"

[29] Widdis, *Visions of a New Land*, p. 3.

President Lyndon B. Johnson had already understood the symbolism inherent in the Soviet conquest of space after the first *Sputnik* launch:

> And as I was sayin', whoever controls the high ground of space controls the world. The Roman Empire controlled the world because it could build roads. Later, the British Empire was dominant because they had ships. In the Air Stage, we were powerful because we had the airplane. And now the Communists have established a foothold in outer space. Pretty soon they'll have damned space platforms so they can drop nuclear bombs on us, like rocks from a highway overpass. Now how in the hell did they ever get ahead of us?![30]

Ever since Galileo's telescopic observations in the early seventeenth century it had been possible to imagine celestial bodies as something to set one's foot on.[31] Now, it had become reality and the first Soviet and American satellites had made space sovereignty an issue of global concern. Humankind had to come to a decision on whether celestial bodies could or should be a subject to national claim of sovereignty or not. The controversy around the question was of concrete and political importance. First the Soviet pennants and medals sent to the Moon surface and now the cartographical act of naming the features on its far side were considered highly controversial.

In response to this concern, the UN General Assembly had established, in December 1958, an ad hoc Committee on the Peaceful Uses of Outer Space. The committee declared that "recognizing the common interest of mankind in outer space and recognizing that it is the common aim that outer space should be used for peaceful purposes only."[32] In December 1966 this committee formulated a treaty on "Principles Governing the Activities of States in the Exploration and Use of Outer Space, including the Moon and Other Celestial Bodies." The treaty declared (among other things) that: "Outer space, including the Moon and other celestial bodies, is not subject to national appropriation by claim of sovereignty, by means of use or occupation, or by any other means."[33]

---

[30] The quote is from Philip Kaufman's film *The Right Stuff* (USA, 1983).

[31] Imaginary voyages to the skies had existed even before Galileo's discoveries, but the journey to the Moon and heavens was then treated merely as an allegory because celestial bodies were not perceived as three-dimensional objects. Frederick I. Ordway, "Dreams of Space Travel from Antiquity to Verne," in Frederick I. Ordway, Randy Liebermann, and Ben Bova (eds.), *Blueprint for Space: Science Fiction to Science Fact* (Washington, DC and London, 1992).

[32] Official Records of the General Assembly: Resolution adopted by the General Assembly: Resolution 1348 (XIII). *Question of the peaceful use of outer space. 792nd plenary meeting, 13 December 1958.*

[33] Official Records of the General Assembly: Resolution 2222 (XXI). *Treaty on Principles Governing the Activities of States in the Exploration and Use of Outer Space, including the Moon and*

Space as an Imperial Project

> Fairy tale is coming true! The dream of man, ever since the first glance at the heavenly skies, is now fulfilled. Is it possible that the secrets of the Universe will unravel? Yes it is, answer the Soviet people.[34]

The idea of conquest [*pokorenie*] accompanied all three Luna missions depicted here. The Luna Program presented a stunning thought: an entirely new dimension of time and space, celestial and interplanetary. Yet this dimension was measurable. There were many techniques to capture infinity: It was scouted and reconnoitered, conquered, mapped, measured, and finally named. All these techniques integrated outer space and specifically the Moon into "Soviet Space."

The questions of nature, space, and territory had been profoundly important in Russian and Soviet history at all times. Besides politics, the race into space seems to have added a new dimension to aesthetics as well, as Russia's proverbial horizontal vastness was amplified with the new Soviet one: vertical expansion toward outer space. The role of visual imagery in this process—photographs and maps—was crucial. The "master narrative" of Socialist Realism treated nature as a resource, measurable and evaluated in economic terms. Nature had to be transformed and bent to human will.[35] This theme is substantial in the Khrushchevian discourse concerning space exploration. Not only was the Soviet Union exploring the universe at a fierce pace, it was creating new celestial bodies: moons, comets, even planets. The Soviet Union was altering the cosmic order— literally everything seemed to be possible. The fact that the United States was simultaneously struggling hard with its own early lunar program made the success even sweeter.[36] Socialist science had no limits.

The role of photography must be seen as indispensable here: The photographs of distant celestial objects enabled viewers to symbolically discover and possess these far-away places. Their capacity to render distant places made them a powerful tool for inspiring people's imagination. To the great public, the conquest of space would not have happened without illustrations: Space as a "colonized frontier" was made real through photographs. And, as photographs, the cosmic ones were even more amazing than ordinary ones: The lunar

---

Other Celestial Bodies.

[34] Sharonov, "K solntsu!," pp. 2–3. All translations, unless otherwise mentioned, are mine.

[35] Douglas R Weiner, *Models of Nature: Ecology, Conservation, and Cultural Revolution in Soviet Russia.* (Bloomington, IN and Indianapolis, IN, 1988), p. 169.

[36] Cargill R Hall, *Lunar Impact: A History of Project Ranger* (Washington, DC, 1977), pp. 6–10.

photographs were not taken by a man, but by a machine, *automatically*. They were *acheiropoieta* [*nerukotvornyi*]: made without human hand.³⁷ In this sense, the photographs from the far side of the Moon were indeed miracles, miracles created by Soviet science.

The most possessive of these imperial endeavors was the act of mapping and naming the lunar scenery. In the context of the cold war, the lunar conquest was of the utmost importance. The cartographical act audaciously hinted that the Moon was to be included in Soviet territory, even if the official political rhetoric (piously perhaps) heralded otherwise. The emphasis on conquest in Soviet propaganda was ambivalent and the written propaganda constantly emphasized that "the Soviet man will walk into the Universe as an explorer and creator, not as a conqueror."³⁸ Still, these acts can be seen as clearly imperial: The mapped and named Moon became an extension of Soviet space.

Domesticated Space

In the course of the 1960s we can see a clear decline of the above-mentioned themes of possession in cosmic depictions. The key shift appeared in conjunction with the first manned space flights. The focus turned from outer space to the Earth's surface. The theme of conquest was increasingly replaced with more earthbound subject matters related to the cosmonauts and the emphasis was on the commonplace, everyday qualities of the cosmonaut heroes' personal life. The cosmonaut's journey beyond Earth's atmosphere and his return from the frontiers of our existence had been thoroughly choreographed in the media.³⁹ The making of the dream and especially any dangers or misfortunes attached to the program had to be kept undisclosed. This eventually created an illusion that space exploration was uncomplicated. Ultimately, it was not so easy to maintain the heroic image attached to the cosmonauts. Because of the "secrecy regime"⁴⁰

---

37   The concept normally refers to icons with particularly great powers alleged to have come into existence without human interference. Brandon Taylor, "Photo-power: Painting and Iconicity in the First Five-Year Plan," in Dawn Ades et al. (eds.), *Art and Power: Europe under the Dictators, 1930–1945* (London, 1995), pp. 249–52.

38   N. Malakhov, "Dolog i truden put...," in *K Zvezdam. Risunki letšika-kosmonavta A. Leonova i hudožnika-fantasta A. Sokolova* (Leningrad, 1970), pp. 5–11.

39   Svetlana Boym and Adam Bartos, *Kosmos: Remembrances of the Future* (Princeton, NJ, 2001), p. 91.

40   Asif A. Siddiqi, "Cosmic Contradictions: Enthusiasm and Secrecy in the Soviet Space Program," in James T. Andrews and Asif A. Siddiqi (eds.), *Into the Cosmos: Space Exploration and Soviet Culture* (Pittsburgh, 2011), pp. 47–76.

surrounding the space program, the cosmonauts seemed to emerge out of nowhere to stand beside the ruling power at Lenin's mausoleum. Their authentic accomplishments seemed more and more irrelevant. As Slava Gerovitch has noted: "bound by secrecy on one side and by propaganda demands on the other, Soviet-era space history was reduced to a set of clichés: flawless cosmonauts flew perfect missions, supported by unfailing technology."[41]

Little by little the cosmic landscape faded and in the end the cosmonaut remained as an earthbound figure. When we examine photographs from popular media this is strikingly true: we can see cosmonauts in ritualistic welcoming ceremonies, in their childhood, in their preparation for the flight, in their daily routines, and during their leisure pursuits.[42] This emphasis on the everyday qualities of the heroes' life was in line with the new official humanism, which defined the arts of the Khrushchev period in general from the end of the 1950s. The actual heroic deed, the conquest of earthly bounds, no longer seemed important. The importance of the cosmic heroes was now on the surface of the Earth, not in the skies. Gone were the cosmic utopia and sublimity found in the cosmic propaganda. As Matthew Cullerne Bown puts it: "the socialist utopia, as it existed in the Soviet Union *circa* 1970, was in fact the only utopia anyone should count on seeing."[43]

In 1970, as if in line with this fading utopian idealism, the International Astronomical Union discovered that two of the major Soviet discoveries from the far side of the Moon were in fact optical illusions: The Montes Sovietici and Mare Desiderii were "not clearly identifiable" and the names were deleted from the lunar nomenclature.[44]

But something still remains untouched: The first lunar probe, the *Luna 1*, is still circling the Sun in an orbit situated between the Earth and Mars. Within her she is carrying the precious heraldic symbols of the late Soviet Union, by all probability to the end of time. One can find a melancholic irony lurking behind this idea: Sealed in a hermetic vacuum, the final remains of the early Soviet imperial space endeavor are eternally traveling in the open void. Only a collision with another heavenly body will end the path of the lonely traveler.

---

[41] Slava Gerovitch, "Creating Memories: Myth, Identity, and Culture in the Russian Space Age," in Steven J. Dick (ed.), *Remembering the Space Age* (Washington, DC, 2008), pp. 203–36.

[42] For instance, RGANTD 1–2211, 1–14923, 1–2209; *Ogonyok* 31 (1961), *Ogonyok* 34 (1962), *Ogonyok* 43 (1964).

[43] Matthew Cullerne Bown, *Socialist Realist Painting* New Haven, CT, (New Haven, CT, 1998), p. 414.

[44] C. de Jager and A. Jappel (eds.), *Proceedings of the Fourteenth General Assembly Brighton, United Kingdom, August 18–27, 1970* (Dordrecht, 1971); Whitaker, *Mapping and Naming*, pp. 231–5.

CHAPTER 12

Eccentric Orbit: Mapping Russian Culture in the Near Abroad

Kevin M.F. Platt

Not all people exist in the same now.
—Ernst Bloch

Not only are the limits of literature—its "peripheries" and border zones—in flux. To the contrary, flux characterizes the "center" itself. It is simply not the case that a single, ancient, and continuous current evolves in the literary center while new phenomena arise only at the margins. Rather, these same new phenomena occupy the very center itself, and the center shifts to the periphery.
—Iurii Tynianov

I. Documentation

> glue's not quite right
> and the eye color hair color height are slightly off
> go easy opening it
> at the border try to look honest
> and smile
> so the seams'll be less obvious
> on the other hand the first and last name are magnifico
> and the age suspiciously young
> while the watermarks are so fine
> that there's totally no reason to flinch
> if someone looks long and hard at your face[1]

---

* Earlier versions of this chapter were presented at the conference convened by *Ab Imperio* in fall 2010, "Empire Studies: A Roadmap for the 2010s," and at the conference "New Perspectives on Empire and Space: Russia and the Soviet Union in Focus" at the University of Helsinki's Aleksanteri Institute in February 2012. I would like to thank all the participants and attendees of these meetings for their questions and discussion, as well as the poets of the Orbit

Since the collapse of the Soviet Union, official identification documents have been tricky business in Latvia. In 1990–91, post-Soviet Latvia was declared to be legally continuous with the interwar Latvian Republic (1922–40), the constitution of which is therefore still in force today. As a result, only citizens of the interwar republic and their descendants gained automatic citizenship in the republic's new era. This left all other residents—many of them born and raised in Soviet Latvia, and many of whom had cast votes in support of independence in a landmark 1991 referendum—to pass through an initially ill-defined naturalization process. In 1995 a new naturalization law and a special category of *"nepilsonis,"* or "noncitizen," was created for this rather large category of former Soviet Latvians—who make up around 15 percent of the republic's present population and the majority of whom self-identify as "Russians" [*Russkie*], although there are many other ethnicities mixed into this category as well.[2] As these numbers perhaps make plain, many noncitizens have refused to naturalize out of disaffection or protest. In a particularly absurd wrinkle, the children of noncitizens are themselves noncitizens—that is, in its present form this category is a permanent feature of the Latvian social landscape that will not disappear. Russians, in their inimitable way, commonly shorten *negrazhdanin*, the Russian translation of *nepilsonis*, to *negr*—the Russian word for "dark-skinned person," which is a term of perhaps debatable significance in some contexts, but is without doubt an ironically charged slur in this instance.

Indignation at the status of noncitizens surfaces now and again in the Russian Federation in media, political discourse, and diplomatic rhetoric—and it should be noted that the media space of Russian-speaking Latvia is far from completely distinct from that of Russia proper. In Russia, too, one finds linguistic complexity concerning the identities of residents of the former Soviet republics. As Vladimir Putin announced in his Address to the Federal Assembly of 2005, in the wake of "the greatest geopolitical catastrophe of the century"—that is, the collapse of the Soviet Union—"tens of millions of our compatriots and fellow citizens found themselves beyond the borders of Russian territory."[3] In Russian political and

---

group who are my subject below. I also must thank Gabriella Safran, Sanna Turoma, Maxim Waldstein, and the members of the University of Pennsylvania Works In Progress group—Paul Saint-Amour, Emily Steiner, and Emily Wilson—for their helpful critiques of the essay.

[1] Semen Khanin, *Orbita* 5 (2009): 174. For the poems quoted in this chapter, see http://orbita.lv. All translations are the author's, unless otherwise indicated.

[2] Population data are derived from the data of the Latvian Central Statistical Bureau. See "Population Census 2011—Key Indicators," www.csb.gov.lv/en/statistikas-temas/population-census-2011-key-indicators-33613.html (accessed April 9, 2012).

[3] Vladimir Putin, "Address to the Federal Assembly" (April 25, 2005), www.kremlin.ru/text/appears/2005/04/87049.shtml (accessed May 18, 2007).

public discourse, the concept of "compatriots abroad" dates to the late 1990s, when it was given legal definition in the law "On the state politics of the Russian Federation with relation to compatriots abroad" [*O gosudarstvennoi politike RF v otnoshenii sootechestvennikov za rubezhom*]. This law gave "compatriots abroad" special rights to travel, access to simplified immigration procedures, and a number of other entitlements. It also dedicated the Russian state to protect the compatriots' legal, economic, and "cultural" interests (such as language use, educational rights, and historical heritage)—the case of Latvia's "noncitizens" has frequently figured at the center of public attention in this regard.[4] Since Putin's speech, both in Russia and in neighboring states with significant ethnic Russian populations, the term "compatriots abroad" has gained a very broad currency. Yet it indexes not so much a concept as a whirlpool of conceptual confusion, despite the best efforts of legal minds.

In public discourse and common parlance, as in Putin's address, the term primarily evokes ethnic Russians who have been stranded outside "Russian territory" by the collapse of the Soviet Union. Yet its legal definition, which has been revised several times since the law's adoption, has failed to clarify the precise boundaries of the category, as a result of the historical "messiness" of Russian ethnic identity. In the first version of the law, in what was more or less a reflection of the dictionary definition of the term "compatriot" in light of the status of the Russian Federation as successor state to the Soviet Union, it seemed that anyone who had been a citizen of the Soviet Union, independently of ethnic identity, could be considered a "compatriot abroad."[5] Since that time, however, the rising importance of patriotic and ethnic nationalist rhetoric in the Russian Federation, as well as the increasing inflows and visibility of nonethnic Russian migratory workers in connection with Russia's rising prosperity and demand for manual laborers, have lent great stridency to political and public discourse surrounding immigration and therefore surrounding the compatriots. Many Russians want to make it easy for "good compatriots" to return to the fold of Russian citizenship, but also to limit the access of "undesirable" former Soviets to easy immigration. The sentiment often seems to be: yes to Latvian Russians, no to Uzbek migratory workers (for instance).

---

[4] See the text of the law as republished by the private firm Konsul'tant Plius at: "O gosudarstvennoi politike RF v otnoshenii sootechestvennikov za rubezhom," www.consultant.ru/online/base/?req=doc;base=LAW;n=102935 (accessed December 4, 2010).

[5] In this initial version, although any former citizen of the USSR could claim the status of "compatriot abroad," descendants of "persons belonging to the titular nations of foreign governments" could not—that is, an ethnic Latvian former citizen of the USSR could be considered a compatriot, yet his children could not. See the 1999 version of the law at: "O gosudarstvennoi politike RF v otnoshenii sootechestvennikov za rubezhom," www.consultant.ru/online/base/?req=doc;base=LAW;n=89945#p36 (accessed December 4, 2010).

From 2006 to 2009 a number of corrections were introduced into the law on "compatriots abroad," intended to narrow the category's applicability. These corrections have failed to eliminate ambiguity. The current redaction specifies that "compatriots abroad" are those persons living in other states and "relating, as a rule, to the peoples who have historically resided on the territory of the Russian Federation," yet who have additionally "made a free choice to be spiritually, culturally, and legally linked to the Russian Federation." This choice can be demonstrated by:

> An act of self-identification, reinforced by social or professional activity for the preservation of Russian language, the native languages of the peoples of the Russian Federation, the development of Russian culture abroad, the strengthening of the friendly relations of the states of residence of the compatriots with the Russian Federation, the support of social organizations of compatriots, and the defense of the rights of compatriots or by other evidence of the free choice of the persons in question of spiritual and cultural linkage with the Russian Federation.[6]

Here, then, we see the collision of the complex social and ethnic identity formations inherited from the Soviet and Russian imperial past with contemporary problems of "disaggregation" of citizenship that have been observed as a global phenomenon.[7] Returning to the matters of documentation with which we began, recent years have brought a Russian legislative project to create a "Russian Card" for "compatriots abroad" that would confirm their special privileges and grant its holders additional rights to work and to various medical, educational, and other entitlements normally associated with citizenship in the Russian Federation. Yet the project of creation of such a card has foundered on a seemingly endless debate over the proper definition of "compatriots" that ranges from obviously unworkable concepts of ethnic belonging via genealogical evidence to inclusive categories that would include all who speak Russian and identify with the Russian people on a "spiritual-cultural" level.[8]

---

[6] "O gosudarstvennoi politike RF v otnoshenii sootechestvennikov za rubezhom," www.consultant.ru/online/base/?req=doc;base=LAW;n=102935

[7] For an example of the rhetorical pitfalls of political debates over identity in Russia, see, for instance, Viktor Khamraev, "'Deputaty pozabotilis' o 'edinom sovetskom narode,'" *Kommersant* (March 3, 2006), www.kommersant.ru (accessed November 3, 2010). From the large literature on the changing nature of citizenship, the author has found particularly helpful: Saskia Sassen, *Losing Control: Sovereignty in an Age of Globalization* (New York, 1996); Seyla Benhabib, *The Rights of Others: Aliens, Residents and Citizens* (Cambridge, 2004). The concept of the "disaggregation" of citizenship is from the latter source.

[8] On the "Russian card," see, for instance, Tamara Miodushevskaia, "'Karta russkogo': novyi proekt pomoshchi sootechestvennikov za rubezhem," *Argumenty i fakty* (June 8,

All of this is to say that the poem by the Russian-speaking Jewish Latvian poet Semyon Khanin that I have taken as an epigraph above touches a nerve concerning citizenship, official documents, and social identities in the post-Soviet periphery. Note that the poem's structure is calculated to impede recognition of the object being described, which is a false document, intended to obscure identity. One may add that the name Semyon Khanin is itself a pseudonym. Identity seems here to recede in a swirl of nesting dolls, all poised on the international border where the controlling structures of state confront the individual, yet perhaps are unable to contain him or her in those categories currently available to make sense of the biographies and subject positions shaped by the history and contemporary reality of this region. Khanin's poem opens a window on pressing questions for individuals in this region—questions of political borders, geography, social, and ethnic identity, and cultural belonging. What does it mean to be a Latvian Russian, or a Russian in Latvia? If the boundaries of the Russian Federation are plain enough, where are the boundaries of "Russian culture" located? To count oneself as a Russian in Latvia, is it enough simply to speak Russian and raise one's children to do so, or must one be more active in asserting a "free choice to be spiritually, culturally, and legally linked" to the Russian Federation? And where does this leave "Russians" who choose not to be so linked—can one be "Russian" in some distinctive "Baltic" manner? What does it mean to promote Russian culture in this region "outside of Russian Territory" or to preserve Russian cultural heritage here—is it enough to write poetry in Russian? Must one write it under one's legal name? Must this poetry participate in recognizably Russian traditions of poetic production? Semyon Khanin is part of a thriving poetry scene in Riga today. I will return to that topic at the end of this chapter, in order to show how attention to this case of cultural production at the margins of Russian geography can give new purchase on the significance of "Russian culture," on the cultural organization of space, and on the operations of culture more generally at the start of the twenty-first century. Yet before zeroing in on poetry, let us take several steps back, in order to capture Russian cultural life in Latvia in a "wide-angle" shot.

II. The Near Abroad

As the above suggests, the term "Russian" is impossible to apply with precision in this territory. In the following, by "Russian" I will refer to the varied population that speaks Russian as a first language in Latvia, regardless of ethnic identity, and

---

2008), www.aif.ru/society/article/19172 (accessed April 9, 2012).

regardless of identification with the populations or social identities of the Russian Federation.⁹ Present-day Latvia's Russian communities result from enormously varied circumstances: from religious minorities who fled persecution to Swedish Livonia as early as the seventeenth century, to families who arrived in the region during the imperial period, to those who fled the October Revolution to relocate in the interwar Latvian Republic during the first part of the twentieth century, to Jewish families with deep roots in the Baltic for whom the Russian language has been native for generations. Yet largely overshadowing all of these groups, both numerically and in the public consciousness, is the large population that settled in Latvia during the late twentieth century, reflecting the population dynamics and social engineering decisions of the Soviet state. In this, Latvia presents a case study in processes of decolonization that involve the collapse of a land-based empire that leaves communities it has shaped in its wake. Note the distinction of the resulting demographic situation from that of former colonies of global sea-based empires, which have been viewed, by and large, as paradigmatic for the study of postcoloniality in recent decades. Present-day Latvia recalls instead Eastern European states such as Poland during the interwar period of the early twentieth century—states defined in an intensely felt context of national revival and newly gained independence that nevertheless included exceedingly large and longstanding minority communities, some of them representative of formerly dominant ethnicities or groups and others of additional nondominant imperial groups and ethnicities.

Latvia is in fact the post-Soviet state including the proportionally largest population of Russians who have been so "stranded" by the USSR's collapse. According to the latest census data, ethnic Russians make up 26.9 percent of the population; other Russian speakers, including Belorussians, Ukrainians, Jews, and other former Soviet ethnicities, are estimated to make up another 10 per cent.¹⁰ It should be added that, in distinction from those earlier postimperial national states, the collapsed empire in this case—the USSR—for all of its nation-making activities and obsessive documentation of "nationality," was devoted to a secular ideal of common Soviet identity that resulted in a high incidence of

---

⁹ This is an intentionally "skewed" use of the term "Russian" that might well provoke objections by many of the individuals I so describe. My use is intended to do so, and thereby to provoke a cognizance of the social fissures and contestation that are in general concealed beneath standard usages—the same sort of cognizance that is generated by any attempt to imagine who might have a right to a "Russian Card" in this territory. Are Russian-speaking Jews "Russian" enough to bear a "Russian Card?" What about Armenians? For that matter, what about "Russified" ethnic Latvians?

¹⁰ See: "Population Census 2011—Key Indicators."

intermarriage among ethnic and national groups.[11] Russian identity constructions have for centuries borne traces of "empire" in their capaciousness with regard to intermarriage and assimilation, but these trends have reached their apogee in Latvia today, and in particular in Riga, where half of Latvia's Russian population resides. Riga has for centuries been an imperial contact zone and multiethnic city. Add to this the repeated political transformations and population movements of the twentieth century, and we arrive in present-day Riga, where Russians are to an extraordinary degree the offspring of ethnically complex genealogies.[12] Note as well that for reasons associated with social and political utility, ethnically mixed families gravitated toward Russian language and culture in the Soviet years, allowing the Latvian enclave to remain far more ethnically homogeneous. The result is a standoff not only of opposed ethnic identities but of opposed constructions of ethnicity, "endogamous" and "exogamous"—taking these terms not as analytically adequate categories, but as ones that capture the politically charged matter of identity formation in this territory.[13]

Both in the scale and genealogical complexity of its Russian population, Latvia therefore presents the most exaggerated case of a complex social condition that is evident in different ways and to differing extents throughout the post-Soviet and post-socialist states of the Baltic, Eastern Europe and Central Asia—the band of states referred to in Russia as the "Near Abroad." In a final excursus at this level of generality, let us pause over this term, which is just as complex as the terms for political identity discussed above, noting first of all its "oxymoronic" construction denoting territory at once "close" and "distant." Latvia today epitomizes this conception of geography. From the perspective of Russia, it numbers among the most "near" spaces—territorially, historically, linguistically,

---

[11] On nationalism and ethnic identity in the Soviet Union, see, among other sources, Terry Martin, *The Affirmative Action Empire: Nations and Nationalism in the Soviet Union, 1923–1939* (Ithaca, NY, 2001); Yuri Slezkine, "The USSR as a Communal Apartment, or How a Socialist State Promoted Ethnic Particularism," *Slavic Review* 53/2 (1994): 414–52.

[12] No hard data is available regarding this claim.

[13] The most extensive study of ethnic identity in Latvia is to be found in David Laitin, *Identity in Formation: The Russian-speaking Populations in the Near Abroad* (Ithaca, NY, 1998). This study, however, is now somewhat out of date and overstates the case for an inevitable assimilation of Russians and others into the ethnic formations of the titular nationalities of post-Soviet states, based on rational-choice models concerning economic and social advantage. For a corrective argument that Baltic Russians may be in the processes of forming a distinct regional ethnic identity, see Daniel A. Kronenfeld, "The Effects of Interethnic Contact on Ethnic Identity: Evidence from Latvia," *Post-Soviet Affairs* 21/3 (2005): 247–77; Daniel A. Kronenfeld, "Ethnogenesis without the Entrepreneurs: The Emergence of a Baltic Russian Identity in Latvia," in Karsten Brüggemann (ed.), *Narva und die Ostseeregion* (Narva, 2004), pp. 339–63.

ethnically, and in terms of economic, social, and familial relationships that bridge the border. In other ways, it is among the most "abroad" spaces—a member state of the European Union, geographically positioned in the west, and defined by a non-Slavic titular nation. A testimonial, likely heavily edited or wholly fictitious, from a site devoted to Russian tourism in Riga, provides a "typical" sketch of the view toward Riga from Russia:

> In the old city are little towers, cathedrals, chapels, winding streets, and quiet—traffic is limited here almost to the point of absolute prohibition. All around are European tourists—well-behaved but also cheerful. The place is glowing with culture. There are no "internationals," gastarbeiters, raggedy individuals in flip-flops or other eyesores of the European capitals. It's nice. You feel at home, although all around is a background made up of all sorts of European languages. Even the Russians here are somehow refined—until they speak, you don't even know where they are from. [...] In general, the Riga service personnel are a separate topic of discussion. Young men and women in any little shop speak at a minimum three languages besides their own—English, German, and Russian.[14]

In short, from the perspective of the Russian Federation, Latvia maximally combines integration into Europe with an almost domestic familiarity. Latvia is at once "theirs" and "ours," near and far, exotic and homey, in an ironically charged conception of political space that correlates precisely with the fragmentation and contestation of social identities in the region.

III. Post-imperial Culture

As the tourist pitch cited above announces, Latvia is "glowing with culture." It's not just in the view toward Latvia from the Russian Federation that the category of "culture" plays a definitive role. To offer an ethnographic confession, my own decision to spend a summer in contemporary Latvia in June of 2003 was precipitated by the same ironic complex of geography described in the citation above—by the homely yet exotic attractions of a version of "Russian culture" in a European landscape—that appealed to me as the perfect place to bring my Russian-speaking Jewish American children when school was out. As I had learned on a previous short visit to Riga, Russians in Latvia are ... different—and they recognize this difference themselves. In a survey of Latvian

---

[14] "Uikend v Rige: neskol'ko vpechatlenii," www.kuda.ua/lenta/38 (accessed December 11, 2010).

residents conducted in 1997 and 1998, a majority of respondents (both Latvians and Russians) reported that Russians in Latvia and Russians in the Russian Federation constitute "different peoples."[15] When one asks Latvian Russians what distinguishes them from Russians in the Russian Federation—as I did in a series of in-depth interviews conducted with residents of the Riga region over the summers of 2007–10—they commonly answer that Russians in Latvia are "more cultured" than they are across the border to the east.[16] In the typical explanation that I heard from the successful Jewish businessman Evgenii Gomberg, being "more cultured" means having a greater respect for the law and high culture and having no tolerance for the absurdities of public life in the Russian Federation and none of the habits that are needed to survive there, which he lumped together under the term "loutishness" or "boorishness" [*khamstvo*].[17]

This use of the term "culture" is both equivocal and affectively loaded. In some respects, it activates the concept of "culturedness" [*kul'turnost*] that primarily references polite behavior in everyday life—greetings to shopkeepers, no public displays of drunkenness or swearing, and so on. Yet in other respects it is high culture that is at stake: As Gomberg elaborated, in Latvia, classic Russian culture is truly valued, as opposed to the often vulgar and debased condition of cultural life in the contemporary Russian Federation. Often, too, informants told me that a better, "purer" Russian is spoken in Latvia. In both registers—that of everyday culture, or *kul'turnost'*. and that of high culture—such conversations are colored by a tincture of nostalgia. *Kul'turnost'* was itself a hallmark social ideal of Soviet public life dating from the Stalinist revival of middle-class values in the

---

[15] Pål Kolstø, *Nation-building and Ethnic Integration in Post-Soviet Societies: An Investigation of Latvia and Kazakstan* (Boulder, CO: 1999), pp. 258–61. See also Daniel Kronenfeld's further analysis of this survey data in his: "Ethnogenesis without the Entrepreneurs."

[16] My results correlate well with those of Kronenfeld, who asked similar questions during in-depth interviews with a similar population in 2000 and 2001. Kronenfeld, "Ethnogenesis without the Entrepreneurs."

[17] I have used fictitious names for all informants other than published authors and public figures. Gomberg, as the sponsor of prominent public art projects that figure in other parts of my overall project, falls into the latter category. For my preliminary publications regarding his activities, see Kevin M.F. Platt, "Okkupatsiia protiv kolonizatsii: kak istorii postsovetskoi Latvii pomogaet provintsializirovat' Evropu," in Dirk Uffel'man [Uffelmann], Aleksandr Etkind, and Il'ia Kukulin (eds.), *Vnutrenniaia kolonizatsiia Rossii* (Moscow, 2012). For other and early attestations to the use of the marker *khamstvo* in the larger territory of the Baltic to distinguish between a positive and negative version of Russian cultural identity, see the late Soviet Estonian case described in Maxim Waldstein, "Russifying Estonia? Iurii Lotman and the Politics of Language and Culture in Soviet Estonia," *Kritika: Explorations in Russian and Eurasian History* 8/3 (2007): 561–96.

1930s, while the high culture that Latvian Russians speak of, often wistfully, consists of the canonical forms of the bygone Soviet era—ballet, opera, Pushkin, etc.[18] In this, the "cultural" identity of Russians in Latvia sometimes resembles a devotion to the values of a lost civilization.

Very often, conversations about the Latvian Russian identity slide from comparison of local Russians with "mainland" Russians to comparison of Russians with Latvians. Here, my informants typically explained that Russian culture, in distinction from Latvian culture, has "world significance." The former dramaturge of the Riga Russian Theater, named Rostislav, explained to me how the progressive rejection of Russian culture by ethnic Latvian society was crippling young people—both Russian and Latvian. Rostislav volunteered the view that Russians in Latvia were more "cultured," in the sense of everyday behavior, as a direct result of the influence of ethnic Latvians' European social habits. Yet, in his view, at the level of high culture, the Russians are unquestionably richer—theirs is a "large nation" in comparison to "small nations" like Latvia. In an inversion of the opposed exogamous and endogamous logics of Russian and Latvian ethnic belonging, Rostislav explained that ethnic Latvian society must maintain openness toward the language and culture of "large nations" like Russia or else risk "becoming narrow." As a corrective, Rostislav has taken up cultural projects—helping to found a nonprofit Russian-language community library in central Riga and also serving as advisor to a youth theater group. At root, Rostislav's stance activates a common historical narrative of postimperial victimhood, according to which the Russian Empire and then the Soviet Union had brought to the formerly undeveloped and peripheral peoples and lands of the Baltic the gifts of culture, modernity, economic advancement, and incorporation into cosmopolitan circuits of social life—a gift that is, in this view, not sufficiently acknowledged by Latvians. In Rostislav's nonprofit library, we may recognize a minor echo of the conception of the Russian and Soviet empires as "cultural projects" writ large—"la mission civilisatrice"—that has been well diagnosed recently in the case of the Caucasus by Bruce Grant.[19]

Yet this historical narrative of postimperial victimhood is not unproblematic or uncontested. First of all, it does not correspond at all to the conceptions of history operative among ethnic Latvians. Dominant voices in ethnic Latvian

---

[18] On the prehistory of *kul'turnost'*, see Sheila Fitzpatrick, *The Cultural Front: Power and Culture in Revolutionary Russia* (Ithaca, NY, 1992), pp. 1–15.

[19] Bruce Grant, *The Captive and the Gift: Cultural Histories of Sovereignty in Russia and the Caucasus* (Ithaca, NY, 2009). For a more extensive discussion of "la mission civilisatrice" of the Russian and Soviet Empires in Latvia, see my "Okkupatsiia vs. kolonizatsiia: istoriia, postcolonial'nost' i geograficheskaia identichnost', sluchai Latvii," *Neprikosnovennyi zapas* 71 (2010): 49–62.

public life view the 1940 Soviet annexation of Latvia as a hostile military takeover entirely analogous to the Nazi invasion that followed it, and therefore resent Russians as, by and large, "occupiers."[20] Consider, for instance, the Riga Museum of the Occupation, devoted to the history of Latvia from the initial Soviet annexation in 1940 through the collapse of the Soviet Union in 1991, which in its very title identifies the years of Nazi and Soviet domination as parts of a single national experience of "occupation." As the museum's main official catalogue explains:

> Fifty-one years of occupation took a heavy toll on Latvia. About a third of the population perished or were [sic] exiled as a result of political murders and genocide, war action, and inhuman treatment in the Gulag, or became refugees at the end of World War II to escape the return of the Soviet regime. In their place, settlers from other parts of the Soviet Union were brought in. They did not speak the Latvian language and were strangers to Latvian culture and traditions. From the very first, both occupation powers tried to deprive the Latvian nation of its national pride and to deny, falsify or distort the history of Latvia and Latvia's historical ties to Europe. Latvia was estranged from the humanistic cultural foundations of Western culture. After war's end, the political, economic and social life in the Western world thrived; at the same time, all progress in Latvia stopped. The Western world forgot Latvia. The name of Latvia disappeared from books of history, as though it never had existed. The borders of the Baltic States disappeared from maps.[21]

According to this story, the wellspring of Latvian civilization is not Russian cultural largesse at all, but instead a fundamental European identity that accords Latvians a special license on "Western belonging"—a Western belonging that was interrupted, impeded, or concealed during the years of Nazi and Soviet occupation. This conception gains greater affective force in light of

---

[20] In 2009 the Latvian President Valdis Zatlers made a public appeal to end the practice, widespread among ethnic Latvians, of applying the term "occupant" [*okupants*] to describe Latvia's Russian population. Although Zatlers's gesture did not lead to the desired result, it did provoke a broad public discussion of the meaning of the usage, which is viewed by many Russians as a discriminatory term of abuse. See n.a., "Papildināta—Zatlers: jāvienojas, ka vārds 'okupants' vairs netiks lietots," *Diena* (December 7, 2009), www.diena.lv/sabiedriba/politika/papildinata-zatlers-javienojas-ka-vards-okupants-vairs-netiks-lietots-702651 (accessed August 23, 2011).

[21] Paulis Lazda, "The Museum of the Occupation of Latvia: Why? What? How?" trans. Baiba Kaugara, introduction to *Latvijas Okupāciajas Muzejs: Latvija zem Padomju Savienības un nacionālsociālistiskās Vācijas varas 1940–1991* (Riga, 2008), pp. 11–13, cit. on p. 11.

its contestation in the context of "Old Europe," where the countries of "New Europe" are frequently subjected to an orientalizing gaze that renders them either *prima facie* "not fully European" or "damaged" by the years of socialism or Soviet domination.[22] In Latvian public discourse concerning history, culture, and geography, this orientalizing gaze is deflected onto the local Russian population and the Russian Federation itself, which are seen as contributing to the erosion or destruction of culture in Latvia, not to its creation.

Yet Rostislav's conception of Latvian Russians as representatives of a beneficent greater Russian civilization is problematic when one turns in the other direction as well—toward the Russian Federation, that is. An elementary school teacher named Vera offered one of the most outspoken articulations of Russian cultural preeminence and unjust Russian victimhood I have heard in Latvia. Vera and I spoke at length concerning Latvian educational policies, which have successively diminished the place of Russian language and culture in Latvian schools over the course of the past 20 years, and have completely eliminated Russian as a language of instruction for higher education. Vera regards these policies as discriminatory—intended to place Russians at an educational disadvantage and to prevent them from preserving their cultural heritage. As part of her struggle to counteract what she views as an all-out attack on Russian culture in Latvia, Vera organizes tours for her pupils to the Russian Federation in order to visit museums, monuments, and the homeland, in general. Yet, ironically, Vera admitted that going to the Russian Federation was a difficult experience. People in Russia are, in her account, rude, lacking in culture, and unpleasant to deal with. Like Gomberg, Vera described Russia as a land of "boorishness."[23] The paradoxical complexities of this situation are plain: Latvian Russians like Vera are drawn to the Russian Federation in order to experience their authentic cultural heritage, yet must overlook the lack of culture there.

---

[22] The tendency to orientalize the populations of the former socialist states is a perpetual sore point for intellectuals of the New Europe, such as Milan Kundera. His longstanding efforts to distinguish Prague from Moscow in the eyes of Western readers are well known, as is the complexity of these efforts in light of recent accusations of his collaboration with the Czechoslovakian secret police. Milan Kundera, "The Tragedy of Central Europe," *The New York Review of Books* 31/7 (April 26, 1984): 33–8; Milan Kundera, "Die Weltliteratur," *The New Yorker* (January 8, 2007): 28–35.

[23] It was only about an hour into our discussion that I learned something of Vera's family history, which added an additional interesting wrinkle to the picture. Vera's surname is Ozoliņa, which is just about the most Latvian name imaginable (the equivalent to a Mrs. Smith or Mrs. Brown in the anglophone context). As it turns out, while her mother is Russian, her father is a Russified Latvian, educated in Soviet Russia. In terms of genealogy, Vera has as much claim to an ethnic Latvian identity as she does to a Russian one, but chooses to identify as Russian.

In part, this is a reflection of the distinction between everyday culture and high culture—in Russia the former is lacking, while the latter is axiomatically present. Yet there are deeper ironic implications here—deriving from local history and the status of culture in Russian social life in general. In the early eighteenth century Peter the Great imported a range of modern European cultural institutions into the Russian Empire—from academies and patterns of secular social intercourse to literary culture and forms of dress. Incidentally, Peter's cultural policies resulted from the same ideological conceptions that led him to wrest Livonia and its ports from the Swedish Empire. Both undertakings were intended to render the Russian Empire a European power. Since that distant era, and eliding many complexities, the inscription of high culture in geography has been ambivalent in Russian social life: Is high culture a vehicle of the Russian national spirit or is it a "Western" category opposed to popular culture, the natural world, and Russia as non-European nation? The geographical expression of this contest is most evident in the rivalry of Moscow and St. Petersburg—the national "center at the center" and the European "center on the periphery" of Russian cultural life.

Now fast-forward to the middle twentieth century, when Soviet Latvia, as European territory *prima facie*, became heir to this same ambivalent inscription of culture into space. In the postwar era, as a result of their peculiar history of transformation from independent European states into Soviet republics, the Baltic territories constituted the Soviet Union's "westernmost" region, if not in geographic terms (strictly speaking, Kaliningrad held this status), then certainly in conceptual ones. When Soviet internal émigrés and tourists traveled to the Baltic, they saw themselves as being transported to "our west." In consumer culture, goods from the Baltic—confections from the Laima chocolate factory, Elite brand cigarettes—bore heightened value derived from this special place in the geographic imagination. On large and small screens, Baltic cities presented the backdrop of dramatic films and TV series set in the "west" (London street scenes for the Soviet serial *Sherlock Holmes*, for instance, were shot in Riga). By the late-Soviet era, the Baltic had become a privileged location for cultural experimentation by virtue of its "western" location—this was the "Europe" of the USSR, a site of both politically and culturally innovative practices. One could mention here the literary and critical journals *Daugava* and *Rodnik*, significant sites for the publication of cutting-edge works of authors from Moscow and St. Petersburg during the 1980s, the edgy productions of the Theater of the Young Viewer under the direction of Adol'f Shapiro during that same decade, or even the Jurmala Competition of Young Performers of Estrada Song, that in the late 1980s became a site of national revival in pop song.²⁴ In short, by virtue of the "western" character of Russian culture per se, Soviet Latvia had itself become a "center at the periphery."

Current conceptions of the "cultured" status of Russian Latvia are heir to this model of Latvia as a cultural homeland away from the homeland. For Vera and for others like her, Russians in Latvia turn out to be "more Russian than Russian Russians" (to use the formulation of a woman who called in to a radio show I participated in on August 10, 2009 in Riga). Yet it must also be said that just as the high culture with which Latvian Russians identify is that of the Soviet past, the privileged position of Latvia as a center at the periphery may in some ways be a thing of history as well. Within the unifying bounds of the Soviet extension of Russian culture, Russians were at home everywhere. In the context of independent Latvia, however, this home away from the homeland becomes rather *unheimlich*. Although Latvia's status as a "space of culture" persists in various registers of public discourse—that of Russian tourists in the Near Abroad, for instance—Latvia's Russians are more often than not represented in a pose of exaggerated victimhood in the russophone media and political rhetoric of Latvia and in that of the Russian Federation as well. Of course, this is in part a reflection of the political utility both in local politics and in international diplomacy of questions concerning the "compatriots abroad" and their rights. Yet one must also admit that questions such as those of access to Russian-language education and the status of noncitizens constitute legitimate targets of complaint and real impediments for Russian cultural activity in the region: As a result of these policies, new generations of Latvian Russians are undoubtedly less broadly educated in the common Russian cultural canon, less polished speakers and writers, and less broadly exposed to contemporary music, theater, and writing of the Russian Federation.

In recent years, Latvian Russian society, often aided by money from Moscow, has supported a number of initiatives intended to compensate for this loss of cultural competence and social prestige. More often than not, however, these projects reflect a "provincialized" version of Russian culture that reiterates the marginality that it is intended to ameliorate. Furthermore, the political imperative of demonstrating the rootedness of Russians in Latvia is in many ways at odds with pretensions to global significance and import in the Russian cultural space. Leafing through the pages of the glossy magazine *Baltic World* [*Baltiiskii mir*], published during the last few years with Moscow money and Baltic editorial and authorial energies, one encounters Russians celebrating patriotic holidays, Russians protesting distortions of history in school curricula, Russians dressed in folk costumes dancing and preparing traditional food—local snapshots and local

---

²⁴ See Kevin M. F. Platt, "Russian Empire of Pop: Post-Socialist Nostalgia and Soviet Retro at the 'New Wave' Competition," *Russian Review* 72 (2013): 447–69.

problems—but few traces of "world-historical significance."²⁵ This uninspiring picture of Latvian Russian communities throws into high relief the radical shift in status that Russian culture has experienced in the last 20 years in the region. Russians here have suffered a double loss: From privileged site of cultural production in the late-Soviet period their enclave is beginning to look more like a community of provincial rubes, an object of patronization and condescension from east and west alike. In part, one suspects, claims concerning the special status of "culture" for Latvian Russians are only a vestige of past glories, a mantra to calm the anxious worry that Russian culture in Latvia may have run its course.

IV. All-Russian Culture

Yet Russian culture in Riga has not yet come to its terminus. In August 2009 I sat in a Riga café with journalist Il'ia Dimenshtein, author of popular history books with provocative titles like *Jurmala—Our Own* [*Nasha Iurmala*].²⁶ Dimenshtein's books are devoted to anecdotal histories that serve the conflicting imperatives of demonstrating the local belonging of Russians in Latvia while also proving the grander significance of local Russian culture, offering a mix of vignettes concerning Latvian curiosities and personalities with others devoted to the regional origins or interests of famous individuals of "all-Russian" and "all-Soviet" import—to translate the Russian terms conferring significance of imperial breadth, *vserossiiskaia* and *vsesoiuznaia*.²⁷ In our discussions, Dimenshtein

---

[25] Another recent project that illustrates the articulation of Russian culture in Latvia as a regional phenomenon was the exhibition "Russians of Latvia," organized at the initiative of Tat'iana Zhdanok, deputy of the European Parliament from Latvia, with the financial support of the European Green fraction the Moscow City Department of Foreign Economic and International Relations, and the Moscow House of Compatriots. The exhibit, organized chronologically and covering Russian life of the region from the seventeenth century to the present, devotes some attention to famous Russians with Latvian origins, but is primarily concerned with the specificity of Russian life in Latvia. Clearly, the project's aim was to demonstrate first and foremost the rootedness of Russians in the region, rather than their character as representatives of a broader, imperial, or Soviet Russian civilization. See: *Russkie Latvii: Katalog Vystavki* (Riga, 2008). Also see materials related to the exhibition at the website "Russkie Latvii," www.russkije.lv/ru/lib/read/exhibition-opening1.html (accessed December 15, 2010).

[26] Il'ia Dimenshtein, *Nasha Iurmala* (Riga, 2009). Other books by Dimenshtein include: *Russkaia Riga: istoricheskie ocherki* (Riga, 2002); *Riga i rizhane 100 let nazad* (Riga, 2007); *Imena russkoi Latvii* (Riga, 2007).

[27] The peculiar construction of the terms *vserosiiskii* and *vsesoiuznyi*, used most commonly to describe cultural and political institutions and events of republican and union scale, denotes significance over a multiplicity of smaller entities and territories—an imperial

expressed the pessimistic view described above in no uncertain terms, telling me that he doubted whether there was any meaningful production of Russian culture at all in present-day Latvia. The key term here is "meaningful." Of course, Russians in Latvia write in the papers, publish books, produce visual art, and so on. Dimenshtein's lament concerned high culture, culture of broad meaning, culture of "all-Russian" significance, at this moment when Russian society in Latvia is seemingly being deflated into a purely provincial phenomenon.

Certain cultural activity, however, escapes Dimenshtein's view. A useful gauge of the contemporary Russian literary world is to be found in the "The New Literary Map of Russia"—an aggregating website organized in uniquely "geographical" manner, devoted to the "reconstruction of the wholeness of Russian [*rossiiskoe*] literary space."[28] The site's main page features an interactive map of the Russian Federation that shows Russian cities in three scales, corresponding to population, but also to political importance—Moscow is the only city shown here in red. No external states or cities appear, rendering Kaliningrad as an island hanging in the middle of emptiness—Latvia, in other words, exists only as a negative space somewhere to the west of Pskov'. However, the index of the site's subpages is broken down into the categories "Cities of Russia" and "Countries of the World," the latter of which includes all countries where Russian literature is to be found—that is to say, where it may be found in the opinion of the editors, who are themselves listed in a political and regional hierarchy that illustrates the dominance of Moscow personnel in the project as a whole.[29] In other words, for all of its admirable aims, "The New Literary Map of Russia" presents cultural geography from the perspective of the center, and aims to "reconstruct" Russian literary space as the hierarchical space of empire. In this virtual literary empire, Latvia's page is particularly well represented—listing more authors than the page for Great Britain, for instance. Four of the 16 authors listed there, including Semyon Khanin, are founding members of the Riga literary group Orbit (Orbita).[30]

---

sweep, reminiscent of medieval czars of "all of the Russias." The principle contrasts with that of other terms denoting the unified entity or territory—*soiuznyi, respublikanskii*.

[28] "O proekte" on the site "Novaia literaturnaia karta Rossii," www.litkarta.ru/about/ (accessed December 12, 2010).

[29] Interestingly, the index list of "Cities of Russia" and "Countries of the World" includes under the latter category Russia. That term, however, links not to any Russia subpage, but back to the index list page itself. In the Borghesian logic of the site, Russia is both a universal category and a subheading.

[30] "Latviia" on the site "Novaia literaturnaia karta Rossii," www.litkarta.ru/world/latvia/ (accessed December 12, 2010). The numbers of authors listed in various regional subpages of the site clearly reflect the specific views of the editors involved and the contingencies of regional subeditors who have been invited to participate in the project,

Orbit, which also has its own subheading on the Latvia page of "The New Literary Map of Russia," is a loose organization comprised of the five poets who created the group in 1999: Khanin, Sergei Timofejev, Zhorzh Uallik, Artur Punte, and Vladimir Svetlov. In addition, the group includes a large number of affiliates active in literature, visual art, music, and so forth. Orbit is a hotbed of activity: a web portal, exhibitions, happenings, and group appearances at festivals in Latvia, Europe, the Russian Federation and publications of various sorts, poetic, artistic, and critical. Although the poets of Orbit write in Russian, the group's publications—including the poetic almanac, *Orbit*, multimedia DVDs, and a variety of other projects—are bilingual Russian–Latvian editions. This practice was adopted with a high degree of intentionality, as Punte explained to me in the summer of 2010, when I conducted several interviews with the founders of the group. Bilingualism is a distinctive feature of Orbit, and it reflects the group's highly self-conscious negotiation of the border between the Latvian and Russian ethnic enclaves, on the local level, and between Russia and Latvia or Eurasia and Europe, in a larger frame. Much of Orbit's activity takes the form of poetic performance in collaboration with ethnic Latvian musicians, composers, artists, and poets in multimedia happenings involving recitals, music (either live or DJ), and projected video art with subtitles in Latvian and at times in English. Many of these performances take place in a rave-party atmosphere that attracts a large audience of young people from both language enclaves. Further, the Orbit poets actively engage in translation practices that bridge Latvia's two language enclaves in various ways. Some recent examples include the Russian-language lyrics that Timofejev has written for the Latvian pop-rock group Brainstorm, which addresses its music to both Russian and European markets, and a number of translation projects that present Latvian poetry to Russian audiences, organized by Aleksandr Zapol', a visual artist and intellectual closely affiliated with the group.[31] In short, in distinction from most

---

rather than any "global" view of the "most successful" or "most significant" russophone literary production in any statistical or economic sense. Yet for this reason it presents an excellent heuristic device to measure the network of relationships that defines the dominant (or domineering) version of Russian cultural space centered on Moscow.

[31] These include an anthology of recent Latvian poetry in Russian translations that makes the interesting typographical gesture of a facing-page layout of works in two languages, with text set in opposite orientations from top to bottom of each page—so that (as Zapol' explained to me) two readers might sit across from one another and read the book in two languages simultaneously. Another recent publication by Zapol' is an anthology of poetry written in Russian by Latvian poets since the late nineteenth century—a volume that includes an excellent essay on the history of translation in Russian imperial and Soviet contexts. See Aleksandr Zapol'

cultural activity in Latvia, Orbit is an intentionally trans-ethnic and trans-linguistic phenomenon.[32]

As Orbit's presence on "The New Literary Map of Russia" suggests, the group handily manages to transcend the narrow provincialism within which Latvia's Russian cultural production is for the most part confined. The poets of Orbit are published in the most significant Russian literary journals, their books are published by prominent Russian publishers, they are nominated for the most prestigious Russian literary prizes, and discussed in critical essays by prominent Russian critics.[33] Then, too, the Orbit poets have been quite successful on the international European literary scene as well—they are regularly invited to festivals and translated into European languages. In part, one may attribute Orbit's "all-Russian" stature to the genealogy that links it to the literary culture of Latvia in the late 1980s. Timofejev, the oldest founding member of the group, in fact was published in the late 1980s in *Rodnik*, and the affiliates of the group include other links to that point of origin, such as poet Sergei Moreino. Another factor in the success of Orbit is clearly technological acuity, which allows these poets to participate in the virtual landscape of Russian poetry that is becoming with each year more and more important as the primary site of new publication and cross-fertilization.[34] A final factor is the web of personal relationships linking

---

(ed. and trans.), *Za nas / Par mums* (Riga, 2009); Aleksandr Zapol' (ed.), *Latyshkaia/russkaia poeziia: stikhi latyshkikh poetov, napisannye na russkom iazyke* (Riga, 2011).

[32] The transliteration employed in the present chapter of Timofejev's name into the Latin alphabet, which follows Latvian transliteration conventions, is a case in point. When I embarked on several publications of Timofejev's work in English translation in 2011, he and I discussed the possibility of using a more standard transliteration (Sergei Timofeev or Sergey Timofeyev), yet settled on retaining the Latvian version as a marker of his distinctive social identity and geographical positioning.

[33] The Orbit poets have been published in the prominent Russian journals *Vavilon*, *Vozdukh*, *TextOnly*, *Znamia*, and others. Sergei Timofejev has been shortlisted for the most prestigious Russian literary prize, the Andrei Bely Prize. In 2002 Il'ia Kukulin, then the poetry editor for the influential Moscow journal *Novoe literaturnoe obozrenie*, devoted a massive review essay to Russian literature in Latvia, with special attention to the Orbit group, as well as in Uzbekistan: Il'ia Kukulin, "Fotografiia vnutrennosti kofeinoi chashki," *Novoe literaturnoe obozrenie* 54 (2002): 262–82. My thinking about Timofejev, in particular, is informed by Kukulin's views.

[34] One may note, incidentally, the beneficial effects of what is from some angles of vision viewed as a scourge—the near absence of any enforcement of copyright in Russian internet space—that in the case of poetry results in a highly dynamic virtual landscape. On the internet and contemporary Russian poetry, see Kevin M.F. Platt, "Poetry in the Cloud: An Experiment, Results, and n+1 Hypotheses," *World Literature Today* 85/6 (November 2011): 40–43.

the Orbit poets to the Moscow and St. Petersburg literary scenes, and therefore to the arbiters of all-Russian cultural significance.

All of which renders Dimenshtein's discounting or ignorance of Orbit as a producer of "important" Russian cultural production in Latvia rather striking. Here, perhaps, we see a reflection of the nearly hermetic isolation of Russian-language communication circuits from Latvian ones in contemporary Latvia. In conversations in 2009 and 2010, Punte explained to me that, although in the first years of the project in the early 2000s, Russian-language newspapers had announced and reported on Orbit's events, at present the group communicates with the regional population in large part through the Latvian-language press. As a result, Orbit's resonance among Russian society in Latvia is limited: Although the group is broadly recognized on the cosmopolitan cultural scene and in the bohemian youth culture of Riga, it is virtually unknown in the Russian society of Latvia as a whole. The marginality of the Orbit poets' activities for Russians in Latvia is compensated to some degree by the group's prominence and success in the Latvian-language cultural sphere. Timofejev, for instance, is currently serving a term as president of the National Committee on Culture, a citizen advisory body to the Latvian Ministry of Culture. The group's works are typically favorably reviewed in the Latvian-language press. And the group has been included in Latvian delegations to such events as the Leipzig Book Fair.[35] Orbit, then, in its practices and resonance, completely inverts what I have described above as the typical geopolitical positioning of Russian culture in Latvia. Their work is well integrated in Latvian-language cultural life, but paradoxically also all-Russian in significance, and completely marginal to "mainstream" Russian

---

[35] See, for instance, the favorable review of a book of translations into German of Orbit poets' works that incidentally also reports on their activities at the Leipzig Book Fair: n.a., "Vācijā iznācis tekstgrupas Orbīta dzejas krājums," *Kulturasdiena* (March 23, 2012), /www.diena.lv/kd/literatura/vacija-iznacis-tekstgrupas-orbita-dzejas-krajums-13938501 (accessed March 24, 2012). According to Timofejev and Punte, the group has at times experienced some resistance on the part of Latvian official institutions to its undertakings. Early in the group's history, shortly after it was founded in the late 1990s, the Ministry of Culture seemed disinclined to offer state grants to the group's publishing projects. In Timofejev's words, the attitude seemed to be: "Why should the Latvian Ministry of Culture support Russian projects?" Yet this phase passed quickly, according to Timofejev, and the same figures were soon including the Orbit poets in their official projects. One may compare this experience with the case of Yuri Lotman's reception in Estonian society during the late-Soviet and post-Soviet periods, as discussed by Maxim Waldstein, which combined both a tendency toward adoption of the theorist as an "honorary" Estonian figure, and some resentment that an ethnic and cultural "other" (Lotman was a Russian-speaking Jew) should be perceived in the world at large as one of Estonia's most prominent intellectual figures. See Waldstein, "Russifying Estonia?," esp. p. 591n.

culture of the Baltic region, which is itself marginal (or provincial) within the larger Russian cultural context.

Let us turn, at this point, to consider some of the textual production of Orbit—in full recognition that a text cannot capture the full significance of the group's work, oriented as it is on multimedia works and performance. Consider a recent poem by Timofejev:

Truths

I want to tell you simple truths,
Reveal important things to you.
Always open doors, step into elevators,
Go upstairs, move down corridors.
Always get into cars, start the engine,
And if it's winter, wait until it warms up.
Always spend money, but sparingly,
And only once in a while spend everything you've got.
In summer it will be summer; in fall it will be fall,
Don't get flustered; don't do anything that disgusts you.
Girls will become young women, and then you'll notice
them crossing the street holding little kids' hands.
Men will somberly weigh the options
But then act according to circumstances, often making mistakes.
Governments are made to fall;
Ships—to glide beneath bridges.
All the same, the lights on the other side of the river
Will never—imagine that—never go out.
Still, if they do, pack your bag—
Only the essentials—and leave the city immediately.
When you arrive in a new place, look around, lean against a tree;
You can light up—if you smoke—stand around, think.
You see, here too in the evening they drink tea and in the morning, coffee.
Blame the mayor and wait for things to get better.
And if there is a river and you see lights on the other side,
That's something to cling to.[36]

---

[36] The poem is available on the Orbit website, in Timofejev's subpage "Znaesh' li ty drug," www.orbita.lv/publications/1115 (accessed December 17, 2010). The translation results from my collaborative work with the poet and with Julia Bloch and Bob Perelman.

This poem is a manifesto of Timofejev's poetic practice, in which he informs us point-blank what his poetic intentions are: "I want to tell you..." Yet let us refrain from further interpretation until we can situate the poem a little better in the larger frame of Russian poetry. In so doing, we will touch on features that are common to the poetics of the group as a whole—although it should also be said (as the members of Orbit often do) that they are each possessed of an individual and irreducible poetic voice. In a number of ways, Timofejev's poem illustrates how the work of the Orbit group is distinct from the poetic mainstream of the Russian Federation. For a start, this is free verse—a marginal and contentious form in Russian poetic production, which in distinction from most European traditions has retained a remarkable devotion to strict poetic forms up to the present day.[37] In a discussion on a Jūrmala beach in 2010, Timofejev recounted to me how a Russian poet once confronted him at a poetry festival in Ukraine, accusing him of a sort of "formal betrayal" of Russian poetry—of writing in free verse in order to produce easily translatable texts. In a separate conversation, Punte recalled with some bitterness his experience in the Magister program for writers and poets at the Gorky Institute in Moscow, where it was explained to him that "real" Russian poetry excludes free verse.[38] The reliance on free verse, along with the Orbit poets' multimedia and performance experiments, in which they have truly been pioneers in Russian poetry, demonstrate the group's orientation toward innovation and their sense of autonomy from "mainland" Russian poetic culture.

Turning a more focused attention on the poem above, its figural and conceptual simplicity resonates with the "new sincerity" proclaimed by some

---

[37] Kukulin relates the free-verse orientation of the group first of all to the higher incidence of this form in Soviet Latvia, where the local writers' union was somewhat more favorably disposed to departures from strict form than in the USSR as a whole. Additionally, he points to the influence of the poet Arkadii Dragomoshchenko on Timofeev himself in the late 1980s. Dragomoshchenko, a poetic outsider, became a leading force for innovation in the Leningrad underground scene in the last decade of the Soviet Union. Kukulin, "Fotografiia vnutrennosti kofeinoi chashki." For an up-to-date consideration of the history and cultural significance of free verse in Russian and Soviet poetic traditions, see Mikhail Gronas, "Naizust': o mnemonicheskom bytovanii stikha," *Novoe literaturnoe obozrenie* 114 (2012): 223–48. The article is accompanied by a number of critical responses and elaborations, including my own: Kevin M.F. Platt, "O iambakh i posledstviiakh, prichinakh i trocheiakh...," *Novoe literaturnoe obozrenie* 114 (2012): 264–8.

[38] Punte offers additional related comments concerning the formally conservative atmosphere of the Gorky Institute in a joint interview with Timofejev: Sergei Timofejev and Viestarts Gailītis, "Krievu orbīta," *Diena* (July 19, 2008), www.diena.lv/izklaide/krievu-orbita-615862 (accessed March 24, 2012).

Moscow and Petersburg poets as an antidote to the highly self-conscious conceptualism of the 1980s and early 1990s.[39] Yet that work, on the whole, has tended toward a conservatism of form and piety toward cultural canons that is entirely lacking here. Timofejev's writing, typically for the work of the group, is sincere and lyrical, yet not invested in any cultural recovery project in particular. Khanin, for instance, explains his own writing as an attempt to produce a poetic language that would be identical with everyday language yet still remain "poetic." Like Khanin, in "Truths" Timofejev is focused on the everyday, on images drawn from daily experience that he combines in an "atmospheric" fabric that lifts these images toward an undefined symbolic or metaphorical significance. In this poem in particular, this heightened metaphoricity is linked to fundamental existential questions, the "simple truths" of space and time. To be more precise, that poem is about the persistence in human experience of movement across thresholds. The poet begins with the seemingly minor and the spatial: "Always open doors, step into elevators, / Go upstairs, move down corridors." He moves out in scale toward the biographical: "spend money, but sparingly, / And only once in a while spend everything you've got"; "Girls will become young women, and then you'll notice / them crossing the street holding little kids' hands." Next he arrives at the level of the impersonal and historical: "Governments are made to fall; / Ships—to glide beneath bridges." And finally at the catastrophic or apocalyptic: "pack your bag— / Only the essentials—and leave the city immediately."

Timofejev grounds this series of gestures firmly in the unremarkable and the quotidian—as if the fall of governments were an order of event entirely comparable to the passage of ships under bridges, or even to movement down a corridor—communicating, it seems, the utter banality of limits and thresholds of all sorts. Perhaps this is an entirely comprehensible insight for those who, like Timofejev, position their social identity and professional practice on the intersection of multiple political and cultural borders, and who have lived through the radical transitions of the fall of the USSR, the economic surge of the 2000s, and the utter crash of the years after the global financial crisis of 2008— and one should note that the effects of boom and bust have been extraordinarily intense in Latvia. Yet, for all that, the lights on the other side of the river have never gone out. The final eight lines of the poem raise this implication to an almost metaphysical level. In the catastrophic moment when the lights *do* go out, when one is forced to flee the city as a refugee—an image of no little

---

[39] Alexei Yurchak, "Post-Post-Communist Sincerity: Pioneers, Cosmonauts and Other Soviet Heroes Born Today," in Thomas Lahusen and Peter Solomon (eds.), *What Is Soviet Now? Identities, Legacies, Memories* (Berlin, 2008), pp. 257–76.

bandwidth in this territory that armies have washed over for centuries—one nevertheless still winds up in a new town much the same as the one that has been abandoned. In sum, this is a poem about the durability of certain forms of experience—modern, urban, hopeful, banal—across all temporal and spatial borders, no matter how grand or minor.

Turning away from this poem and back toward the practices of Orbit as a whole, we may observe that Timofejev's focus on motion and the thresholds is truly a master trope in the writings of the group. Starting with the name "Orbit," an image of motion around a distant center, one may extend this observation with regard to any number of other texts and projects. Khanin's poem above is a case in point; the larger cycle of his recent works, to which that text belongs, is devoted to trips to determined and undetermined locations; Zapol' has produced large format photos that narrativize a seemingly frivolous relationship conducted in the course of a banal tourist trip divided between Moscow and Riga. Other recent works by Timofejev include the monologue of a provincial thief who aspires to move to the "capital" and the fairy-tale story of the romance of "Man with woman, Riga boy and Moscow girl."[40] Or consider, for instance, a programmatic recent work by Punte (who confessed to me "I have problems with identity")—a meditation on urban estrangement entitled "Gastarbeiters," from which I will reproduce only a single stanza for reasons of space:

> And if we recount how we found our way into the center by guesswork,
> trying not to attract attention, concealing in our bags stencils
> (the kind every decent person has, we thought),
> and having quite specific plans in relation to your city…
> How we moved along walls, concealing those same stencils in our bags,
> passing relay baton spray cans … losing along the way (countless)
> tiny parts from our favorite childhood erector set…
> How in the afternoon we hopped up and down behind posing tourists,
> so that we'd show up in their snapshots (show up in photographs) that we
> would never see—there are already quite a few photos like that around.[41]

Punte's poem superimposes the social roles of migratory worker and urban youth or graffiti artist to articulate an amalgamation of belonging and alienation, inscription via unsanctioned art and commando existence at the limits of the

---

[40] Cited from Timofejev's subpage on the Orbit website, "Znaesh' li ty drug," www.orbita.lv/publications/1115 (accessed December 17, 2010).

[41] The poem is available on the Orbit website, in Punte's subpage "Stikhotvoreniia," www.orbita.lv/publications/1113 (accessed April 9, 2012).

permissible. In sum, the Orbit poets self-consciously focus on their own location at the margins of Russian culture and on the border between Russian and Latvian enclaves, Russian and European contexts, and mine this location for poetic possibility, dramatizing the identities of subjects balanced across linguistic, political, and social fractures in a geographical "tarrying with the negative."

What is the result of this intentional rejection of that version of Russian culture in Latvia that I describe above—the provincialism and postimperial victimhood oriented on recovery of a rooted and whole ethnic identity—that dominates regional conceptions of cultural production? The politics and practice of the Orbit group is one of cosmopolitan hybridity, rather than nostalgic loyalty to Russian ethnic wholeness. Yet, oddly enough, it is the trajectory of Orbit out of the cultural center that itself makes possible a recuperation of relevance on the larger scene of Russian culture—an "all-Russian" significance. As in Timofejev's poem—crossing the border brings these poets home. In part, this is a reflection of the logic of cultural innovation operative in modern societies everywhere, for it is precisely their dedication to innovation and departure from tradition that places these poets "at the forefront" of Russian literature. In their case, one may add, the inherently temporal logic of innovation has been turned "on its side" and inscribed into a cultural geography, becoming movement across the borders of languages, polities, and imagined cultural wholes. Orbit, in other words, is exploiting the logic of limits that is constitutive of modern cultural life—for, as Peter Stallybrass and Allon White observed some decades ago, "cultural identity is inseparable from limits, it is always a boundary phenomenon and its order is always constructed around the figures of its territorial edge."[42] Yet this spatialized temporal scheme may be projected back into history as well. Turning to Orbit's broader international successes in ethnic Latvian social life and in Europe as a whole, we must observe that it is this same rejection of the "center" of Russian culture that allows the group to realize the postimperial dream of contributing once more to "world-significant Russian culture" in Latvia. By the same token, the rejection of the culture and politics of post-Soviet nostalgia allows these poets to preserve the cultural geography of the late Soviet period, by which Riga was a locus of innovative Russian cultural and political practices, a "center on the periphery."

Yet we should not confuse Orbit's orientation on margins and innovation with autonomy or independence from the larger, albeit highly complex and contested, mechanisms of transnational Russian cultural life. In fact, one may note a certain parity between "mainstream" Russian culture in the Baltic,

---

[42] Peter Stallybrass and Allon White, *The Politics and Poetics of Transgression* (Ithaca, NY, 1986), p. 200.

supported by Moscow money and initiatives intended to foster the cultural integrity of "compatriots abroad," on one hand, and Orbit, which thrives on elite Russian publishing contracts and recognition from sites like "The New Literary Map of Russia," on the other. Most of the time, these relationships activate separate circuits and distinct political valences. As Punte recounted, although Orbit has applied for funding from the Russian embassy, the request came to naught as a result of the group's unwillingness to engage the issues that interest cultural attachés, which, according to the poet, are largely restricted to political wedge issues like the history and memory of World War II. Yet it should also be noted that Timofejev was the recipient of the "Russian Prize" in 2010, an award that recognizes a Russian-language author residing outside of the Russian Federation, which is sponsored by the Eurasian Integration Fund and self-consciously intended to assert the cultural wholeness of former Soviet space.[43] Nevertheless, granting that two distinct spatial and temporal logics govern the dynamic relationship of periphery and center, corresponding to the discrete mechanisms of cultural innovation and consolidation, we must also recognize that these processes are integrated in the complex scene of Russian culture *in toto* in which, as Yurii Tynianov explains in the second epigraph to this chapter, with the passing of years and decades, the center may become periphery in one historical moment, and then revert to center again in the next.[44] Of course, in Tynianov's account the "center" and "periphery" were merely metaphors referring to generic categories and their position in the literary system. Yet in my account these metaphors gain an actual spatial and geographical significance. In short, in Latvia we are witness to culture's perpetual noncoincidence to itself, as this noncoincidence becomes visible in the cultural significance of space and the spatial mapping of culture.

Let me close by returning to the questions with which I began: What does it mean to be a Latvian Russian, to make a "free choice to be spiritually, culturally, and legally linked" to the Russian Federation—or not to make this choice? Quite obviously, "culture" is key here, yet there are as many different answers to these questions as there are ways one may perform and produce

---

[43] See the official site of the Russian Prize [*Russkaia premiia*], which explains that the prize "was established in 2005 for the preservation and development of the Russian language as a unique phenomenon of world culture and for the support of Russian-language authors of the world." In fact, the prize was originally awarded only to authors resident in the Near Abroad, yet was broadened to apply to world authors in 2008. "Russkaia premiia," www.russpremia.ru (accessed April 9, 2012).

[44] Yurii Tynianov, "Viktoru Shklovskomu: Literaturnyi fakt," in his *Poetika. Istoria literatury. Kino*, ed. E.A. Toddes, A.P. Chudakov, and M.O. Chudakova (Moscow, 1977), pp. 255–69, cit. on p. 257.

Russian culture. In this connection, I may note that the analysis presented in the present chapter, in its somewhat reductive binarism, must be taken only as a heuristic tool: Russophone Latvian culture includes a great many cultural practices that articulate a range of individually nuanced and particular relationships between the cultural and social life of the Russian Federation and Latvia. For in Latvia, Russian lives and Russian culture "jut out" from under the "cover" of authoritative Russian political and social categories, allowing the very terms "Russian" and "culture" to wander and realize their multifarious potential.

Here, we catch a glimpse of the multiplicity of the term "culture." Over the past two decades anthropologists have reacted against an earlier tendency to think of "cultures" in a unitary and bounded way, recognizing instead the internal fragmentation and contested boundaries of human communities and the meanings and identities that they produce. As a result, the discipline has manifested a tendency to reject or avoid the term "culture" as a whole.[45] Yet, regardless of the discipline's avoidance of the term, "culture" retains its force in human societies—a potency that is in fact buttressed by the term's projection of unity in the face of multiplicity. As we have seen above, various registers of "one culture" work simultaneously in different geographies and different temporal modalities. As Bloch wrote, "not all people exist in the same now"—or, we may add, in the same "there."[46] By one logic of cultural life, Russian identity in Latvia is produced by means of return—to the past, to folk holidays and dances, to historical documents and canonical forms. By another, the gesture toward margins, peripheries, borders, and limits—and beyond—is productive of culture and identity. Yet both are bound into the integral logic of the relationship between the cultural center and the periphery in their own fashion. Each modality of culture, through its distinct concatenation of time and space, produces "the Russian," just as truly as each Russian produces culture. Yet these many different articulations of Russian culture are locked in a tense flux of competing, unsettled visions of the Russian cultural being, posited as singular and whole, yet always riven by fractures and internal divisions, which are themselves productive in the long term of new wholes and new fragments.

---

[45] For an influential argument against "culture," see Lila Abu-Lughod, "Writing against Culture," in Ellen Lewin (ed.), *Feminist Anthropology: A Reader* (Malden, MA, 2006), pp. 153–69. For a cogent discussion of the term and its problems, see William H. Sewell, Jr., "The Concept(s) of Culture," in Victoria E. Bonnell and Lynn Hunt (eds.), *Beyond the Cultural Turn: New Directions in the Study of Society and Culture* (Berkeley, CA, 1999), pp. 35–61.

[46] Ernst Bloch, "Nonsynchronism and the Obligation to Its Dialectics," trans. Mark Ritter, *New German Critique* 11 (1977): 22–38, cit. on p. 22.

Bibliography

Manuscript Sources

Bakhmeteff Archive of Russian and East European Culture at Columbia University [BAR]

N.S. Trubetskoi to P.N. Savitskii, n.d. [1935]. George Vernadsky Papers, Box 8, Folder "Petr Nikolaevich Savitskii 1935."
P.N. Savitskii to G. Vernadskii, December 9, 1956. George Vernadsky Papers, Box 8, Folder "Mordovskaia ASSR 1945–46 gg."

Bibliothèque nationale de France, Departement de Musique [BNF, DdM].

N.S. Trubetskoi to P.P. Suvchinskii, February 15, 1926. BNF, DdM.
N.S. Trubetskoi to P.P. Suvchinskii, n.d. [Fall 1927]. Not catalogued.
N.S. Trubetskoi to P.P. Suvchinskii, n.d. [Fall 1927]. Not catalogued.
Nikolai Trubetskoi to Vera Guchkova-Suvchinskaia (later Traill), n.d. [before 1926]. Not catalogued.
Nikolai Trubetskoi to Petr Suvchinskii, March 5, 1926. Not catalogued.

Bundesarchiv [Federal Archive of Germany] [BArch]

BArch DY24 – 9345.
BArch DY24 – 11222.
BArch DY24 – 16993.
BArch DY24 – 17043.
BArch DY24 – 20203 Thälmann Brigade, Bd. 1.
BArch DY34 – 25150.

George Vernadsky Collection

Vernadskii, Georgii, "Kn. Trubetskoi i ukrainskii vopros," BAR, George Vernadsky Collection, Box 96.
Vernadskii, Georgii, "Kratkoe izlozhenie evraziiskoi tochki zreniia na russkuiu istoriiu," BAR, George Vernadsky Collection, Box 96.

Vernadskii, Georgii, "O rode Vernadskikh," BAR, George Vernadsky Collection, Box 98.

MIT Archives

MC 72 (Roman Jakobson Papers), Box 43, Folders 33 and 34.
MC 72 (Roman Jakobson Papers), Box 43, Folder 28.
MC 72, Box 119, Folder 95.
MC 72, Box 28, Folder 103.

State Archive of Russian Federation (GARF), Moscow

Circular of All-Russian Central Executive Committee (VTsIK), April 30, 1920, f. 5677, op. 2, d. 2, l. 27.
Explanatory circular on the decree of the Council of People's Commissars (Sovnarkom), "On the Changing of Borders" of January 27, 1918, dated May 11, 1918, f. 5677, op. 2, d. 2, l. 20.
Khmelev, A.N., "Istoriia administrativno-territorial'nogo deleniia Rossii. Opyt vvedeniia i isuzhenie voprosa," unpublished ms, undated [early 1920s], f. 6984, op. 1, d. 217, p. 127.
Sovnarkom decree, July 15, 1919, stipulating that border changes required the authorization of the Russian People's Commissariat for Internal Affairs (NKVD), f. 5677, op. 2, d. 2, l. 23.
Summary, undated, of Sviatlovskii's talk of August 17, 1922, f. 5677, op. 3, d. 394, ll. 24–30.

Der Bundesbeauftragte für die Unterlagen des Staatssicherheitsdienstes der ehemaligen Deutschen Demokratischen Republik (Federal archive of the state security service of the former GDR) [BstU]

BstU, MfS, BV Karl-Marx-Stadt, IM-file XIV 18/82, "Christian Schulze," page 100, 30.10.86.
BstU, MfS, HA XVIII 1827, Bd 2, 1974–1978, Bericht 12.9.1978.
BstU, MfS, BV Karl-Marx-Stadt, IM-file XIV 18/82, "Christian Schulze," page 100, 30.10.86.

Other

Trassenmuseum Deutzen (a self-organized museum of the former pipeline workers in Deutzen near Leipzig, visited in 2008).

Primary Sources

Aleksandrov, I.G., "Osnovy uykhoziaistvennogo raionirovanie SSSR," in G.M. Krzhizhanovskii (ed.), *Voprosy ekonomicheskogo raionirovaniia SSSR. Sbornik materialov i statei (1917–1929 gg.)* (Moscow, 1957).
Arsen'ev, Konstantin I., *Statisticheskie ocherki Rossii* (St. Petersburg, 1848).
Barabashov, N.P., (ed.), *Atlas of the Other Side of the Moon* (Oxford, 1961).
Bely, Andrei, *Petersburg*, trans. David McDuff (London, 1995).
Berg, Lev S., *Natural Regions of the U.S.S.R.* (New York, 1950).
——, *Ocherki po istorii russkikh geograficheskikh otkrytii* (Moscow, 1946).
——, "Opyt razdeleniya Sibiri i Turkestana na landshaftnye i morfologicheskie oblasti," *Sbornik v chest' 70–letiya D.N. Anuchina* (Moscow, 1913), 117–51.
Bitov, Andrei, *A Captive of the Caucasus*, trans. Susan Brownsberger (New York, 1992).
Blagonravov, A., "*Mechanics Illustrated* zajavljajet pravo na lunu," *Ogonyok* 29 (1957): 22.
Bogdanchikov, M., "Zadachi ekonomicheskoi geografii na sovremennom etape," in *Na metodologicheskom fronte geografii i ekonomicheskoi geografii* (Leningrad, 1932).
Bor'ba raionov za proizvodstvo khleba (Moscow, 1930).
Brodsky, Joseph, *Collected Poems in English* (New York, 2000).
——, *Sobranie sochinenii* (Petersburg, 1997), vol. 2.
Brounov, Petr I., "K voprosu o geograficheskikh rayonakh Evropeyskoy Rossii," *Sovremennye voprosy russkogo sel'skogo khozyaystva* (St. Petersburg, 1904), 23–45 2nd pagination.
Bulgak, V.B., "Rynok diktuet novye resheniya," speech at the enlarged meeting of the Collegium of the Ministry of Transport of RF, *Transport Rossii* 2 (1998): 2.
Center for Strategic Research, "Tranzitnyi potentsial, kak faktor stimulirovaniya ekonomicheskogo razvitiya i novogo geopoliticheskogo pozitsionirovanija Rossii," Moscow March 14, 2000. Proceedings of a seminar held at the Center for Strategic Research. http://www.mintrans.ru/pressa/Tranzit.htm (accessed March 20, 2000).
Chelintsev, Aleksandr N., *Sel'skokhozyaystvennye rayony Evropeyskoy Rossii kak stadia sel'skokhozyaystvennoy evolyutsii i kul'turnyi uroven' sel'skogo khozyaystva v nikh* (St. Petersburg, 1911).
Danilov, A., "Tsentrografiia," in *Bol'shaia Sovetskaia Entsiklopediia* (Moscow, 1934), vol. 60.
de Jager, C., and A. Jappel (eds.), *Proceedings of the Fourteenth General Assembly Brighton, United Kingdom, August 18–27, 1970* (Dordrecht, 1971).

de Pauly, Théodore, *Description ethnographique des peuples de la Russie* (St. Petersburg, 1862).
Declaration 1998. Declaration of the International Euro-Asian Conference on Transport, St. Petersburg, Russia, May 12–13, 1998.
Declaration 2000. Declaration of the Second International Euro-Asian Conference on Transport, St. Petersburg, Russia, September, 12–13. 2000.
Declaration 2003. Declaration of the Third International Euro-Asian Conference on Transport, St. Petersburg, Russia, September 11–12, 2003.
Denim, M., "Taezhnaia neft," *Vokrug sveta* 5 (1964): 6–8.
Dokuchaev, Vasilii V., *K voprosu o pereotsenke zemel' Evropeyskoy i Aziatskoy Rossii, s klassifikatsiey pochv* (Moscow, 1898).
Edinaya Lenta Novostei 20.1.2006 15:22 MSK, "Vladimir Yakunin: podpisannoe segodnya soglashenie o sotrudnichestve mezhdy OAO 'RZhD' i MID RF yavlyaetsya v vysshei stepenii aktual'nym," http://www.rzd.ru/agency/pnews.html?pnews_id=39668&he_id=652.
"Ekonomicheskaia geografiia," in *Bol'shaia Sovetskaia Entsiklopediia* (Moscow, 1933), vol. 63.
Fortunatov, Aleksei F., "K geografii preobladayushchikh yarovykh posevov," *Sovremennye voprosy russkogo sel'skogo khozyaystva* (St. Petersburg, 1904), 3–19 2nd pagination.
———, "K voprosu o sel'skokhozyaystvennykh rayonakh v Rossii," *Trudy Imperatorskogo Vol'nogo Ekonomicheskogo Obshchestva* 5 (1896): 1–12 2nd pagination.
Frank, Sergei, "Ob itogah raboty transportnogo kompleksa v 1999 godu," speech at the Collegium of the Ministry of Transport of Russia, Moscow, Russia, 16 February 2000, http://www.mintrans.ru/pressa/doklad_000216htm (accessed December 3, 2001).
———, "Razvitie mezhdunarodnyh transportnyh koridorov na territorii RF," speech at the meeting of the government of the RF, Moscow, Russia, September 7, 2000, http://www.mintrans.ru/pressa/doklad_000907.htm (accessed December 3, 2001).
———, "Realizatsiya tranzitnogo potentsiala dlya stimulirovaniya ekonomicheskogo razvitiya i novogo geopoliticheskogo pozitsionirovaniya Rossii," speech at the Seminar "Modernization of the Economy," Center for Strategic Development, Moscow, Russia, March 14, 2000, http://www.mintrans.ru/pressa/doklad_000314.htm (accessed December 3, 2001).
———, speech at the First international Euro-Asian Transport Conference, St. Petersburg, Russia, May 12–13, 1998, http://www.eatu.ru.page(DOC).doc(245)html (accessed December 3, 2001).

———, speech at the Second International Euro-Asian Transport Conference, St. Petersburg, Russia, September 12, 2000, http://www.mintrans.ru/pressa/doklad_000912.htm (accessed December 3, 2001).

———, "V MTK nuzhno vlozhit" 450 mrd rublei," *Kommersant*, 8 May 2001, http://www.mintrans.ru/pressa/doklad/_010508_1.htm (accessed December 3, 2001).

Government of the RF, Postanovlenie Pravitel'stva RF N848, "O federal'noi tselevoi programme 'Modernizatsiya transportnoi sistemy Rossii (2002–2010),'" December 5, 2001, http://www.mintrans.ru/Pressa/N_848.htm (accessed December 12, 2001).

Government of the RF, Press release N663, September 7, 2000, "Osnovnie napravlenie formirovaniya i razvitiya mezhdunarodnyh transportnyh koridorov na territorii RF." http://www.government.ru/data/news_text.html?he_id=103&news_id=1032 (accessed December 3, 2001).

Gurvich, L., *Vokrug sveta* 3 (1964): 53.

"Imia Rossii. Istoricheskii Vybor 2008." http://www.nameofrussia.ru (accessed April 18, 2012).

Kachosvily, L., "Sputnik III Moskovan yllä," *Neuvostoliitto Tänään* 11–12 (1958): 19.

Kaempffert, Waldemar, "The Week in Science—Shifting Populations. Soviet Studies Rearrangement of People and Industries," *New York Times*, June 16, 1935, XX8.

Keller, Karl, "Zur Frage der Rassenstatistik," *Allgemeines Statistisches Archiv* 24 (1934/35): 129–42.

Kotel'nikov, A.N., "K voprosu ob organizatsii statistiki naseleniya v Rossii," *Trudy Imperatorskogo Vol'nogo Ekonomicheskogo Obshchestva* 2/5 (1895): 135–8.

Kruber Aleksandr, "Fiziko-geograficheskie oblasti Evropeyskoy Rossii," *Zemlevedenie* 14/3–4 (1907): 163–220.

———, "Opyt razdeleniya Evropeyskoy Rossii na rayony," *Zemlevedenie* 3–4 (1898): 175–84.

Krylov, Yu, "Mezhplanetnaya trassa prolozhena...," *Ogonyok* 39 (1959): 6.

Krzhizhanovskii, G.M. (ed.), *Voprosy ekonomicheskogo raionirovaniia SSSR. Sbornik materialov i statei (1917–1929 gg.)* (Moscow, 1957).

Kulebyako-Koretskii, Nikolai G., "Rayony khlebnoy proizvoditel'nosti Evropeyskoy Rossii i Zapadnoy Sibiri," *Trudy Imperatorskogo Vol'nogo Ekonomicheskogo Obshchestva* 4–5 (1903): 40–84.

Latvian Central Statistical Bureau, "Population Census 2011—Key Indicators," www.csb.gov.lv/en/statistikas-temas/population-census-2011-key-indicators-33613.html (accessed April 9, 2012).

Lenin, V.I., "Materializm i Empiriokrititsizm. Kriticheskie zametki ob odnoi reaktsionnoi filosofii," in *Polnoe Sobranie Sochinenii*, 5th edn. (Moscow, 1961), vol. 18.

Livshits, R.S., *Ocherki po razmeshcheniiu promyshlennosti SSSR* (Moscow, 1954).

Ljapunov, B., "Natshalo kosmitsheskoij ery," *Ogonyok* 41 (1958): 6–7.

Malakhov, N., "Dolog i truden put...," in *K Zvezdam. Risunki letšika-kosmonavta A. Leonova i hudožnika-fantasta A. Sokolova* (Leningrad, 1970).

Maselvich, A.G., "Skazka stala bylju!," *Ogonyok* 40 (1959): 8.

Mendeleev, D.I. (1890), "Materialy dlia peresmotra obshchago tamozhennago tarifa Rossiiskoi Imperii po Evropeiskoi torgovli," in *Sochineniia* (Leningrad and Moscow, 1950), vol. 17.

——, (1892), "Tolkovyi tarif, ili issledovanie o razvitii promyshlennoi Rossii v sviazi s ee obshchim tamozhennym tarifom 1891 g.," in *Sochineniia* (Leningrad and Moscow, 1950), vol. 19.

——, (1896), "Fabrichno-zavodskaia promyshlennost" i torgovlia Rossii," in *Sochineniia,* (Leningrad, Moscow, 1952), vol. 21.

——, *Granits poznaniiu predvitet" nevozmozhno*, ed. Iu.I. Solov'ev (Moscow, 1991).

——, *K' poznaniiu Rossii* (St. Petersburg, 1906).

——, *Nauchnyi arkhiv. Osvoenie krainego Severa. Tom 1.Vysokie shiroty severnogo ledovitogo okeana* (Moscow, 1960).

——, *Problemy ekonomicheskogo raxvittia Rossii* (Moscow, 1960).

——, *S dumoiu o blage rossiiskom. Izbrannye ekonomicheskie proizvedeniia*, ed. S.V. Kazantsev (Novosibirsk, 1991).

——, *Sochineniia* (25 vols., Leningrad and Moscow, 1934–1936).

——, *Zavetnye mysli. Polnoe izdanie (vpervye posle 1905g.)* (Moscow, 1995).

Mihailov, Nikolai, M., "Zima i leto (ocherki o nashem climate)," *Vokrug sveta* 1 (1954): 18–25.

Ministry of Foreign Affairs of the RF, transcript of remarks and reply to a media question by Russian Minister of Foreign Affairs Sergey Lavrov after signing a cooperation agreement between the Foreign Ministry and OAO Russian Railways, Moscow, January 19, 2006, www.mid.ru (accessed January 25, 2006).

Mintrans, Federal'naya tselevaya programma modernizatsiya transportnoi sistemy Rossii (2002–2010 gody), Podprogramma Mezhdunarodnye transportnye koridory, Moscow, December 5, 2001. http://www.mintrans.ru/pressa/FZP/FZP_VV.htm?lvl=2 (accessed December 12, 2001).

——, "Transportnaya strategiya RF na period do 2020," Moscow, May 12, 2005. http://www.mintrans.ru/pressa/TransStrateg_VV.htm?!vl=2 (accessed June 6, 2005).

Motylev, V. "Ekonomicheskaia geografiia," in *Bol'shaia Sovetskaia Entsiklopediia* 63 (Moscow, 1933), p. 246.
Müller, Johannes, "Die Stellung der Statistik in neuen Reich," *Allgemeines Statistisches Archiv* 24 (1934/35): 241–50.
Nikolai, M. Sibirtsev, "O trekhverstnoy pochvennoy karte," *Trudy Imperatorskogo Vol'nogo Ekonomicheskogo Obshchestva* 2/5 (1893): 125–35.
Official Records of the General Assembly: Resolution 2222 (XXI). *Treaty on Principles Governing the Activities of States in the Exploration and Use of Outer Space, including the Moon and Other Celestial Bodies.* http://www.unoosa.org/oosa/OOSA/index.html
Official Records of the General Assembly: Resolution adopted by the General Assembly: Resolution 1348 (XIII). *Question of the peaceful use of outer space. 792nd plenary meeting, 13 December 1958.* http://www.unoosa.org/oosa/OOSA/index.html
Putin, Vladimir, address to the Federal Assembly of the RF, Moscow, the Kremlin, May 26, 2004, http://www.kremlin.ru/eng/text/speeches/2004/05/26/1309_type70029_71650.shtml (accessed July 14, 2007).
———, "Address to the Federal Assembly," April 25, 2005, www.kremlin.ru/text/appears/2005/04/87049.shtml (accessed May 18, 2007).
———, "Rabotat' na perspektivu," speech at the All-Russian Scientific-practical Conference Transport of Russia at the Turn of the Century, Moscow, December 6, 1999; published in *Transport Rossii*, December 3–19, 1999.
———, speech at the meeting of the State Council of the RF, Kremlin, Moscow, October 29, 2003, http://www.kremlin.ru/appears/2003/10/29/1555_type63378_54670.shtml (accessed May 13, 2005).
Rikhter, Dmitrii I., "Opyt razdeleniya Evropeyskoy Rossii na rayony po estestvennym i ekonomicheskim priznakam," *Trudy Imperatorskogo Vol'nogo Ekonomicheskogo Obshchestva* 4 (1898): 46–91 2nd pagination.
———, "Popytki razdeleniya Rossii na rayony po estestvennoistoricheskim i ekonomicheskim priznakam," in *Sovremennye voprosy russkogo sel'skogo khozyaystva* (St. Petersburg, 1904), 49–78 2nd pagination.
———, "Zamechaniya na pochvenno-otsenochnyi proekt V.V. Dokuchaeva," *Trudy Imperatorskogo Vol'nogo Ekonomicheskogo Obshchestva* 1/1 (1898): 42–59 2nd pagination.
Rossiiskaya Gazeta, Advertisement of the DGTV Group, March 23, 2005.
Rossiiskaya Gazeta, Sergei Kuznetsov, "Transport Rossii nuzhdaetsya v chastnyh investitsiyah," May 25, 2003.
Rossiiskaya Gazeta, Aleksei Tsitskin, "Na temy dnya. Prognozy ne pospevayut za koridorami," February 11, 1998.

Semenov, Petr P. (ed.), *Zhivopisnaya Rossiya: Otechestvo nashe v ego zemel'nom, istoricheskom, plemennom, ekonomicheskom i bytovom znachenii* (12 vols, St. Petersburg; Moscow, 1881–1901).

Semenov-Tyan-Shanskii, Veniamin P., *O mogushchestvennom territorial'nom vladenii primenitel'no k Rossii: ocherk po politicheskoy geografii* (St. Petersbourg, 1915).

———, *Tipy mestnostey Evropeyskoy Rossii i Kavkaza: ocherk po fizicheskoy geografii v svyazi s antropogeografiey* (St. Petersburg, 1915).

———, *To, chto proshlo. Tom 2, 1917–1942* (Moscow, 2009).

Sharonov, V., "K solntsu! K zvezdam!" *Ogonyok* 3 (1959): 2–3.

Skvortsov, Aleksandr I., *Khozyaystvennye rayony Evropeyskoy Rossii* (St. Petersburg, 1914).

"Soedinennye zasedaniya Pochvennoy i Statisticheskoy komissii 1–3 marta 1895 g.,"

Statisticheskiy vremennik Rossiyskoy imperii 2/1 (1871).

Statistika pozemel'noy sobstvennosti i naselennykh mest Evropeyskoy Rossii (St. Petersburg, 1880–85).

Sviatlovskii, E.E. (ed.), "Die zentrographische Methode und ihre Entwicklung in Theorie und Praxis," *Allgemeines Statistisches Archiv* 24 (1934/35): 21–40.

———, "La centrographie," in *Comptes rendus du Congrès international de géographie* (Warsaw, 1937), vol. 3, p. 379.

———, "Méthodes centrographiques (Résumé du rapport au Congrès International de Géographie, 1934)," in *Congrès International de Géographie. Varsovie, 1934. Résumés des Communications* (Warsaw, 1934), 137–8.

———, *Tsentrograficheskaia laboratoriia im. D.I. Mendeleeva k piatnadtsatiletiiu Oktiabria (1917–1932). Tsentrografiia. I* (Leningrad, 1933).

———, with the collaboration of Walter Crosby Eells, "The Centrographical Method and Regional Analysis," *The Geographical Review* 27/2 (1937): 240–54.

Sytin, Viktor, "Chelovek realnoj mechty," *Ogonyok* 38 (1957): 12–13.

Tanfil'ev, Gavriil I., "Fiziko-geograficheskie oblasti Evropeyskoy Rossii," *Trudy Imperatorskogo Vol'nogo Ekonomicheskogo Obshchestva* 1 (1897): 1–30 2nd pagination.

———, *Glavneyshie cherty rastitel'nosti Rossii* (St. Petersburg, 1903).

Tillo, A.A., "Raspredelenie tsentrov materikov na poverkhnosti zemnogo shara," *Izvestiia Russkogo Geograficheskogo Obshchestva* 23 (1887): 750–53.

Torgovlya i promyshlennost' Rossii po rayonam, vol. 1 (St. Petersburg, 1900).

Transport Rossii, Boris Primochkin, "Za logistikoi – budushchee," 7 (1998).

Transport Rossii, Pavel Kolesnikov, "Effektivnost' i bezopasnost'," December 27–31, 1999.

Transport Rossii, Speech of Minister of Transport of RF Nikolai Tsakh, "Doklad ob itogah sotsial'no-ekonomicheskogo razvitiya transportnogo kompleksa za 1997 god ob osnovyh zadachah na 1998 god," 2 (1998).
Transport Rossii, Yaroslav Sibirtsev, "Obshcherossiiskii forum transportnikov," December 6–12, 1999.
Trotskii, Lev, "D.I. Mendeleev i marksizm," in *Sochineniia*, vol. 21: *Kul'tura perekhodnogo perioda* (Moscow and Leningrad, 1927), pp. 268–90; available at: http://www.magister.msk.ru/library/trotsky/trotl961.htm (accessed 18 April 2012).
Trudy Imperatorskogo Vol'nogo Ekonomicheskogo Obshchestva 5 (1895): 110–80.
USSR in Construction 8 (1932).
Vail, Petr, and Aleksandr Genis, *60-e: mir sovetskogo cheloveka* (Ann Arbor, MI, 1988).
Vasilev, Sergei, "Razvedtšikam nebesnyh glubin," *Pravda*, October 6, 1957, p. 1.
Vazar, Vasiliy E., "Pochvennaya karta Chernigovskoy gubernii v svyazi s voprosom o statisticheskom issledovanii pochv," *Trudy Imperatorskogo Vol'nogo Ekonomicheskogo Obshchestva* 1/2 (1895): 143–51.
"Veber, Al'fred," in *Bol'shaia sovetskaia entsiklopediia*, 1st edn. (Moscow, 1928), vol. 9, 123–4.
Veber, A. [Alfred Weber], *Teoriia razmeshcheniia promyslennosti*, abr. and trans. N.V. Morozov, foreword by Nikolai Baranskii (Leningrad and Moscow, 1926).
Vernov, S.N, "Razvedka glubin kosmosa," *Ogonyok* 44 (1957): 5.
Vinogradov, A., and L. Krivenko, "Navstrechu utrennei zare," *Vokrug sveta* 1 (1964): 6–7.
von Thünen, Johann Heinrich, *Der isolierte Staat in Beziehung auf Landwirtschaft und Nationaloekonomie* (Jena, repr. 1910).
Weber, Alfred, Über den Standort der Industrie (Tübingen, 1909).
Weinberg, V.P., "Polozheniia tsentra naselennosti Rossii s 1613 po 1913 g.," *Izvestiia Russkogo Geograficheskogo Obshchestva*, 51/6 (1915): 385–408.
——, "Polozheniia tsentra poverkhnosti Rossii ot nachala kniazhestva Moskovskogo do nastoiashchego vremeni," *Izvestiia Russkogo Geograficheskogo Obshchestva* 51/6 (1915): 365–84
Zahn, Friedrich, "Vom Wirtschaftswert des Menschen als Gegenstand der Statistik," *Allgemeines Statistisches Archiv* 24 (1934/35): 461–4.

Secondary Sources

A Tribute to Roman Jakobson, 1896–1982 (Berlin and New York, 1983).

Aaltola, Mika, "Agile Small State Agency: Heuristic Plays and Flexible National Identity Markers in Finnish Foreign Policy," *Nationalities Papers* 39 (2011): 257–76.
Abu-Lughod, Lila, "Writing against Culture," in Ellen Lewin (ed.), *Feminist Anthropology: A Reader* (Malden, MA, 2006).
Aho, Juhani, *Hajamietteitä kapinaviikoilta* (Porvoo, 1918).
Akhundov, M.D., *Kontseptsii prostranstva i vremeni: istoki, evoliutsiia, perspektivy* (Moscow, 1982).
Alampiev, Petr, M., *Ekonomicheskoe rayonirovanie SSSR* (Moscow, 1959).
Aleksandrov, D.A., "Pochemu sovetskie uchenye perestali pechatat'sia za rubezhom: stanovlenie samodostatochnosti i izolirovannosti otechestvennoi nauki, 1914–1940," in *Voprosy istorii estestvoznaniia i tekhniki* 3 (1996): 3–24.
Alevras, Natalia, "G.V. Vernadsky and P.N. Savitsky: Istoki evraziiskoi kontseptsii," in *Rossiia i Vostok: problemy vzaimodeistviia / Tezisy dokl. i soobshch. k mezhdunar. nauch. konf.* (Cheliabinsk, 1995): 121–4.
——, "Nachala evraziiskoi kontseptsii v rannem tvorchestve G.V. Vernadskogo i P.N. Savitskogo," *Vestnik Evrazii* 1 (1996): 5–17.
Alkio, Santeri, *Talonpoika ja Suomen vapaus* (Vaasa, 1922).
Almgren, Beverly S., "D.I. Mendeleev and Siberia," *Ambix* 45/2 (1998): 50–66.
Anderson, Benedict, *Imagined Communities: Reflections on the Origin and Spread of Nationalis,* (London, rev. edn. 2006).
Andreev, E.S., "Osnovnye etapy razvitiia otechestvennoi geopoliticheskoi mysli," *Vlast,'* 4 (2010): 146–7.
Andreyev, Catherine, and Ivan Savický, *Russia Abroad: Prague and the Russian Diaspora, 1918–1938* (New Haven, CT, 2004).
Antonov, M.F., "Genii russkoi ekonomicheskoi mysli," *Molodaia gvardiia* 3 (2000).
——, "Mendeleev—Chlen Soiuza russkogo naroda," available at: http://www.hrono.ru/biograf/bio_m/mendeleev_di.php (accessed April 18, 2012).
Antoshchenko, Aleksandr (ed.), *Evraziia ili "Sviataia Rus"? Rossiiskie emigranty v poiskakh samosoznaniia na putiakh istorii* (Petrozavodsk, 2003).
——, *O Evrazii i evraziitsakh (bibliograficheskii ukazatel')* (Petrozavodsk, 2000).
Apunen, Osmo, and Helena Rytövuori, "Ideas of 'Survival' and 'Progress' in the Finnish Foreign Policy Tradition," *Journal of Peace Research* 19 (1982): 61–82.
Apunen, Osmo, "Beauty and the Beast: Semiotic Perspectives on the Formation of Finnish/Russian National Characters," Paper presented at the IV Pan-European IR Conference, September 9–10, 2001.
Avtonomova, Natalia, and Mikhail Gasparov, "Jakobson, Slavistics and the Eurasian Movement: Two Moments of Opportunity, 1929–1953," in

Henryk Baran et al. (eds.), *Roman Jakobson. Teksty, dokumenty, issledovania* (Moscow, 1999).

Bailes, Kendall, E., *Science and Russian Culture in an Age of Revolutions: V.I. Vernadsky and His Scientific School, 1863–1945* (Bloomington, IN, 1990).

Bakuła, Bogusław, "Colonial and Postcolonial Aspects of Polish Discourse on Eastern 'Borderlands,'" in Janusz Korek (ed.), *From Sovietology to Postcoloniality: Poland and Ukraine from a Postcolonial Perspective* (Stockholm, 2007).

Balibar, Etienne, "The Nation-Form: History and Ideology," in Etienne Balibar and Immanuel Wallerstein (eds.), *Race, Nation, Class: Ambiguous Identities* (London, 1991).

Balkin, Jack, M., "Nested Oppositions," in *Yale Law School Legal Scholarship Repository. Faculty Scholarship Series*. Paper 281, http://digitalcommons.law.yale.edu/fss_papers/281, 1990.

Balmaceda, Margarita M., "Der Weg in die Abhängigkeit. Ostmitteleuropa am Energietropf der UdSSR," *Osteuropa* 54/9–10 (2004): 162–79.

Baran, Henryk, et al. (eds.), *Roman Jakobson. Teksty, dokumenty, issledovania* (Moscow, 1999).

Barańska, Katarzyna, and Claudia Snochowska-Gonzalez, "Wojna chamsko-pańska," *Recykling Idei* 10 (2008).

Baranskii, Nikolai, N., *Moya zhizn' v ekonomgeografii* (Moscow, 2001).

Barnes, Trevor, "Envisioning Economic Geography: Three Men and their Figures," *Geographische Zeitschrift* 86/2 (1998): 94–105.

Barnett, Vincent, "Catalysing Growth?: Mendeleev and the 1891 Tariff," *Research in the History of Economic Thought and Methodology* 22-A (2004): 123–44.

Baron, Nick, "Nature, Nationalism and Revolutionary Regionalism: Constructing Soviet Karelia, 1920–1923," *Journal of Historical Geography* 33/3 (2007): 565–95.

——, "New Spatial Histories of 20th-century Russia and the Soviet Union: Exploring the Terrain," *Kritika: Explorations in Russian and Eurasian History* 9/2 (2008): 433–47.

——, "New Spatial Histories of Twentieth-century Russia and the Soviet Union: Surveying the Landscape," *Jahrbücher für Geschichte Osteuropas* 55 (2007): 374–400.

——, *Soviet Karelia: Planning, Politics and Terror in Stalin's Russia, 1920–1939* (London, 2007).

——, "Stalinist Planning as Political Practice: Control and Repression on the Soviet Periphery, 1935–38," *Europe-Asia Studies* 56/3 (2004): 439–62.

Baskakov, Petr, "JSC Russian Railways as an Integrator of Transport Services in the Markets of Europe and Asia," *Round Table at the 23rd German Logistics Congress*, Berlin, October 18–20, 2006.

Bassin, Mark, "'Classical' Eurasianism and the Geopolitics of Russian Identity," *Ab Imperio* 2 (2003): 257–66.

———, "Geographical Determinism in Fin-de-siècle Marxism. Georgii Plekhanov and the Environmental Basis of Russian History," *Annals of the Association of American Geographers* 82/1 (1992): 3–22.

———, *Imperial Visions: Nationalist Imagination and Geographical Expansion in the Russian Far East, 1840–1865* (Cambridge, 1999).

———, "Reductionism Redux? Or the Convolutions of Contextualism," *Annals of the Association of American Geographers* 83/1 (1993): 163–6.

———, "Russia between Europe and Asia: The Ideological Construction of Geographical Space," *Slavic Review* 50/1 (1991): 1–17.

Bassin, Mark, Christopher Ely, and Melissa Stockdale (eds.), *Space, Place, and Power in Modern Russia: Essays in New Spatial Histories* (DeKalb, IL, 2010).

Baykov, Alexander, *The Development of the Soviet Economic System: An Essay on the Experience of Planning in the USSR* (Cambridge, 1946).

Bazhanov, Valentin, "A Note on A.S. Panarin's *Revansh Istorii*," *Europe-Asia Studies* 51/4 (1999): 705–8.

Beauvois, Daniel, "Mit 'kresów wschodnich' czyli jak mu położyć kres," in Wojchiech Wrzesiński (ed.), *Polskie mity polityczne XIX i XX wieku* (Wrocław, 1994).

Beissinger, Mark, "Rethinking Empire in the Wake of Soviet Collapse," in Zoltan Barany and Robert G. Moser (eds.), *Ethnic Politics after Communism* (Ithaca, NY, 2005).

———, "Soviet Empire as 'Family Resemblance,'" *Slavic Review* 65/2 (2006): 294–303.

Beisswenger, Martin, "Konservativnaia revoliutsiia v Germanii i dvizhenie evraziitsev—tochki soprikosnoveniia," *Konservatism v Rossii i v mire* 3 (2004): 49–73.

———, *Petr Nikolaevich Savitskii (1895–1968): A Bibliography of His Published Works* (Prague, 2008).

Belen'kii, M., *Mendeleev* (Moscow, 2010).

Belonin, N.N., "D.I. Mendeleev kak kartograf," *Naukovy Zapiski* 7/8, *Trudy Naukovo-Doslidnogo Institutu Geografii* 2 (1942): 223–33.

Benhabib, Seyla, *The Rights of Others: Aliens, Residents and Citizens* (Cambridge, 2004).

Berg, Leo S., *Natural Regions of the U.S.S.R.* (New York, 1950).

———, *Nomogenesis or Evolution Determined by Law* (London, 1926).

———, "Nomogenez, ili Evoliutsia na osnove zakonomernostei," in Lev S. Berg, *Trudy po teorii evoliutsii, 1922–1930* (Leningrad, 1977).

———, *Nomogenez, ili Evoliutsia na osnove zakonomernostei. Trudy Geograficheskogo Instituta*, vol. 1 (Petrograd, 1922).

———, *Ocherki po istorii russkikh geograficheskikh otkrytii* (Moscow, 1946).

Bhabha, Homi K., *The Location of Culture* (London, 1994).

Black, Edwin, *IBM and the Holocaust: The Strategic Alliance between Nazi Germany and America's Most Powerful Corporation* (Rockville, MD, 2009).

Black, J.L., "Opening up Siberia: Russia's 'Window on the East,'" in Alan Wood (ed.), *The History of Siberia: From Russian Conquest to Revolution* (London, 1991).

Bloch, Ernst, "Nonsynchronism and the Obligation to Its Dialectics," trans. Mark Ritter, *New German Critique* 11 (1977): 22–38, cit. on p. 22.

Boiarintsev, Vladimir, *Evreiskie i Russkie uchenye. Mify i real'nost'* (Moscow, 2001).

Bojanowska, Edyta, *Nikolai Gogol: Between Ukrainian and Russian Nationalism* (Cambridge, MA, 2006).

Bolkhovitinov, Nikolai, "Zhizn' i deiatel'nost' G.V. Vernadskogo (1887–1973) i ego arkhiv," *Slavic Research Center Occasional Papers* 82 (2002): 1–63.

———, *Russkie uchenye-emigranty (G.V.Vernadsky, M.M.Karpovich, M.T.Florinsky) i stanovlenie rusistiki v SShA* (Moscow, 2005).

Böss, Otto, *Die Lehre des Eurasier. Ein Beitrag zur russischen Ideengeschichte des 20. Jahrhunderts* (Wiesbaden, 1961).

Bourdieu, Pierre, *L'Ontologie politique de Martin Heidegger* (Paris, 1988).

———, *The Logic of Practice* (Cambridge, 1990).

Bown, Matthew Cullerne, *Socialist Realist Painting* (New Haven, CT, 1998).

Boym, Svetlana, and Adam Bartos, *Kosmos: Remembrances of the Future* (Princeton, NJ, 2001).

Bradford, Richard, *Roman Jakobson: Life, Language, Art* (New York, 1994).

Bretanitskaia, Alla (ed.), *Petr Suvchinsky i ego vremia* (Moscow, 1999).

Briese, Olaf, "Symbolische Siege. Die Talsperren und ihr Double," *Zeitschrift für Geschichtswissenschaft* 51/6 (2003): 510–36.

Brooks, Nathan M., "Mendeleev and Metrology," *Ambix* 45/2 (1998): 116–28.

———, "Mendeleev, Dmitrii Ivanovich," in Noretta Koertge (ed.), *New Dictionary of Scientific Biography* (New York, 2008), vol. 5.

Brubaker, Rogers, and Frederick Cooper, "Beyond Identity," *Theory and Society* 29 (2000): 1–47.

Brubaker, Rogers, *Nationalism Reframed: Nationhood and the National Question in the New Europe* (Cambridge, 1996).

Buchowski, Michał, "The Specter of Orientalism in Europe: From Exotic Other to Stigmatized Brother," *Anthropological Quarterly* 79/3 (2006): 463–82.

Buck-Morss, Susan, *Dreamworld and Catastrophe; The Passing of Mass Utopia in East and West* (Cambridge, 2000).

Bull, Hedley, *The Anarchical Society: A Study of Order in World Politics* (London, 1977).

Burbank, Jane, and David Cooper, *Empires in World History: Power and Politics of Difference* (Princeton, NJ, 2010).

Burbank, Jane, Mark von Hagen, and Anatolyi Remnev (eds.), *Russian Empire: Space, People, Power* (Bloomington, IN, 2007).

Burke, Peter, *History and Social Theory* (Cambridge, 2005).

Burton, Antoinette (ed.), *After the Imperial Turn: Thinking with and through the Nation* (Durham, NC, 2003).

——, "Thinking beyond the Boundaries: Empire, Feminism and the Domains of History," *Social History* 26/1 (2001): 60–71.

Bush, Barbara, review of *The New Imperial Histories Reader* in *Reviews in History*, http://www.history.ac.uk/reviews/review/989 (accessed April 13, 2012).

Buzan, Barry, Charles Jones, and Richard Little, *The Logic of Anarchy: Neorealism to Structural Realism. New Directions in World Politics* (New York, 1993).

Calhaun, Craig, Frederick Cooper, and Kevin W. Moore (eds.), *Lessons of Empire: Imperial Histories and American Power* (New York and London, 2006).

Carr, E.H., and R.W. Davies, *A History of Soviet Russia: Foundations of a Planned Economy, 1926–1929*, vol. 1 (London, 1969).

Cassedy, Steven, "Review of Imperial Knowledge: Russian Literature and Colonialism by Ewa M. Thompson," *Slavic Review* 60/4 (2001): 880.

Castells, Manuel, *The Information Age: Economy, Society and Culture. Vol. 1: The Rise of the Network Society* (Oxford, 1996).

Cavanagh, Claire, "Postcolonial Poland," *Common Knowledge* 10/1 (2004): 82–92.

Chakrabarty, Dipesh, *Provincializing Europe: Postcolonial Thought and Historical Difference* (Princeton, NJ, new edn. 2007).

Chappell, John, "Social Darwinism, Environmentalism, and Ideology," *Annals of the Association of American Geographers* 83/1 (1993): 160–66.

Chilton, Paul A., *Security Metaphors: Cold War Discourse from Containment to Common House* (New York, Bern, and Frankfurt am Main, 1996).

Chinyaeva, Elena, "Ruska emigrace v Ceskoslovensku: vyvoj ruske pomocne akce," *Slovansky prehled* 1 (1993).

——, *Russians outside Russia: The Emigré Community in Czechoslovakia, 1918–1938* (Munich, 2001).

Clark, Katerina, *Petersburg, Crucible of Cultural Revolution* (Cambridge, MA, 1995).
Coen, Deborah, R., "Imperial Climatographies from Tyrol to Turkestan," *Osiris* 26/1 (2011): 45–65
Cohen, Bernard, *Interactions: Some Contacts between the Natural Sciences and the Social Sciences* (Cambridge, MA, 1994).
Condee, Nancy, *The Imperial Trace: Recent Russian Cinema* (Oxford, 2009).
Cooper, Frederick, *Colonialism in Question: Theory, Knowledge, History* (Berkeley, 2005).
Corten, Irina H., *Vocabulary of Soviet Society and Culture: A Selected Guide to Russian Words, Idioms, and Expressions of the Post-Stalinist Era, 1953–1991* (Durham, NC, 1992)..
Costlow, Jane, "'For the Bear to Come to Your Threshold': Human–Bear Encounters in Late Imperial Russian Writing," in Jane Costlow and Amy Nelson (eds.), *Other Animals: Beyond the Human in Russian Culture and History* (Pittsburgh, PA, 2010).
Darrow, David W., "The Politics of Numbers: Zemstvo Land Assessment and the Conceptualization of Russia's Rural Economy," *Russian Review* 59/1 (2000): 52–75.
Davies, R.W., *Crisis and Progress in the Soviet Economy, 1931–1933* (London, 1996).
Deleuze, Gilles, "Postscript on the Societies of Control," *October* 59 (1992): 3–7.
Derrida, Jacques, "Structure, Sign, and Play in the Discourse of the Human Sciences. Discussion," in Richard Macksey and Eugenio Donato (eds.), *The Structuralist Controversy: The Languages of Criticism and the Science of Man* (Baltimore, MD, 2007).
Dimenshtein, Il'ia, *Imena russkoi Latvii* (Riga, 2007).
——, *Nasha Iurmala* (Riga, 2009).
——, *Riga i rizhane 100 let nazad* (Riga, 2007).
——, *Russkaia Riga: istoricheskie ocherki* (Riga, 2002).
Dirks, Nicholas B., *Castes of Mind: Colonialism and the Making of Modern India* (Princeton, NJ, 2001).
Dobb, Maurice, *Soviet Economic Development since 1917* (London, 1948).
Dobrenko, Evgeny, and Eric Naiman (eds.), *The Landscape of Stalinism: The Art and Ideology of Soviet Space* (Seattle, WA, 2003)
Domańska, Ewa, "Obrazy PRL w perspektywie postkolonialnej. Studium przypadku," in Krzysztof Brzechczyn (ed.), *Obrazy PRL. Konceptualizacja realnego socjalizmu w Polsce* (Poznań, 2008).

Doronchenkov, Aaskold, *Emigratsiia "pervoi volny" o natsional'nykh problemakh i sud'be Rossii* (St. Petersburg, 2001).
Dosse, François, *History of Structuralism. Vol. 1: The Rising Sign, 1945–1966*, trans. Deborah Glassman (Minneapolis, MN, 1997).
Douglas, Mary, *Purity and Danger* (London, 2002).
Doyle, Michael, *Empires* (Ithaca, NY, 1986).
Dronin, Nikolai, M., *Evolyutsiya landshaftnoy kontseptsii v russkoy i sovetskoy fizicheskoy geografii (1900-e–1950-e gg.)* (Moscow, 1999).
Drozdek, Michał, *Istota sporu CENTRUM kontra ROAD* (Warsaw, 1990).
Dugin, Aleksandr, "Apokalipsis stikhii," *Elementy* 8 (1997): 56.
——, *Misterii Evrazii*, republished in *Absoliutnaia rodina* (Moscow, 1999).
Dziubenko, P.V., *D.I. Mendeleev i tamozhennyi tarif. Tamozhenno-tarifnaia politika v nauchnom nasledii D.I. Mendeleeva: Uroki dlia Rossii* (Moscow, 2003).
Egorov, Konstantin, D. (ed.), *Rayonirovanie SSSR: Sbornik materialov po rayonirovaniyu s 1917 po 1925 gg.* (Moscow and Leningrad, 1926).
Eijbergen, B., et al., *Russia: The Transport Sector*, World Bank Policy Note, 2006. http://www.worldbank.org.ru/ECA/Russia.nsf/ECADocByUnid/3447E75C1AE221EAC3256F0E00246EB9/$FILE/Transport_PN_eng.pdf. Changed September 13, 2004.
Eisenstadt, Shmuel, *Political Systems of Empires* (New York, 1963).
Epstein, Mikhail, "Russo-Soviet Topoi," in Evgeny Dobrenko and Eric Naiman (eds.), *The Landscape of Stalinism. The Art and Ideology of Soviet Space* (Seattle, WA and London, 2003).
Erasov, Boris, "O geopoliticheskom i tsivilizatsionnom ustroenii Evrazii," *Evraziia* 5 (1996): 30.
Esakov, Vasilii A., *Geografiya v Moskovskom universitete: Ocherki organizatsii, prepodavaniya, razvitiya geograficheskoy mysli (do 1917 g.)* (Moscow, 1983).
Etkind, Aleksandr, "Internal Colonization and Russian Cultural History," *Ulbandus* 7 (2003): 17–25.
——, *Internal Colonization: Russia's Imperial Experience* (Cambridge, 2011).
Evtuhov, Catherine, "The Roots of Dokuchaev's Scientific Contributions: Cadastral Soil Mapping and Agro-Environmental Issues," in Benno P. Warkentin (ed.), *Footprints in the Soil* (Amsterdam and Oxford, 2006).
Fanon, Frantz, *Wyklęty lud ziemi* (Warsaw, 1985).
Faye, Jean Pierre, and Léon Robel, *Le Cercle de Prague* (Paris, 1969).
FDJ, *Fragen und Antworten zum Zentralen Jugendobjekt "Erdgastrasse"* (Berlin, 1986).

Fedotova, Anastasiya, A., "Botaniki v Nizhegorodskoy ekspeditsii V.V. Dokuchaeva: "starye" territorii, novye zadachi," *Istoriko–biologicheskie issledovaniya / Studies in the History of Biology* 2/4 (2010): 66–83.

Figurovskii, N., *D.I. Mendeleev* (Moscow, 1961; rev. edn. 1983).

Finnegan, Diarmid, A., "The Spatial Turn: Geographical Approaches in the History of Science," *Journal of the History of Biology* 41 (2008): 369–88.

Fitzpatrick, Sheila, *The Cultural Front: Power and Culture in Revolutionary Russia* (Ithaca, NY, 1992).

Fiut, Aleksander, "Polonizacja? Kolonizacja?," *Teksty Drugie* 6 (2003): 150–56.

Florovskii, Georgii, "Evraziiskii soblazn," *Sovremennye zapiski* 34 (1928): 312–46.

Foucault, Michel, "Questions on Geography," in *Power/Knowledge: Selected Interviews and other Writings 1972–1977*, trans. Colin Gordon (New York, 1980).

——, *Discipline and Punish: The Birth of the Prison* (New York, 1977).

——, *Power/Knowledge: Selected Interviews and other Writings, 1972–1977* (New York, 1980).

French, R.A., "Geography and Geographers in the Soviet Union," *The Geographical Journal* 127/2 (1961): 159–65

Fyodorov, Nikolai, "Filosofiia obshchego dela," in Svetlana Semenova and Anastasiia Gacheva (eds.), *Russkii kosmizm. Antologiia filosofskoi mysli* (Moscow, 1993).

Fyren, "Vem har mördat Rysslands tsarer?" *Fyren* 8–9 (1921).

Galaburdy, V.G., et al. (eds.), *Edinaya transportnaya sistema* (Moscow, 1996).

Galan, František W., *Historic Structures: The Prague School Project, 1928–1946* (Austin, TX, 1984).

Gasparov, Boris, "The Ideological Principles of Prague School Phonology," in Krystyna Pomorska, E. Chodakowska, H. McLean, and B. Vine (eds.), *Language, Poetry and Poetics. The Generation of the 1890s: Jakobson, Trubetzkoy, Majakovskij. Proceedings of the First Roman Jakobson Colloquium, at the Massachusetts Institute of Technology, October 5–6, 1984* (New York and Berlin, 1987).

Gatrell, Peter, *The Tsarist Economy, 1850–1917* (London, 1986).

Generalov, Sergei, "Investments into Russian Logistics and Transportation Industry," *Round Table at the 23nd German Logistics Congress, October 18–20, 2006, Berlin*.

Geppert, Alexander C.T., "Space *Personae*: Cosmopolitan Networks of Peripheral Knowledge," *Journal of Modern European History* 2 (2008): 262–85.

Gerasimov, Ilya, Jan Kusber, and Alexander Semyonov, *Empire Speaks Out: Languages of Rationalization and Self-description in the Russian Empire* (Leiden, 2009).

Gerasimov, Ilya, Sergey Glebov, Aleksandr Kaplunovski, Marina Mogil'ner, and Aleksandr Semyonov, "In Search of a New Imperial History," *Ab Imperio* 1 (2005): 33–56.

Gerasimov, Ilya, Sergei Glebov, Aleksandr Kaplunovskii, Marina Mogil'ner, and Aleksandr Semenov (eds.), *Novaia imperskaia istoriia postsovetskogo prostanstva* (Kazan, 2004).

Gerovitch, Slava, "Creating Memories: Myth, Identity, and Culture in the Russian Space Age," in Dick, Steven J. (ed.), *Remembering the Space Age* (Washington, DC, 2008).

Gestwa, Klaus, und Johannes Grützmacher, "Infrastrukturen," in Stefan Plaggenborg (ed.), *Handbuch der Geschichte Rußlands. Band 5: 1945–1991. Vom Ende des Zweiten Weltkriegs bis zum Zusammenbruch der Sowjetunion* (Stuttgart, 2003).

Glebov, Sergei, "A Life with Imperial Dreams: Petr Nikolaevich Savitsky, Eurasianism, and the Invention of 'Structuralist' Geography," *Ab Imperio* 3 (2005): 299–329.

——, "Granitsy imperii kak granitsy moderna: Antikolonial"naia ritorika i teoriia kul"turnykh tipov v evraziistve," *Ab Imperio* 2 (2003): 267–92.

——, "Whither Eurasia: History of Ideas in Imperial Situation," in *Ab Imperio* 8/2 (2008): 345–76.

Glenny, Michael, and Norman Stone (eds.), *The Other Russia* (London, 1990).

Glymour, Clark, "Social Science and Social Physics," *Behavioural Science* 28/2 (1983): 126–34.

Go, Julian, "The "New" Sociology of Empire and Colonialism," *Sociology Compass* 3 (2009): 1–14.

Gordin, Michael D., "Making Newtons: Mendeleev, Metrology and the Chemical Ether," *Ambix* 45/2 (1998): 96–115.

——, "Measure of All the Russias: Metrology and Governance in the Russian Empire," *Kritika* 4/4 (2003): 783–815.

——, *A Well-ordered Thing: Dmitrii Mendeleev and the Shadow of the Periodic Table* (New York, 2004).

Gorsuch, Anne E., and Diane P. Koenker (eds.), *Turizm: The Russian and East European Tourist under Capitalism and Socialism* (Ithaca, NY, 2006).

Gorsuch, Anne E., ""There is no place like home": Soviet Tourism in Late Stalinism," *Slavic Review* 62/4 (Winter 2003): 760–85.

Gottmann, Jean (ed.), *Centre and Periphery: Spatial Variation in Politics* (Beverly Hills, CA, 1980).

Grant, Bruce, *The Captive and the Gift: Cultural Histories of Sovereignty in Russia and the Caucasus* (Ithaca, NY, 2009).

Gritsai, O.V., G.V. Ioffe, and A.I. Treivish, *Tsentr i periferiia v regional'nom razvitii* (Moscow, 1991).

Guha, Ranajit, *Dominance without Hegemony: History and Power in Colonial India* (Cambridge, MA, 1997).

Gumilev, Lev, *Etnogenez i biosfera zemli* (Leningrad, 1990).

——, *Drevniaia Rus' i Velikaia step'* (Moscow, 1989).

——, "Etnogenez i biosfera zemli," *Priroda i chelovek* 4 (1992): 59.

——, "Izmenenie klimata i migratsii kochevnikov," *Priroda* 4 (1972): 44–52.

——, "Menia nazyvaiut evraziitsem," *Nash sovremennik*, 1 (1991): 24.

——, "Pis'mo v redaktsiiu 'Voprosov filosofii,'" *Voprosy filosofii* 5 (1989): 161.

——, *Ritmy Evrazii. Epokhi i tsivilizatsii* (Moscow, 1993).

Gurvich, G.Ts., *Ekonomicheskie vzgliady D.I. Mendeleeva* (Minsk, 1951).

Guseinov, Rashad, "Logistic Market of Russia Today and Tomorrow," *Round Table at the 23nd German Logistics Congress, Berlin, October 18–20, 2006.*

Gyidel, Erenst, "Ob 'ukrainofil'stve' Georgiia Vernadskogo, ili variatsiia na temu natsional'nykh i gosudarstvennykh loial'nostei," *Ab Imperio* 4 (2006): 329–46.

Hagemeister, Michael, "The Conquest of Space and the Bliss of the Atoms: Konstantin Tsiolkovskii, in Eva Maurer, Julia Richers, Monica Rüthers, and Carmen Scheide (eds.), *Soviet Space Culture: Cosmic Enthusiasm in Socialist Societies* (New York, 2011).

Hall, Cargill R., *Lunar Impact: A History of Project Ranger* (Washington, DC, 1977).

Halle, Morris, "On the Origins of Distinctive Features," in Morris Halle (ed.), *Roman Jakobson: What He Taught Us* (Columbus, OH, 1983).

Halperin, Charles, "George Vernadsky, Eurasianism, the Mongols, and Russia," *Slavic Review* 41/3 (1982): 477–93.

——, "Russia and the Steppe: George Vernadsky and Eurasianism," *Forschungen zur Osteropäischen Geschichte* 36 (1985): 55–194.

Harford, James J., "Korolev's Triple Play: *Sputniks* 1, 2, and 3," in Roger D. Launius (ed.), *Reconsidering* Sputnik: *Forty Years since the Soviet Satellite* (Amsterdam, 2000).

Harley, J.B, "Maps, Knowledge, and Power," in Denis Cosgrove and Stephen Daniels (eds.), *The Iconography of Landscape: Essays on the Symbolic Representation, Design and Use of Past Environments* (Cambridge, 1989).

Harvey, David, *Spaces of Global Capitalism: A Theory of Uneven Geographical Development* (London, 2006).

Hayashi, Tadayuki (ed.), *The Construction and Deconstruction of National Histories in Slavic Eurasia* (Sapporo, 2003).

Hechter, Michael, *Internal Colonialism: The Celtic Fringe in British National Development* (Berkeley, CA, 1975).

Hill, Fiona, and Clifford Gaddy, *The Siberian Curse: How Communist Planners Left Russia Out in the Cold* (Washington, DC, 2003).
Hirsch, Francine, "Towards an Empire of Nations: Border-making and the Formation of Soviet National Identities," *The Russian Review* 59/2 (2000): 201–26.
——, *Empire of Nations: Ethnographic Knowledge and the Making of the Soviet Union* (Ithaca, NY, 2005).
Hoffman, David L., and Yanni Kotsonis (eds.), *Russian Modernity: Politics, Knowledge, Practices* (New York, 2000).
Holenstein, Elmar, *Roman Jakobson's Approach to Language: Phenomenological Structuralism* (Bloomington, IN, 1976).
Holquist, Peter, "Dilemmas of Progressive Administrator: Baron Boris Nolde," *Kritika: Explorations in Russian and Eurasian History* 7/2 (Spring 2006): 241–73.
Hooson, David, "The Development of Geography in Pre-Soviet Russia," *Annals of Association of American Geographers* 58/2 (1968): 250–72.
——, "Methodological Clashes in Moscow, 1962," *Annals of the Association of American Geographers* 52 (1962): 469–75.
——, "Some Recent Developments in the Content and Theory of Soviet Geography," *Annals of the Association of American Geographers* 49 (1959): 73–82.
Hosking, Geoffrey, "First through Kiev," *Times Literary Supplement*, June 1, 2007.
Howe, Stephen (ed.), *The New Imperial Histories Reader* (London, 2010).
Il'in, Viktor, and Aleksandr Panarin (eds.), *Rossiia: opyt natsional'no-gosudarstvennoi ideologii* (Moscow, 1994).
Immonen, Kari, *Ryssästä saa puhua... Neuvostoliitto suomalaisessa julkisuudessa ja kirjat julkisuuden muotona 1918–1939* (Keuruu, 1987).
Ionidi, P.P., *Mirovozrenie D.I. Mendeleeva* (Moscow, 1959).
Ionov, Igor, "Puti razvitiia tsivilizatsionnogo soznaniia v Evrazii i problema evraziistva," *Tsivilizatsii* 6 (2004): 158–87.
Ivanov, Viacheslav V., "Buria nad N'iufaundlendom. Iz vospominanii o Romane Jakobsone," in Henryk Baran et al. (eds.), *Roman Jakobson. Teksty, dokumenty, issledovania* (Moscow, 1999).
Jakobson, Roman (ed.), *K kharakteristike evraziiskogo iazykovogo soiuza* (Paris, 1931).
——, *N.S. Trubetzkoy's Letters and Notes* (The Hague, 1975).
——, "O teorii fonologicheskikh iazykovykh souiuzov mezhdu iazykami," in Roman Jakobson, *Izbrannye raboty* (Moscow, 1985).

———, "Sur la théorie des afinities phonologiques entre les langues," in N.S. Troubetzkoy, *Principes de phonologie* (Paris, 1949).

———, "Über die heutigen Voraussetzungen der russischen Slavistik," *Slavische Rundschau* 1 (1929): 629–46.

Jakobson, Roman, and Krystyna Pomorska, *Besedy* (Jerusalem, 1982).

Jałowiecki, Bohdan, "Przestrzeń historyczna, regionalizm, regionalizacja," in Bohdan Jałowiecki (ed.), *Oblicza polskich regionów* (Warsaw, 1996).

Jangfeldt, Bengt, "Roman Jakobson v Shvetsii, 1940–1941," in Henryk Baran et al. (eds.), *Roman Jakobson. Teksty, dokumenty, issledovania* (Moscow, 1999).

Janion, Maria, *Niesamowita słowiańszczyzna. Fantazmaty literatury* (Cracow, 2006).

———, "Polska między Wschodem a Zachodem," *Teksty Drugie* 6 (2003): 131–49.

Jaruzelski, Wojciech, "Towarzysze, głosujcie 'za'. Z Wojciechem Jaruzelskim rozmawiał Jarosław Kurski," *Gazeta Wyborcz*, May 30, 2003, p. 16.

Jasny, Naum, "A Soviet Planner—V.G. Groman," *Russian Review* 13/1 (1954): 52–8.

———, *Soviet Economists of the Twenties: Names to be Remembered* (Cambridge, 1972).

Jessop, Bob, "The Regulation Approach, Governance, and Post-Fordism: Alternative Perspectives on Economic and Political Change?," *Economy and Society* 24/3 (1995): 307–33.

Kaika, Maria, "Dams as Symbols of Modernization: The Urbanization of Nature between Geographical Imagination and Materiality," *Annals of the Association of American Geographers* 96/2 (2006): 276–301.

Kalashnikova, T.M., *Ekonomicheskoe raionirovanie* (Moscow, 1982).

Kangas, Anni, "Beyond Russophobia: A Practice-based Interpretation of Finnish–Russian/Soviet Relations," *Cooperation & Conflict* 46 (2011): 40–59.

———, *The Knight, the Beast and the Treasure: A Semiotic Inquiry into the Finnish Political Imaginary on Russia, 1918–1930s* (Tampere, 2007).

Karimov, Aleksei, E., *Dokuda topor i sokha hodili: Ocherki istorii zemel'nogo i lesnogo kadastra v Rossii XVI – nachala XX v.* (Moscow, 2007).

Karlov, Viktor, "Evraziiskaia ideia i russkii natsionalizm: Po povodu stat'i V.A. Shnirel'mana 'Evraziiskaia ideia i teoriia kul'tury,'" *Etnograficheskoe obozrenie* 1 (1997): 1–13.

———, "O evraziistve, natsionalizme i priemakh nauchnoi polemiki," *Etnograficheskoe obozrenie* 2 (1997): 125–32.

Katkov, George, "Lenin as Philosopher," in Leonard Shapiro and Peter Reddaway (eds.), *Lenin: The Man, the Theorist, the Leader; a Reappraisal* (London, 1967).

———, "Masaryk's Guests" in Michael Glenny and Norman Stone (eds.), *The Other Russia* (London, 1990).

Katzman, Julie E., "The Euro-Siberian Gas Pipeline Row: A Study in Community Development," *Millennium—Journal of International Studies* 17/1 (1988): 25–41.

Keller, Karl, "Zur Frage der Rassenstatistik," *Allgemeines Statistisches Archiv* 24 (1934/35): 129–42.

Kern, Stephen, *The Culture of Time and Space, 1880–1918* (Cambridge, MA, 1986).

Khachaturian, Valeriia, "Istoki i rozhdenie evraziiskoi idei," *Tsivilizatsii* 6 (2004): 187–201.

Khamraev, Viktor, "'Deputaty pozabotilis' o 'edinom sovetskom narode,'" *Kommersant*, March 3, 2006, www.kommersant.ru (accessed November 3, 2010).

Khou, Stiven [Stephen Howe], "Iz Manchestera v Moskvu," *Ab Imperio* 1 (2011): 89–90.

Kirzhaev, S.N., and V.A. Tolstov (eds.), *Iz epistoliarnogo naslediia V.I. Vernadskogo: Pis'ma ukrainskim akademikam N.P. Vasilenko i A.A. Bogomol'tsu* (Kiev, 1991).

Klinge, Matti, *Keisarin Suomi* (Espoo, 1987).

Knorr Cetina, Karin, Theodore R. Schatzki, and Eike von Savigny (eds.), *The Practice Turn in Contemporary Theory* (London:, 2000).

Kochanowicz, Jacek, "Polish Kingdom: Periphery as a Leader," paper prepared for the XIV International Economic History Congress in Helsinki, Finland, August 21–25, 2006.

Kohonen, Iina, "The Space Race and Soviet Utopian Thinking," in David Bell and Martin Parker (eds.), *Space Travel and Culture: From* Apollo *to Space Tourism* (Oxford, 2009).

Kojevnikov, Aleksei, "The Great War, the Russian Civil War, and the Invention of Big Science," *Science in Context* 15/2 (2002): 239–75.

Kol'tsov, Anatolii, V., *Sozdanie I deyatel'nost' Komissii po izucheniyu estestvennykh proizvoditel'nykh sil Rossii* (St. Petersburg, 1999).

Kolstø, Pål, *Nation-building and Ethnic Integration in Post-Soviet Societies: An Investigation of Latvia and Kazakstan* (Boulder, CO, 1999).

Konstantinov, O.A., "Ekonomicheskaia geografiia v Geograficheskom Obshchestve za sorok let Sovetskoi vlasti," *Geograficheskii sbornik* 11 (1957): 131–87.

Korek, Janusz, "In the Face of the West and the East: The Formation of the Identity of the Polish Intelligentsia after the End of World War II," in Janusz

Korek (ed.), *From Sovietology to Postcoloniality: Poland and Ukraine in the Postcolonial Perspective* (Stockholm, 2007).
Koshik, Viktor, *Konstantin Leont'ev, razmyślenija na slavjanskuju temu* (Moscow, 1997).
Kotkin, Stephen, "Mongol Commonwealth? Exchange and Governance across the Post-Mongol Space," *Kritika* 8/3 (2007): 487–532.
Kozikov, I.A., "Proekt modernizatsii Rossii D.I. Mendeleeva," *Sotsial'no-gumanitarnye znaniia* 5 (2009): 235–55.
Krasnodębski, Zdzisław, "Adam Mickiewicz' politische Theologie," in Zdzisław Krasnodębski and Stefan Garsztecki (eds.), *Sendung und Dichtung: Adam Mickiewicz in Europa* (Hamburg, 2002).
Krivulin, Viktor, "Zaveshchanie v zanaveshennom zerkale (K tretei godovshchine Iosifa Brodskogo)," *Novoe literaturnoe obozrenie* 37(1999): 382–6.
Królikowski, Jeremi, "Metamorfozy polityki imperialnej—od soboru na placu Saskim do Pałacu Kultury i Nauki," in Dariusz Konstrantynów and Piotr Paszkiewicz (eds.), *Kultura i polityka. Wpływ polityki rusyfikcji na kulturę zachodnich rubieży Imperium Rosyjskiego (1772–1915)* (Warsaw, 1994).
Kronenfeld, Daniel, A., "The Effects of Interethnic Contact on Ethnic Identity: Evidence from Latvia," *Post-Soviet Affairs* 21/3 (2005): 247–77.
——, "Ethnogenesis without the Entrepreneurs: The Emergence of a Baltic Russian Identity in Latvia," in Karsten Brüggemann (ed.), *Narva und die Ostseeregion* (Narva, 2004).
Kudriatseva, T.S., and Shekhter, M.E., *D.I. Mendeleev i ugol'naia promyshlennost'* (Moscow, 1952).
Kukulin, Il'ia, "Fotografiia vnutrennosti kofeinoi chashki," *Novoe literaturnoe obozrenie* 54 (2002): 262–82.
Kundera, Milan, "Die Weltliteratur," *The New Yorker*, January 8, 2007, pp. 28–35.
——, "The Tragedy of Central Europe," *The New York Review of Books*, 31/7 (April 26, 1984): 33–8.
Kuzio, Taras, "History, Memory and Nation Building in the Post-Soviet Colonial Space," *Nationalities Papers* 30/2 (2002); 241–64.
Laitin, David, *Identity in Formation: The Russian-speaking Populations in the Near Abroad* (Ithaca, NY, 1998).
Lamanskii, Vladimir, *Geopolitika panslavizma* (Moscow, 2010).
Laruelle, Marlène (ed.), *Sovremennye interpretatsii russkogo natsionalizma* (Moscow, 2008).
——, "A-t-il existé des précurseurs au mouvement eurasiste? L'obsession russe pour l'Asie au tournant du siècle," *Revue des études slaves* 3–4 (2004): 437–54.
——, *Ideologiia russkogo evraziistva ili mysli o velichii imperii* (Moscow, 2004).

——, *L'Idéologie eurasiste russe, ou comment penser l'empire* (Paris, 1999), trans. into Russian as: *Ideologiia russkogo evraziistva. Mysli o velichii imperii* (Moscow, 2004).

——, *Russian Eurasianism: An Ideology of Empire* (Washington, DC, 2008).

Lass, Andrew, "Poetry and Reality: Roman O. Jakobson and Claude Lévi-Strauss," in Christofer Benfey and Karen Remmler (eds.), *Artists, Intellectuals and World War II: The Pontigny Encounters at Mount Holyoke College, 1942–1944* (Amherst, MA, 2006).

Lavrov, S.B., and B.B. Rodoman (eds.), *Geografiia i khoziaistvo. Vyp. 3. Tsentrograficheskii metod v ekonomicheskoi geografii* (Leningrad, 1989).

Lazda, Paulis, "The Museum of the Occupation of Latvia: Why? What? How?" trans. Baiba Kaugara, introduction to *Latvijas Okup*āciajas Muzejs: Latvija zem Padomju Savienības *un nacionālsociālistiskās Vācijas varas 1940–1991* (Riga, 2008).

Lehár, Bohumil, *Rada vzájemné hospodářské pomoci: sborník dokumentů o vývoji a činnosti RVHP (1978–1983)*, (Prague, 1984).

Lévi-Strauss, Claude, "L'Analyse structurale en linguistique et en anthropologie," in *Word* 1 (1945): 1–2.

——, *De près et de loin* (Paris, 1988).

——, *Structural Anthropology*, vol. 2 (New York, 1963).

——, "Structure et dialectique," in *For Roman Jakobson: Essays on the Occasion of His Sixtieth Birthday* (The Hague, 1956).

Liberman, Anatoly, "N.S. Trubetzkoy and His Works on History and Culture" in Trubetzkoy, Nikolai, *The Legacy of Genghis Khan* (Ann Arbor, MI, 1991).

Lie, John, *Modern Peoplehood* (Cambridge, 2004).

Lincoln, Bruce W., *Nikolai Miliutin: An Enlightened Russian Bureaucrat* (Newtonville, MA, 1977).

——, *In the Vanguard of Reform: Russia's Enlightened Bureaucrats, 1825–1861* (DeKalb, IL, 1982).

Lisiak, Agata A., "The Making of (Post)colonial Cities in Central Europe," *CLCWeb: Comparative Literature and Culture* 12/1 (2010).

——, "Disposable and Usable Pasts in Central European Cities," *Culture Unbound. Journal of Current Cultural Research* 1(2009): 431–52.

Liuks, Leonid, "Zametki o "revoliutsionno-traditsionalistskoi" kul'turnoi modeli 'evraziitsev,'" *Forum noveishei vostochnoevropeiskoi istorii i kul'tury* 2 (2004): 1–17.

Livingstone, David, N., "The Spaces of Knowledge: Contributions towards an Historical Geography of Science," *Environment and Planning. D. Society and Space* 13 (1995): 5–34.

———, *Putting Science in Its Place: Geographies of Scientific Knowledge* (Chicago, IL, 2003).
———, *The Geographical Tradition: Episodes in the History of a Contested Enterprise* (Oxford, 1992).
Lotman, Yuri M., *Universe of the Mind: A Semiotic Theory of Culture* (Bloomington, IN, 1990).
Lovejoy, Arthur O., *The Great Chain of Being: A Study of the History of an Idea* (Cambridge, 1936).
Luelsdorff, Philip A. (ed.), *The Prague School of Structural and Functional Linguistics: A Short Introduction* (Philadelphia, PA, 1994).
Lukashevich, Stephen, *Konstantin Leontev: A Study in Russian "Heroic Vitalism"* (New York, 1967).
Luks, Leonid, "Evraziistvo i konservativnaia revoliutsiia. Soblazn antizapadnichestva v Rossii i Germanii," *Voprosy filosofii* 6 (1996): 57–69.
Makarov, Vladimir, "'Pax Rossica'. Istoriia evraziiskogo dvizheniia i sud'by evraziitsev," *Voprosy filosofii* 9 (2006): 102–17.
Makarov, Vladimir, and A.M. Matveeva, "Geosofiia P.N. Savitskogo: mezhdu ideologiei i naukoi," *Voprosy filosofii* 2 (2007): 123–35.
Maksimov, Semyon A., *P.I. Brounov—osnovopolozhnik sel'skokhozyaystvennoy meteorologii* (Leningrad, 1952).
Malmstad, John, "K istorii 'evraziistva': M. Gorky and P.P. Suvchinsky," *Diaspora: Novye materialy* 1 (2001): 327–47.
Marks, Steven, *Road to Power: The Trans-Siberian Railroad and the Colonization of Asian Russia, 1850–1917* (Ithaca, NY, 1991).
Martin, Terry, *The Affirmative Action Empire: Nations and Nationalism in the Soviet Union, 1923–1939* (Ithaca, NY and London, 2001).
Masłowska, Dorota, *Snow White and Russian Red* (New York, 2005).
———, *Wojna polsko-ruska pod flagą biało-czerwoną* (Warsaw, 2002).
McKinney, William M., "Carey, Spencer and Modern Geography," *The Professional Geographer* 20/2 (1968): 103–6.
Meinander, Henrik, *Suomen historia: linjat, rakenteet, käännekohdat* (Helsinki, 2006).
Mendeleev, D.I. (1884), "O vozbuzhdenii promyshlennogo razvitiia v Rossii," in *Sochineniia* (Leningrad and Moscow, 1950), vol. 20.
Mespoulet, Martine, "Une lutte pour l'autonomie professionnelle: Etre statisticien dans une région au début des années 1920," *Le Mouvement social* 196 (2001): 63–88.
———, "Statisticiens des zemstva: Formation d'une nouvelle profession intellectuelle en Russie dans la période prérévolutionnaire (1880–1917). Le cas de Saratov," *Cahiers du monde russe* 40/4 (1999): 573–624.

Miller, Aleksei, *"Ukrainskii vopros" v politike vlastei i russkom obshchestvennom mnenii (vtoraia polovina XIX v.)* (St. Petersburg, 2000).

———, "Dualizm identichnostei na Ukraine," *Otechestvennye zapiski*, 1 (2007): 84–96.

———, *Imperiia Romanovykh i natsionalizm* (Moscow, 2006).

———, *The Romanov Empire and Nationalism: Essays in the Methodology of Imperial Research* (Budapest and New York, 2008).

Miodushevskaia, Tamara, "'Karta russkogo': novyi proekt pomoshchi sootechestvennikov za rubezhem," *Argumenty i fakty* (June 8, 2008), www.aif.ru/society/article/19172 (accessed April 9, 2012).

Mitin, Ivan, and Dmitry Zamiatin (eds.), *Voobrazhenie prostranstva, prostranstvo voobrazheniia* (Moscow, 2009).

Mladenstev, M.N., and V.E. Tishchenko, V.E., *Dmitrii Ivanovich Mendeleev, ego zhizn' i deiatel'nost'* (Moscow, 1938).

———, and Tishchenko, V.E., *Dmitrii Ivanovich Mendeleev, ego zhizn' i deiatel'nost: universitetskii period, 1861–1890* (Moscow, 1993).

Mogil'ner, Marina, *Homo imperii. Istoriya fizicheskoy antropologii v Rossii (konets XIX – nachalo XX v.)* (Moscow, 2008).

Moore, David Chioni, "Colonialism, Eurasianism, Orientalism: N.S. Trubetzkoy's Russian Vision," *Slavic and East European Journal* 41/2 (1997): 321–40.

———, "Is the Post- in Postcolonial the Post- in Post-Soviet? Toward a Global Postcolonial Critique," *PMLA* 116/1 (2001): 111–28.

Mosse, W.E., *Economic History of Russia, 1856–1914* (London, 1996).

Naiman, Anatolii, "'Hava Nagila'—A Memoir," *Commentary*, July 1997: 34.

Naiman, Eric, "Introduction," in Evgeny Dobrenko and Eric Naiman (eds.), *The Landscape of Stalinism: The Art and Ideology of Soviet Space* (Seattle, WA and London, 2003).

Nikitin, Nikolai, P., "Dorevolyutsionnaya ekonomicheskaya geografiya," in Nikolai N. Baranskii (ed.), "A.F. Fortunatov," in Nikolai N. Baranskii (ed.), *Ekonomicheskaya geografiya v SSSR. Istoriya i sovremennoye razvitiye* (Moscow, 1965), pp. 405–10.

———, *Ekonomicheskaya geografiya v SSSR. Istoriya i sovremennoye razvitiye* (Moscow, 1965), pp. 9–53.

Nowak, Andrzej, "Between Imperial Temptation and Anti-imperial Function in East European Politics: Poland from the Eighteen to Twenty-first Century," in Kimitaka Matsuzato (ed.), *Emerging Meso-areas in the Former Socialist Countries: Histories Revived Or Improvised* (Hokkaido, 2005).

——, "From Empire Builder to Empire Breaker, or There and Back Again: History and Memory of Poland's Role in Eastern European Politics," *Ab Imperio* 1 (2004): 255–89.

——, *History and Geopolitics: A Contest for Eastern Europe* (Warsaw, 2008).

"O gosudarstvennoi politike RF v otnoshenii sootechestvennikov za rubezhom," www.consultant.ru/online/base/?req=doc;base=LAW;n=89945#p36 (accessed December 4, 2010).

"O proekte" on the site "Novaia literaturnaia karta Rossii," www.litkarta.ru/about/ (accessed December 12, 2010).

Ollus, Simon-Erik, and Heli Simola, *Russia in the Finnish Economy* (Helsinki, 2006), http://www.sitra.fi/julkaisut/. Changed 12 June 2006.

Ordway, Frederick I., "Dreams of Space Travel from Antiquity to Verne," in *Blueprint for Space: Science Fiction to Science Fact* (Washington, DC and London, 1992).

Owen, Thomas, "The Russian Industrial Society and Tsarist Economic Policy, 1867–1905," *Journal of Economic History* 45/3 (1985): 587–606.

Pagden, Anthony, *Lords of All the World: Ideologies of Empire in Spain, Britain, and France c. 1500–c. 1800* (New Haven, CT, 1995).

Palmgren, Raoul, *Suur linja Arwidssonista vallankumouksellisiin sosialisteihin: kansallisia tutkielmia* (Helsinki, 1948).

Panarin, Aleksandr, *Rossiia v tsiklakh mirovoi istorii* (Moscow, 1995).

——, *Pravoslavnaia tsivilizatsiia v global'nom mire* (Moscow, 2002).

"Papildināta—Zatlers: jāvienojas, ka vārds 'okupants' vairs netiks lietots," *Diena* (December 7, 2009), www.diena.lv/sabiedriba/politika/papildinata-zatlers-javienojas-ka-vards-okupants-vairs-netiks-lietots-702651 (accessed August 23, 2011).

Parkhomenko, V.I., *D.I. Mendeleev i russkoe neftianoe delo* (Moscow, 1957).

Peet, Richard, "Reinventing Marxist Geography: A Critique of Bassin," *Annals of the Association of American Geographers* 83/1 (1993): 156–60.

Pertsik, Evgenii, N., *K.I. Arsen"ev I ego raboty po raionirovaniyu Rossii* (Moscow, 1960).

Plamper, Jan, "Foucault's Gulag," *Kritika* 3/2 (2002): 255–80.

Platt, Kevin M.F., "Okkupatsiia protiv kolonizatsii: kak istorii postsovetskoi Latvii pomogaet provintsializirovat' Evropu," in Dirk Uffel'man [Uffelmann], Aleksandr Etkind and Il'ia Kukulin (eds.), *Vnutrenniaia kolonizatsiia Rossii* (Moscow, 2012).

——, "Poetry in the Cloud: An Experiment, Results, and n+1 Hypotheses," *World Literature Today* 85/6 (November 2011): 40–43.

——, "Okkupatsiia vs. kolonizatsiia: istoriia, postcolonial'nost' i geograficheskaia identichnost', sluchai Latvii," *Neprikosnovennyi zapas* 71 (2010): 49–62.

Plokhii, Serhii, *Unmaking Imperial Russia: Mykhailo Hrushevsky and the Writing of Ukrainian History* (Toronto, 2005).
Polian, Pavel M., "Ocherk istorii Russkoi tsentrografii," in S.B. Lavrov and B.B. Rodoman (eds.), *Geografiia i khoziaistvo. Vyp. 3. Tsentrograficheskii metod v ekonomicheskoi geografii* (Leningrad, 1989).
——, *Veniamin Petrovich Semenov-Tyan-Shanskiy, 1870–1949* (Moscow, 1989).
Poppe, Nikolaus, "The Economic and Cultural Development of Siberia," in George Katkov, Erwin Oberländer, Nikolaus Poppe, and Georg von Rauch (eds.), *Russia Enters the Twentieth Century* (London, 1973).
Porter, Philip W., "What is the point of Minimum Aggregate Travel?," *Annals of the Association of American Geographers* 53/2 (1963): 224–32.
Poulsen, Thomas M., "Centrography in Russian Geography," *Annals of the Association of American Geographers* 49/3 (1959): 326–7.
Pratt, Mary Louise, *Imperial Eyes: Travel Writing and Transculturation* (London, 1994).
Procyk, Anna, *Russian Nationalism and Ukraine: The Nationality Policy of the Volunteer Army during the Civil War* (Edmonton and Toronto, 1995).
Prokhanov, Aleksandr, "Kosmizm-leninism," *Pravda*, 16/857 (April 21, 2010), http://www.zavtra.ru/cgi/veil/data/zavtra/10/857/11.html
Pursiainen, Christer, *Russia between Integration and Protectionism: International Road Transport, Ports, and the Forestry Sector* (Stockholm, 2007).
Pynnöniemi, Katri, "In Celebration of Monumentalism: Transport Modernization in Russia," in Markku Kangaspuro and Jeremy Smith (eds.), *Modernization in Russia since 1900,* (Helsinki, 2006).
Pynnöniemi, Katri, *New Road, New Life, New Russia: International Transport Corridors at the Conjunction of Geography and Politics in Russia* (Tampere, 2008).
Pynnöniemi, Katri, *The Political Constraints on Russia's Economic Development: The Visionary Zeal of Technological Modernization and Its Critics* (Helsinki, 2010).
Riabchuk, Mykola, "Culture and Cultural Politics in Ukraine: A Post-Colonial Perspective," in Taras Kuzio and Paul J. D'Anieri (eds.), *Dilemmas of State-led Nation Building in Ukraine* (Westport, CT, 2002).
Riasanovsky, Nicholas. "The Emergence of Eurasianism," *California Slavic Studies* 4 (1967): 39–72.
——, *Russian Identities: A Historical Survey* (Oxford, 2005).
Rikhter, Gavriil D., "D.I. Rikhter," in Nikolai N. Baranskii (ed.), *Ekonomicheskaya geografiya v SSSR. Istoriya i sovremennoye razvitiye* (Moscow, 1965), 411–18.

Rodchenko, Aleksandr, *Inventarnaia Prostranstvo*, ed. Peter Noever (Vienna, 2006).
Rokicki, Konrad, and Sławomir Stępień (eds.), *W objęciach Wielkiego Brata: Sowieci w Polsce, 1944–1993* (Warsaw, 2009).
Rokkan, Stein, *State Formation, Nation-building, and Mass Politics in Europe. The Theory of Stein Rokkan. Based on His Collected Works, Selected and Rearanged by Peter Flora with Stein Kuhnle and Derek Urwin* (Oxford and New York, 1999).
——, "Territories, Centres, and Peripheries: Toward a Geoethnic-Geoeconomic-Geopolitical Model of Differentiation within Western Europe," in J. Gottmann (ed.), *Centre and Periphery: Spatial Variations in Politics* (Beverly Hills, CA and London, 1980).
Ruder, Cynthia A., *Making History for Stalin: The Story of the Belomor Canal* (Gainesville, FL, 1998).
Rudy, Stephen, *Roman Jakobson, 1896–1982: A Complete Bibliography of His Writings* (New York, 1990).
Ruggie, John G., "Territoriality and Beyond: Problematizing Modernity in International Relations," *International Organization* 47/1 (1993): 139–74.
Russkaia, ukrainskaia i belorusskaia emigratsiia v Chekhoslovakii mezhdu dvumia mirovymi voinami. Rezul'taty i perspektivy issledovanii. Fondy Slavians Pomorska *koi biblioteki i prazhskikh arkhivov* (Prague, 1995).
Russkie Latvii: Katalog Vystavki (Riga, 2008).
Rutland, Peter, *The Myth of the Plan. Lessons of Soviet Planning Experience* (London and Melbourne, 1985).
Rybakov, Sergei, "Istorik-evraziets Georgii Vernadsky," *Voprosy istorii* 11 (2006): 157–64.
Rybczynski, Witold, "Shipping News," *The New York Review of Books* 53/13 (2006): 9–11.
Said, Edward W., *Culture and Imperialism* (New York, 1994).
——, *Orientalism* (New York, 1978).
——, *Orientalizm* (Warsaw, 1991).
Sakwa, Richard, *Putin: Russia's Choice* (London, 2004).
Salischeva, Nadeshda, "Main Institutions of the Russian Administrative Law in the Sphere of the Administration of Economy," in Juha Tolonen and Boris Topornin (eds.), *Legal Foundations of Russian Economy* (Helsinki, 2000).
Sassen, Saskia, *Losing Control: Sovereignty in an Age of Globalization* (New York, 1996).
Savickij, Petr, "Les Problèmes de la géographie linguistique du point de vue du géographe," *Travaux du Cercle linguistique de Prague* 1 (1929): 145–56.
Savický, Ivan, *Praga i zarubezhnaia Rossiia* (Prague, 2002).

Savitskii, Petr, "Evropa i Evraziia. (Po povodu broshiury kn. N.S. Trubetskogo 'Evropa i Chelovechestvo')," *Russkaia mysl* 2 (1921).
——, "Geograficheskie i geopoliticheskie osnovy evraziistva," *Kontinent Evraziia* (Moscow, 1997).
——, *Geograficheskie osobennosti Rossii* (Pargue, 1927)
——, "Introduction," in *Tridtsatye Gody. Utverzhdeniia evraziitsev* (Prague, 1931).
——, *O zadachakh kochevnikovedeniia. Pochemu skify i gunny dolzhny byt' interesny dlia russkogo?* (Prague, 1928).
——, "Pod'em' i 'depressia' v drevnerusskoi istorii," *Evraziiskaia Khronika* 9 (1935): 65–100.
——, *Rossiia—osobyi geograficheskii mir* (Prague, 1927).
Schlögel, Karl, *Im Raume lesen wir die Zeit:* Über Zivilisationsgeschichte und Geopolitik (Munich, 2003).
Scott, James C., *Seeing Like a State: How Certain Schemes to Improve the Human Condition Have Failed* (New Haven, CT, 1998).
Semenova, Svetlana, and Anastasiia Gacheva (eds.), *Russkii kosmizm. Antologiia filosofskoi mysli* (Moscow, 1993).
Serapionova, Elena. *Rossiiskaia emigratsiia v Chekhoslovatskoi respublike* (20–30 gody) (Moscow, 1995).
Sergeev, A., and A. Tiurin, "Istoriia poluvekovoi druzhby," *Minuvshee: Istoricheskii almanakh* 18 (1995): 353–425.
Sériot, Patrick, *Discours sur la langue et souffrance identitaire en Europe centrale et orientale* (Paris, 2010).
——, *Struktura i Tselostonost'. Ob intellektual'nykh istokakh strukturalizma v Tsentral'noi i Vostochnoi Evrope, 1920–1930* (Moscow, 2001).
——, *Structure et totalité: Les Origines intellectuelles du structuralisme en Europe centrale et orientale* (Paris, 1999).
Sewell, William H., Jr., "The Concept(s) of Culture," in Victoria E. Bonnell and Lynn Hunt (eds.), *Beyond the Cultural Turn: New Directions in the Study of Society and Culture* (Berkeley, CA, 1999).
Seymor, M. Lipset, and Stein Rokkan (eds.), *Party Systems and Voter Alignments: Cross-National Perspectives* (New York, 1967).
Shaw, Denis J.B., and Oldfield, Jonathan D., "Landscape Science: A Russian Geographical Tradition," *Annals of the Association of American Geographers* 97/1 (2007): 111–26.
Shaw, Denis J.B., and Oldfield, Jonathan D., "Scientific, Institutional and Personal Rivalries among Soviet Geographers in the Late Stalin Era," *Europe-Asia Studies* 60/8 (2008): 1397–418.
Shevtsova, Lilia, *Putin's Russia* (Washington, DC, 2005).

Shirinskii-Shikhmatov, Yuri, "Rossiiskii natsional-maksimalizm i evraziistvo," *Evraziiskii sbornik* 6 (1929): 28.

Shlapentokh, Dmitry (ed.), *Russia between East and West: Scholarly Debates on Eurasianism* (Leiden, 2007).

Shnirel'man, Viktor, "Evraziiskaia ideia i teoriia kul'tury," *Etnograficheskoe obozrenie* 4 (1996): 3–16.

——, "Evraziistvo i natsional'nyi vopros. Vmesto otveta V.V. Karlovu," *Etnograficheskoe obozrenie* 2 (1997): 112–25.

——, "The Fate of Empires and Eurasian Federalism: A Discussion between the Eurasianists and Their Opponents in the 1920s," *Inner Asia* 3 (2001): 153–73.

——, *Who Gets the Past? Competition for Ancestors among Non-Russian Intellectuals in Russia* (Washington, DC, 1996).

Siddiqi, Asif A., "Cosmic Contradictions: Enthusiasm and Secrecy in the Soviet Space Program," in James T. Andrews and Asif A. Siddiqi (eds.), *Into the Cosmos: Space Exploration and Soviet Culture* (Pittsburgh, PA, 2011).

Simonov, Yurii G., *Isoriya geografii v Moskovskom universitete: sobytiya i lyudi*, vol. 1. *Nachala universitetskoy geografii: Anuchinskiy etap v ee razvitii, pervye geography-professionaly v Moskovskom universitete* (Moscow, 2008).

Siukonen, Jyrki, *Uplifted Spirits, Earthbound Machines: Studies on Artists and the Dream of Flight 1900–1935* (Helsinki, 2001).

Skórczewski, Dariusz, "Dlaczego Polska powinna upomnieć się o swoją postkolonialność?," *Znak* 628 (2007): 145–53.

——, "Modern Polish Literature: Through a Postcolonial Lens—The Case of Pawel Huelle's Castorp," *Sarmatian Review* 26/3 (2006): 12–29.

——, "Postkolonialna Polska—projekt (nie)możliwy," *Teksty Drugie* 1/2 (2006): 100–112.

Sladek, Zdenek, "Prag: Das 'russische Oxford,'" in Karl Schlögel (ed.), *Der Grosse Exodus. Die russische Emigration und ihre Zentren 1917 bis 1941* (Munich, 1994).

Slezkine, Yuri, "The USSR as a Communal Apartment, or How a Socialist State Promoted Ethnic Particularism," *Slavic Review* 53/2 (1994): 414–52.

Smith, Gerald S., *D.S. Mirsky: A Russian-English Life, 1890–1939* (Oxford, 2000).

Smith, Jeremy (ed.), *Beyond the Limits: The Concept of Space in Russian History and Culture* (Helsinki, 1999).

Smith-Peter, Susan, "Defining the Russian People: Konstantin Arsen'ev and Russian Statistics Before 1861" *History of Science* 45/1 (2007): 47–64.

Soja, Edward, D., "Taking Space Personally," in Barney Warf and Santa Arias (eds.), *The Spatial Turn: Interdisciplinary Perspectives* (London, 2009), pp. 11–45.

———, *Postmodern Geographies: The Reassertion of Space in Critical Social Theory* (London, 2nd edn. 2011).
Solovey, Tatyana, D., "Institutsionalizatsiya nauki v Moskovskom universitete (Zhizn' i trudy D.N. Anuchina v kontekste epokhi)," *Vestnik Moskovskogo universiteta, seriya 8: istoriya* 6 (2003): 3–38.
Sowa, Jan, *Fantomowe ciało króla: Peryferyjne zmagania z nowoczesną formą* (Cracow, 2011).
Stallybrass, Peter, and Allon White, *The Politics and Poetics of Transgression* (Ithaca, NY, 1986).
Stanziani, Alessandro, "Statisticiens, zemstva et Etat dans la Russie des années 1880," *Cahiers du Monde russe et soviétique* 32/4 (1991): 445–67.
Steinmetz, George (ed.), *Sociology and Empire: Colonial Studies and the Imperial Entanglements of a Discipline* (Durham, NC, 2012).
Stites, Richard, *Revolutionary Dreams: Utopian Vision and Experimental Life in the Russian Revolution* (Oxford and New York, 1989).
Stoler, Ann Laura, "Considerations on Imperial Comparisons," in Ilya Gerasimov, Jan Kusber, and Aleksandr Semyonov (eds.), *Empire Speaks Out: Languages of Rationalization and Self-description in the Russian Empire* (Boston, MA and Leiden, 2009).
Sukhova, Natalia G., *Razvitie predstavleniy o prirodnom territorial'nom komplekse v russkoy geografii* (Leningrad, 1981).
Sunderland, Willard, "The 'Colonization Question': Visions of Colonization in Late Imperial Russia," *Jahrbücher für Geschichte Osteuropas* n.s. 48/2 (2000): 210–32.
Suny, Ronald Grigor, "The Empire Strikes Out: Imperial Russia, 'National' Identity and Theories of Empire," in Ronald Grigor Suny and Terry Martin (eds.), *A State of Nations: Empire and Nation-making in the Age of Lenin and Stalin* (New York, 2001).
Suny, Ronald Grigor, and Terry Martin (eds.), "Introduction," in Ronald Grigor Suny and Terry Martin (eds.), *A State of Nations: Empire and Nation-making in the Age of Lenin and Stalin* (Oxford, 2001).
Sviatopolk-Mirski, Dmitrii. "Natsional'nosti SSSR," *Evraziia* 22 (Paris, 1929).
Swyngedouw, Eric, "Modernity and Hybridity: Nature, Regeneracionismo, and the Production of the Spanish Waterscape, 1890–1930," *Annals of the Association of American Geographers* 89/3 (1999): 443–65.
Sytnik, Konstantin, Stepan Stoiko, and Elena Apanovich, *V.I. Vernadsky: Zhizn' i deiatel'nost' na Ukraine* (Kiev, 1984).
Szmeja, Maria, *Niemcy? Polacy? Ślązacy!* (Cracow, 2000).
Tagirova, Nailya, "Mapping the Empire's Economic Regions from the Nineteenth to the Early Twentieth Century," in Jane Burbank, Mark von

Hagen, and Anatolyi Remnev (eds.), *Russian Empire: Space, People, Power, 1700–1930* (Bloomington, IN, 2007), 125–38.
Taubman, William, *Khrushchev: The Man and His Era* (London, 2003).
Taylor, Brandon, "Photo-power: Painting and Iconicity in the First Five-Year Plan," in Dawn Ades et al. (eds.), *Art and Power: Europe under the Dictators, 1930–1945* (London, 1995).
Tazbir, Janusz, "O czym się pisać nie godziło," *Gazeta Wyborcza*, 27 December, 2003, pp. 16–17.
Thompson, Ewa, *Imperial Knowledge. Russian Literature and Colonialism* (Westport, CT, 2000).
——, "Postkolonialne refleksje," *Porównania* 5 (2008): 113–26.
——, "Praising the Kaczynski brothers," *Washington Times*, April 8, 2007.
——, "Said a sprawa polska. Przeciwko kulturowej bezsilności peryferii," *Europa*, 29 June 2005, p. 11.
——, *Trubadurzy imperium. Literatura rosyjska i kolonializm* (Cracow, 2000).
——, "W kolejce po aprobatę. Kolonialna mentalność polskich elit," *Europa*, September 15, 2007.
Timofejev, Sergei, and Viestarts Gailītis, "Krievu orbīta," *Diena*, July 19, 2008, www.diena.lv/izklaide/krievu-orbita-615862 (accessed March 24, 2012).
Todes, Daniel P., *Darwin without Malthus: The Struggle for Existence in Russian Evolutionary Thought* (New York, 1989).
Todorova, Maria, *Imagining the Balkans* (New York, 1997).
Tolstoy, Nikita, "N.S. Trubetskoi i evraziistvo," in N.S. Trubetskoi, *Istoriia. Kul'tura. Iazyk* (Moscow, 1995).
Toman, Jindrich, *The Magic of a Common Language: Jakobson, Mathesius, Trubetzkoy, and the Prague Linguistic Circle* (Cambridge, 1995).
Toporov, V., "Nikolai Sergeevich Trubetskoi—ucheny, myslitel,' chelovek," in *Pis'ma i zametki N.S. Trubetskogo* (Moscow, 2004); Russian edn.: *N.S. Trubetzkoy's Letters and Notes*, prepared for publication by Roman Jakobson with the assistance of H. Baran, O. Ronen, and Martha Taylor (The Hague and Paris, 1975).
Treadgold, Donald W., *The Great Siberian Migration: Government and Peasant in Resettlement from Emancipation to the First World War* (Princeton, NJ, 1957).
Troitskii, Evgenii, *Opora na sobstvennye sily i neokolonializm. Russko-slavianskii vzgliad* (Moscow, 1999).
——, *Russkaia etnopolitologiia i natsional'naia ideia* (Moscow, 2006).
——, *Russkii narod v poiskakh pravdy i organizovannosti (988–1996)* (Moscow, 1996).

———, (ed.), *Istoriko-metodologicheskie aspekty izucheniia russkoi (pravoslavno-slavianskoi) tsivilizatsii* (Moscow, 1994).

——— (ed.), *Russkaia ideia, slavianskii kosmizm i stantsiia Mir* (Kaluga, 2000).

——— (ed.), *Slavianstvo v usloviiakh globalizatsii i informatsionnoi voiny* (Moscow, 2002).

Trubetskoi, Nikolai, *Istoriia. Kul'tura. Iazyk* (Moscow, 1995).

———, "Mysli ob indo-evropeiskoi probleme," *Voprosy iazykoznaniia* 1 (1958): 65–77.

———, "O turanskom elemente v russkoi kul'ture," *Istoriia, kul'tura, yazyk* (Moscow, 1995).

———, "Obshcheevraziiskii natsionalizm," *Evraziiskaia khronika* 9 (1927): 24–31.

———, "Vavilonskaia Bashnia i smeshenie iazykov," *Evraziiskii Vremennik* 3 (1923): 116–17.

———, *The Legacy of Genghis Khan* (Ann Arbor, MI, 1991).

Tsymburskii, Vadim, *Ostrov Rossii. Geopoliticheskie i khronologicheskie raboty* (Moscow, 2007).

Turoma, Sanna, *Brodsky Abroad, Empire, Tourism, Nostalgia* (Madison, NJ, 2010).

Tynianov, Yurii, "Viktoru Shklovskomu: Literaturnyi fakt," in E.A. Toddes, A.P. Chudakov and M.O. Chudakova (eds.), *Poetika. Istoria literatury. Kino* (Moscow, 1977).

"Uikend v Rige: neskol'ko vpechatlenii," www.kuda.ua/lenta/38 (accessed December 11, 2010).

Ulivi, Paolo, and David Harland, *Lunar Exploration: Human Pioneers and Robotic Surveyors* (Berlin, Heidelberg, and New York, 2004).

"Vācijā iznācis tekstgrupas Orbīta dzejas krājums," *Kulturasdiena* (March 23, 2012), /www.diena.lv/kd/literatura/vacija-iznacis-tekstgrupas-orbita-dzejas-krajums-13938501 (accessed March 24, 2012).

Valenius, Johanna, *Undressing the Maid: Gender, Sexuality and the Body in the Construction of the Finnish Nation* (Helsinki, 2004).

Vandalkovskaia, Margarita, *Istoricheskaia nauka rossiiskoi emigratsii: "Evraziiskii soblazn."* (Moscow, 1997.

Vernadskii, Georgii, *Opyt istorii Evrazii* (Berlin, 1934).

———, "Protiv solntsa. Rasprostranenie russkogo gosudarstva k Vostoku," *Russkaja mysl'* 1 (1914): 4.

Vernadskii, Vladimir, *Biosfera i noosfera* (Moscow, 2002).

Vernadskii, Georgii, "Gosudarevy sluzhilye i promyshlennye liudi v Vostochnoi Sibiri XVII veka," *Zhurnal Ministerstva narodnogo prosveshcheniia* 4 (1915): 352–4.

———, *Nachertanie russkoi istorii* (Prague, 1927).

———, "O dvizhenii russkikh na vostok," *Nauchno-istoricheskii zhurnal*, 2 (1914).
———, *Opyt istorii Evrazii* (Berlin, 1934).
———, "Protiv solntsa: Rasprostranenie russkogo gosudarstva k vostoku," *Russkaia mysl* 1 (1914): 56–79.
———, *Russkaia istoriografia* (Moscow, 1998).
Vernadskii, Vladimir, *Dnevniki. 1917–1921. Ianvar' 1920 – mart 1921* (Kiev, 1997).
———, *Dnevniki. 1917–1921. Oktriabr' 1917 – ianvar' 1920* (Kiev, 1994).
———, *Dnevniki. Mart 1921 – avgust 1925* (Moscow, 1998).
———, *Dnevniki. 1926–1934* (Moscow, 2001).
———, *Dnevniki. 1935–1941* (2 vols., Moscow, 2006).
———, *Publitsisticheskie stat'i* (Moscow, 1996).
Vinokur, Grigorii, "Moskovskii Lingvisticheskii Kruzhok," *Nauchnye Izvestiia Akademicheskogo Tsentra Narkomprosa*, vol. 2 (1922).
Vishnevskii, Anatolii, *Serp i rubl': Konservativnaia modernizatsiia v SSSR* (Moscow, 1998).
Vladimirskii, Boris, and N.A. Temuryants, *Solar Activity and the Biosphere: Heliobiology. From A.L. Chizhevsky to the Present* (Moscow, 1999).
von Hagen, Mark, "Empires, Borderlands, and Diasporas: Eurasia as Anti-paradigm for the Post-Soviet Era," *American Historical Review* 109 (April 2004): 445–68.
———, "Writing the History of Russia as Empire: The Perspective of Federalism," in Catherine Evtuhov, Boris Gasparov, Aleksandr Ospovat, and Mark von Hagen (eds.), *Kazan, Moscow, St. Petersburg: Multiple Faces of the Russian Empire* (Moscow, 1997).
———, "Empires, Borderlands, and Diasporas: Eurasia as Anti-paradigm for the Post-Soviet Era," *The American Historical Review* 109/2 (2004): 445–68.
von Laue, Theodore H., *Sergei Witte and the Industrialization of Russia* (New York and London, 1963).
Vucinich, Alexander, *Darwin in Russian Thought* (Berkeley, CA, 1988).
———, "Mendeleev's Views on Science and Society," *Isis* 58/3 (1967): 342–51.
Wajda, Andrzej, "Świątynia Józefa Stalina czy zabytek sowieckiej architektury z lat 50.?," *Gazeta.pl Warszawa*, 6 May 2008.
Waldstein, Maxim, "Observing Imperium: A Postcolonial Reading of Ryszard Kapuscinskis Account of Soviet and Post-Soviet Russia," *Social Identities* 8/3 (2002): 481–99.
———, "Russifying Estonia? Iurii Lotman and the Politics of Language and Culture in Soviet Estonia," *Kritika: Explorations in Russian and Eurasian History* 8/3 (2007): 561–96.
———, *The Soviet Empire of Signs* (Saarbrücken, 2008).

———, "Theorizing the Second World: Challenges and Prospects," *Ab Imperio* 1 (2010): 98–118.
Walicki, Andrzej, *Philosophy and Romantic Nationalism: The Case of Poland* (Oxford and New York, 1982).
Warf, Barney, and Santa Arias (eds.), *The Spatial Turn: Interdisciplinary Perspectives* (London, 2009).
Warner, Marina, *Monuments and Maidens: Allegory of the Female Form* (London, 1996).
Weber, Eugen, *Peasants into Frenchmen: The Modernization of Rural France, 1870–1914* (Stanford, CA, 1976).
Weber, Max, *Economy and Society: An Outline of Interpretative Sociology* (Berkeley, CA< 1968).
Weiner, Douglas R., *Models of Nature: Ecology, Conservation, and Cultural Revolution in Soviet Russia* (Bloomington, IN and Indianapolis, IN 1988).
Werness, Hope B., *The Continuum Encyclopedia of Animal Symbolism in Art* (New York, 2004).
Westwood, J.N., *Soviet Railways to Russian Railways* (New York, 2002).
Whitaker, Ewen A., *Mapping and Naming the Moon: A History of Lunar Cartography and Nomenclature* (Cambridge, 1999).
Widdis, Emma, "To Explore or to Conquer?: Mobile Perspectives on the Soviet Cultural Revolution," in Evgeny Dobrenko and Eric Naiman (eds.), *The Landscape of Stalinism: The Art and Ideology of Soviet Space* (Seattle, WA and London, 2003).
———, *Visions of a New Land. Soviet Film from the Revolution to the Second World War* (New Haven, CT and London, 2003).
Wiederkehr, Stefan, "Eurasianism as a Reaction to Pan-Turkism," in Dmitry Shlapentokh (ed.), *Russia between East and West: Scholarly Debates on Eurasianism* (Leiden, 2007).
Wilson, Kathleen (ed.), *A New Imperial History: Culture, Modernity, and Identity* (Cambridge, 2004).
Wittgenstein, Ludwig, *Philosophical Investigations* (Oxford, 2001).
Wolff, Larry, *Inventing Eastern Europe: The Map of Civilization on the Mind of the Enlightenment* (Stanford, CA, 1994).
Wortman, Richard S., *Scenarios of Power: Myth and Ceremony in Russian Monarchy. Vol. 1: From Peter the Great to the Death of Nicholas I* (Princeton, NJ, 1995).
Young, Glennys, "Fetishizing the Soviet Collapse: Historical Rupture and the Historiography of (Early) Soviet Socialism," *Russian Review* 66 (January 2007): 95–122.

Young, Robert, *Colonial Desire: Hybridity in Theory, Culture, and Race* (London, 1995).
Yurchak, Alexei, *Everything Was Forever, Until It Was No More* (Princeton, NJ, 2006).
——,"Post-Post-Communist Sincerity: Pioneers, Cosmonauts and Other Soviet Heroes Born Today," in Thomas Lahusen and Peter Solomon (eds.), *What Is Soviet Now? Identities, Legacies, Memories* (Berlin, 2008)
Zaleski, Eugène, *Planning for Economic Growth in the Soviet Union, 1918–1932* (Chapel Hill, NC, 1971).
Zapol, Aleksandr (ed. and trans.), *Za nas/ Par mums* (Riga, 2009).
—— (ed.), *Latyshkaia/russkaia poeziia: stikhi latyshkikh poetov, napisannye na russkom iazyke* (Riga, 2011).
Zarycki, Tomasz, "History and Regional Development: A Controversy over the "Right" Interpretation of the Role of History in the Development of the Polish Regions," *Geoforum* 38 (2007): 485–93.
——, "The Persistence of the Borders on the Territory of Poland," in Olga Brednikova and Viktor Voronkov (eds.), *Nomadic Borders / Кочующие Границы. Proceedings of the seminar held in Narva, November, 13–15.1998* (St. Petersburg, 1999).
——, "Politics in the Periphery: Political Cleavages in Poland Interpreted in Their Historical and International Context," *Europe-Asia Studies* 52/5 (2000): 851–73.
——, "The Power of the Intelligentsia: The Rywin Affair and the Challenge of Applying the Concept of Cultural Capital to Analyze Poland's elites," *Theory and Society* 38/6 (2009): 613–48.
——, "Uses of Russia: The Role of Russia in the Modern Polish National Identity," *East European Politics and Societies* 18/4 (2004): 595–627.
Zdziechowski, M., *Wpływy rosyjskie na duszę polską* (Cracow, 1920).
Zolberg, Aristide R., "The Ecole Libre at the New School, 1941–1946," *Social Research* 65/4 (1998): 921–51.
Zvereva, Galina, "Diskurs gosudarstvennoi natsii v sovremennoi Rossii," in Marlène Laruelle (ed.), *Sovremennye interpretatsii russkogo natsionalizma* (Moscow, 2008).
Zwierzchowski, Piotr, "Obraz Rosjan w kinie PRL," in Konrad Rokicki and Sławomir Stępień (eds.), *W objęciach Wielkiego Brata: Sowieci w Polsce, 1944–1993* (Warsaw, 2009).

Unpublished Papers and Dissertations

Almgren, Beverly, "Mendeleev: The Third Service, 1834–1882," Ph.D. diss. (Brown University, 1968).

Bräu, Richard, "Zum Erscheinen und zur Rezeption von Alfred Webers Werk 'Über den Standort der Industrien' (1909) 1926 in der Sowjetunion—eine wissenschaftshistorische Recherche," unpublished paper presented at Alfred Weber Institut für Sozial- und Staatswissenschaften, January 19, 1995 (revised January 1988).

Butorac, Mark, "From the Other Oil Field: Mendeleev, the West and the Russian Oil Industry," Ph.D. diss. (McGill University, 2001).

Granitsy, Sergei, "The Challenge of the Modern: The Eurasianist Ideology and Movement, 1920–29," Ph.D. diss. (Rutgers University, 2004).

Lewis, Cathleen S., "The Red Stuff: A History of the Public and Material Culture of Early Human Spaceflight in the U.S.S.R.," Ph.D. diss., History (George Washington University, 2008).

Stackenwalt, Francis, "The Thought and Work of Dmitrii Ivanovich Mendeleev on the Industrialization of Russia, 1867–1907," Ph.D. diss. (University of Illinois at Urbana, 1976).

Titov, Alexander, "Lev Gumilev, Ethnogenesis and Eurasianism," Ph.D. diss. (University College London, School of Slavonic and Eastern European Studies, 2005).

Index

Ab Imperio (journal) 10, 17
administrative-territorial division 111, 113, 117, 135, 155
Alekseev, Nikolai 47
Alexander I 221
Alexander II 134, 229, **230**, 238
Alexander Nevsky Orthodox Cathedral in Warsaw 211
Anderson, Benedict 7, 12, 16
Annenskii, Nikolai 142, 144, 145,
anti-semitism 36, 39, 40, 97, 98, 230
Anuchin, Dmitrii 56 152,153, 155,
Arapov, Petr 35, 46
Arctic 98, 110, 110n19, 128
Arctic Ocean 92
Armenia 6, 36, 52, 240, 252–5, 276
Around the World (journal) 240–46, 256
Arsen'ev, Konstantin 111, 137–8, 140, 147, 299, 327
Austria 38, 163, 199, 200
autocracy 85, 106, 115, 116, 132

Baer, Karl von 56–7
Bakuła, Bogusław 209
Baltic region 290
Barańska, Katarzyna 214
Baranskii, Aleksandr 155–6
Bassin, Mark 92n22
bear (symbol of) 229, 235, 236, 237
Beauvois, Daniel 210
Beissinger, Mark 219
Beissinger, Mark 9n27, 219, 249n23,
Beketov, Andrei 147
Belarus 196, 209
Belarusians 51,52, 70, 71, 81, 180, 210

Bely, Andrei 109, 254, 254n35
  Andrei Bely Prize 288n33
Berg, Lev 56–7, 153, 155
Berlin 88, 180
Bhabha, Homi 209
biosphere 87n4, 92, 93, 94n30, 95
Bitov, Andrei 240, 252–6
Black Sea 52, 149, 249
Bloch, Ernst 271, 296
Boas, Franz 53
Bodin, Jean 94
Bogatyrev, Petr 47
Bolkhovitinov, Nikolai 63, 66
Bolshevik conceptions of 118, 118n43, 132
Bolshevik Revolution 99, 193, 206, 230; *see also* October Revolution
Bolsheviks and Bolshevism 37, 65, 74, 98, 108n11, 118, 118n43, 132, 206, 220, 224, 226, 231, 233, 234, **237**
Borzov, Aleksandr 153
botanists, *see also* plant geographers 142, 145, 146, 147, 149, 150, 152
botany, *see also* plant geography 140
Bourdieu, Pierre 18, 32
Brodsky, Joseph 239, 240, 244–5, 247–9, 256
Bromberg, Iakov 47
Brounov, Pyotr 149–53
Buchowski, Michał 210–11
Bukharin Nikolai 125, 126, 127, 131
Bulgakov, Sergei 96
Burbank, Jane 10, 12, 16
Büsching, Anton Friedrich 148

cadastral surveys 21, 141–6, 148, 150, 152–4, 155, 156
capitalism 116, 128, 164, 250; *see also* print capitalism 12
cartography 251, 266
Catholic Lublin University 204
Caucasus 110, 115n31, 149, 252, 280
Cavanagh, Claire 207
Celtic mythology 214
Central Asia 138, 241, 277
Central Statistical Committee (CSC) 138, 140, 142, 154
centrality 4, 32, 54, 113, 120
  cultural 27
  geographical 93
  nested 4
centre and periphery vii, 17, 17n53, 18, 21, 27, 28, 193, 255, 271, 283, 284, 294, 295, 296; *see also* periphery
centrographical method, *see* centrography
centrography 117, 120–22, 126n66, 128–32
Charents, Yegishe 253
Chelintsev, Aleksandr 151–2
Chizhevskii, Aleksandr 95, 99, 259
Chkheidze, Konstantin 47
Chubais, Anatoli 86
CIA 201
citizenship 272, 273, 274, 274n7, 275
Civic Platform (Platforma Obywatelska, PO) 203, 213
Civil War (Finnish) 223, 235, 237, 238
Civil War (Russian) 20, 42n29, 66n19, 67, 68n28, 74n44, 87, 89, 120, 155, 225, 227
Cold War 15, 160, 250, 258, 266, 269
colonial domination, *see* domination
colonialism 2, 5–8, 13, 17, 19, 62, 192
  internal 205–6, 210 see internal colonization
  Russian 66, 198, 202, 208
  Soviet 198, 208, 214
COMECON 159, 162
Commission fort the Study of the Natural Resources (KEPS) 154, 155
communism 24, 63, 85, 99, 116, 120, 121, 160, 168, 249–51
  and Finland 228–41
  and Poland 191–215
  Soviet communism 209
compatriots abroad 273, 274, 284, 295
Congress Kingdom 210
Congress of Vienna 199
constructivism 118n43
Cooper, Frederick 10, 12, 16
Correlations, method of 49
cosmism 21, 26, 87n4, 99, 259
cosmos 85, 86, 87, 87n4, 93, 95, 96, 97, 99, 100, 101, 258, 263,
Crimea 74, 89, 148, 201
CSC, *see* Central Statistical Committee
Cuban Crisis 250
cultural belonging 275
cultural capital 199
cultural identity, *see* identity
culture
  post-imperial 278–85
  Russian 26–7, 74n44, 76, 97, 200–201, 239, 274–5, 285–96
  Russian culture in Latvia 271–96
  Soviet 26, 118, 205, 240, 260
Custine, Astolphe marquis de 211

Danilevskii, Nikolai 55–7
decentering 2–5, 11, 19–20, 26–7, 86, 101, 173, 245–6
  of modernity 8; *see* de-provincialization (of Russia, continental empires); *see* provincializing Europe
decolonization 85, 276

Democratic Left Alliance (Sojusz Lewicy Demokratycznej, SLD) 194, 200, 203
Denikin, Anton 89
Denim, M. 244–5
de-provincialization (of Russia, continental empires) 2, 5, 9, 19
Derrida, Jacques 4
destiny 21, 79, 85, 86, 87, 90, 93, 98, 100, 101, 194
determinism 21, 86, 87, 93, 94, 108n22, 127
    geographical determinism 21, 86–7, 101
Dimenshtein, Il'ia 285, 286, 289
Dokuchaev, Vasilii 42–5, 56, 140–56
Domańska, Ewa 198, 208–10, 214
domination
    colonial 8, 57
    imperial 6–7, 13, 223
    Soviet 192–3, 199, 203, 213, 215, 281–2
    Russian 192, 211, 213
    Western 213–15, 219, 214–15
Donets 110
Dostoevskii, Fedor Mikhailovich 55
Douglas, Mary 222
Doyle, Michael 6, 7, 13
Dugin, Aleksandr, 21, 98–9

eagle (symbol of) 25, 221, 223, 224, 235
Eastern Germany 159, *see also* GDR
Eastern Slavs 81, 214
economic development 8, 105, 111, 138, 187, 189, 200
economic geographers 136
economic planning 127, 136
education 118, 166, 170, 186, 198, 245, 273, 282, 284
emigration 46, 86, 87, 88, 240
empire ii, vii–viii, 1–22, 24–7, 33, 60, 69, 82–3, 85–92, 96–7, 99–101, 107, 109–13, 115–16, 123, 137–40, 146, 148, 151–4, 156, 200, 205–6, 211, 219–25, 227–33, 238–40, 248, 249–51, 255–6, 261, 266, 276–7, 280, 286
    British 6n15, 99, 267
    as a "category of practice" 3, 25, 219
    colonial 1, 2, 6–10, 12, 13, 18–19, 82, 192–3, 203, 209
    communist 1
    continental 6–7, 10, 12, 19, 22, 98
    definitions of 6–8, 12–13, 219–20
    Habsburg 13, 36, 85, 156
    liberal 86
    maritime vii
    modern vii, 7, 10
    multiethnic 66, 70, 82
    Ottoman 6, 85
    Roman 214, 248, 267
    Romanov 82
    Russian 10–13, 19–20, 25, 31, 52, 60–61, 65–70, 77–9, 82–3, 85–101, 111–12, 115–16, 135, 137–9, 146–7, 154–6, 198, 205, 209, 220–21, 225–9, 232, 234, 249, 254, 280, 283–4
    Soviet Union as 10, 18, 193, 204, 206, 219–25, 228, 238, 250, 280
    style of 85
    Western 10, 198
empire-building 7, 251
England 236, 250
Estonia 50, 247, 252–5, 279n17, 289n35
ethnicity 148–9, 253n31, 277
    multi(poly)ethnicity 10, 65, 83
Etkind, Alexander 205–6, 210
Eurasia (newspaper) 46
Eurasia 1, 11, 19, 23, 31, 32, 35, 41–54, 56–61, 64–6, 78, 83, 89, 97, 175, 178, 287

Eurasianism 11, 19–21, 29–59, 61–83, 85–99, 189, 239n2; *see also* neo-Eurasianism
  and anti-colonialism 32, 78n54
  and geography 43–44, 49, 78, 80–81, 87, 89–91, 94
  and linguistics 32, 33, 36, 45, 47, 48–54, 55n79, 58
  and modernity 32, 33, 41, 47
  and positivism 34n11
  and "Russian science" 42– 7
  and spatiality, *see* spatiality
  and structuralism 32, 33, 47–60
  as a political movement 35, 40, 46, 59
  leaders of 35, 40
Eurasian language union 47–9, 52–3
Eurasian space, *see* space
European Union 197, 203, 278
Evolution, regular 56

Fanon, Frantz 192
Far North, *see* Arctic
federalism 20
FES, *see* Free Economic Society
Finland 25, 51, 178, 178n9, 179, 219–38, 254,
Fiut, Aleksander 210,
Five-Year Plan 124, 126, 127, 129, 131n81, 261, 269n37
Florenskii, Pavel 96
Fortunatov, Aleksei 140–41, 146–7, 149–52
Foucault, Michel 4, 14, 16, 161, 161–2, 253
France 17, 35, 250
Frank, Sergei 185, 186–9
Free Economic Society (FES) 140, 141, 143, 144, 146, 147, 153, 154
FRG (Federal Republic of Germany) 163, *see also* West Germany
Fukuyama, Francis 96

Fyodorov, Nikolai 55, 87n4, 88, 96, 99, 100, 259

Gasparov, Boris 60
Gazeta Wyborcza (newspaper) 212
Gdańsk shipyard 195
GDR (German Democratic Republic) 159, 163, **165**–71; *see also* Eastern Germany
Genis, Aleksandr 240, 249–51, 256
geographical determinism, *see* determinism
geography
  cultural 27, 135, 286, 294
  economic 122, 127, 131, 135, 141, 199
  geographical knowledge 21, 103
  physical 78, 133, 135, 136, 141, 149, 150, 153, 154, 226
  plant 147, 149, 150, 152, 153
  Russian 136–54
  Soviet 25, 135–7, 140, 154, 155, 156
Geopolitics 21, 22, 23, 24, 47, 61, 62, 65, 76, 82n64, 90, 96, 98, 131, 134, 161, 161n6, 164, 166, 171, 184, 189, 191, 195, 272, 289
Georgia 80, 252
geosophy 90
German geographical tradition 141, 154
German Statistical Society 129
German Statistical Society 129
German University in Prague 38
Germans 43, 214
Germany 44, 88, 131, 159, 163, 171, 177, 214, 278, 289n35
Giedroyć, Jerzy 196–7
Gomberg, Evgenii 279, 279n17, 282
Gorbachev, Mikhail 194
Gosplan 120, 121, 122, 124, 126, 128, 129, 129n75, 155
Grand Duchy (of Finland) 25, 220, 222, 226

Great Britain 205, 286
Great Russians 63, 66, 70, 71, 76, 77n50, 81
Grigor'ev, Aleksandr 155
Guha, Ranajit 13
Gulag 95, 161n6, 281
Gumilev, Lev 21, 87, 92–6
    concept of territory 94

Halperin, Charles 67
Harvey, David 4
Hechter, Michael 205
Herder, Johann Gottfried 94
Hettner, Alfred 154
historiography 15
    Eurasianist 20, 93
    European 85
    German 214
    Polish 197, 208,
    Russian 63, 64, 66
    Western 85
Holy Roman Empire 214; *see also* empire
Homo-Sovieticus 200, 211
Howe, Stephen 5, 37
hybridity 5, 8–9, 11, 20, 27, 294
    postcolonial 8
    Russia's 11, 14

identity
    anticommunist 193
    cultural 3, 254, 279n17, 280, 294
    ethnic 273, 274, 275, 277n13, 294
    Eurasian 82
    European 281
    Finnish 221
    hybrid 21, 71–3
    imperial 13, 135, 252, 255
    Latvian 282n23
    national 1, 21, 39, 63, 65–72, 86, 135, 195, 221, 249–55, 277n11
    Polish 195, 196, 198, 203, 210, 215
    political 3, 13, 25, 92, 277
    problems of 293
    Russian 27, 74, 88–9, 99, 132, 251, 254, 256, 273, 277, 279n17–280, 296
    social 288n32, 292
    Soviet 25, 240–41, 246–7, 251–6, 276
    spatial 26, 132, 240–41, 251, 256
Il'in, Vladimir 47, 97
immigration 273
imperial contact zone viii, 277
imperial domination, *see* domination
imperial expansion 2, 9n26, 224, 238
imperial experience vii, 3, 14, 19, 221
imperial formation vii, viii, 2, 3n9, 10, 16, 24, 223, 225, 238
imperial identity, *see* identity
imperial power viii, 192, 228, 233, *see also* empire
imperial situation vii, 3, 5, 10, 14, 17, 21, 25, 33, 58, 256
imperial space, *see* space
imperial spatiality, *see* spatiality
imperialism vii, 1, 2, 5n14, 6, 16, 41, 130, 191–215, 266
    cultural 41
    epistemological 89
    Russian 198, 206, 209
    Soviet 191
    Western (European) 41, 89, 198
industrialization 116, 127, 136, 243
industry 106, **112**, 148, 152, 163, 181, 182, 243, 258
    energy 23, 110, 159–63
Institute for National Remembrance (IPN) 200
Intelligentsia 39, 70–72, 198, 201, 205, 210, 239, 249, 252, 256
interface periphery, *see* periphery
internal colonization 8, 205
International Astronomical Union 266, 270

International Geographical Union 122, 130
International Transport Corridor 173, 174, 175, 183, 186, 187, 188, 189, 190,
Internationalism 22, 159, 162, 164, 166, 172
IPN, see Institute for National Remembrance
Ireland 214
Irkutsk 244, 247
Isto, Eetu 221, **222**, 223
Italy 163, 250

Jakobson, Roman 20, 31–60, 68n26, 78n52
Jałowiecki, Bohdan 210
Janion, Maria 207, 209, 214
Japan 241, 256
Jaruzelski, Wojciech 194, 197
Jew/ish 36, 37, 40, 47, 97–99, 195, 230, 275, 276, 278, 279, 289; see also anti-semitism
John Paul II 196
Joliot-Curie, Frédéric 265

Kaczyński, Jarosław 204
Kalinin, Mikhail 245
Kaliningrad 247, 283, 286
Karsavin, Lev 88
Katyń Massacre 195
Kazakhstan 247
KEPS, see Commission fort the Study of the Natural Resources
Khanin, Semyon 275, 287, 292, 293
Khara-Dava, Erzhen 47
Khrushchev, Nikita 26, 240, 241, 243, 258, 259, 259n5, 262, 268, 270
Kozyrev, Nikolai 93
Krasnov, Andrei 152, 155
Kremlin 23, 194, 249
Kresy 209–10, 214

Krivulin, Viktor 256
Królikowski, Jeremi 211–12
Kruber, Aleksandr 153
kul'turnost 279, 280n18
Kultura (monthly) 196–7
Kulyabka-Koretskii Nikolai 147, 149, 150–51
Kwaśniewski, Aleksander 197

Lamanskii, Vladimir 88
language-game 25, 220, 221, 223, 227, 229, 230, 233, 234, 235, 236, 237, 238; see also Wittgenstein, Ludwig
Latvia 24, 26, 27, 50, 178n7, 210, 271–96
Law and Justice (Prawo i Sprawiedliwość, PiS) 203–4, 212
Le Roy, Edouard 93n27
Lefebvre, Henri 4
Lenin, Vladimir 47, 108, 118, 232–5, 270
Leningrad 75, 92, 121, 126, 130, 131, 247, 248, 249, 254, 255, 256, 291n37
Leningrad Polytechnic Institute 126
Leont'ev, Konstantin 56, 88
lion (symbol of) 225
Lipset, Seymor 193
Lisiak, Agata Anna 212
Lithuania 50, 68, 149, 178n9, 196, 203, 207–8, 210, 248–9
Little Russians 70
Lomonosov, Mikhail 86, 265
London 197, 283
London government, see Polish government in exile
Lotman, Yuri (Iurii) 17, 18, 279, 289
Luna program 26, 259, 261, 268

macrocosmos 88

maiden (symbol of) 25, 221, 223, 226, 232, 233
maps and mapping (*see* Cartography)
martial law (in Poland) 195, 197
Marxism 46, 108n12
Masłowska, Dorota 214–15
materialist versus idealist conceptions of 21, 108, 117–18, 132, 133
Mayakovskii, Vladimir 36, 40
Mendeleev, D.M. 21, 22, 105–34
  Eurasianism of 107, 113, 133
  evolutionism of 105, 115, 121, 132, 133
  interest in centralities 112, 112n25, 132
  new cartographic projection of 113
  spatial conception of 21, 106–16, 132–4
messianism 11, 21, 86, 98, 99, 100, 101
metropole vs. colony viii, 5–9, 11, 16–17, 22, 24, 85, 156, 198, 220, 229, 238, 249, 254–5
Mickiewicz, Adam 195
migratory workers (gastarbeiters) 273
Mikhailov, Nikolai 241–3
Miller, Alexei 10, 36
Ministry of Agriculture (Russian) 146, 150, 151, 154
Ministry of State Domains (Russian) 139, 148, 150, 156
Mirsky, D. S. (Dmitrii Petrovich Sviatopolk-Mirskii, prince) 39
MLC, *see* Moscow Linguistic Circle
mobility 14, 26, 161, 162, 172, 245, 246
modernity 2, 3, 5, 6, 8, 13, 14, 19, 32, 33, 36–7, 47, 51, 105–34, 163, 280
modernization 10, 13, 14, 21, 23, 25, 105, 106, 107, 107n7, 111, 111n21, 116, 129, 133, 134, 163n11, 174, 174n3, 175, 177, 180–84, 186, 189, 243, 244, 245, 246, 256
Montesquieu 86, 94
Moore, David Chioni 202
Moreino, Sergei 288
Moscow 24, 27, 36, 37, 63, 68, 72, 73, 74n44, 85, 89, 91, 96, 98, 100, 115, 131, 146, 151, 153, 155, 174, 175, 176, 178, 180, 185, 189, 192, 194, 200, 211, 223, 234, 235, 242, 246, 247, 257, 259, 282n22, 283, 284, 286, 287n30, 288n33, 289, 291, 292, 293, 295,
Moscow Linguistic Circle (MLC) 36, 37
Moscow the Third Rome 249
Moscow University 36, 72, 152
Mount Ararat 253
Murmansk 241
Muscovy 249, 264, 266
Museum of the Occupation, Riga 281, 281n21

narodnichestvo 205
national space, *see* space
nationalism 1, 6, 8, 10, 11, 12, 20, 24, 27, 36, 68n28, 82, 83, 83n68, 106, 119, 133
  ethnic 70, 77n50, 82, 273, 277n11
  dissident 86
  Eurasian 41, 65, 79, 80
  Latvian 27
  methodological 6, 10, 11
  Polish 206, 208
  Russian 20, 62n6, 71, 76, 77n50, 86, 96, 99, 100, 101, 206
  Ukrainian 70, 71, 77n50
nation-building 2, 6, 7, 14, 245, 279
nationhood 7, 13, 25, 221, 255
naturalists, *see also* botanists, plant geographers, soil scientists 140, 141, 143, 144–51, 154, 156

Nazi Germany 195
"near abroad" 85, 86, 271, 275, 277, 284, 295n43
neo-Eurasianism 21, 87, 96, 99, 239n2,
nested oppositions 4, 18, 22, 24, 173
New Alexandria Institute of Agriculture and Forestry in Pulawy 146, 151, 153
new imperial histories 4–9
New Literary Map of Russia 286–8, 295
new spatial histories 14–15
Nizhnii Novgorod 141–7, 152
    Nizhnii Novgorod and Poltava expeditions 141–7, 152, 156
NKVD 117n40
noncitizens 272, 273, 284,
Novorossiiskii University in Odessa 152
Nowak, Andrzej 206–7

occupation 267, 281
    Nazi occupation 38, 210, 281
    Soviet occupation 210, 214, 281
October Revolution 19, 20, 87, 276; *see also* Bolshevik Revoltuion
Ogonyok 264
Omsk 115, 122
Orange Revolution 197
Orbit (Orbita) poetry group 27–8, 271–2, 286–95
Orientalism 7, 16, 24, 62, 192, 205
    internal 210
Orthodoxy 41, 47, 48, 53, 59, 70, 73, 86, 87n4, 96, 97, 98, 100, 101, 133, 224, 225
outer space, *see* space
Ovid 249

Palace of Culture and Science in Warsaw 211–13
Palanga 247–8
Panarin, Aleksandr 21, 96–8
    idiom of space 97

Pan-European transport corridor 173–4, 190
Pasternak, Boris 36, 39
People's Commissariat of Transport 126
Perestroika 194, 239
Periodic system of being 58
periphery 3n9, 6, 16, 18, 22, 25, 26, 52, 73, 108, 111, 193, 195, 198, 207, 245, 246, 275; *see also* center and periphery
    interface periphery 207
Peter I, the Great 75, 283
Petrograd 155, 226,
Petrovskaya Agricultural Academy in Moscow 146
Phonological union 52, 57
Phonology 31, 32, 38, 40, 42, 47, 49, 53, 57, 58
photography 268
physical geographers 136, 141, 149
pigration 90, 107, 116, 120, 138, 154, 277, *see* also emigration and immigration
Piłsudski Square in Warsaw (formerly Saxon Sq. and Victory Sq.) 211
pipelines 23, 163, 164, 173, 182
Pipes, Richard, 63
PIS, *see* Law and Justice
plant geographers, *see also* botanists 153, 155
plant geography, *see also* botany 147, 149, 150, 152, 153
Platforma Obywatelska, *see* Civic Platform
PO, *see* Civic Platform
Poland 24, 146, **165**, 191–215, 236, 237, 276
Polish government in exile 196
Polish Peasants' Party (Polskie Stronnictwo Ludowe) 203
Polish United Workers Party 194
Polish Uprisings of 1831 and 1863 206

Polish-Bolshevik War, *see* Polish-Soviet War
Polish–Lithuanian Commonwealth 203, 208
Polish–Soviet War 206, 236
Politburo 125
Political police, Soviet 131
Polskie Stronnictwo Ludowe, *see* Polish Peasants' Party
Poltava
Pomorska, Krystyna 53
population movement, *see* Migration
population resettlement, *see* Migration
postcolonial studies vii, 1, 5, 205, 207
postcolonial theory 7, 11, 191–2, 202–7, 211–15
postcoloniality 7–8, 191, 196, 209, 276
post-imperial vii, 12, 27, 209, 220, 228, 234, 238, 276, 280, 294; *see also* culture
postmodern/ity 22
post-socialism 24, 162n9, 277
post-Soviet 6, 15, 21, 22, 23, 26, 27, 61, 87, 96, 106, 106n2, 162, 173–4, 185, 239, 239n2, 256, 272, 275, 276, 277, 277n13, 289n35, 294
post-Soviet space, *see* space
post-Stalin, *see* Stalin, Josef
Poznań University 210
practice turn 220
pragmatist turn 220
Prague Linguistic Circle 35, 41, 49, 88
Pravda 125
Prawo i Sprawiedliwość, *see* Law and Justice
Prokhanov, Aleksandr 99
propaganda 165, 186, 241, 257, 258, 262, 266, 269, 270
Propertius 248–9
protectionism 111, 111n21; *see also* tariffs

provincialism 77, 288, 294
provincializing Europe (Dipesh Chakrabarty) 2, 8
Prussia 199–200
Punte, Artur 287, 289, 291, 293, 295
Putin, Vladimir 23, 175, 181, 182, 183, 272, 273

Ratzel, Friedrich 44
regionalization 22, 135–56
    Russian imperial 111, 111n24, 151–4
    Soviet 117, 118, 120, 120n49, 120n50, 121, 122, 154–6
Regularity 40, 44, 58
resurrection 46, 68, 87n4, 88
RGS, *see* Russian Geographical Society
Riga 27, 151, 275, 277, 278, 279, 280, 281, 283, 284, 285, 286, 289, 293, 294
Rikhter, Dmitrii 147, 148, 149–51, 152
Rokkan, Stein 193, 207
Russian Empire, *see* empire
Russian Federation, the 85, 111, 183, 185, 272–9, 282, 284, 286, 287, 291, 295, 296
Russian Geographical Society 119, 121, 122, 129n75, 129n76, 131, 138, 139, 140, 154
Russian idea 86
Russians 26, 27, 41, 43, 48, 53, 68, 70–81, 97–100, 134, 139, 232, 240
    Baltic Russians 277n13
    and Poles 199, 202, 205–7, 211, 214–15
    Russian in Latvia 271–97
Russification 25, 70, 71, 211, 212, 221, 233, 251

Said, Edward 7, 13, 16, 24, 192, 204
Saratov 115n31, 123, 143n19, 150

Savitskii, Petr 20, 31–49, 54–9, 63–8, 78, 88–92
Saxon Square, *see* Piłsudski Square in Warsaw
Semenov-Tian-Shanskii, Piotr, 138–40, 147
Semenov-Tian-Shanskii, V.P. (Veniamin) 121, 129n75, 131
Sériot, Patrick 32, 58
SGGW, *see* Warsaw University of Life Sciences
Shapiro, Adol'f 283,
Shirinskii-Shikhmatov, Yuri 89
Siberia 25, 51, 66, 91, 98, 107n4, 108, 108n8, 115, 123, 126, 147, 163, 179, 241, 243, 244, 246, 249–51
Sibirtsev, Nikolai 144, 145, 146, 149, 150, 151, 153
Sikorski, Radosław 213
Skórczewski, Dariusz 198, 204–5
Skvortsov, Aleksandr 151
Slavic mythology 214
Slavophiles 86, 249
SLD, *see* Democratic Left Alliance
Snochowska-Gonzalez, Claudia 214
sobornost 86
social physics 112, 112n25
socialism 22, 23, 99, 116, 132, 162, 171, 212, 240n3, 282
socialist 22, 159, 167, 169–72
Sofia (city) 88, 89
soil science 140, 145, 146, 153
soil scientists 140, 143, 145, 149, 150, 153
Soja, Edward 4
Sojusz Lewicy Demokratycznej, *see* Democratic Left Alliance
Solidarity movement 195, 197
Solov'ev, Vladimir 56, 96
Solzhenitsyn, Aleksandr 208
  Solzhenitsyn Prize 96
Sonderweg 11, 14, 20, 33

South America 210
Soviet Army 209
Soviet culture, *see* culture
Soviet domination, *see* domination
Soviet empire, *see* empire
Soviet identity, *see* identity
Soviet nation 245, 255
Soviet nationalities 86, 135
Soviet nationhood 255
Soviet regime 23, 86, 100, 119, 206, 235, 249, 281
Soviet space, *see* space
Soviet space program 260, 261, 261n12, 270
Soviet territory, *see* territory
Soviet Union 1, 3, 4, 6, 9, 9n27, 10, 12, 13, 13n39, 15, 19, 21, 22, 24, 26, 37, 56, 61, 82, 83, 85, 101, 120, 122, 124, 128, 135, 136, 156, 159, 160, 162, 163, 166, 173, 203, 219, 230, 235, 239, 241, 244, 248–55, 256, 258, 259, 260, 262, 264, 266, 268, 270, 272, 273, 276, 277n11, 280, 281, 283, 291n37; *see also* USSR
  and Poland 191–209, 214
  as empire, *see* empire
  collapse of vii, 1, 9, 15, 61, 135, 136, 163, 219, 240, 255, 272, 273, 276, 281
  international building sites in, 168–71
Sowa, Jan 208
space
  Bolshevik conceptions of 118, 118n43, 132
  cultural 11, 109, 254, 284, 287n30
  Eurasian 20, 40, 53, 79, 80, 239n2
  geocultural 65
  geographical 210, 211, 239–41, 250
  idiom of, *see* Panarin

imperial 14–19, 21–2, 26, 27, 33, 79–82, 105, 107, 112, 148, 233, 246–7, 249, 255–6, 270
and infrastructure 14, 23, 117, 162–3, 173–90, 245
materialist versus idealist conceptions of 21, 108, 117–18, 132, 133
national 16, 23, 133, 168, 255
outer 26, 257–270
post-Soviet 22–3, 27, 173–90
program, see Soviet space program
socialist 22, 159, 167, 169–72
Soviet 14, 132, 174, 239, 244–7, 251, 255–6, 261, 268–9, 295
Stalinist conceptions of 21, 26, 128–9, 133, 136, 211, 246
Spalding, Henry Norman 46
spatial change 106, 107, 112, 115, 133
spatial control 161
spatial development 106, 115
spatial history 15
spatial ideology 26, 245–6
spatial planning and policy 21, 105, 106, 110, 113
  Russian imperial 106, 110, 113
  Soviet 117–32
spatial science 21, 103, 105, 133
spatiality vii, 4n10, 20, 27, 91, 176, 246, 256
  and Eurasianism 20
  imperial spatiality 14, 17, 19, 26, 249, 256
Sputnik
  Soviet satellite 257, 258, 260, 261, 264, 267
  Soviet travel agency 241, 242, 246
St. Petersburg 20, 27, 63, 70, 72, 75, 85, 140, 142, 143, 146, 149, 150, 153, 154, 174, 187, 189, 212, 254, 283, 289
St. Petersburg University 140, 142, 147, 150, 152

St. Vladimir University in Kiev 150
Stalin, Josef, 25, 133, 134n91, 211, 212, 213, 239, 241, 242n6, 243, 244, 249, 250, 251, 253n31, 256, 257
Stalinism 21, 26, 99, 128, 129, 130, 136, 155, 193, 195, 201, 211, 246, 246n18, 259n5, 260, 279
State Geographical Society, see Russian Geographical Society
State Planning Commission, see Gosplan
statistics 118, 119, 121, 130, 138, 139, 145, 146, 148, 153, 156
Stoler, Ann L. 10, 11
Strakhov, Nikolai 56
Structuralism 20, 31, 33, 37, 45, 54, 55, 60
Strumilin, S.G 121, 129, 129n75, 131
Struve, Petr 89
subaltern 9n26, 12
subaltern studies 5
subalternity 4
Suny, Ronald G. 6
Supreme Council for the National Economy (Vesenkha), Institute for Industrial-Economic Research 125
surveillance 23, 171
Suvchinskii, Petr (Souvctchinsky, Pierre) 35, 39, 40, 46, 47, 56, 67, 88
Suvorov, Victor 208
Svetlov, Vladimir 287
Sviatlovskii, E.E. 105, 119–32
Sweden 38, 50, 221, 226, 276, 283

Tambov 115, 122
Tanfil'ev, Gavriil 45n38, 146, 147, 148, 149, 150, 151, 152, 153, 155
tariffs 116, 132, 179,
Tatar 51, 80
Teilhard de Chardin, Pierre 93n27
teleology 32, 55–7, 128

temporality 27, 91, 97
territorial planning, *see* spatial planning
territoriality, *see* territory
territory; *see also* administrative-territorial division; interface periphery; near abroad
    administrative 70
    colonial 202
    Containment and 160
    Eurasian 47, 63, 79–80, 90–93, 184
    Eurasian concepts of 78, 90
    European 283
    geographical 27, 78
    national 16, 166, 253
    and nationalism 99, 101
    neo-Eurasiant concepts of; *see* Dugin; Gumilev; Panarin
    and Orthodoxy 96, 101
    political-economic 107
    Russian 23, 26, 45, 63, 92, 106, 108, 115, 134, 173, 175, 189–90, 226, 239, 272–5, 285n27
    and sovereignty 159, 175
    Soviet 25–6, 123, 136, 163, 173, 239, 240–47, 252–4, 259, 261, 269, 285n27
    transformation of territoriality 160–62
    virtual 209–10
theology 86, 101
Thompson, Ewa 202–8, 213
Timofejev, Sergei 287, 288, 288n33, 289, 289n35, 290–95
Tobol'sk 107n4, 115
Tomsk 115
topogenesis 90
tourism 240, 241, 245, 245n12, 278
transport diplomacy 187
Transport network 23
    and late Imperial Russia 107, 107n7, 110, 111, 116
    and early Soviet Russia 117, 126, 128, 131n81
    and post-Soviet Russia 173–90
Trans-Siberian Railway 123, 179
Trautfetter, Ernst Rudolf 147
Trest, monarchist organization 46
Troitskii, Evgenii 21, 99–100, 101
Trotskii, Lev 110n16, 119, 119n46
Trubetskoi, Nikolai 20, 31, 32, 34, 35, 36–7, 38–59, 64, 65, 68, 78n54, 88, 91, 92
Tsiolkovskii, Konstantin 87n4, 95, 99, 259, 260, 261, 265
Tsymburskii, Vadim 96
turizm, *see* tourism
Tynianov, Iurii 271, 295

Uallik, Zhorzh 287
Ukraine 61, 64–83, 108, 149, 151, 163, 168, 196, 206, 210, 291
Ukrainians 63, 68, 70–77, 80–81, 207, 276
Upper Silesia 210
urbanization 107
USSR 46, 52, 79, 85, **123**, 128, 132, 159, 163, 164, 167, 169, **177**, 224, 229, 230, 242, 265, 273n5, 276, 283, 291, 292; *see also* Soviet Union

Vail, Petr 240, 249–51, 256
Varga, Eugen 118
Vavilov, Nikolai 56
Vernadskii, Georgii (George Vernadsky) 20, 47, 58, 61–75, 80–88, 91–3, 99, 259
Vernadskii, Vladimir 20, 42n29, 64, 69, 72–7, 87n4, 93, 259
Verne, Jules 260, 265
Vertov, Dziga 239
Victory Square, *see* Piłsudski Square in Warsaw

Vistula (river) 212
Vokrug sveta, *see* Around the World
Volga, river 123, 151
Von Hagen, Mark 61, 83
von Thünen, Johann Heinrich 118, 119n45, 128
VTsIK Administrative Commission 117n41, 120n49, 155

Wajda Andrzej 212
Wałęsa, Lech 195
Warsaw 130, 131, 194, 211–13
Warsaw University of Life Sciences 211
Weber, Alfred 118, 118n44, 119n45, 128, 130
Weber, Eugen 8
Weber, Max 235

Weinberg, V.P. 119, 119n47, 123
West Germany 160, *see also* FRG
Witte, Sergei 116
Wittgenstein, Ludwig 25, 238
World War I 154, 199, 211
World War II 38, 60, 64, 161, 162, 281, 295
Wortman, Richard 229
Wrangel, Petr 73, 89

Yeltsin, Boris 86, 181

Zapol', Aleksandr 287, 293
zemstva 140, 142, 143, 144, 146, 150, 154, 155, 156
zemstvo statisticians 142, 143–7
Zielona Góra Festival 208